MOTHERING MAGAZINE'S

HAVING A BABY,
NATURALLY

Also by Peggy O'Mara

Natural Family Living

MOTHERING MAGAZINE'S

HAVING A BABY, NATURALLY

The *Mothering* Magazine Guide
to Pregnancy and Childbirth

Peggy O'Mara,
Editor and Publisher

WITH **Wendy Ponte**

ILLUSTRATED BY **Jackie Facciolo**

PRODUCED BY
THE PHILIP LIEF GROUP, INC.

ATRIA BOOKS
NEW YORK   LONDON   TORONTO   SYDNEY   SINGAPORE

ATRIA BOOKS
1230 Avenue of the Americas
New York, NY 10020

ISBN: 0-7434-3963-5

First Atria Books trade paperback edition August 2003

10   9   8   7   6   5   4

ATRIA BOOKS is a trademark of Simon & Schuster, Inc.

For information regarding special discounts for bulk purchases,
please contact Simon & Schuster Special Sales at 1-800-456-6798
or business@simonandschuster.com

Designed by Christine Weathersbee

Manufactured in the United States of America

This book is dedicated to all those who work tirelessly

in the face of discouragement and resistance to inspire

women to reclaim the ecstatic experience and

transformative mystery of normal birth.

Acknowledgments

I first and foremost want to thank Wendy Ponte for her hard work, dedication, rigor and kind friendship during the writing of this book. My special gratitude to the hardworking staff of *Mothering,* who tolerated my absences from the office. Thank you to Judy Linden and Lynne Kirk, two top-notch, uncompromising editors who challenged me to new levels, and to Emily Bestler, for her vision of this book and her ever gracious demeanor and regard.

I am indebted both in this book and in my own life to thinkers and writers who have come before me in the arena of childbirth reform. I am very grateful to the women I learned from about birth. Thank you to Stephanie, Viola, Libby, Maggie, Veronica, my old friend Pam and my sister Sue. We learned about birth together. Thank you also for the safe haven of my La Leche League friendships during the early years. I was inspired as a new mother by the writings of Sheila Kitzinger, Suzanne Arms, Doris Haire, Jeannine Medvin O'Brien (now Jeannine Parvati Baker), Juliette deBarclai Levy, Selma Fraiberg, Eda LeShan, Arlene Rossen Cardozo, Walt Whitman and Rudolph Steiner. During the writing of this book, I have learned from the books of Penny Simkin, Janet Whalley, Ann Keppler, Judith Rooks, Marsden Wagner, Aviva Jill Romm, Barbara Holstein, Mindy Pennybacker, Aisha Ikramuddin, Jyoth Larson, Lynn Moen, Judy Laik, Vimala Schneider McClure, Sandy Jones, and Tine Thevenin. Carol Huotari, reference librarian at La Leche League, International, and Barbara Loe Fisher and Kathi Williams of the National Vaccine Information Center were especially helpful in providing information. I'm encouraged by the hard work of Laura Maxon and the vision of Santa Cruz County, whose December 2000 Strategic Plan calls for access to home births and birth center births for all women.

Thank you to Phyllis and Marshall Klaus for giving me my first copy of Murray Enkin's book *A Guide to Effective Care in Pregnancy and Childbirth,* and to the Cochrane Pregnancy and Childbirth Group for maintaining the international database. I used this book as the basis for the recommendations in *Having a Baby . . . Naturally.*

Above all, I must acknowledge and thank my children, Nora, Bram, Finnie and Lally, who taught me how to be brave, and my parents, Ruth and Oliver O'Mara, who gave me optimism and always believed in me.

CONTENTS

CONTENTS

CONTENTS

Congratulations! You're pregnant. You are now wondering how to create the best possible environment for you and your baby, and the environment that you have the most control over is your mental one. It is important that you have a good inner opinion of yourself during pregnancy. Rest assured that your body is already equipped for the challenges of pregnancy and birth. You can educate your mind, develop trust in your body, and fortify your spirit with accurate and objective information. And you can trust yourself to act in your own best interests and in the best interests of your child.

With pregnancy, you may be surprised to find how deeply your choices have been influenced by the beliefs, attitudes, and customs of society, by the opinions of family members, and by your general lack of exposure to birth. Unless you have witnessed them, pregnancy and birth can seem strange and frightening when in fact they are simple and natural. Several factors contribute to our collective belief that pregnancy and birth are complicated. The overmedicalization of childbirth in the United States, the human tendency to be intimidated by custom and authority, and the fact that insurance companies often only cover hospital birth make real choices in childbirth difficult if not impossible.

In 1982 psychiatrist Ronald Laing wrote, "We do not see childbirth in many obstetric units now. What

we see resembles childbirth as much as artificial insemination resembles sexual intercourse. And, birth, as a home and family event, has virtually been cultured out." Laing believed this change was a matter of power. "Women are allowed or not to have their babies at home. In hospital, they are allowed or not to move, scream or sing, stand, walk, sit or squat. Women are allowed or not to have their babies after birth. . . . To allow is to exercise as much, if not more power, than to forbid." Laing pleaded for genuine choice, asking, "Why should any one way have to be imposed on all? Why cannot two or more ways coexist in the same society? Why should there be any monopoly on what is available?"

Understanding Your Choices: Informed Consent

Pregnancy and birth are normal biological events. They are not medical events, but they take place within a cultural context and are colored by the beliefs and attitudes of the community at large. Hopefully, this book will give you a bigger sense of these events as they occur in this larger community, and help you to find the information and support you need to plan for your own birth environment and the arrival of your new baby.

You deserve to have true informed consent regarding the decisions you make during this time. While it sounds like a fancy term, informed consent simply means that you have the right to know the risks and benefits of treatment, and the right to choose which procedures you want during pregnancy and birth, regardless of how commonly they are used. All too often, we undergo procedures passively, without being aware that we could question or even decline a treatment.

Informed consent has been a legal principle for 100 years in the United States. This doctrine requires practitioners to disclose all information needed to make a decision, and requires that consent be given voluntarily and without coercion. The concept of informed consent is critical: in thousands of letters to *Mothering* magazine, women have said that they regret that they had not known more about their choices during pregnancy and birth.

The advice and suggestions in this book are based not only on scientific evidence but on the experiences of these women who have come to trust *Mothering* magazine as a respected authority on natural family living.

About Our Sources

Mothers-to-be are often confused by the conflicting medical literature that is available. For example, guests on talk shows routinely quote contradictory findings to prove a specific point. In addition, practices in common use are not always supported by medical research. As a pregnant woman, you will want to look carefully at the evidence, so I have sought out a definitive and objective resource.

The recommendations in this book are based on Oxford University's *Effective Care in Pregnancy and Childbirth,* a 1,500-page, two-volume book that summarizes the most authoritative international studies available on the effects of care practices during pregnancy, during childbirth, and after the baby is born. The first edition, published in 1989, was widely acclaimed as a landmark publication. For the first time, evidence-based information on the

effects of pregnancy and childbirth care was made readable and accessible to all who needed and wanted it.

The second edition won first prize in the British Medical Association 1995 Medical Book Competition in the Primary Health Care category, and has been translated into several languages. The third edition of this book was prepared by the editors of the Cochrane Pregnancy and Childbirth Group, along with Murray W. Enkin, M.D., a prominent physician and author of the first edition.

Effective Care in Pregnancy and Childbirth has been compiled into an electronic database consisting of a register of over 9,000 controlled studies from almost 400 medical journals, in 18 different languages, from 85 different countries—as well as a systematic review of their results. The suggestions here are based on the latest, most comprehensive scientific evidence, providing you with the most up-to-date information on which to compare choices for yourself during pregnancy and childbirth.

Why Natural?

As the title implies, this book focuses on natural pregnancy and childbirth, subjects *Mothering* magazine has been reporting on for over twenty-five years. During that time, we've learned that women who experience natural childbirth not only report greater satisfaction with their birth experiences than those who do not, but also feel less pain and discomfort during the early weeks and months of motherhood. It is unfortunate, therefore, that these concepts have been misunderstood in recent years. For instance, some consider a birth "natural" simply if the mother is conscious, while others, more accurately, understand that a natural childbirth is a drug-free birth. Even more unfortunate is the fact that so few women are helped and encouraged to have a natural birth.

You may be frightened when the subject turns to drugs in labor and wonder if natural birth means that your choices will be limited. Some of you would hate to have drugs foisted on you; others want to make sure that you have access to the comfort level of your choice. In pregnancy and birth, what you want is simply choice. And yet you may not realize how much your choices are limited by the constructed culture of birth, by custom unsupported by evidence, and by our general lack of exposure to and discomfort with birth. For example, most women will experience ultrasound scans during their pregnancies, even though ultrasound is not recommended for routine use by the American College of Obstetricians and Gynecologists. Electronic fetal monitors are routinely used in hospital birth, yet they have never been shown in scientific studies to be any more effective than a simple stethoscope. And it may surprise you to learn that birth is safe in any setting—home, hospital, birth center—although only 1 percent of births in the United States take place outside of a hospital.

Twenty-three other countries have better birth outcomes than we do in the United States. All of these countries spend less money on health care than we do. Even with all of our technology, we are not protecting as many babies and mothers as other countries do with less. American insurance companies define pregnancy as a disability; obstetrical medicine acts defensively to ward off malpractice suits; pharmaceutical companies and manufacturers of birth technology entice practitioners to try their products by offering incentives; in short, as a culture, we are uncomfortable with the intimate physical events of pregnancy, birth, and breastfeeding.

What do those twenty-three countries have in common—those who spend less money yet have better birth outcomes than the United States? All of them rely on midwives. In New Zealand, for example, midwives attend 70 percent of births. In the United States, midwives attend nearly 10 percent of births.

Compare these labor and delivery outcomes for low-risk mothers who were clients of certified nurse-midwives (CNMs) with the clients of physicians (M.D.s):

Labor and Delivery Procedure	CNMs	M.D.s
Oxytocin induction*	8.5%	15.2%
Oxytocin augmentation**	11.7%	37.2%
Internal electronic fetal monitor	16.2%	43.5%
Epidural anesthesia	17.3%	32.7%
Episiotomies	10.8%	35.4%
Third- and fourth-degree lacerations †	6.6%	23.3%
Operative deliveries ‡	11.0%	30.1%

* Oxytocin induction is the use of the drug oxytocin to attempt to end pregnancy and stimulate labor to begin.
** Oxytocin augmentation is the use of oxytocin to attempt to increase the strength or effectiveness of labor contractions.
† Third- and fourth-degree lacerations are tears of the perineum, usually following an episiotomy, that extend into the rectum.
‡ Operative deliveries include those delivered by vacuum extraction, forceps, or cesarean section

The Institutes of Medicine, the Office of Technology Assessment of the U.S. Congress, and the National Commission to Prevent Infant Mortality have all published statements of support for the development of nurse midwifery in the United States. In 1989, the National Birth Center Study was published in the *New England Journal of Medicine,* a study that demonstrated positive results of care of 12,000 birthing women by certified nurse midwives. The study showed that compared to hospital births, birth center births had a lower risk of cesareans, less infant death, and no maternal death.

More Evidence for Natural Birth

In her 1990 book *Safer Childbirth,* British statistician Marjorie Tew published overwhelming evidence for the safety and superiority of skillful midwifery and home birth. In fact, no study of matched populations has ever shown home birth to be unsafe.

In a report published in March 1992, the British House of Commons stated, "We conclude that the choices of a homebirth or birth in small maternity units are options which have been substantially withdrawn from the majority of women in this country. . . . The policy of encouraging all women to give birth in hospitals cannot be justified on the grounds of safety. . . . Hospitals are not the appropriate place to care for healthy women."

A 1998 National Institutes of Health study published in the *Journal of Epidemiology and Community Health* found that patients of certified nurse midwives have 19 percent lower infant mortality rates than doctors, 31 percent less neonatal mortality, and 33 percent less incidence of low birth weight.

A 1999 Stanford University dissertation by Peter F. Schlenzka provided even more evidence of the safety of natural childbirth. He examined nearly 816,000 births from 1989 and 1990, comparing both low-risk and high-risk births occurring both at home and at the hospital. Schlenzka found no difference in mortality rates for infants born in the hospital or in other settings. His findings clearly show that the natural approach is as safe for both groups.

In California, Santa Cruz County has cited Schlenzka's research as the basis for ballot initiatives calling for expanded birth services for local residents. The county's December 2000 Strategic Plan called for adopting the goals of the "Mother Friendly Childbirth Initiative," a document defining ten prerequisites for a mother-friendly birthing environment; making midwifery care available at the local hospital; providing every pregnant woman with a "Midwifery Model of Care" brochure; funding development of a freestanding birth center; ensuring financial support for women who desire out-of-hospital birth; and awarding grants to helping services and nonprofits. These initiatives are significant because they mark the first time a county government has recommended alternatives to hospital birth.

The History of Childbirth

If midwifery care and natural birth are actually safer and more satisfying, why are they not more popular? To answer this question, it is important to understand the cultural context, which determines to a large extent both our choices and our experiences regarding pregnancy and childbirth. For nearly 200 years, midwives, physicians, and nurses have competed in one way or another to be the main care providers for pregnant and birthing women. The enduring influences of this competition have affected our choices regarding place of birth, birth attendant, birth interventions, and pain management, as well as physical contact with our babies, breastfeeding, postpartum care, and early family life.

EARLY MIDWIVES AND OBSTETRICIANS

Not until the Revolutionary War did educated doctors seek to attend births. Before then, physicians regarded care of the pregnant woman as beneath their dignity and expertise. In addition, childbirth was viewed as a life-threatening event that could result in death, regardless of who attended the birth. Midwifery was not considered part of medicine, and the few men who did attempt to practice midwifery were widely ridiculed for their intrusion into an exclusively female profession. Midwives were generally women who had birthed several of their own children, and had learned by assisting at friends' births or learning from an established midwife. Organized training programs and schools for midwives did not exist until 1848, when the Boston Female Medical College opened in the United States.

Midwives were often the only source of health care, and they were respected members of the community. Many came as colonists, some as slaves, and others as immigrants. While some had received training in other countries, learning was most often passed on through the apprenticeship method, and yet most midwives were isolated from one another, busy with their own families, and did not think of themselves as members of a profession.

With the development of obstetrical forceps in the 1750s in England, obstetrical practices began to change rather dramatically, both in England and subsequently in the United States. Midwives who had maintained an unquestioned monopoly found themselves in competition with male practitioners—now claiming to have superior knowledge in the form of obstetrical instruments.

At first, physicians were only called to assist at difficult births, but gradually it became more common for forceps to be used to hasten the process of normal delivery. By the early 1800s, it was popular for upper- and middle-class women to have forceps deliveries with male physicians.

By the mid-1800s, medicine was becoming professionalized: the American Medical Association, founded in 1847, recognized obstetrics as one of its four special sections as early as 1859. By 1888, the American Association of Obstetricians and Gynecologists was formed. Physicians sought legislation that would create state licensing requirements allowing only physicians to practice medicine.

Unfortunately, there was no effort at that time to educate and license midwives. Midwifery practices were diverse, and laws were mainly local. In fact, it was not until the 1920s that most midwives practiced under some type of regulation. By that time, there were not enough schools to certify professional midwives in sufficient numbers.

By 1900, physicians were attending about 50 percent of all births in the United States, and virtually 100 percent of the births of middle- and upper-class women. Midwives primarily took care of poor women. At this time, misguided advocates for women, including female physicians, male obstetricians, and others, demanded the abolition of midwifery, claiming that it was unsafe. They called for the prohibition of midwives, especially in areas where doctors were available.

In the years to come, midwives were systematically outlawed as state after state succumbed to intense medical pressure. Meanwhile, in England, Germany and most European nations, midwives were trained to become established and independent practitioners.

THE RISE OF MEDICAL BIRTH

The struggle between midwife and physician for dominance in the care of pregnant and birthing women peaked between 1910 and 1935. The Carnegie Foundation's 1910 Flexner Report focused on medical education in the United States in general and found it to be of poor overall quality, with obstetrics making the worst showing. The report concluded that medical progress required obstetric physicians to take over the supervision of childbirth, adding that there was not enough time to educate and certify midwives.

The prejudices of the time supported this view, and the most influential obstetricians publicly participated in the defamation of midwives as untrained and therefore unsafe. The 50 percent of births still attended by midwives were seen as a missed opportunity for obstetrical training.

In addition, experts of the early 1900s argued that childbirth was a dangerous condition that damaged most women and warranted routine medical intervention. In fact, they believed that forceps delivery was safer than unassisted labor, which was assumed to hinder a woman's sexual functioning and possibly damage her baby's brain. The campaign to eliminate midwives was part of the attempt by obstetricians to establish the credibility of their own fledgling profession.

The 1900s saw the beginning of the American migration to cities, the development of the modern hospital, and the rise of allopathic, or Western, medicine. By 1939, the use of sterile techniques and the development of antibiotics improved the safety of birth, particularly in hospitals, where infections after childbirth were common.

In addition, economic factors made hospital birth more acceptable. Prior to the 1930s, individuals paid for all of their own medical expenses. The Great Depression spurred the creation, in 1943, of the Emergency Maternity and Infant Care (EMIC) program, which eventually provided free hospital obstetric care to over a million mothers and babies. Within three years, it covered one of every seven births in the United States, and therefore made hospital birth affordable. By the late 1940s, half of all births took place in the hospital.

In the 1940s, the "modern way" to give birth was under total anesthesia. "Twilight sleep," the method of choice, involved injecting a laboring woman with morphine and then giving her the amnesiac, or memory-impairing, drug scopolamine. At the time, the development of twilight sleep was hailed as a breakthrough, although the birthing woman was so drugged that she could seldom participate in the birth, requiring multiple interventions such as episiotomies and forceps delivery.

By 1960, nearly all women gave birth in the hospital. Over 90 percent of white women and 74 percent of African-American women were anesthetized during delivery. Eventually it was recognized that morphine contributed to maternal deaths, that scopolamine didn't actually kill pain (only the memory of pain), and that general anesthesia depressed the mother's as well as the baby's respiratory and nervous system. Sadly, home birth had virtually been eradicated by the mid-1970s, and 99 percent of births took place in the hospital.

NATURAL CHILDBIRTH IS REBORN

Counter to this increased medicalization of childbirth were two breakthroughs. One was the 1944 publication of Grantly Dick-Read's book *Childbirth without Fear: The Principles and Practice of Natural Childbirth,* a book that discussed for the first time in the popular press the role that emotions play in birth. Dick-Read, a British obstetrician, proposed the then-novel idea that fearing the pain of labor increases the pain of labor. Dick-Read concluded that educating women about childbirth could prepare them to withstand its rigors.

Dick-Read became the first to advocate the use of controlled breathing and relaxation techniques during labor. Results with the Dick-Read method at Yale New Haven Hospital Clinic in 1946 showed that women who were educated in breathing and relaxation techniques used less medication than unprepared women.

The second breakthrough came in 1951 when two French obstetricians, Fernand Lamaze and Pierre Vellay, traveled to Russia to observe the so-called psychoprophylactic (mind-over-matter) obstetrical practices in use there. In 1956 *Painless Childbirth,* Lamaze's classic book on this practice, was published. His method relied heavily on the use of distraction techniques during contractions. The most famous of these techniques involves structured, controlled breathing.

In 1960 Elisabeth Bing, a physical therapist, and Marjorie Karmel, a mother who had trained with Dr. Lamaze while pregnant in France, introduced and popularized this technique as "the Lamaze method" in the United States.

SIGNIFICANT STRIDES

Meanwhile, despite persecution from obstetricians, midwifery care continued to evolve. In 1911, amid studies that concluded that mothers and babies in the United States were dying more often than they were in many western European countries, the commissioner of health for New York City criticized the United States as being the only "civilized" country in the world that did not safeguard the care of mothers and babies by training and regulating midwives.

In 1918 the Maternity Center Association, the first woman-centered birthing organization in the United States, created the nation's first prenatal-care pilot project, as well as another significant first—classes for expectant parents. A report on the association's first twenty years of operation appeared in 1955 in the *American Journal of Obstetrics and Gynecology.* Of 5,000 births attended by association midwives, 87 percent took place in the home. Women cared for by these midwives were nearly three times less likely to die in childbirth than the average woman, who typically gave birth in a hospital setting without a midwife present.

In 1925 Mary Breckenridge, a British-trained midwife, established the Frontier Nursing Service in the Appalachian Mountains of southeastern Kentucky, creating a new model for rural health care and sowing the seeds of nurse-midwifery. Sixteen graduates of the Frontier Nursing Service formed the first nurse-midwifery organization in the United States, the Kentucky Association of Midwives, in 1929. This group went on to become the American Association of Nurse-Midwives, originally affiliated with the National Organization for Public Health Nursing, and later established as the American College of Nurse-Midwives.

VOICES OF A NEW GENERATION

In the 1960s the voices of pregnant and birthing women began to be heard. In 1960, the International Childbirth Education Association was founded to promote family-centered maternity care and freedom of choice based on knowledge of alternatives. Sheila Kitzinger's revolutionary book *The Experience of Childbirth*, published in 1962, introduced the idea that birth is a highly personal event. She recommended that labor pains be accepted as "pain with a purpose."

In 1965 Robert Bradley, M.D., published *Husband Coached Childbirth*, adding American innovations to the Dick-Read relaxation and breathing methods. Bradley especially encouraged husbands to participate as coaches during the birth process. It was not until the 1970s, however, that fathers were actually "allowed" in the delivery room with mothers.

Birth activism came of age in the 1970s, with the publication of three landmark books: Doris Haire's *Cultural Warping of Childbirth;* Suzanne Arms's *Immaculate Deception;* and Ina May Gaskin's *Spiritual Midwifery.* In 1976, *Mothering* magazine was founded as a voice of this activism. The Seattle Midwifery School opened in 1978 as the first modern midwifery school in the United States that did not require a nursing degree for admittance.

That same year the cesarean section rate for the United States hit 18 percent; it was 7 percent in 1960. Many lay and professional people were deeply concerned about the state of modern obstetrical care, and in 1978 and 1979 congressional hearings were held on the risks and benefits of common obstetrical interventions, including cesarean sections. The result

was a call for a reduction in the rate of cesarean sections and an increase in access to prenatal care. At the same time, the American College of Obstetrics and Gynecologists, the American Academy of Pediatrics, and the American Medical Association approved a resolution against home birth, despite a great deal of scientific evidence backing its safety.

A RENAISSANCE OF MIDWIFERY

Laws were revised during the 1970s to regulate and define the practice of midwifery. Although many states were in a political ferment, the percentage of out-of-hospital births more than doubled (from 0.6 percent in 1970 to 1.5 percent in 1977) and was 5 percent or higher in several states, including California and New Mexico.

In the 1980s, normal birth was finally rediscovered in the United States. The Carnegie Foundation reversed its 1910 Flexner Report and encouraged the growth of midwifery care in the United States. It also suggested that midwifery competence could be attained through multiple pathways of learning: for example, through apprenticeship, nursing education, and institutional learning. In 1982, the Midwives Alliance of North America was formed as a group to unify all midwives, regardless of educational background.

At this time, society learned more about natural pregnancy and childbirth. South American obstetrician Roberto Caldeyro-Barcia advocated birth in the upright position, a posture that enhances the natural gravity of the body during birth. As a result, spontaneous pushing rather than "bearing down" during the second stage of labor began to be recommended, and women were encouraged to birth in positions like squatting and on hands and knees. French surgeon Michel Odent made tubs of water available to women during labor and birth, and found that water enhanced relaxation.

A LOOK AHEAD

While much progress has been made in our understanding of a woman's experience of pregnancy and childbirth, over 30 percent of women—about a million and a half each year—give birth surgically, and more than 70 percent undergo multiple, unnecessary interventions during childbirth. We can do better than this.

However, more choices are available now than ever before in the arena of pregnancy and childbirth care. Depending upon the state in which she lives, today's mom-to-be can choose a midwife, an obstetrician, a nurse practitioner, a physician's assistant, or a naturopath to assist her during birth.

While pregnancy and birth customs come and go, the questions facing prospective parents are the same as they've always been. What will make me feel well cared for during pregnancy? Where would I feel safest giving birth? Who will I want to be with me? As you ask yourself these questions, realize that the choice is completely yours, and don't be unduly influenced by anyone else.

There's No "Right" Way!

Let's face it: You can do everything "right," eating all the right foods, reading all the books, and talking to all the right practitioners, yet you still can't control your pregnancy or birth. This can lead you to feel personally responsible when things do not proceed as expected. There is no "right way" to give birth. Birth is not a contest. It is a creative process, and as such, every birth is unique. If we give paints, brushes, easels, and canvases to a group of women and ask them to paint the same scene, each painting will be distinctly different—just as each pregnancy and birth will be a unique experience.

Because each birth is a totally unique and unpredictable event, no amount of preparation or good character can assure a specific result in birth. However, there are some things that have been shown to contribute to a satisfying birth experience: childbirth preparation with a teacher who is independent and not affiliated with any institution or practitioner; suggestions for nondrug pain relief; continuous labor support from another woman; and giving birth in a setting where you feel safe and free from dogmatic beliefs or practices.

This book encourages you to explore drug-free childbirth because nondrug pain relief actually works—and it offers more of a real sense of control than do drugs. It seems sadly ironic that we protect our bodies from drugs throughout pregnancy, only to flood our bloodstream and our baby's with them during birth. Using drugs during childbirth also raises many questions about both the immediate and long-term effects on mothers and babies.

Birth is a normal event, and no two are alike. There is no single way to prepare all women for childbirth, because birth is unpredictable by nature. Perhaps the best way to prepare yourself for pregnancy and childbirth is to become comfortable with the unexpected. Learn to surrender to things as they are. Rely on your own inner resources, trust your body's responses, and take joy in preparing for the new life that is now becoming a part of yours.

Trusting your body means relying on your body, believing in yourself, and getting to know your own limitations. We often underestimate our body's powerful physical demands. By learning to appreciate your body's natural functions and listening to its needs, you can prepare for the powerful physical focus of birth.

Birth: A Powerful Focus

The news that you're pregnant tends to be accompanied by emotions of joy. Why, then, does the anticipation of birth evoke fear? Our beliefs and attitudes about birth come from stories we heard as children, as well as the experiences of friends and family. We are further shaped by our own birth experiences, by our view of women in general and of women in our own families in particular, as well as by personal, spousal, family, religious and societal beliefs about sex, pregnancy, pain, authority, doctors, midwives, and hospitals.

As you read this book, examine your beliefs and

attitudes about each of these words with a friend or with your partner. Doing this will reveal a lot about what you have learned regarding trusting your body during pregnancy and childbirth.

You can develop trust in your body by getting to know yourself in operation. Even though you may be tired intermittently at the beginning of your pregnancy, as your energy returns, you will want to choose a vigorous physical project that engages you. Perhaps you've always wanted to take yoga. Or maybe you set yourself the challenge of walking a bit farther every day. How about getting rid of your inhibitions by regularly dancing around your living room? During my first pregnancy, I chopped down tumbleweeds on our farm. A pregnant friend in Maine helped to dig a shallow well on her property. These physical tasks helped us to focus on our strength, our ability to accomplish new tasks, and our willingness to stretch our physical boundaries.

This is a joyful time in your life—a time when you may wish to deepen your relationship with the contemplative, spiritual, or sacred. Traditions will also become important to you, as friends welcome your new baby with showers. Recent generations have begun to borrow on indigenous traditions, hosting ritual ceremonies such as Blessingways to honor the pregnant woman. These ceremonies invite the larger community to support you and your family.

Consider keeping a dream or reflective journal during your pregnancy. Record thoughts about your growing baby, as well as your reactions to classic or religious images of mother and child.

Your pregnancy and birth experiences mirror your life. They are peak experiences and can be intense microcosms of some of your unfinished business. It would be unrealistic to expect to transform all aspects of your life during pregnancy. However, such things as exploring attitudes and beliefs about pregnancy and birth will deepen your relationship with both.

And don't forget to balance your serious, thoughtful preparation with play! Make time in your life for experiences that allow you to play, sing, dance, and laugh as much as possible.

This Book

Drawing from the material published in *Mothering* magazine, along with the most cutting-edge information available, this book outlines the full spectrum of choices available during your pregnancy and childbirth. It is divided into seven parts that follow the sequence of pregnancy, labor, delivery, and the time after the baby is born.

- **PART ONE:** *The First Trimester (chapters 1 through 3).* This section addresses adjusting to pregnancy, making time for yourself, and natural remedies for common concerns of the first three months. An extensive chapter on diet includes cooking, shopping, and menu tips for vegetarians, vegans, and meat eaters, as well as current recommendations regarding nutritional supplements during pregnancy. Part 1 ends with detailed information on choosing your place of birth and birth attendant. We put this right up front because these choices will influence everything that follows in your pregnancy.

- **PART TWO:** *The Second Trimester (chapters 4 through 9).* By your second trimester, you will be reflecting more deeply on your pregnancy; this section offers some guidance in self-reflection and self-awareness during pregnancy. You will have to make choices during this trimester regarding prenatal testing, and this chapter provides an overview of the most current practices. In this section, good labor support is strongly recommended. You'll learn how to find it, as well as excellent childbirth preparation. To guide your choices, you'll find objective data on mother-friendly birth care. This section ends with information about children attending the birth of a sibling, as well as a discussion about breastfeeding.

- **PART THREE:** *The Third Trimester (chapters 10 through 14).* This section delves deeper into preparing for your baby's birth. Here you'll be encouraged to reevaluate the birth choices of your first trimester to see if they still suit you. You'll find straight talk about fear and pain in labor, and strategies for avoiding the cascade of medical interventions that often lead to surgical birth. In this section, we suggest some natural means of induction for when it's truly needed, and some practical tips for getting ready for baby.

- **PART FOUR:** *Labor and Delivery (chapters 15 through 20).* In this section, you will find birth stories that show the unique and individual nature of birth. The section provides help for early labor and again revisits your birth intentions. A variety of birth positions are offered, and unnecessary medical interventions such as electronic fetal monitors and episiotomies are discussed.

- **PART FIVE:** *Postpartum (chapters 21 through 26).* The postpartum period is often ignored or given little coverage in books about pregnancy and childbirth. This book provides an extensive chapter on taking care of yourself as a new mother, in addition to getting to know your beautiful new baby. A breastfeeding review is included, as well as a look at how a new baby can affect your marriage or relationship. Honest information on postpartum realities is provided, as well as help for mothers who suffer from postpartum depression. The section ends with helpful suggestions for addressing the dilemma of work and motherhood.

- **PART SIX:** *Special Circumstances (chapters 27 through 29).* This section offers support for those who find themselves in special circumstances—sometimes unexpectedly—during their pregnancies and births. A comprehensive chapter on miscarriage and stillbirth, and one on premature babies, is included, as well as information on other special considerations.

- **PART SEVEN:** *Just for Fathers (chapters 30 through 32).* This chapter provides an overview of important issues, including learning to be a father, fathers at birth, balancing work and family, breastfeeding and sexuality, and sharing household tasks.

Each of the thirty-two chapters will also include three short, easy-to-read sidebars:

> Natural Soothers: Home-care recipes including complementary and alternative remedies, food and nutritional advice, at-home spa treatments, and natural beauty treatments that your pregnant body will love.

> Body Wise: Simple yoga postures, dance exercises, walking and hiking tips, and suggestions for other movement opportunities during pregnancy.

> Higher Ground: Affirmations, inspirational quotes, and poetry for pregnancy and birth, as well as suggestions for spiritual practices such as meditation, and rituals including Blessingways.

In addition, you'll find these invaluable resources at the end of the book:

- A one-of-a-kind "Birth Report Card" that will allow you to evaluate the practitioners you are considering according to the standards of the World Health Organization, the Coalition for Improving Maternity Services, and the national averages.

- An exhaustive resource list that is regularly updated on the magazine's Web site: *www.mothering.com.*

This book is for you if you want real informed consent. Do you want to read extensively about pregnancy and birth, participate fully in decision making, and make educated, personal choices from the full range of options available? Do you have faith in a time-tested, nonmedical approach to birth that is proven safe and that offers nondrug pain reduction techniques? Read on to learn how you can make the best possible choices to protect your new baby's health.

PART ONE

The First Trimester

What's Happening in My Body?

MONTH ONE. During the first month, you often don't even know you're pregnant. It's not until you miss your first period that you begin to suspect. You may feel tired, your breasts may be tender, and you may urinate more frequently.

MONTH TWO. During the second month, your uterus will begin to expand, and if this is your first pregnancy, it will be about as big as a tennis ball. With subsequent pregnancies, your uterus will become larger earlier in your pregnancy. Some women feel occasional nausea or morning sickness during month two, and you may respond with stronger emotions than usual. Pregnancy hormones may cause mood swings. You may feel very tired this month and next, but this will pass by the beginning of the second trimester.

MONTH THREE. During the third month, you will begin to settle into your pregnancy, and later this month, you will begin to feel less tired because your heart will be better adjusted to pumping more blood, 25 percent of which now goes to the baby. Your uterus will be about the size of a grapefruit when you touch your abdomen. You will begin to gain weight, and your clothes may begin getting tight. By the end of the third month, the risk of miscarriage and birth defects will be significantly reduced because the critical period of early organ development will be passed.

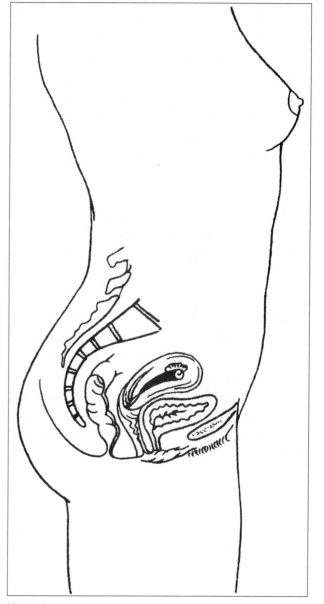

Month I

What's Happening with My Baby?

MONTH ONE. During the first month, your baby is a microscopic fertilized egg that is dividing again and again, forming a ball of cells with separate layers that will grow into your baby's body. A yolk sac nourishes your baby until all major organs have formed. At the end of one month, your baby will be about the size of a small pea and will weigh less than one ounce.

MONTH TWO. The central nervous system and all the body systems of your baby start to form at five weeks but will take months to fully develop. From now until the twelfth week the baby is susceptible to birth defects. The controlled environment of the amniotic fluid surrounds the baby by six weeks.

Your baby's face, eyes, ears, and mouth are all forming during the second month, and brain cells are growing. By the end of the second month, the placenta begins to grow. The baby, now officially called a fetus, is about one inch long and still weighs less than an ounce.

MONTH THREE. The baby now has teeth buds, and the soft cartilage of the skeleton has begun to turn into bone. The nose, eyelids, eyebrows, eyelashes, nails, and skin are formed. By the third month, the baby's entire body is covered by a downy hair called lanugo. Your baby can now roll over in the amniotic fluid, open and close her mouth, swallow, make a fist, smile, and squint. The heartbeat of your baby is growing stronger. By the end of the twelfth week, the external genital organs of your baby are formed and recognizable. The baby has finally reached one ounce in weight and is now about the size of a walnut.

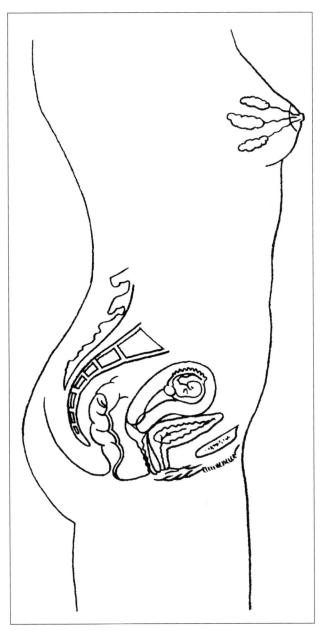

Month 2

> Becoming a parent may happen on purpose or by accident,
> but however it comes about, parenting itself is a calling.
>
> —MYLA AND JON KABAT-ZINN, *Mindful Parenting*

No matter how much you have been looking forward to having a baby, it still takes you by surprise. Perhaps you've been trying to have a baby for a long time, or maybe conception came much more quickly than you expected it to. Either way, there is, at first, something almost unreal about finding out that you are going to become a mother. You may not feel entirely prepared. Perhaps the timing doesn't feel absolutely perfect. Whether you feel ready or not, however, you can count on your body and mind to be equal to this very special task.

This is a time for celebration, for taking your place in the line of generations upon generations of women who have given birth. In our culture, pregnancy is often handled as if it were a medical condition. Nearly all women are treated as if something could go wrong at any time, and they're subjected to a number of routine medical procedures. In fact, only a small number of pregnant women require such interventions. You can make a special effort to enjoy the normalcy of pregnancy and be nourished and sustained by the grandmothers who have come before you.

In other cultures—and when life was simpler in our own—pregnancy was a routine part of the everyday fabric of life. Pregnant and postpartum women were honored with rituals and practices intended to ensure a safe birth by supporting and nurturing the mother and child. Somewhere between these old ways and the complex medical intervention pregnancy has become, there lies a comfortable balance that each woman must stake out for herself.

Discovery

To begin with, how do you know you are pregnant? Some women will have guessed even before a pregnancy test confirms their suspicions. Symptoms of pregnancy can appear quickly and may include extreme fatigue, tender breasts (similar to how some women's breasts feel right before menstruation), a need to urinate more frequently than usual, and, of course, missing a menstrual period. Some women will bleed a bit and may think their period is beginning, when it is actually just the result of the egg implanting itself into the uterus. It is rare for a woman to have a normal menstrual period when she is pregnant, but occasionally this does happen. Some women will experience no immediate symptoms, and this is normal, too. Many of these symptoms will fade as you move further into your pregnancy (see "First Trimester Common Concerns" later in this chapter for more details).

Home pregnancy tests are very accurate and easy to use. They will usually give results as soon as you have missed the first day of your period. They work by measuring the level of human chorionic gonadotropin (hCG) in your urine. This hormone is released by the embryo into the mother's bloodstream. The hCG levels are most concentrated first thing in the morning, so this may be the best time to take your test.

The hCG levels can also be detected by means of a blood test that can give you an answer before the first missed menstrual period, often as early as ten days after conception.

After six weeks' gestation, pregnancy can be confirmed by a midwife or doctor with an internal examination. Changes in the size and firmness of the uterus and cervix can be detected at that point.

The Due Date

Of course one of the first things you will want to know once pregnancy is confirmed is when the baby is due. Not so long ago doctors would give a very rough estimate of arrival, telling their patients to expect the baby in late January or early February, for example. Nowadays, midwives and doctors calculate due date in the following way: the woman will be asked what the first day of her last menstrual period was. Fourteen days will then be added to that date, which is the guesstimated date of ovulation. Then 266 days are added to that, and the resultant date is "it."

However, most people don't realize how rough this calculation really is, even when it is combined with a first trimester ultrasound to measure the baby's size. Eighty percent of pregnancies last somewhere between thirty-eight and forty weeks. Only 5 percent of babies arrive on their actual due date. Some 10 percent more go beyond forty weeks, if they are not medically induced first. Also, the standard calculation counts on a woman remembering exactly when she last menstruated and assumes that she ovulates on day 14 of the cycle. Many women ovulate on other days.

Additionally, women who have been on the pill before conception may have extremely irregular cycles (it takes at least three months after terminating use of the pill to regularize menstruation), thus making an estimate of due date very difficult.[1] Finally, women who were breastfeeding at the time of conception may not have been menstruating at all, and may have no idea where in their cycles they were when they conceived.

If you know exactly what date you conceived, you can add 280 days (about ten lunar months) to that and come up with a somewhat more accurate due date (see "The First Trimester" Web site list in appendix 2 for where to find a lunar month due date calculator). Even this, however, is just a guess. Due date may be affected by many factors, such as maternal age, ethnicity, and possibly even caffeine consumption. Getting too attached to a specific date and deeming the pregnancy early or late based on that can lead to unnecessary medical interventions and a sense that others know more about when your baby should be born than nature does.

Taking Stock

Part of this early time of celebration of your new pregnant state includes taking stock of your life, and of your health. Are you living a life that is compatible with the growth of a new human being? Are there changes you need to make?

Most people start by questioning their health practices. You want to know what to eat, what medicines to avoid, and how much you can move about. Most women have been pregnant for just a few weeks before they realize it, and some may not realize they are pregnant for a month or more. "What about that glass of wine I had, or the cappuccino I drink every morning?" many women worry.

We'll get into some ideas for healthy living and eating later, but first it's important not to get too hung up on what you've done before this moment. You can't change the past, but you can start to take care of yourself and your baby now.

Tobacco, caffeine, and alcohol habits are areas to look at first. These substances can have a big effect on the health of pregnant women, but even more on the health of their developing babies. The first trimester of pregnancy is an explosion of growth for the fetus. This is the time when the central nervous system, the heart and kidneys, even the face and eyes, are forming. By the tenth week your baby will already have fingers, toes, eyes, and ears.

CAFFEINE

The effects of caffeine on pregnancy have been well documented. Caffeine stays in your bloodstream for four to six hours after you have consumed it, and the placenta does not protect your baby from its effects. Consuming it at a rate of only two cups of regular caffeinated coffee per day may double your chances of miscarriage. It can alter the baby's heart rate and depress respiration. The effects on respiration can last into childhood.[2] There are also some preliminary studies that suggest heavy coffee drinkers (four cups per day or more) may increase the risk of sudden infant death syndrome (SIDS).[3]

Aside from this, too much caffeine will affect your sleep, which may already be hard to come by, as it is for many pregnant women. Caffeine increases stomach acids and will therefore increase heartburn, an ailment that affects even non-caffeine-consuming pregnant women.

Just to give you an idea of how much caffeine is in your daily cup of joe:

Coffee	8 oz. cup	135 mg
Black tea	8 oz. cup	20 to 100 mg (depends on length of diffusion)
Häagen-Dazs coffee ice cream	1 cup	58 mg
Diet Coke	12 oz.	46.5 mg
Pepsi-Cola	12 oz.	37.5 mg
Green tea	8 oz. cup	12 to 30 mg
Chocolate bar	1.5 oz.	27 mg
Decaf coffee	8 oz. cup	5 mg
Chocolate milk	8 oz. glass	5 mg[4]

TOBACCO

Practically everyone knows that smoking cigarettes is extremely detrimental to general health. Nicotine from your bloodstream will pass into the baby's bloodstream. This speeds up her heart rate and interrupts her respiratory movements. Nicotine in your body will also constrict blood vessels in the placenta so less oxygen and nutrients can reach your baby.[5]

Mothers who smoke typically have babies who weigh less. Smokers are also more likely to have a premature infant, or experience other birth complications. If you smoke, you are 33 percent more likely to experience a miscarriage or have a stillborn baby. Maternal smoking doubles, and possibly even triples, the risk of sudden infant death syndrome (SIDS).[6] Smoking can have other effects most people are unaware of. One recent study, for example, from the American Society of Plastic Surgeons suggests that women who smoke between one and ten cigarettes per day have a 50 percent higher chance of having a baby with cleft lip or palate.[7]

ALCOHOL

Another question most newly pregnant women have is about alcohol consumption. Research has shown clearly that excessive drinking during pregnancy can result in fetal alcohol syndrome. The American College of Obstetricians and Gynecologists defines excessive drinking as two or more drinks on a daily basis or binge drinking, more than three drinks on one occasion.[8] There is also some evidence to indicate that even a single binge can damage the fetus in early pregnancy. A baby born with fetal alcohol syndrome may have abnormal facial features, heart defects, club foot, low weight, and many other problems.

There is, however, no research that has studied the effects of mild or moderate alcohol consumption during pregnancy. For ethical reasons, it isn't likely that a complete double-blind study will ever be done.

In the United States, any kind of drinking during pregnancy is generally frowned upon. In other countries, however, women do continue to have the occasional glass of wine with dinner, and there is no evidence to indicate that this is harmful. Ultimately, each woman must make her own decisions about this issue.

RECREATIONAL DRUGS

It also makes sense to avoid using all recreational drugs. Some of them, such as cocaine, can seriously damage the developing embryo after even a single use. Some, such as marijuana, have been studied but have not proven harmful.[9] Many others have not been fully studied, but that doesn't mean they are not dangerous. Since their effects are not fully known, why risk it?

Steps toward a Healthy Lifestyle

There are a number of different approaches to giving up substances such as tobacco and caffeine that have become part of our lives. Some women may join a group such as Smokenders to help them work through this process, while others may find the group dynamic is not to their taste. Others have sworn by nicotine patches, twelve-step programs, hypnosis, or acupuncture to reduce tobacco cravings.

Here is a four-point plan that can get you started and lay a foundation for whichever method you ultimately choose.

Commit yourself 100 percent. It is the easiest and most loving way to tackle this challenge. Pick a day to start: it may be tomorrow, or it may be the beginning of next week. Muster up all your determination. Most of all, be prepared to spend some concentrated time and energy on making this change. Changing habits requires intense focus at first.

Evaluate yourself honestly. Exactly how much do you smoke or drink caffeinated beverages now? What factors trigger the desire to use one of these substances: a time, a place, a feeling, a situation? Which cigarette or cup of coffee do you enjoy the most?

Take a look at your support system. Can you think of three or four people who will really get behind you and encourage your change? Do you have a friend, family member, or coworker who has successfully gone through this situation and would act as your sponsor? You may want the support of a trusted health professional, as well. It is possible to do this alone, but it is much easier to have someone's help available should your resolve begin to waver.

Plan on a slow and gradual change. This is much healthier for your body than an abrupt "cold turkey" approach. Upon finding out they are pregnant, most women feel compelled to try to make an instant change in their negative habits. Taking it a bit more gradually, though, will cut down on stress and minimize cravings, which helps to ensure success. Start by eliminating one-quarter of your daily caffeine or tobacco consumption each week for four weeks. Cut out the easiest ones first, and save that most pleasurable cigarette or cup of coffee for week four, when you have had the strength of three weeks of success behind you.

Concentrating on a nourishing diet with plenty of variety can help (see chapter 2). If you use a cigarette or a glass of cola to either relax or energize you, consider what else might have the same effect. A glass of carrot juice or a short walk can give your body a big boost, for example, and a cup of herbal tea with honey or a five-minute meditation can relax you. Drinking plenty of water is essential while you are trying to quit. Your body will be eliminating toxins that were stored in cells and tissues.

Taking stock of your life includes an evaluation of activities that affect the health of the mind and emotions, as well. You may find yourself more deeply affected by violent films or books than you once were, for example. If you know that certain situations, such as a confrontation with a relative, are difficult to handle emotionally, then avoid them if you reasonably can. This is a time to take care of yourself on all levels.

Making Time for Yourself

You do not become a mother just at the moment of birth. You have already become a mother. You already want to do what is best for your baby. Taking care of yourself in all ways—emotionally, physically, psychologically, and spiritually—is the best beginning for your life as a mother and the best beginning for your child.

Pregnancy can be the first time that you take time for yourself. It helps if you can get into the habit of doing this from the beginning of your life as a mother. The moment you conceive, you become a mother to your baby, even though he or she is not yet born. It helps to remember this because most of us, in this age of hurry and change, will tend to expect ourselves to carry on as before.

Your baby needs you already, however, and keeping up with the physical and emotional changes you are going through requires you to slow down and pay attention to the cues your mind and body are giving you. You are, day by day, changing profoundly. Most big life changes call for thoughtful reorganization of our daily patterns. And this change is one that will be ongoing for years to come once your baby is born and grows into a child.

If you listen carefully to yourself, you may realize that you are just too tired to go to the party you'd planned to attend, even though you promised you'd be there. Your body needs more rest than usual. You may find yourself thinking almost obsessively about a certain food. Perhaps these limitations and cravings are your body's way of telling you what is right for you.

Look for ways to slow down and focus on yourself and your baby. If meditation has not been a part of your life before, early pregnancy is a great time to start. Meditation may sound intimidating to someone who has not had any previous experience with it. However, it does not need to be complicated or mysterious, and it's a great way to learn the ability to focus on one moment at a time, which will help you during delivery. Meditation can be as simple as observing your breath or even sitting in a rocking chair and quietly knitting.

There are an abundance of step-by-step guidebooks written on the subject of meditation. Many

yoga and adult education centers offer short workshops in meditation as well.

It isn't necessary to attend a workshop, however, to have a successful meditation practice. Simply sit in a well-supported position, either in a chair that holds your back upright or cross-legged on the floor, perhaps with a thin pillow underneath your buttocks. Some people meditate lying down, while others find this position tends to put them to sleep. It is best to remain awake and aware during meditation, although if you do repeatedly fall asleep during the process, it may be just what your body needs. Here are a few suggestions for simple meditations to get you started:

- Close your eyes and observe your breath as it enters and then leaves your body. You may accompany each breath by silently thinking the words "rising" as you inhale and "falling" as you exhale. As thoughts come into your mind, simply observe them and let them go.

- Close your eyes and repeat a simple mantra that you are comfortable with, such as the classic "ohm." You can repeat it in time with your breath, if you like.

- Try "walking meditation." You can do this in a quiet place outdoors or even in your own living room. Walk very slowly, try to feel each part of your foot as it contacts the ground (you may want to do this barefoot). Observe what is in front of you. If thoughts begin to rise, simply observe them and let them go.

MAKE TIME FOR EXERCISE

Early pregnancy is also an excellent time to start a regular exercise program that fits in with your changing body and energy levels. Movement is good for your health and for your baby's health, of course. It can also help you to get to know your body. Merely taking time out for yourself to exercise can enhance your self-worth. Focusing on yourself through movement will help you to understand the language of your body. You might discover areas that are tense and need release. And finally, increasing your awareness of your body through movement during pregnancy will prepare you to listen to your body during labor and birth.

It is important to consult with your care provider before beginning an exercise program. For the most part, though, you will find you can do whatever feels right. Recent studies indicate not only that exercise is safe during pregnancy but that regular and vigorous exercise helps to increase the rate of on-time delivery and lessen your chances of going into preterm labor and having a premature baby. This seems to be true even for women who are at risk for early delivery. In order to benefit from this, and other good effects of exercise, a woman must expend at least 1,000 calories per week exercising. This usually means about three hours of aerobics of some kind, or four to five hours of brisk walking each week.[10]

The American College of Obstetricians and Gynecologists recommends that you do not exercise so hard that you are not able to have a conversation while working out.[11] This is because too great an increase in your heart rate will heat your core up too much, which is not safe for the fetus. For this same reason, it is important to avoid saunas and very hot baths throughout your pregnancy. Generally speaking, activities that can result in a fall are also best avoided. That might include rollerblading, bike riding, and skiing, among others. As your pregnancy progresses, you will discover that certain positions are not as comfortable as they once were or that you need to limit certain kinds of stretches.

If you've already been running, lifting weights, or doing other very intense exercise, you will likely be able to continue these in a modified form (speak to your health care provider about what that might mean for *you*). Pregnancy is probably not the best time to start jogging, if you haven't been doing it before, but it is a fine time to start doing yoga, tai chi, or walking, just to name a few of the many options.

Yoga is particularly good for expectant women be-

BODY WISE
Modified Sun Salutation

This is an excellent way to stretch and invigorate your body, and it incorporates two other yoga positions, the Wheelbarrow and the Downward Dog. Go slowly at first and learn each step thoroughly. Then allow each step to flow to the next one. Inhale and exhale deeply evenly as you execute each step, keeping your head and neck relaxed.

1. Stand up straight with your feet slightly apart and your hands in prayer position at chest level.

2. Inhale deeply as you lift your arms and open them above your head.

3. Slowly bend down at the waist, keeping your knees bent and your head down as you place your palms on the floor.

4. Extend your right leg behind you, placing the ball of your right foot on the floor.

5. Extend your left leg behind you, placing the ball of your left foot on the floor.

6. Walk your hands back until you can press your heels to the floor and your body is in an inverted V, a posture called Downward Dog. Your toes should be slightly apart and turned in a bit.

7. Drop your head toward your knees. Bend your knees to the floor and pull yourself back into a sitting position.

8. Open your knees wide and allow your pelvis to hang down between them as you reach your fingertips as far out in front of you as possible.

cause it teaches you to focus on one part of the body at a time, and relax other parts. That's why you'll find yoga exercises throughout this book, many of them in the "Body Wise" sidebars. This training will come in handy during labor. You can look for a class geared just for pregnant women or find a gentle hatha yoga class, if you are a beginner. There are some poses that pregnant women should avoid, so be sure to ask the instructor about that. Dance may be another activity to explore, and there are a wide variety of options available: African, jazz, ballet, ballroom, and more. The ability to express deep emotion during dance may make it the perfect exercise for pregnancy. These days it is easy to find many organized classes of all kinds for expectant women who want exercise, as well as many videotapes.

All the benefits of working out that apply to women in general also apply to pregnant women, including speeding up a sluggish digestive system, relieving constipation, improving your mental outlook, avoiding depression, and keeping you fit for the work of labor that is ahead. There is also a social component to exercise. You may meet other pregnant women and pick up valuable tips on pregnancy and parenting.

First Trimester Common Concerns

As mentioned in the beginning of this chapter, many women experience pregnancy symptoms immediately. Some even figure out they are pregnant because of those symptoms, while others do not feel in any way unusual. Many mothers observe that pregnancy feels different for them with each child. There are very few rules about what's "normal" when it comes to having babies.

Fatigue. Most women notice changes in their energy levels during their pregnancy. Many women feel extreme fatigue right from the very beginning. It can feel like a nap is urgent, or you may find yourself nodding off at dinner, even though you normally stay up until midnight.

It's good to listen to your body's cues, as much as you reasonably can. You need extra rest—your body is going through huge hormonal changes right now. Take a fifteen-minute catnap when you can, or put your feet up for a few minutes. Realize that your normal evening regime may need to change a little, at

least during the first trimester. Most women, though not all, notice that they get a lot of their energy back again in the second trimester.

Breast changes. Sore breasts are a pregnancy symptom that many women notice immediately. Women who tend to get sore breasts with their periods may even think they are about to menstruate, not realizing they are pregnant. Other women may not feel any tenderness at all.

For some women the pain of sore breasts can be intense. Fortunately this symptom, too, usually fades away as the second trimester approaches. You may need to wear a much more supportive bra, or an athletic bra. Many women find it helpful to wear one to bed.

Increased breast size is very common in the early weeks. Women with smaller breasts may notice this change sooner. Other changes that can happen to the breasts are noticeably darker areolas and more prominent Montgomery's tuberoles (the little bumps on the areola).

Changes in skin, hair, and nails. As your pregnancy unfolds, you may discover that you've got thicker hair and stronger nails. You may also see changes in your skin. For some women this means they suddenly have a beautifully clear complexion, while others will find themselves with acne for the first time in their lives! If you do get pimples, try dabbing a little undiluted lavender oil on them. For inflamed pustules, use one drop of tea tree oil. Try to keep your skin extra clean and indulge in an occasional clay mask or facial.

Morning sickness and nausea. These are two of the most common complaints of the first trimester of pregnancy. Some women will experience just a bit of queasiness when they first wake up. Others might experience it at a different time of the day. Some women will feel sick enough to vomit at times. Still others will notice that they have very marked food likes and dislikes during this time. All in all, almost three-quarters of expecting women will experience some form of this problem.[12]

Despite its prevalence, the causes of morning sickness are not known for certain. Some possible reasons for it include:

- *Adjustment to the increased level of hormones.* The early pregnancy months are marked by an increase in estrogen and HCG (human chorionic gonadotropin), which is the hormone that maintains the body's estrogen levels. By the second trimester most women's bodies adjust to the higher levels all by themselves.

- *Low blood sugar.* This may be why some women experience a feeling of nausea first thing in the morning or after a prolonged time without food. In the early part of pregnancy the fasting blood sugar level reaches lower levels than in the nonpregnant state. The body's basal metabolic rate also speeds up, and therefore the symptoms of low blood sugar (nausea, shakiness, and fatigue) can happen much more quickly than usual.

- *Changes in the production of stomach acids and digestive enzymes.* When a woman becomes pregnant, her digestive functions slow down to allow for greater absorption of nutrients. Part of this slowing down includes lesser production of hydrochloric acid and other digestive enzymes. This may contribute to a feeling of nausea and explain why heartburn is a symptom for some women.

- *B-complex deficiencies.* Some women may need more B-complex vitamins than they are getting in their daily diets, especially vitamin B6, which helps the body to metabolize protein. This seems to be particularly true for women who are under a great deal of stress, have taken birth control pills recently, or are prone to motion sickness. Overcooked and overprocessed foods contribute to a lack of B vitamins in our diets.

- *Fatigue.* Some women discover that becoming overtired increases the tendency to feel nauseous.

- *Stress.* Pregnancy is stressful because it is a time of change. The changes may be desirable, but require a great deal of adjustment nonetheless.

NATURAL SOOTHER
Pregnancy Pick-Me-Up

This is a great drink for relieving morning sickness and helps to restore the body's balance after vomiting or diarrhea. It also helps keep electrolytes high and is good to drink during labor.

> 1/3 cup lemon juice
>
> 1/3 cup honey
>
> 1 teaspoon salt
>
> 1 crushed dolomite (calcium/magnesium carbonate) tablet

Stir in enough water to make 1 quart of solution. Pour over ice and sip slowly.

A Variation
For those who experience low blood sugar, which may contribute to extreme nausea in pregnancy, try this simple drink.

> 1 teaspoon honey
>
> 1 teaspoon apple cider vinegar

Stir into a glass of warm water and sip. This mixture can be made and drunk throughout the day and if you get up at night.

- *Protection.* There is some speculation that morning sickness may be nature's way of protecting the fetus from toxins present in some strong vegetables or spices.

To help cope and cut down on the amount of morning sickness and digestive problems you experience, try these tips:

- Increase your levels of protein. This may help to stabilize your blood sugar.
- Try to eat frequent small meals throughout the day. Take small snacks, such as trail mix, with you whenever you go out. Some women find it

helpful to have food by the side of their beds so they can nibble something during the night or first thing in the morning, before they even stand up. Eating saltines is one of those clichés of pregnancy, but it does seem to help many women. Granola bars, bread, protein smoothies, and bananas may help as well and add more nutrients than a cracker will.

- Avoid foods that are spicy, high in fat, rich, or high in sugar. It may also make sense to completely avoid caffeine.

- Eating in a healthy way when you're extremely nauseous can be challenging. Taking a prenatal vitamin can help ensure adequate vitamin levels, although it should not be used as a substitute for a good diet. Experiment with the best time of day to take your supplement, because taking it on an empty stomach may contribute to nausea. Taking it with a meal is usually best.

- Listen to your body. If you are having strong cravings or aversions to certain foods, there may be reasons for it. Give your body what you feel comfortable with.

- To avoid frequent heartburn, try papaya enzyme (papain) with your meals, consuming acidophilus in yogurt or kefir drinks, drinking liquids between meals rather than with them, or drinking bubbly mineral water, which makes you burp.

- Increase your consumption of B-complex vitamins. B6 seems to be particularly helpful. B6-rich foods include blackstrap molasses, wheat germ, yeast, wheat bran, bananas, avocados, dried beans, eggs, and meat. Try adding .5 to 2 milligrams of it to your daily diet. You can get about half a milligram by eating 1 banana, 1 slice of watermelon, a serving of salmon, or a large baked potato.

- Some women find that the smell of food and cooking odors are so overwhelming that they need to avoid them as much as possible. Here's a good excuse to have someone else do the cooking for a while! Other odors, such as perfumes, may also present a problem.

- Get adequate rest. Many women report that simply lying down helps relieve symptoms. Try, however, to get at least a little exercise, even if it seems like moving about will make you feel worse. Light exercise, such as walking or yoga, seems to alleviate pregnancy nausea.

- Ginger is a very effective natural remedy for nausea. You can purchase it as a tea or make your own from 1 teaspoon of fresh grated ginger or 1/2 teaspoon of dried ginger, or take one or two 500-milligram capsules. Nibbling on crystallized or candied ginger can also help. The effects will last at least four hours. Taking ginger in very large quantities has been known to help women with severe vomiting in early pregnancy, although this should be done only under medical supervision. Ginger has been well studied and is known to be safe, although its blood-thinning effects mean you should avoid it in the final weeks of pregnancy.

- Chamomile, peppermint, spearmint, fennel, raspberry leaves, and wild yam have been shown to be helpful in relieving digestive problems during pregnancy. You can use these in tea form or purchase tinctures and add them to a small amount of water. Herbal scents can also soothe. Try filling a small bag or cloth bundle with cloves, cinnamon, rosemary, or other herbs and breathing in the scent when you feel ill. These particular herbs are safe for use during pregnancy, but not all herbs are. See chapter 2 for advice on which ones to avoid.

- Try these acupressure techniques for relief. Probe each point shown on page 12 until you feel a twinge. Then stimulate each one for a few minutes. The first point to try is two thumb widths above the crease on the inner surface of the wrist, directly in line with the middle finger. Another point is between the breasts, directly over the sternal notch. The hollow at the base of the front of the neck is another to try, especially to reduce the urge to vomit. You can also try the motion sickness pressure-point bands available at most pharmacies. These are worn like bracelets, and have been shown to be extremely effective.

- Acupuncture, which uses fine needles to stimulate certain points, is an excellent aid for nausea and other digestive problems. You need to find a licensed practitioner for this treatment.
- Try this aromatherapy technique for morning sickness: mix 3 drops of lavender essential oil with 1 drop of peppermint essential oil, put this into an aromatherapy diffuser or a bowl of warm water, and allow it to scent the room. To help relieve nausea, try placing a cool lavender oil compress on your forehead and a warm lavender oil compress over the front of your rib cage. Make these by mixing either cool or warm water with a few drops of lavender oil, and then soaking a washcloth in it. It can also help to inhale peppermint oil on its own, or drink a cup of strong peppermint tea. Aromatherapy can also help with actual vomiting. Add 7 drops of lemon or lavender oil to 1 ounce of carrier oil: massage over the abdomen, or simply inhale the essences.
- Several homeopathic remedies can help. *Nux vomica* is recommended for vomiting and vertigo. *Ipecacuanhua* is a remedy for nausea with irritability. It is safe to take these in potencies of 12X or 30X. It is best to consult with a professional homeopath who can prescribe mixtures that are just right for you.

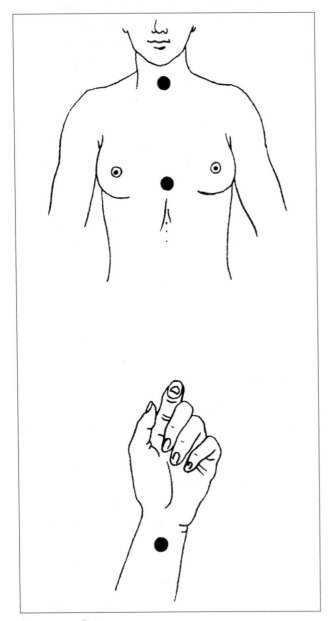

Acupressure Points

Luckily, morning sickness usually goes away by the fourth month. A few women may experience some nausea throughout their pregnancies, but these cases are rare. Many women do continue to have problems with heartburn, however.

It may also help to know that there seems to be a positive side to morning sickness and nausea. Studies show a significantly lower risk of miscarriage and stillbirth if nausea or vomiting is present. Also, fewer low-birthweight babies are born to women who experience these symptoms.

If your nausea and vomiting are so severe that you cannot eat, it is important to seek outside help. Consult with your midwife or doctor right away. Different types of antihistamines are generally used to help control severe nausea. Although avoiding medications as much as you can in pregnancy is advisable, these drugs appear to be safe for the fetus[13] and help the mother to keep herself, and her growing baby, well nourished.

Occasionally a woman's nausea is severe enough to warrant hospitalization and/or intravenous therapy in order to prevent dehydration and electrolyte imbalance. This condition is known as hyperemesis gravidarum. Interestingly, many women with hyperemesis seem to get instant relief just from hospitalization, even without any medicines or intravenous therapy.[14] Some doctors theorize that simply getting away from the stresses in their daily lives may be all that is needed. It could be that not having to breathe in food and cooking odors contributes to the change as well. Again, though, this type of severe nausea is quite rare.

Constipation. Many women find themselves experiencing occasional or frequent constipation right from the beginning. This is another one of those symptoms caused by increased hormone levels. They make the intestines relax and become less efficient.[15] Drink as much water as you can, and try to get sufficient fiber from fruits, vegetables, and whole grains in your diet. Exercise will also help keep things moving.

Try blending 2 ounces of sweet almond oil with 20 drops of marjoram and 5 drops of rose geranium essential oils. Use this aromatherapy blend to massage the lower back and lower abdomen. This may help relieve constipation.

If constipation becomes unbearable you will need to see your caregiver for further help.

Bleeding. It is not uncommon to spot-bleed during the first trimester, so don't panic if this happens to you. If you bleed a bit just after intercourse or a vaginal exam, there is no cause for worry, but call your midwife or doctor who may ask you to come in for an exam. Sometimes the bleeding does mean that a miscarriage is happening (see chapter 27), but only in about 30 percent of cases. If there is no discernible cause for the bleeding, your care provider may suggest you rest as a precaution. There is no proof that resting will prevent a miscarriage from happening or stop incidental bleeding, but it certainly can't hurt.

Sinusitis. This is a condition some women will experience throughout their entire pregnancies.[16] They may feel as though they have a permanent cold—complete with stuffed-up ears. What happens is that the mucous membranes inside the nostrils and sinuses swell up during pregnancy because of increased hormone levels. Drinking extra water may relieve your symptoms a bit. Try a humidifier in your bedroom and add some eucalyptus essential oil to it, or to a diffuser.

Headaches. During pregnancy, you may experience more headaches than you usually do. This could be because of tension, which is the most common reason for all headaches. Low blood sugar and increased sinus congestion might also cause headaches. Avoid aspirin and ibuprofen products (such as Advil and Motrin) during pregnancy. Acetaminophen products (such as Tylenol) are usually considered to be safe. Check with your practitioner. Before using painkillers, though, try these headache-relieving techniques:

- Use a cold compress or ice pack on your forehead.
- Rub peppermint oil on your forehead and temples, or place peppermint oil in an aromatherapy diffuser.
- Ask your partner to massage your head and temples. If you like, ask him to rub your forehead with Tiger Balm, a Chinese herbal paste available in most health food stores.
- Lie down in a dark room if you suspect your headache is tension-based. Try to incorporate more meditation and exercise into your daily schedule to help prevent tension.
- Be sure to eat regularly in order to avoid headaches that are the result of low blood sugar.

About 70 percent of women who normally get migraine headaches find they do not have them at all during pregnancy. The other 30 percent who continue to have them might benefit from trying biofeedback to relieve pain.

Depression. Some women will experience depression in the first trimester of pregnancy. It can feel almost as if you are being followed around by a black cloud. For most women it is minor and manageable. It usually goes away, sometimes almost overnight, by the end of thirteen weeks. If it continues, or if it feels as though you just can't manage it, seek out professional help. Do not take any antidepression medication, including the herb Saint-John's-wort, without consulting with your doctor or midwife.

For mild depression, try using an uplifting essential oil, such as bergamot or geranium, in an aromatherapy diffuser or warm bath. The homeopathic treatment *Pulsatilla* may also help.

Be sure you are getting enough protein in your diet (see chapter 2) and plenty of exercise. Aerobic exercise can alleviate mild depression by releasing your body's endorphins, naturally occurring chemicals that reduce stress and improve mood. A daily walk outdoors, or other vigorous exercise, can be particularly good for relieving depression.

Weight gain. Most women worry a great deal about gaining weight, even in the early months. As with everything else in pregnancy, there is no real "normal" range by which to gauge proper weight gain. Some women actually lose weight in the first trimester, especially if they have had a lot of nausea. Other women, particularly those on a second pregnancy, may gain quite a lot of weight. Many women report a thickening of the waist in the very early weeks, which they notice when they try to close the buttons of tighter-fitting jeans.

Fully experiencing the changes of your pregnant body, the extra storage of fat for nurturing, the full and heavy feeling of your growing baby, can often bring up negative self-images. We live in a society where "thin is beautiful." But thin is not beautiful for a pregnant woman and her baby. A strong, sturdy, well-rounded body is.

For many of us, it is an internal battle to feel excited about a weight gain of one or two pounds a week when most of our lives are spent watching our weight or trying to lose that proverbial last five or ten pounds. We know it's "better for the baby" and "probably" better for us and that we'll lose it later,

but growing into pregnancy and gaining weight can nevertheless present a challenge.

A simple visualization exercise to replace negative images within your psyche with positive images can be helpful in adapting to pregnancy weight gain. To begin a visualization, find a comfortable position of relaxation. Choose a person to lead you through the visualization whom you feel comfortable with. Let this person know what parts of your body feel heaviest and most uncomfortable to you. You can also tape-record your own voice if you prefer.

You can start with a relaxation process, using the imagery of your breath to focus on certain parts of your body, flowing from head to toe such that by the end of this process you are not only relaxed but centered inside your body. For example: "Now let your attention focus in the throat, and as you breathe in, your throat will become more and more loose, more and more open. With each breath, you will massage the inside of your body. Feel each breath create more and more room as your throat becomes relaxed and open.

"Now let this breath imagery move on through the body, stopping at the places of largest weight gain. Embrace with your breath the insides of your thighs, your upper arms, your buttocks, your face. Let your breath caress and warm the growing fat cells of your body as they pulsate nourishment and new life to your baby. See the food from the inside of your body transformed into liquid gold speeding through the placenta to your rapidly growing baby. See the link between you and your baby."

Other image ideas to work with are: imagine yourself ten pounds heavier, floating in water as your baby floats in water inside you; imagine yourself as a huge, powerful boulder, or as a whale swimming gracefully as queen of the ocean. Use imagery to replace ideas you may have as to what your body should look like. See yourself as a strong, complete, whole, and stable woman, bringing new life into your body, supported and nurtured by each mouthful of food.

End your visualization by focusing your breathing away from your body and back into the room and by slowly becoming aware of the room or space in which you are lying.

You may be wondering precisely where in your body the weight you've gained is going. After all, the average baby only weighs seven or eight pounds. Where does all the rest go? Here's where it goes in the "average" pregnancy (but remember, every pregnancy is different):

Baby	7.5 pounds
Your breasts	2 pounds
Extra maternal stores of protein, fat, and other nutrients	7 pounds
Placenta	1.5 pounds
Uterus	2 pounds
Amniotic fluid	2 pounds
Extra blood	4 pounds
Extra body fluids	4 pounds[17]

Sex. Can you have normal sex during pregnancy? The answer, for all normal pregnancies, is yes. Whether you will feel the same, sexually speaking, is another story. Some women find they have stronger sexual urges than usual. Other women feel much less. This may depend on how you are feeling. Being exhausted or feeling nauseous is not great for most people's sex drives!

Environmental hazards. It seems that the news announces yet another environmental hazard for us to be concerned about on a daily basis. There are indeed many contaminants and pollutants out there, and it pays to educate yourself as much as possible. At the same time, it is possible to go overboard and become afraid of everything, adding to stress levels just at a time when you want to try to decrease them. Here are a few specific things to watch out for:

- Secondhand smoke is almost as dangerous for your baby as if you were smoking a cigarette yourself. Try to avoid smoke-filled rooms. Ask your friends to kindly step out of the room if they must smoke.

- Electromagnetic fields (EMFs), emanating from power lines and electrical appliances, have been linked with reproductive problems as well as cancer. Although the research is inconclusive, it is probably best to limit your exposure to these potential hazards. Stand back or leave the room when using a microwave oven. Avoid electric blankets (try using a hot water bottle instead). Keep electric clocks, radios, and fans at least thirty inches from the head of your bed. Almost all major brands of computers now come equipped with low-emission terminals. To check yours, ask the manufacturer if it is TCO or MPR2 compliant. Sit at least thirty inches from the front of a video display terminal or television set. Of greater concern are EMFs emanating from office equipment such as copiers or laser printers. Sit at least four feet away from the back or sides of these machines, where the EMFs are strongest (even if a wall separates you from the machine). The same goes for television sets. Several studies have attempted to show a link between miscarriage and the daily use of computer monitors by pregnant office workers. So far these studies have been inconclusive.

- X rays are another cause of concern. If you are counseled to get an X ray while you are pregnant or trying to get pregnant, always ask, "How much will it help? Is it indispensable? And how much exposure will there be?"

- The fumes from paints, some cleaning supplies, glues, and other noxious products can harm a baby in utero, particularly during the first trimester.

- By the same token, breathing in the fumes from nail polish and polish remover may best be avoided. Other cosmetic applications, such as hair dye, have not been well studied in terms of their effects on the fetus, but you might want to stay away from them as much as possible until they have been shown to be safe.

- Avoid food additives and pesticides as much as you can during pregnancy. Recent research indicates that a woman who has a family history of allergic reactions such as asthma, eczema, or hay fever should completely avoid eating peanuts while pregnant or breastfeeding. Eating even traces of them during pregnancy (including from peanut oil) can actually sensitize a fetus to peanuts and create a future, potentially severe food allergy.

- Dental amalgam (silver-colored) fillings are the subject of controversy. Mercury makes up about 50 percent of a filling, and there is serious concern that this has been the cause of both short-term health effects, such as chronic fatigue syndrome and depression, and long-term effects, such as autism and Alzheimer's disease. It was once thought that the mercury in amalgam was inert. In other words, once it was in your mouth, it stabilized. That has now been proven to be untrue.[18] In some countries pregnant women are advised to completely avoid amalgam. It is best, in general, to avoid any medical interventions you can while you are pregnant, and that includes dental work (with the exception of cleanings, which are even more important for women who are expecting). If you absolutely *must* have a tooth filled, talk to your dentist about nonmercury alternatives.

Medicines. You may be wondering what medications are safe to use during pregnancy. A good rule of thumb is to avoid taking any medications, over-the-counter or prescription, during pregnancy and to ask your care provider about any substance you are at all unsure of. Here is a rundown of a few commonly used types of drugs:

- *Painkillers.* Aspirin (and white willow bark, which is a natural form of aspirin), ibuprofen (Motrin, Advil), codeine, and naproxen should not be used. Most care providers will recommend acetaminophen (Tylenol) if pain relief is absolutely necessary. (Also see "Headaches" on page 13 for some natural pain-relieving remedies.)

- *Antibiotics.* Penicillin seems to be safe for use in pregnancy—but don't ever use it without checking with your care provider. Sulfonamides (such as ampicillin) seem to be largely safe, except for the last few weeks of pregnancy, as they may cause jaundice in the newborn.[19] Many other antibiotics, such as streptomycin, for example, are dangerous and should never be used during pregnancy.

- *Tranquilizers and sleeping pills.* These can have a sedative effect on the baby as well as you. Newborns whose mothers use these drugs can show poor muscle control and have trouble breathing and eating.[20]

- *Laxatives.* Bulking agents and detergent stool-softeners appear to be safe for use in pregnancy. Others, including mineral oil and saline cathartics, are not safe for various reasons.[21] Check with your health provider before choosing a laxative. It's probably a good idea to try natural laxatives first, though, such as extra water and fruits, vegetables, and fiber.[22]

- *Asthma medications.* In some cases, the effects of a prolonged asthma attack may be more likely to harm your baby than the drugs will. Discuss this with your doctor.

- *Antidepressants and antipsychotic drugs.* Some of these drugs have been proven harmful during pregnancy, and others have not yet been well studied. You need to discuss this with your doctor to develop a strategy that will get you through the pregnancy without harming your growing baby.

Toxoplasmosis. You might not even know what toxoplasmosis is, but if you change cat litter or do a lot of gardening, you may be at risk for getting it. *Toxoplasma gondii* is a parasite carried by cats, in their feces, and also found in the soil. If you get it, you may have no symptoms or just mild flu-like ones. The real danger is to your baby, because infection can lead to miscarriage, birth defects, and premature birth. It's best, while pregnant, to have someone else change the cat litter, or to wear gloves if no one else is available. It's also a good idea to wear gloves while you are gardening. Toxoplasmosis can also be a food-borne infection. Avoid undercooked meats and wash fruits and vegetables well.

Listeriosis. This infection is caused by another type of bacteria found in foods. There are only about 2,500 cases of listeriosis per year in the United States, but fully one third of those infections happen to pregnant women. Listeria bacteria can be found in soft foods that have not been stored at sufficiently low temperatures. Avoid soft and unpasteurized cheeses and patés.

Herpes. Women with the herpes virus are greatly concerned about how it will affect their babies. There are two types of this virus: type 1 usually appears in the form of cold sores on the lips, and type 2 usually appears as watery blisters on the genitals. Unless the virus is actually contracted during pregnancy, it will not harm the baby growing inside your uterus. In fact, women with long-standing infections actually pass on natural protection against herpes infection to their babies.[23] It is well known that herpes recurrences can be brought on by stress—so you may find that you have more outbreaks during pregnancy. Whatever you can do to relieve stress in your life will help: slow down and try meditation. Avoid sunburn, saunas, and other high heat situations (which should be avoided by all pregnant women, anyway). Sitz baths and baking soda poultices may help relieve symptoms. Hydrogen peroxide or iodine kills the surface virus and speeds up the drying of lesions. Lemon balm cream (also called melissa extract) is a good topical treatment for sores.

Zinc, echinacea, chaparral leaves, chlorophyll powder, clay water, and the amino acid L-lysine may also help, but it is important to check with your care provider before taking some of these during pregnancy.

There is some evidence that a diet high in the amino acid lysine and low in arginine may reduce herpes outbreaks. Eat fish, chicken, beef, mung bean sprouts, brewer's yeast, milk, cheese, and most fruits and vegetables (but not peas). Avoid gelatin, chocolate, soybeans, wheat germ, wheat flours, and oats.[24]

If a woman is infected for the first time while she is pregnant, it is possible to pass the infection on to the fetus. This can result in mental retardation and other serious complications, or even death, so it's especially important to be cautious.

Long-standing cases of herpes will not present a problem during the birth itself unless it happens to coincide with an outbreak of blisters. If the blisters are in the genital area, it is possible that your caregiver will order a cesarean section. Blisters that are on the buttocks or thighs may be covered over with bandages to prevent passing the infection to the newborn. Sometimes even blisters in the genital area, if they are on the outer labial area, may not automatically indicate a C-section if the care provider feels it is possible to keep them from touching the baby.

Your age. How much of an issue is a woman's age when it comes to giving birth? The medical profession has historically had a bias for women who gave birth at early ages. In medical literature, women over age thirty-five and having their first babies are actually referred to as being in the "elderly primipara." While older studies showed that women over thirty-five were at higher risk for everything from infant mortality to longer labor, most of these studies have been shown to be faulty. Factors such as socioeconomic status, birth order, and general health were not taken into account. The poor picture of older women may also have been the result of a preexisting bias on the part of researchers against older mothers.

The only definitively known risks of giving birth over age forty have to do with genetics. Women over age thirty-five do have an increased chance of having a fetus with a chromosomal abnormality, such as Down syndrome, the most common and well-known of these abnormalities. One out of 1,000 babies born to women age twenty-nine will have Down syndrome. At age thirty-five, the risk rises to 2 or 3 per 1,000; and at age forty it is about 8 or 9 per 1,000. The worldwide frequency of genetic disorders, including Down syndrome and all others, is 6 in 1,000.[25]

Like most things in the world, there are pluses and minuses to delaying childbirth. Many older women feel they have reached most of their career goals and are really ready to become mothers now. They feel they are in a place where they can dedicate themselves to motherhood in a way they could not have as ambitious 30-year-olds. The average woman over age forty will find she proceeds with pregnancy pretty much the same way her younger sisters do, with all the ups and downs associated with childbirth. Other women may find it harder to adjust to change than they might have when they were younger. And there is no doubt that pregnancy is a time of huge change, a time when we really have to learn to let go and allow for forces that are bigger than we are, no matter what our age.

What to wear. This becomes an issue for many women almost right away. In the beginning you may find that many of your closer-fitting clothes don't work anymore or are just plain uncomfortable. Most maternity clothes are created for women who are in the second trimester, at the earliest.

Even later, when you can fit into maternity clothing, you may discover some difficulties. First of all, maternity clothing tends to be quite expensive. On the other hand, you'll tend to get more use from your maternity clothing than regular clothes, so you may feel this helps to balance out the higher prices. Finding styles you like can be tricky. Historically, fashions for pregnant women have tended to be a bit on the juvenile side. Amazingly, many maternity clothes are "dry clean only," which adds to the expense, inconvenience, and toxicity at a time when you need simplicity and safety in your life.

There has been a trend, more recently, for many big-name clothing stores to create maternity lines with clothing modeled by pregnant celebrities. Some of these clothes fit right in with the latest styles. Many of these lines steer completely away from the previous more juvenile look of maternity clothing. Some of them make no effort to mask the tummy

and try, instead, to show it off. After all, what's to hide?

If you don't live near these stores, though, you must order via catalog or online, and that can be tricky. How do you know what looks good on a body you've never had before? Fortunately, most catalogs have excellent return policies, so you can try things on at home and return them if they don't look right.

If you'd like to spend less on maternity clothing, or if the idea of being creative seems fun to you, try these tips now and for the coming months:

- In the early weeks you may be able to get by with loose-fitting clothing that you already own.
- Look through thrift stores and tag sales. Check out the men's section as well as the women's. In the later months you may find good buys in maternity clothes at thrift stores as well.
- Other good thrift-store finds: leggings in cotton, velour, and other stretchy fabrics that can be snipped at the waistline and have a bit of elastic added to them to span the gap; skirts that you can extend by snipping off the waistband and sewing its raw edge to the top part of a slip, which serves as a maternity panel; vintage smocks and Mexican and Guatemalan huipiles (sack dresses); and high-waisted dresses that fit under the bustline in chiffon fabrics.
- Invest in overalls, either short or long. Overalls are a good beginning because they can be worn very loosely at first and still be stylish. You can even wear them with the sides unbuttoned as you grow larger. You can wear a variety of shirts under them. Button-down shirts that are too small can be worn partially unbuttoned and won't show.
- You may find more clothing variety in plus-size shops. Some of these clothes are very stylish yet are less expensive than maternity clothes. Not all large styles work, however. Check the hems of shirts and dresses to make sure they are even.
- If you sew, try this trick: buy large T-shirts or

sweatshirts, cut them along the side seams, and insert contrasting upholstery fabrics cut like very tall, thin isosceles triangles. This will widen the bottom to make room for your wonderful belly. Try a black brocade fabric with a black cotton T-shirt, for example.

- Borrow from previously pregnant friends. In the early months you might also borrow from friends who are larger than you are, or have clothes that are now too large for them. This might tide you over until you reach "maternity clothing size."

HIGHER GROUND

Large and Lovely

Now I know my body

Is really a vessel,

Able to transform itself

At the service of life,

Able to stretch big

With life,

To swell small breasts

Large with milk,

To grow narrow pelvis

Open for birth,

To reach open arms

Out for comfort.

—Peggy O'Mara

When I use the words *eating well,* I mean using food not only to influence health
and well-being but to satisfy the senses, providing pleasure and comfort.

—ANDREW WEIL, M.D., *Eating Well for Optimum Health*

There is probably nothing in the life of women today that pushes their buttons the way the subject of diet can. Hearing the word *diet* immediately conjures up the idea of losing weight for most women, and when it comes to weight loss, women have heard it all: "Eat lots of proteins and cut out carbohydrates," "Eat lots of fruits and vegetables and cut out all meat," "Count your calories," "Count servings instead of calories," and even "Diets don't work at all." It's hard to know how to eat properly at all, let alone when you're pregnant.

Probably the biggest disservice the diet industry has done to women is to give them the message that there is some formula that will solve all their eating problems. The trouble is, of course, that following someone else's menu plans never takes into account what you might really feel like eating *today* (and maybe what your body really needs). Then, when you don't follow the diet properly, you start a downward slide of guilt, followed by rebellious eating, more guilt, and finally weight gain—and a pile of very negative feelings about yourself.

The good news is that pregnancy is an opportunity to unlearn a lot of old, not-so-good eating attitudes. Since you aren't trying to lose weight (the opposite, in fact), this is the perfect time to learn more about nutrition and, more important, to learn to listen to your body instead of everyone else's advice on what to put into it. It's possible that you can completely change your relationship to food, not only during your pregnancy but afterward as well.

Changing your relationship with food might include redefining what food and eating mean to you. Using food as a way to take loving care of yourself may help you to stop seeing your urges as the enemy. Eating can be a community event, for example, or you might use food in a spiritual way to soothe yourself.

In this chapter you will learn the basics about nutritional needs during pregnancy, and you'll be given a few suggestions on how to implement this information. There are tips for different types of eaters, from vegans to vegetarians to red meat eaters. You can decide for yourself how you will put the information together and choose what to eat. At the end of this chapter you'll find some guidelines on how to learn to listen to your body and give yourself what you seem to want and need *today*.

How Much Does Diet Matter during Pregnancy?

"Now you are eating for two," goes the old cliché. This is true, but for many women that could mean getting even more obsessed about eating and having more guilt when they don't do it "properly." If you eat a hot fudge sundae or something else that is considered to be "bad," are you harming your growing baby?

Like many other health-related questions, this one has few clear answers. Other than a few specifics, studies have not been able to pinpoint precisely how the mother's diet affects a baby's growth while it is still in the womb. Trials that study the effects of a specific vitamin or mineral on pregnancy, like zinc for example, have usually failed to show anything conclusive[1] (there are a few exceptions, and we will discuss them below). Trying to observe how a woman's eating habits affect a fetus and rule out all other contributing factors (such as socioeconomic ones, for example) is quite difficult.

Some studies do suggest that pregnancy diet can have an impact on a child's long-term health, perhaps even well into adulthood. Many of these studies relate certain future health problems to an infant's weight at birth. For example, one trial done on adult women concluded that those with a birth weight of less than 5.5 pounds had a 23 percent greater risk of heart disease as an adult, compared to those who weighed more.[2] This study took all their present health conditions into account in order to isolate the real effect of their birth weights on their risk.

Other studies have suggested that babies undernourished in the first trimester are at risk for becoming overweight as adults. Conversely, babies who are very large at birth, 10 pounds or more, are also at a much higher risk for becoming overweight adults.[3] Many other studies show a relationship between nutrition in the womb and risks for schizophrenia, asthma, diabetes, breast cancer, and more. Naturally, diet in the womb is not the only factor contributing to adult disorders. Many other factors, such as your child's future lifestyle, will affect adult health.

Nonetheless, it makes sense to arm yourself with some basics about human nutrition and to learn to provide yourself with the very best fuel. You've got a hard job to do over the next few months, and good nutrition can only help you in your mission.

The Basics of Nutrition

What holds true for the average adult, in terms of nutrition, applies to expecting women as well. Here are a few bottom-line basics about nutrition, along with some special tips for pregnant women. If you want additional information about nutrition during pregnancy, you can check out one of the books suggested in appendix 2.

Macronutrients. Our bodies require energy in order to function, and that energy is received, of course, from food. The foods we eat provide our bodies with three types of macronutrients:

- *Protein.* Protein makes up most of the body's weight, aside from water. Your body uses it to repair and maintain itself and to build muscles and skin. Protein can be found in eggs, meats, poultry, fish, soy products, nuts, and milk products, and in many other foods in lesser amounts.

- *Carbohydrates.* All of the body's tissues can use glucose (which is what carbohydrates are converted to in the body) as fuel. Some parts of the body, the brain for example, can only use glucose, except in starvation situations, as fuel.[4] It is found in grains, fruits, vegetables, legumes, and sugars.

- *Fat.* Aside from making food taste better, fat makes an essential contribution to our health. Essential fatty acids (EFAs) are used to make hormones, build cell membranes, and control blood pressure. Fats can be obtained from vegetable sources like nuts, oils and avocados, just to name a few, or from animal sources such as meat, fish, poultry, and dairy products.

Many foods provide more than one type of macronutrient. Soy products, for example, which are high in protein, also provide carbohydrates. Mushrooms, which are high in carbohydrates, also contain a goodly amount of protein.

Our bodies need all the fuel that macronutrients

provide, in proper proportion, in order to function well. Diets such as the recently popular Atkins diet that advocate wiping out one category of nutrients altogether (carbohydrates in this case) may be effective in the short term for weight loss but can in the long term wreak havoc with the body's operating systems.

The most important thing to know about macronutrients is their proper proportions in the daily diet. Experts do vary slightly in their suggestions on this, but most call for providing 10 to 25 percent of calories from protein, 50 to 60 percent from carbohydrates, and 20 to 30 percent from fats.

During pregnancy there are a few important facts to note about macronutrients:

Protein. During pregnancy, the body's blood volume increases by 50 percent. Protein is needed to facilitate this and to produce breast milk later on. Therefore, pregnant women need to take in more protein than they regularly do. Women who are carrying twins need to be even more careful to keep their protein intake up.

Proteins are made up of amino acids. Animal proteins and soy proteins are known as "complete proteins" because they contain all of the amino acids that human beings need. Plants also contain protein but are "incomplete" because they contain only some of the amino acids. To obtain all the amino acids, you need to combine a variety of plants.

How much protein is enough? If you included all of the following items in your daily diet, you'd have it pretty well covered, as long as you were also eating a balance of other nutritious foods:

- 1 egg *or* 1/2 cup granola *or* 1/4 cup of cottage cheese, and
- 1 cup soy *or* cow's milk yogurt, and
- 1/2 cup of mac 'n' cheese (health-food-store variety) *or* a small handful of roasted soy nuts, and
- 1 cup of baked beans *or* 1 cup serving of pasta *or* 1 cup of miso soup, and
- 1 cup of either soy or cow's milk (but not rice

milk, which does not have high protein content) *or* a handful of almonds, and
- 1 serving meat or fish *or* a tempeh burger on a roll.

Women on vegetarian diets can concentrate on milk, yogurt, cheeses, and eggs to increase their protein intake. Vegans can emphasize soy products such as tempeh, textured vegetable protein (TVP), soy milk, and miso. Women on macrobiotic diets can get their extra protein from fish.

Pregnant women, however, should restrict consumption of certain seafoods that contain moderate to very high levels of mercury to once a month or less often. Here are some fish to be cautious of: grouper,

---

NATURAL SOOTHER

Baby Nog

This is a great drink to have at the beginning of your day. It's packed with protein for energy, and B vitamins to calm and sustain you. Both yeast and molasses are good sources of iron. Adapt the drink to your particular tastes and food persuasions. It's good throughout pregnancy and during the breastfeeding years as well.

1 cup cow, soy, or rice milk

1 raw egg (optional)

1 tablespoon nutritional yeast (if the drink gives you gas, start with 1 teaspoon and gradually increase to 1 tablespoon)

1 tablespoon blackstrap molasses (again, start with less and build up if the taste is strong for you)

1 tablespoon honey

Blend until frothy and serve in a chilled glass.

Atlantic halibut, lobster, mackerel, orange roughy, Atlantic pollock, Pacific rockfish, shark (highest in mercury), snapper, striped bass, swordfish, and tuna. Pregnant women should have no more than 12 ounces of any kind of cooked fish per week, according to the Food and Drug Administration. Some environmental groups think even that is too much.

Anyone can enjoy beans and grains, which also provide a great deal of good quality protein. Women on nonmeat diets can always boost their protein intakes by eating soy-based protein powder occasionally.

Carbohydrates. Carbohydrates are really "the staff of life." Each culture has a specific high-carbohydrate food that is its staple for survival. In Japan it is rice; in Tibet, barley. The Mexicans use corn in most of their main dishes, and the Irish grow potatoes. Here in the United States, as in much of the Western world, bread made from refined wheat flour has been our main staple.

The study of a relatively new concept called glycemic index (GI) has changed the way scientists look at the consumption of carbohydrates. As mentioned earlier, carbohydrates are converted into glucose by the body and used as a basic fuel. Foods with a high GI are converted very quickly into glucose and cause a strong insulin response from the body, raising blood sugar to high levels. Foods with a lower GI are converted into energy much more slowly. This slower insulin response is altogether better for the body. As a point of reference, pure glucose has a GI of 100.

It probably won't come as much of a surprise to learn that refined and processed foods tend to have a much higher GI than unprocessed foods. White rice has a GI of 72, for example, whereas brown and basmati rice have GIs of 55 and 58, respectively. Gatorade has a GI of 78, orange juice 46. Dried dates have a GI of 103; raisins have a GI of 64.

Interestingly, whole wheat bread does not have a significantly lower GI than white bread, unless it includes a lot of whole grains and seeds or is stone-ground. In general, the crunchier a food is, the lower the GI, and the better it is for you. Pasta cooked al dente has a lower GI than overcooked, mushy pasta.

While your carbohydrate needs do not change during pregnancy, it is a good idea to avoid highly processed, sweetened, and refined foods. Eat plenty of low-GI carbohydrates such as oatmeal, beans, whole grains, and legumes, as well as low-GI fruits such as apples, pears, plums, and peaches.

Fat. There are three types of fat: saturated, polyunsaturated, and monounsaturated. In terms of calories and the energy they provide, they are all the same. A tablespoon of butter contains exactly the same amount of calories as a tablespoon of extra-virgin olive oil.

In terms of benefits to the body, however, they are not at all equal. Of the three, monounsaturated fats are generally preferable for the major part of your fat consumption. Monounsaturated oils include olive (which experts think is the hands-down best choice), canola, peanut, and avocado oils, as well as avocados themselves, and some nuts, including almonds, cashews, macadamias, pistachios, and walnuts. Pumpkin seeds are another good source.

Some polyunsaturated fats are all right to include in the diet, especially those that contain omega-3 fatty acids (see more on these below). Sunflower, safflower, sesame, corn, and soybean oils, and cold-water fish oils (like salmon and mackerel) are among the best choices.

Saturated fats are the least healthy and are best used in small amounts. Go easy on butter, fat found in meats, coconut, coconut oils, and palm oil.

One very important note about fats has to do with a type that is not naturally occurring but is extremely prevalent in processed and prepared foods these days. When you read labels, look for the words *trans-fat, hydrogenated,* or *partially hydrogenated fats.* These fats are potentially worse for your arteries than saturated animal fats. Manufacturers use them because they increase the shelf life of foods. It's really best to avoid these altogether.

Omega-3 fatty acids. This is a fairly new area of nutrition research, but important enough to warrant its own section. The omega-3 essential fatty acids are important components of cell membranes. They are also used to make hormones that keep blood from clotting abnormally and inflammation from getting out of control.[5] Countries such as Japan that consume more omega-3 in their diets seem to have lower rates of depression. Consuming enough of it may protect you against heart attacks, stroke, macular degeneration (which can cause blindness), and many cancers and reduce symptoms of inflammatory and autoimmune diseases.

As if that weren't enough, omega-3 is particularly important for pregnant women in the third trimester, and for women who are breastfeeding. These are the times when the baby's brain is developing at an amazing rate. Babies deficient in omega-3 may have a higher risk of autism, attention deficit disorder, and depression or adult degenerative diseases like Alzheimer's or Lou Gehrig's disease.

Many researchers believe that our proportions of omega-3 fatty acids to another fatty acid, omega-6, got turned upside down hundreds of years ago, once agriculture became an integral part of humans' lives. While both types of fatty acid are necessary to human health, it seems that the twentieth century has done even more to contribute to overconsumption of omega-6 (found in meats, corn oil, cottonseed oil, and soybean oil, for example) and also add to what may be a widespread deficiency of omega-3. This is because our ancestors ate wild foods such as game and fish, that in turn consumed high quantities of omega-3 from grasses and other plants. These days most of the meats we consume are fed corn, which simply does not provide this essential fatty acid. Some experts think this may explain the huge increase in heart disease in the twentieth century, along with other health problems such as depression, attention deficit disorder, autism, Alzheimer's disease, and more.

The bottom line is that we all need to eat much more omega-3. You can find it in these foods:

- Oily, cold-water fish like salmon and sardines: this is probably the very best source of omega-3. Try to get a couple of servings a week.
- Canola oil.
- Flax seeds and flax seed oil: this is particularly good for non-meat eaters. Grind up flax seeds and sprinkle them on salads or vegetables, or bake them in muffins. Try to have a couple of tablespoons per day.
- Walnuts and walnut oil.
- Pumpkin seeds.
- Soybeans.
- Hemp seeds.
- Purslane, a lesser-known leafy vegetable used more commonly in the Mediterranean and in Mexico.
- Dark leafy green vegetables.
- Fortified eggs: hens are fed a diet that contains omega-3. You'll find these in health food stores, but more and more commonly in supermarkets as well.

Micronutrients. Micronutrients include vitamins, minerals, fiber, and phytochemicals. While contributing very little in the form of energy (calories) to the body, micronutrients are vital to a number of its functions. Becoming deficient in certain vitamins, for example, can result in a range of diseases or even death.

Below are descriptions of the micronutrients that are particularly important for you to be aware of while you are pregnant:

Folate. Advertising campaigns are beginning to make the term *folic acid* well known, and with good reason. Consuming enough folic acid can reduce the incidence of severe neural tube defects (such as spina bifida) by as much as two-thirds. This matters early on in the pregnancy—right from the very beginning, in fact, since a baby's spinal column and brain are already fully formed by week four.[6] For this reason most experts advise all women of childbearing age to take folate, since 50 percent of pregnancies are unplanned. Aside from pregnancy, folate is also important for the synthesis of DNA, and it acts with vitamin B12 to help form red blood cells.

The minimum amount to consume is 400 mcg daily, according to the RDA requirements, but some experts think it best to take more, up to 800 mcg per day. A pregnant woman needs at least 600 mcg daily. It's usually best to try to get your vitamins through diet, but this can be challenging. Since getting enough folate is so critical, you might consider taking some of it as a supplement. If you are taking a prenatal vitamin, it will probably provide at least 400 mcg.

The highest concentrations of folate can be found in beans and peas, leafy green vegetables, asparagus, sunflower seeds, whole grains, papaya, oranges, blueberries, and strawberries.

You can get about 400 mcg of folate in your daily diet if you eat:

- 1 glass of orange juice *or* 1/4 cup of wheat germ *or* a small handful of dried soybeans, *and*
- 1 egg *or* 2 slices whole-wheat bread *or* 1/4 of a cantaloupe, *and*
- 1 cup of pinto, black, or navy beans *or* two cups of cooked turnip greens, spinach, or asparagus *or* 1 tablespoon brewer's yeast.

Vitamin B6. B6 aids in protein metabolism and red blood cell formation and helps with normal brain function. As discussed on page 10, B6 may also help women who suffer from morning sickness and nausea during the first trimester.

The amount of B6 recommended daily for pregnancy is 1.9 mcg. You can get your daily requirement by eating:

- 1 banana *or* a slice of watermelon *or* a potato (with skin), *and*
- a serving of salmon, chicken, *or* a pork chop *or* 1/2 cup garbanzo beans *or* 1 cup oatmeal, *and*
- 1 cooked rainbow trout *or* a handful of dried soybeans *or* 1 tablespoon of brewer's yeast *or* a cup of green peas *or* brown rice, *and*

- 1/4 cup of wheat bran *or* a handful of walnuts *or* sunflower seeds *or* a cup of tomato juice *or* 1/2 cup of sliced avocado.

Vitamin B12. B12 helps maintain healthy nerve cells and red blood cells and is used to make DNA. This vitamin is of particular importance to vegetarians because it is much harder to provide in nonmeat foods. Breastfed infants of some strict vegetarians can show signs of B12 deficiency when consumption of this vitamin has been neglected. You need to consume 2.6 mcg of this vitamin daily.

If you eat meat or fish, you can get enough B12 in your diet by eating just one rainbow trout or a serving of salmon or beef daily. If you eat dairy products and eggs, you can get enough by consuming two cups of milk and two eggs, or one egg and two ounces of cheese. If you are a vegan and do not consume dairy products, look for well-fortified cereals that provide 100 percent of the daily requirement, or check with your health care provider about supplements.

Calcium. Calcium is important for all women because of the now well-known dangers of osteoporosis, a reduction in bone mass, which can be crippling. The danger for women who are pregnant is that if they are not taking in enough calcium every day, the developing fetus will use the stores of it that are in the mother's bones. This is because calcium is necessary for the baby's own skeleton to develop. Studies also show that sufficient calcium may reduce the risk of developing high blood pressure during pregnancy.[7]

Most women need to take 1,000 mg per day of calcium. During pregnancy and lactation, that amount should increase to at least 1,200 mg. Most prenatal vitamins do not contain adequate amounts of calcium, and the balance needs to be made up for, preferably through the diet. If you decide to take an additional calcium supplement, take it at a different time of day than you take your prenatal vitamin. Calcium is absorbed better when not taken with iron. It does help, however, to take your calcium with vitamin C and vitamin D (at least 400 IU daily) in order to get maximum absorption. Taking your calcium supplement before bed may help you to sleep.

You can get about 1,000 mg of calcium by consuming:

- 1 cup of milk *or* fortified soy or rice milk, and
- 1 cup yogurt *or* fortified soy or rice yogurt *or* 1 cup of cooked collard or turnip greens, and
- 3 ounces of sardines *or* 1 stalk of broccoli and 1 cup of cooked turnip greens.

Other good sources of calcium are cottage cheese, seaweed, almonds, beans, cheeses, tofu, and leafy green vegetables. If you are a vegan or on a macrobiotic diet, try sprinkling toasted sesame seeds on greens, such as steamed or sauteed kale or collard greens.

New research on calcium is beginning to make some experts think that getting the body to *retain* calcium stores is much more crucial in the prevention of osteoporosis than how much of it you consume. Consuming too much alcohol and caffeine and eating a high-protein diet seem to deplete the body of its calcium stores more quickly. Exercising helps the body to hold on to its calcium supply.

Iron. Most of the iron in your body is found in hemoglobin, the protein in red blood cells that carries oxygen to your body's tissues. It helps to form myoglobin, which carries oxygen to your muscles. Your body also stores extra iron for use when it needs it.

For men, adequate iron is rarely a problem, but for women, who lose blood every month when they menstruate, it is. Before they even become pregnant, many women are already anemic without knowing it. This means they do not have enough iron in their red blood cells, leaving them prone to fatigue and low energy. Then they enter pregnancy, a time when the blood volume in their bodies increases. They need iron now more than ever so that the extra red blood cells can function properly. Taking in adequate amounts of iron in the diet will help reduce fatigue. Getting enough iron during pregnancy may also reduce the risk of premature delivery and low birth weight.[8]

Iron is another nutrient that is challenging to get enough of in the diet. This is particularly true for nonmeat eaters, because the type of iron available in meat sources is much more easily absorbed by the human body. Vegetarians and vegans need to be vigilant about taking in enough iron. It can help, if you are a vegetarian, to consume vitamin C with iron sources, because this increases the body's ability to absorb it. Concentrate on dark green leafy vegetables such as spinach and kale. Also eat plenty of whole grains, seaweed, soy products, and fortified cereals.

You need 27 mg of iron in your daily diet. You can get enough of it by consuming:

- 1/2 cup of cream of wheat (fortified) *or* 2 servings of beef, turkey, or clams *or* 1 cup of lentils, and
- 1 cup of lima *or* kidney beans *or* black-eyed peas *or* 1/2 cup of prune juice, and
- 1 wedge of watermelon *or* 12 dried apricot halves *or* 1 tablespoon of blackstrap molasses *or* 2 eggs, and
- 1 cup of cooked spinach *or* 2 cups of cooked kale *or* 4 oysters, and
- 2 slices of whole wheat bread *or* 1/2 cup of tofu *or* 1 chicken leg.

If you are anemic, or a vegetarian, you may need an iron supplement. Most prenatal vitamins will provide the amount of iron necessary for expecting women. It is very important, however, to check with your health care provider before taking any additional iron supplements because too much of it can be toxic.[9] Also keep in mind that some women will experience more constipation with increased iron supplementation.

Zinc. Like vitamin B6, zinc helps the body to metabolize protein. Zinc keeps your immune system healthy and aids in the healing of cuts and wounds. During pregnancy your zinc requirement increases, and you should get 11 to 15 mg per day. You can get enough zinc by eating:

- 1 cup of milk *or* a bran muffin, and
- 1 cup of cereal *or* 1 cooked crab, and

- 1 cup of garbanzo or kidney beans *or* a handful of pumpkin seeds or almonds, and
- 1 serving beef *or* 1/4 cup wheat germ, and
- 1 yogurt *or* 1 1/2 ounces of cheddar cheese *or* 1 small handful of walnuts.

You can also get more than one day's zinc requirement by eating just three oysters. Legumes, soy products, nuts, eggs, whole grains, and wheat germ are nonmeat foods that contain zinc.

Fiber. Fiber is important for everyone, but for pregnant women it is even more vital because it helps to keep constipation at bay. Fiber is found only in plants, not in animal foods. It comes in two forms: *soluble,* which absorbs water, and *insoluble,* which does not. The body needs both types to function optimally, and most fruits, vegetables, and grains contain both types. If you suffer from constipation, however, you need to lean more heavily on the insoluble fibers. They work best when plenty of fluids are included in the diet.

Foods with high amounts of insoluble fiber are: apples (with skin), bananas, grapes, pears, corn, peas, black-eyed peas, kidney and pinto beans, sesame seeds, almonds, oat bran, and whole wheat pasta.

Phytochemicals. There are over 12,000 phytochemicals identified so far. They are protective compounds found in fruits, vegetables, and grains. They contain antioxidants, protect against a range of ailments from heart disease to cancer, stop DNA mutation, and stimulate the immune system. And this is just the tip of the iceberg. New benefits are being discovered every day.

No one knows the precise amount the body needs of any given phytochemical in order to function optimally. Researchers do know, however, that most of us are not getting enough of them. They recommend a minimum of nine servings of fruits and vegetables on a daily basis. The best way to ensure you are getting all the phytochemicals you need is to eat a rainbow variety of fruits, vegetables, and whole grains.

HIGHER GROUND
Self-Demand Feeding

Pregnancy may be the first time in your life that you allow yourself to eat as you please. If you have turned to food to meet emotional needs in the past, or if you simply want to view your pregnancy as an opportunity to have a better relationship with food, try "self-demand feeding."

Self-demand feeding is simple: Eat when you're hungry; eat foods that you choose yourself; stop when you're full. You decide what, when, and how much to eat. Here are some guidelines:

- Have a wide range of foods available in your home.
- Focus on physical hunger rather than the time of day as the reason for eating.
- Be prepared to deal with your own biases about how, what, and when you should eat.
- Do not impose any eating or any rules about eating on yourself.
- Allow yourself to develop new personal tastes and eating styles.

Self-demand feeding is based on the principle that all people, if left to their own devices, will eat a balanced diet over time.

The Food Groups

The United States Department of Agriculture's Food Guide Pyramid was created so that people could have an easy way to know if they are consuming enough of the necessary macro and micronutrients.

Used as a rough guide, the Food Guide Pyramid can come in handy. Some nutritionists do have a few problems with it, however. Many believe the quantities of fruit and vegetables on the lower end of the scale (two to four servings) are way too low. They recommend a daily consumption of eight or nine servings of fruits and vegetables. Others feel the protein section (meats, fish, etc.) may encourage people to eat way too much red meat on a daily basis. Furthermore, they argue that those who are lactose-intolerant or vegan will not be able to eat the suggested dairy portions, and will need to adjust the food guide to make sure they get adequate calcium.

Check out this food guide, which we have modified from the USDA Food Guide Pyramid to suit the needs of pregnant women. This guide takes some of the more recent research about nutrition into account.

THE FOOD GROUPS

- *Grain products:* Five to eleven servings. Include whole grain bread, corn tortillas, rolls, bagels, muffins, whole grain waffles or pancakes, hot grain cereals, rolled oats, cracked wheat, wheat germ, cold cereal, granola, whole grain pastas, brown rice, millet, and bulgur.
- *Vegetables:* Five servings or more. Include a colorful variety of vegetables such as spinach, yellow squash, red peppers, pumpkin, corn, arugula, collard greens, carrots, turnip greens, dandelion leaves, purslane, chard, sweet potatoes, white potatoes, broccoli, and endive.
- *Fruits:* Four servings or more. Include oranges, papayas, tomatoes, lemons, rose hips, berries, watermelon, cantaloupe, apricots, pineapples, apples, and peaches.

- *Milk products and other calcium sources:* Three to five servings. Include milk, yogurt, buttermilk, rice milk, soy milk, kefir, tofu, broccoli, blackstrap molasses, cheese, soy cheese, almonds, sesame seeds, tahini, carob, sea vegetables (kelp, nori, wakami, hijiki, dulse), and mustard greens.
- *Protein sources:* Three servings. Include eggs, fish, chicken, beef, tofu, tempeh, sardines, salmon, cheese, milk, cottage cheese, tuna, and pork.
- *Fat sources:* Use sparingly. Include olive oil, canola oil, salmon, nut butters, avocado, and flax seeds.

Just what is a serving, anyway? The guide below can give you an easy way to guesstimate what a serving actually is.[10]

Food Group	One Serving	Visual Equivalent
Grain products	1/2 cup rice or pasta	Tennis ball
	1 slice bread	CD case
Vegetables/fruits	1 cup raw	Tennis ball
	1/2 cup cooked	Small fist
Calcium sources	1 oz. cheese	Pair of dice
Proteins	3 oz. cooked meat	Cassette tape
Fats	1 tsp. olive oil	Half-dollar

Fluids. Drinking enough liquid while you are expecting is vital. When you are pregnant, your body increases all its normal needs for fluids. Water moves nutrients through your body and to your growing baby. It also removes toxins from your body and keeps it at the right temperature for fetal growth. Water will also make you feel better, cut down on constipation, and help avoid fatigue.

You need eight to twelve 8-ounce glasses of water

every day. You can drink this water straight or make teas, juice, or soups with it. It might help to put your targeted water consumption into a pitcher or water bottle every morning and then drink it throughout the day.

Shopping and Cooking Tips

Once you understand the basics of nutrition and are ready to make some healthy changes in your daily diet, you are ready to put it all into practice. Feeding yourself well involves more than just knowing what the correct nutrients are, however. What you buy for yourself and how you put it all together matters.

Shopping tips. Where should you shop? How important is it to purchase organic foods? What about genetically engineered foods? Experts are divided on all of these issues. More and more of them, though, are beginning to recommend that crops be grown using organic farming techniques.

A study in 1999 reported that pesticide levels in a number of commercially grown fruits and vegetables were too high for children, according to standards set by the EPA. Even a single serving of certain fruits and vegetables, including peaches, winter squash, apples, and grapes, can exceed those safe daily limits.

Some experts are also beginning to wonder about the addition of synthetic hormones to foods, particularly to dairy products. Bovine growth hormone (rBGH) is injected into cows to make them produce milk for much longer periods of time than they naturally would. The jury is still out on whether this may have serious consequences on human health. There is some concern that these hormones may be causing young girls to reach puberty at much earlier ages. The hormones may also cause cancer. What is certain is that synthetic hormones, such as rBGH, have negative health consequences for the cows they get injected into, and for the nutritional quality of the milk they produce. Cows injected with hormones have significantly higher rates of infection, causing them to need a lot of antibiotics. The United States is now the only major nation that has not banned the use of hormones in food growth.

Genetically engineered (GE) foods are also banned by many other countries (there is a general moratorium against them in the European Union, for example), but not by the United States. Biotechnology firms splice genes from bacteria, viruses, insects, hormones, or other plants into plant or animal DNA to create a new product that is more resistant to disease (such as virus-resistant oysters) or to create produce that looks fresher, or is larger, or grows faster (like GE salmon or trout). Some plants are designed to repel insects by producing a sort of inner insecticide.

The problem is that no one really knows what the long-term effects will be of these new creations. The process may introduce new allergens or toxins into foods and even spread allergens into the environment via pollen. GE crops that spread into the wild may upset the food chain, with serious longer-term effects on the ecosystem. It is also much harder to judge the quality of GE products just by looking at them because produce, for example, is often genetically designed to look fresh and luscious for much longer than its age actually warrants.

Use of genetic engineering is already widespread in the United States. Common GE products include canola oil, soybeans and soy oil, chicory, cotton, papaya, potatoes, squash, tomatoes, and dairy products—and even the cows themselves. Currently there are no regulations requiring manufacturers to label their products as "genetically engineered." Those who wish to may voluntarily do so, or can state that their product is not modified. Many processed foods have been shown to contain genetically modified organisms (GMOs).

Buying organically grown foods ensures that you are not only eating foods with minimal amounts of pesticide residues, hormones, antibiotics, and GMOs, but also that you are supporting local and smaller farms. Yes, these foods are generally more expensive than nonorganics. But if you balance your purchases of organic foods with a reduction in junk and processed foods, you may find it comes out pretty much the same.

Try these shopping tips:

- Purchase a variety of foods. Try to buy a wide variety of fruits and vegetables to ensure you are getting all the necessary nutrients. This will also protect you against consuming too many toxins that may be present in one particular type of produce.
- Buy locally produced organic foods as much as possible. Check out local farmers markets, health food stores, co-ops, and cooperative farm organizations. You might also consider starting your own vegetable and herb garden.
- Join a community-supported agriculture (CSA) farm that will deliver fresh organic produce weekly (see appendix 2 for more about CSAs).
- If you can't afford to buy only organic foods, try to at least purchase the following foods organically: strawberries, bell peppers, spinach, U.S. cherries, peaches, Mexican cantaloupe, celery, apples, apricots, green beans, Chilean grapes, and cucumbers. These are foods that seem to have the highest amounts of pesticide residue on them when purchased. Or opt instead for these safer bets: avocados, corn, onions, sweet potatoes, cauliflower, Brussels sprouts, U.S. grapes, bananas, plums, green onions, watermelons, and broccoli.[11]
- Try to purchase fresh produce in season.
- Avoid processed foods. These tend to be high in sodium, not to mention preservatives and trans-fats.
- If you like smoked meats or bacon, try to find products that are nitrate-free.
- Trim any visible fat and skin off fish before cooking it. This will cut down on toxins that tend to congregate in fatty tissues.
- Many bottled beverages, such as iced teas and juices, are made with high-fructose corn syrup. It is best not to have too much of this because it has a high glycemic index. This means it raises your blood sugar levels higher than other sweet-

eners might. If you can, try to purchase drinks that are naturally sweet, such as juices or flavored seltzer waters.
- Purchase foods in their whole state; for example, choose fresh fruit over fruit juices. Buy raw nuts instead of roasted nuts.
- Try to avoid genetically engineered foods. Some products will be marked GE-free, so check the label. Your best bet is to shop in health food stores that avoid purchasing GMOs and to purchase as much certified organic foods as possible.

Cooking tips. You might be the type of person who loves to experiment with food and make up your own wild recipes. Or you may prefer to use tried-and-true recipes created by expert chefs (check out some of the books in appendix 2). Then again, maybe you like to keep cooking to a minimum, opting for quickie meals. There is no one right way to handle it, but no matter how much cooking you do, it helps to know a few tips on healthy preparation.

- Cook foods in a variety of ways. Try to include foods with a variety of tastes: sweet, sour, bitter, bland, astringent. This is a good way of ensuring you will eat a large variety of nutrients. It's also much more interesting!
- Wash all fruits and vegetables before using them. You can use one of the products made specifically for washing produce, or use a very diluted solution of dishwashing liquid and water.
- Be cautious when handling raw poultry, meats, and fish. Wash your hands and any tools or counter space you've used with warm, soapy water afterward. This will help guard against food-borne illness.
- Defrost foods in the refrigerator, not on the counter or in the sink.
- Do not overcook vegetables. Steaming them briefly will keep more of the nutrients in them.
- Eat your pasta al dente. This is not just an aesthetic taste, it turns out. Pasta that is not overcooked has a lower glycemic index, which

means it will not raise your blood sugar levels as much as the mushy stuff.

- Use olive oil as your main fat when preparing foods.
- Keep oils in a cool and dark space. Try to purchase them in small amounts, or keep larger quantities stored in the refrigerator. If the oil has a rancid smell or taste, this means it has gone bad and needs to be thrown away.

Vitamins and Herbs

Generally speaking, it is best to try to meet all your nutritional needs with the foods you eat. While it isn't a good idea to *rely* on a vitamin pill to supply you with good nutrition, you and your health care provider may decide a prenatal vitamin is a good insurance policy. Earlier, we discussed the importance of getting enough folic acid, iron, and B12 during pregnancy. Obtaining these through diet alone might be challenging.

Vitamin A is a supplement to be cautious of during pregnancy. Intakes above the level of 10,000 IU have been shown to cause birth defects.[12] Check your supplement to be sure it does not exceed this limit (most prenatal vitamins won't). Generally speaking, you don't need to worry about overconsuming this vitamin, or others, in your food intake.

Many herbal products can be very helpful, and some are much gentler solutions for health care problems than traditional medications and nutritional supplements. Herbs can come in many forms. The flowers, roots, stems, leaves, and other parts of the plant may be dried, powdered, put into capsules, or immersed in a liquid. While all treatments, herbal or otherwise, are best kept to a minimum during pregnancy, some herbs are considered to be safe to take occasionally. Check with your health care practitioner to see which herbs are safe for you.

Echinacea is an herbal treatment that has been shown to be effective in preventing colds and flu if taken at the very first signs of symptoms. Though once considered "alternative," it is now widely available in pharmacies and department stores as well as in health food stores. Recent studies[13] show echinacea is safe to use during pregnancy. It can be purchased in capsule form or as a tincture. However you choose to take it, it is important to use it in cycles. Many people suggest taking it a few times a day for up to two weeks, and then taking a two-week break before starting again.

Ginger is another herb that can be extremely useful during pregnancy, especially in the early weeks when many women battle with morning sickness and nausea. See chapter 1 for the best way to take this herb for digestive ailments.

There are several herbs, though, that should *not* be used during pregnancy, except under the direction of a trained herbal specialist, and many that have not been adequately studied as of yet.

- *Herbs that stimulate uterine contractions:* Birthwort, blue cohosh, cinchona, cotton root bark, ergot, goldenseal, gotu kila, Peruvian bark. (Note that blue cohosh and black cohosh can be used later in pregnancy to stimulate contractions, under the care of a qualified health care practitioner.)

- *Herbs that stimulate menstrual flow:* Agave, angelica, bethroot, black cohosh, chicory, feverfew, hyssop, horehound, lovage, milk thistle, motherwort, mugwort, nasturtium seed, osha, fresh parsley leaves,* pennyroyal, poke root, pulsatilla, rue, saffron, sumac berries, tansy, thuja (white cedar), watercress, wormwood, yarrow.

- *Herbs that can stimulate or irritate the uterus:* Eucalyptus, barberry, bloodroot, broom, goldenseal, coffee, mandrake, tea, nutmeg, osha, yerba mansa, and the mint family members basil,* catnip, lemon balm, marjoram,* oregano,* peppermint, pennyroyal, rosemary,* true sage,* and thyme.*

* Culinary herbs, used in normal small amounts for cooking, are perfectly safe.

- *Herbs that affect hormonal function:* Dong quai, licorice, motherwort, wild yam.

- *Harsh herbal laxatives:* Aloe, cascara sagrada, purging buckthorn, rhubarb, senna, and yellow dock (in large amounts).

- *Strong herbal diuretics:* Juniper berries, uva ursi (bearberry).

Certain essential oils are best avoided while expecting, for both external and internal use. They include:

Basil
Cinnamon bark
Clove
Hyssop
Marjoram
Myrrh
Oregano
Pennyroyal
Sage
Savory
Thyme
Wintergreen

One essential oil that is generally useful in helping pregnant women with digestive problems and nausea is peppermint. Ask your health care practitioner if it's right for you. Peppermint oil should be avoided, however, while you are taking any homeopathic treatments, as it may counteract their effects.[14]

Changing Your Relationship to Food

As we stated at the beginning of this chapter, pregnancy is the perfect time to examine the way you eat as well as the way you relate to food and to eating.

Most of us have grown up learning to ignore our intuition when it comes to food. We are taught to eat at certain times of the day, whether or not we are hungry. We are discouraged from eating certain foods because they are not appropriate for certain meals, like having chicken soup for breakfast, for example. Some of us have been taught that we must eat everything on our plates, even if we are full. This is common, despite the fact that most children, if left to their own devices, will eat a generally good balance of healthy foods, as long as they are given the opportunity and variety to do so.

Trying to relearn healthy eating habits is not easy. These suggestions will help you get started:

- Declare all "food bans" to be null and void. Give yourself permission to eat whatever you like, without regulations. While at first it may seem like you will eat an entire elephant, you will likely find that it was the ban itself that caused you to binge. Once there is nothing to rebel against, you may find your bingeing pattern reduces or disappears.

- Listen carefully for the actual physical feeling of hunger. This can be tricky at first. Sometimes psychological hunger can feel like physical hunger. When you do recognize hunger, sit with it for just a moment and try to think of what food would most satisfy you. Try a "dress rehearsal" of foods and imagine yourself eating it and swallowing it. Does it satisfy? If not, try another. Then attempt to give yourself the food you really want. Many women have distinct cravings during pregnancy. Try to satisfy them.

- If you decide to make particular changes in your diet, go slowly. Make a couple of changes a week. For example, switch from red meat to poultry and fish, and use whole grain bread instead of white the first week. Buy brown rice instead of white, and drink an extra cup of milk or fortified soy or rice milk the next week. Replace some of your sugary desserts with fresh fruit concoctions. If you try to do it all at once and eat the "perfect" diet, you may find it very difficult to adjust. Be kind to yourself.

- It's difficult to love the body that fashion tells you is not in style. And now it's getting even

BODY WISE
The Corpse Pose

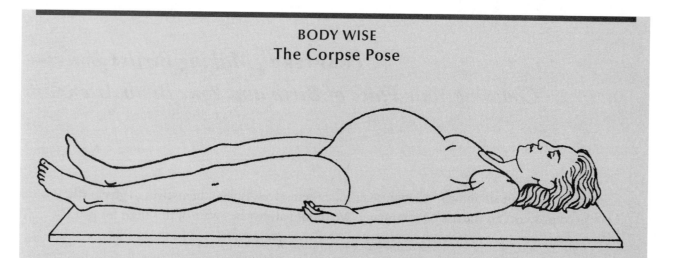

This pose is best done during the first half of your pregnancy while you are still comfortable lying on your back. The Corpse Pose makes a perfect accompaniment to the visualization exercises suggested in chapter 11. It can also be done before bed to prepare for sleep.

- Turn on some relaxing music and/or dim the lights.
- Lie on your back on the floor.
- Put a pillow underneath the small of your back.
- Allow your legs and arms to rest comfortably on the floor.
- Cover yourself with a light blanket, if needed.
- Close your eyes.
- Take several deep breaths.
- Notice the rise and fall of your breathing. Notice your abdomen moving up and down.
- If you notice that you are distracted by busy thoughts, return your attention to your breathing.

Stay in this relaxed pose as long as you are comfortable. Even ten minutes can be deeply relaxing.

bigger! Try walking around naked in the privacy of your home or bedroom. Look at yourself in the mirror and validate the tremendous job your body is doing right now: growing another human being! Every four weeks, take a picture of yourself with nothing on, or just a bathing suit or leotard, to record the changes you are going through. Try the visualization exercises suggested on page 14 to help you be at peace with your body.

CHAPTER 3 *Making Birth Choices—*
Choosing Your Place of Birth and Your Birth Attendant

Human beings are mammals. All mammals hide themselves, isolate themselves to give birth.
They need privacy. It is the same for humans. We should always be aware of this need for privacy.

—MICHEL ODENT, M.D., *Birth Reborn*

It might seem like a backward approach to you, initially, but it makes sense to choose the place in which you will give birth even before you choose a care practitioner, such as a midwife or obstetrician, who practices in that setting. Why choose the setting first? Because studies indicate that a feeling of comfort and safety in your surroundings might be the biggest contribution to a smooth labor. Data from countries such as Japan indicate that environment is strongly related to the need for medical interventions and even to overall infant mortality rate. Having a baby in a Japanese hospital, for example, means having individualized, low-tech care in neonatal units with dimmed lights, no noise, and very few drugs. Many experts believe that this environment explains the Japanese cesarean section rate of only 7 per 100 births, compared to the U.S. rate of 24.4 per 100 births.

Environment can actually affect the *progress* of labor, as well. Nurses who tended laboring women during the Gulf War took note of just how dramatically environment can affect labor. During missile attacks, women in labor began to skip the latent phase altogether and go directly into active labor. If sirens warning of missile attacks sounded in the middle of active labor, many women's contractions would stop, and would not resume until the All Clear message sounded.

While you are unlikely to have to deal with a crisis like this during your baby's birth, the choice you make about where to give birth might make all the difference in terms of the speed of your labor, your comfort level, how much medical intervention you experience, and your overall satisfaction with the whole labor and birth.

Choosing a Place for Your Baby's Birth

Which birth environment is safest? Surprisingly, home births, births in birthing centers, and hospital births are equally safe. Recent studies show definitively that there is no improvement in outcome, for mother or baby, in hospital births as compared to those that happen at home or in a birthing center. The data that supports this clearly shows this to be true for low-risk *and* high-risk pregnancies. In fact, there is an indication that outcome is actually slightly better in low-risk births *out* of the hospital.[1] Low-risk pregnancies are ones in which the woman is in generally good health and no particular difficulties are anticipated during delivery. Low-risk pregnancies comprise about 60 to 90 percent of all births.

A high-risk pregnancy is one in which the woman has some type of serious health concern, such as diabetes, is delivering twins, or has had previous diffi-

NATURAL SOOTHER

Heavenly Scents

Your sense of smell is heightened during pregnancy. You may be intensely attracted to some odors and strongly repelled by others. To keep the air in your home or office appealing, use an aromatic diffuser or simply place a few drops of essential oil in a bowl of water so that they can evaporate, naturally scenting the room. You can also boil a pot of water on the stove and add a few drops of your favorite essential oil to the pot.

To make a recipe effective in alleviating morning sickness and headache, use 3 drops of lavender *(Lavandula officinalis* or *Lavandula vera)* with 1 drop of peppermint *(Mentha piperita).* If colds or flus are in the air, add 1 drop of eucalyptus *(Eucalyptus globulus)* as a preventative.

To help comfort nausea, place a cool lavender oil compress on your forehead and a warm lavender oil compress over the front of your rib cage. To make the compress, add a couple of drops of lavender oil to cool water in a sink or bowl. Soak a clean washcloth in the water, wring out, and apply. Repeat with a second cloth for the warm water compress.

A deep whiff of peppermint oil will often cure nausea, as will a cup of tea or honey water prepared with 1 drop of peppermint oil. Peppermint tea also works well. (Do not overuse peppermint, as it can have stimulating effects, and do not take essential oils internally on an empty stomach. It is contraindicated if you are taking homeopathic remedies.)

cult pregnancy experiences. Interestingly, however, only between 10 and 30 percent of women who are classified high-risk during pregnancy actually experience adverse birth outcomes, and between 20 and 50 percent of women who deliver premature babies are classified low-risk. Risk screening is not an absolute.

Home births, and births in birthing centers, have enjoyed a recent renaissance in the United States. However, there is still a lingering societal question about the safety of such births, and most women continue to go to the maternity ward of the hospital where their caregiver practices. Choosing to do something different may take real courage, as friends and relatives may be particularly concerned about the safety of your choice.

Another advantage of birth in alternative settings has to do with money. Using midwives to attend low-risk births, advocating natural approaches, and reserving obstetrical interventions for the cases with complications could lower the cost of childbirth by 40 percent. The fee for giving birth in a freestanding birthing center, attended by a midwife, is about half of that for a hospital vaginal birth, attended by an ob/gyn.[2] Insurance companies may be beginning to appreciate this cost difference, and in the future we will likely see more and more out-of-hospital births happening in the United States. (See appendix 3 for a comparative chart on the costs of childbirth.)

A more important "cost" to assess, however, has to do with the effects that birth trauma and general hospital-style treatment have on the bonding between a mother and her child. High levels of stress incurred in hospital settings can seriously affect a parent's ability to function well in the difficult weeks after birth. Many women agonize about their negative birthing experiences, including unnecessary interventions and unkind or patronizing treatment, for months or even years after the birth. Since birth sets the stage for your early parenting experiences, it makes sense to avoid anything that increases stress for you or reduces your ability to bond with your child. Making a decision on where your baby's birth will take place is second in importance only to making the decision to become parents in the first place! Take time to explore all the options you have.

Home birth. A home birth is defined as any birth that does not take place in a facility, such as a birth center or hospital. It doesn't actually have to be *your* home; it could be your parents' or your best friend's.

Reasons to choose home birth:

- It is the birthing environment you will have the most control over. In your own home you have the best shot at deciding what visual elements, sounds, smells, and faces will surround you when your baby is born. You can lower the lights, play reggae music, or invite anyone you want to have around you to attend, if you like. Women who give birth at home do report a greater sense of control over the experience, and this sense of control generally contributes to greater overall satisfaction with the birthing experience.

- At home you avoid unnecessary medical interventions such as episiotomy or constant fetal monitoring. A carefully conducted study compared the cesarean section rates between patients who used midwifery services for their home births from The Farm, a well-respected birth center in Iowa, to physician-attended hospital births. The hospital C-section rates were 16.46 percent of all the births. The Farm had a C-section rate of only 1.46 percent![3] Many other studies have confirmed the markedly lower C-section rates in home births. With home birth, your baby's birth will proceed gently and naturally unless a real emergency occurs. If you are transported to a hospital during a home birth, statistics indicate that you and your baby are just as likely to have a good outcome as if you had started out in a hospital setting.

- Many experts believe that you, and your baby, will have a reduced chance of getting an infection if you are not in a hospital. Hospitals are notorious for spreading staph, and other infections, around to patients. You are already used to the bacteria present in your home and have probably developed some immunity to them.

Reasons not to choose home birth:

- You live more than thirty minutes away from a hospital.

- You have a preexisting medical condition, such as diabetes, epilepsy, anemia, or high blood pressure, that makes it advisable to plan on a hospital birth right from the start.

- During pregnancy, if you have bleeding, premature labor contractions, high blood sugar, or protein in your urine.

- You are in generally poor health, smoke heavily, or are extremely overweight.

- You know you are having twins. Most midwives are not willing to try to deliver twins at home.

- You have had a previous cesarean. Depending on the standard of care in your area, it may be difficult to find a birth practitioner to attend a home birth after a cesarean.

- You are living in a home you don't feel is comfortable enough right now, or you don't like the environment.

- There is very little privacy where you live, or you live with people, such as housemates or in-laws, whom you would rather not be with during the actual birth.

- You are unable to find a practitioner who is willing or able to assist you in a home birth.

- You feel so insecure about the concept of home birth that you feel you will be unable to relax or feel safe during the birth.

- Your insurance will not cover the cost of a midwife or doctor unless you are in a hospital, and you cannot afford other choices.

There are very few absolute risk factors; many are relative. For example, home births after a cesarean can be safe, but they are uncommon. Discuss your questions about risk factors with a practitioner experienced in home birth.

Freestanding birthing centers. A freestanding birth center is a facility devoted solely to the care of pregnant and laboring women. It is not physically attached to a hospital, although some are hospital-owned.

Reasons to choose a freestanding birth center:

- The National Association of Childbearing Centers reports birth centers to be as safe as hospital births—with the added benefit of a significantly lower rate of cesarean sections. Birth centers, which generally service low-risk pregnancies, average only 4.4 percent C-sections, less than half the rate for low-risk women in hospital settings. In one survey, there were no maternal deaths reported and a neonatal mortality rate of less than 1 per 1,000 births, if severe birth defects are excluded. These rates are almost identical to those of hospitals.[4]

- A birthing center offers you a homelike setting in which to give birth. You will not see a lot of high-tech machinery around you. You may, instead, see a Jacuzzi, which can be extremely helpful during labor, a room for your family to sleep in, or even a kitchen your family can use to prepare meals during your stay. It is most likely to have been carefully decorated and arranged to make you and your family feel comfortable and welcome.

- Families are encouraged to take full part in the birth and postpartum care.

- You will not find a lot of people coming and going out of your room, the way you would in a hospital. The staff will probably be small and familiar to you. Your privacy will be respected.

- You will have just one area for your stay, where you will labor, deliver the baby, and recover. Many hospitals move women from room to room for the different parts of labor.

- The center you choose may be where you will go for all your prenatal checkups and your childbirth education classes. The same center may also offer parenting workshops or breastfeeding support groups for postpartum, or sibling classes if you have older children. By the time you arrive for your baby's birth, you are likely to feel quite comfortable and familiar with the environment.

- There are still rural settings in this country that are many miles away from the nearest maternity hospital. It may be that a midwife-operated birthing center is your closest option.

- Most major insurance carriers do cover the cost of using a birth center.

Reasons not to choose a freestanding birth center:

- You have a preexisting medical condition, such as diabetes, epilepsy, anemia, or high blood pressure, that makes it advisable to be in a hospital setting right from the start.

- You have been defined as high-risk, which means that you have a medical condition that necessitates a hospital birth, such as diabetes, epilepsy, anemia, or high blood pressure, a previous cesarean section, or twin birth. Most birth centers are geared toward low-risk pregnancies. Some birth centers are willing to deliver twins and previous C-sections, but not all, so you need to ask.

- You have already chosen a care provider with whom you wish to deliver the baby, and they are not affiliated with a birth center.

- You want even more control over your environment than a birth center can provide. Home birth may be most appropriate for you.

Teaching/large hospitals. This is where most births have taken place in recent years. Teaching hospitals are somewhat less expensive than other hospitals because you, the patient, are providing students with a living example of what they need to know to become doctors and nurses.

Reasons to choose a teaching/large hospital:

- You are a high-risk patient. You are most likely to need access to the latest medical technology that a teaching hospital has to offer.

- Your midwife attends births in a hospital, and you prefer to use her for the birth over anyone else. Having a midwife-supervised birth in a large facility can improve the hospital experience immensely.

Reasons not to choose a teaching/large hospital:

- During doctor-attended hospital births, labor is generally expected to conform to a certain pattern that the hospital has deemed "normal." If and when labor begins to deviate in some way from that pattern, a series of steps are likely to be taken to attempt to bring the labor closer to conformity. For example, if your labor does not progress at a rate more or less in accordance with standard expectations, it is likely to be "sped up" with pitocin or similar drugs. One of the prime reasons for this conformity has to do with litigation. Hospitals are geared toward protecting themselves against lawsuits. Although the vast majority of births are relatively uneventful, hospitals treat all births as if something could go wrong and as if they will be called upon to show they did everything properly.

- A teaching hospital is where, statistically, a woman is most likely to deliver by a cesarean section.

- A large hospital is the birth setting in which you are least likely to have control. Hospitals come complete with long lists of regulations that may include who and how many persons attend the birth, whether or not you can walk around, when you can eat (hospitals generally forbid laboring women to eat because they want a woman to be prepared for general anesthesia, which requires an empty stomach), or whether you must wear a fetal monitor continuously. Some hospitals insist on whisking babies away from their mothers right away for a checkup. Some require infants to be in the nursery during visiting hours.

- There will probably be a lack of consistency. You may be moved to different rooms for labor, delivery, and postpartum. You will have a changing array of nurses and doctors to deal with.

- Although hospital decor has certainly improved, you can expect your labor and delivery rooms to feel like a hospital. You will be surrounded with medical apparatus and most likely attended to by people in uniform.

- There is a lack of privacy. Anyone who spends time in a hospital will experience people going in and out of their rooms at all hours of the night and day. Many of these will be people you have never seen before in your life. They include nurses, technicians, janitors, dieticians—even doctors with a crew of students trailing behind them. Some will knock before entering, and some will not.

OTHER OPTIONS

Smaller hospitals. A smaller hospital is likely to be your best bet in terms of individualized care and attention, if a hospital birth is what you have chosen or need. Hospital protocol may be a bit more relaxed in a smaller hospital, and you will experience greater privacy. Some smaller hospitals are now becoming more open about their standard practices. Some are now even offering water births as an option. Smaller hospitals, however, do have slightly higher rates of cesarean sections than do larger community hospitals.

Alternative birthing center (ABC) within a hospital. There are not many birthing centers housed within hospitals, but this seems to be a growing trend. You will generally find a much more comfortable and homelike atmosphere in these centers than in a regular labor or maternity ward. In some hospitals, however, there isn't much difference between the two, so you'll have to check out the facility. Hospital-based birthing centers, as a rule, are very careful about the type of pregnancy they will accommodate. You must be strictly low-risk, with absolutely no complications. Women giving birth to twins or who have had cesarean sections in past pregnancies will likely be turned away.

Water birth. If you have decided that a water birth is what you want, you must, of course, take this into consideration when choosing your place of birth. Many birthing centers and hospitals now have

BODY WISE
Walking

Walking is one of the best ways to exercise during pregnancy or at any time. Develop a walking routine that fits into your lifestyle. Put together a comfortable outfit to wear on your walks in all kinds of weather. Choose shoes or boots that are comfortable and won't slip.

Lay out your outfit and shoes in your room so that they'll be ready for you, and go on your walk first thing in the morning. If you have a child, bring him or her in a backpack or baby jogger. Maybe the morning just does not work for you. Can you end your day with a walk or take a walk after dinner? If you work, can you walk to and from work or during your lunch hour? Are there places you drive to during your day that you can walk to? Take stairs instead of elevators. Park your car farther away than necessary when you park and get in a little walk. Remember that you can get the benefit of exercise even when you only do it in fifteen-minute segments. Several fifteen-minute blocks a day will build your stamina as much as exercising an hour at a time.

Jacuzzi baths or large tubs for use during labor, because water has been shown to be an excellent aid in managing pain. Not all of them, however, will accommodate water births. If you are unable to find one, your only alternative may be to rent a tub for use in your home. In this case your choice of a health provider will be key, as you will want someone who has experience with water birth.

Choose Mother-Friendly

The Coalition for Improving Maternity Services (CIMS) was formed in 1996. It is made up of midwives, physicians, hospital associations, public health workers, doulas, scientists, and many others. As a group they meet to review scientific reports and make recommendations for evidence-based obstetric practices in birth centers and hospitals.

To qualify for CIMS designation, a birth center, hospital, or home birth service must fulfill these Ten Steps of Mother-Friendly Care:

1. Offer all birthing mothers unrestricted access to: birth companions of her choice, continuous emotional and physical support, and professional midwifery care.
2. Provide to the public accurate descriptive and statistical information about its birth care practices and procedures.
3. Provide culturally competent care—that is, care that is sensitive and responsive to the specific beliefs, values, and customs of the mother's ethnicity and religion.
4. Provide the birthing woman freedom of movement and discourage the flat-on-your-back birth position.
5. Have clearly defined policies regarding: continuity of care, follow-up well-baby care, and breastfeeding support.
6. Not routinely employ procedures unsupported by scientific evidence, including but not limited to: shaving, enemas, IV, withholding nourishment, early rupture of membranes, and electronic fetal monitoring. Other interventions are limited as follows: oxytocin (a chemical used to make labor start or speed up) induction rate of 10 percent or less, episiotomy rate of less than 20 percent, with a goal of 5 percent, cesarean rate of less than 10 percent and VBAC (vaginal birth after cesarean) rate of 60 percent or more, with a goal of 75 percent or more.
7. Educate staff in nondrug pain relief and not promote the use of analgesic or anesthetic drugs.

8. Encourage touching, holding, and breastfeeding of all babies.

9. Discourage nonreligious circumcision of the newborn.

10. Strive to achieve the WHO/UNICEF "Baby-Friendly Hospital Initiative" to encourage breastfeeding (see more on this in chapter 9).

When considering a certain hospital or birthing center, ask if they have been designated by CIMS as a mother-friendly institution. This will assure you that you are receiving the best care. If they are not designated, it does not necessarily mean they don't follow these standards. You will just have to ask, point by point, about the specifics. You can use the following list to help you interview a prospective place of birth.

WHAT TO LOOK FOR AND WHAT TO ASK WHEN MAKING YOUR CHOICE

- What is your gut reaction to the environment? Does it feel warm? Do you feel welcomed? Do you like the people who are showing you around? Are they the same people you will have contact with during the birth?

- How does the facility look and sound? Is there a "hospital room" feeling? Is there street noise to deal with? Can the lights be dimmed during the birth?

- What is the facility's policy on birth attendants? Can you include friends, children, and relatives, or only your partner? If it is a hospital, is a doula allowed? (See more on doulas in chapter 7.)

- What is the policy on walking around during labor? Will you be required to wear a fetal monitor the whole time you are in labor?

- If it is a hospital, do they routinely start an intravenous line? Are women routinely given enemas or pubic shaves?

- Are you allowed to eat and drink during labor?

- Can you wear your own clothing, or is a hospital gown required?

- What is the facility's cesarean section rate? What is its rate of episiotomies?

- How are emergencies handled? If it is a freestanding birth center, how are transfers done and what hospital is used as a backup?

- What is the policy on mother/baby separation? Will your naked baby be handed directly to you at birth for skin-to-skin contact, which has been shown to be best for the baby? How long can you hold her? Will the baby sleep in your room? Will the baby be taken away from you for exams, or can you attend these as well?

- If the baby should need intensive care, are parents encouraged to hold him? Is breastfeeding encouraged in the intensive care unit?

- Does the facility have a lactation specialist who can help you with early breastfeeding? Can you specify that no bottles are to be given to your baby?

- If it is a birth center, is it licensed? About thirty-seven states currently license birth centers, so check to see if your state does.

Once you have had a chance to explore all the options, you should make a decision from your heart instead of your head. Since all of the options are statistically safe, the best place for you to give birth is where you feel emotionally safest. It is that simple, really—your baby's birth will proceed most smoothly where you feel most comfortable.

Choosing Your Birth Attendant

After choosing the place for your baby's birth, your next important decision will be choosing the person who will care for you during the next nine months and attend the birth.

In order to find the care provider who is best suited to you, let's take a look at the different possibilities. There are three types of providers you can choose from:

Midwives. Throughout the history of the world, a

midwife, either formally or experientially educated, has been the most common type of birth attendant. In days past a midwife was generally an older woman in the community considered to be a "wise woman." Today, midwives attend about 80 percent of births worldwide. In the year 2001, in the United States, they attended almost 10 percent of all births, but that number grows each year.

In the United States, several types of midwives are available. Some start out as nurses, and some receive their training through apprenticeships or various midwifery certification programs. Some consider their role to be that of a spiritual aide, and some are well prepared to handle all emergencies.

It's important to understand the distinctions and the various terms used to describe midwives, so that you can be sure you are receiving precisely the kind of care that suits you best.

- *Certified nurse-midwife (CNM) and certified midwife (CM).* A CNM is a registered nurse who has had two years of advanced practice in caring for pregnant and birthing women in a certified CNM program. Certification is done by the American College of Nurse-Midwives Certification Council. This same group also awards the credential of certified midwife (CM). CMs receive their training as direct-entry midwives—in other words, they do not start out as nurses but enter midwifery through apprenticeship training or midwifery school. About 85 percent of CNMs and CMs practice in a hospital setting, but some also attend births in birth centers or at home.

- *Certified professional midwife (CPM).* A CPM has received her credentials from the North American Registry of Midwives (NARM), an international certification agency. These midwives have received their training in different ways, some through apprenticeship, some through established midwifery training programs and schools. They are required to have had some out-of-hospital training to qualify for the CPM credential. It is possible for a midwife to be both a CNM and a CPM. A few CPMs practice in hospitals, but most attend home births or work in birthing centers.

- *Direct-entry midwives (DEM).* These midwives have gained experience through apprenticeship, self-study, or through a midwifery program distinct from the discipline of nursing. Some of them may go on to get certification through one of the above-mentioned programs. They normally attend out-of-hospital births. Lack of certification, however, does not necessarily mean lack of training or expertise. You will need to ask her about her professional experience.

- *Lay midwife or traditional midwife (also called independent or granny-midwife).* This type of midwife has gained her experience through on-the-job training, possibly as an apprentice, rather than through any type of specific training program. She attends out-of-hospital births. You will need to check her qualifications by carefully interviewing her, or by listening to the experiences of other women who have used her services.

Several states in the United States license or register midwives. In these states, midwives can take a test and receive a state midwifery license: Each state recognizes different qualifications and also differs in its handling of the license.

Amazingly, ten states in the United States (Washington, D.C., Illinois, Indiana, Iowa, Kentucky, Maryland, Missouri, North Carolina, Virginia, and Wyoming) prohibit the practice of midwifery, other than nurse-midwifery, despite the fact that no studies provide any good reason to doubt the safety of midwifery. In fact, several studies prove the opposite: better outcomes with midwives. If you live in one of these states, you'll have to look harder to find a good, certified midwife, since they may not publicly advertise. Many women in these states use midwives despite the regulations and have satisfying birth experiences.

Keep in mind that the regulations concerning midwives are in constant flux. Each year, as legal authorities begin to recognize their value, midwives are finding it easier to practice their profession.

Obstetricians. Obstetricians are medical doctors who have had four years of residency training in the field of obstetrics and gynecology following medical school. Because of their dual specialty, such doctors are frequently referred to as "ob/gyns." Where and when they received their training may strongly influence how progressive they are, or how open they are to input from patients. Younger doctors may be more open-minded, especially if they have obtained supplementary training in a complementary or integrative medicine modality such as acupuncture or homeopathy. Few doctors, however, receive education about home birth and midwifery, and some don't receive much education about breastfeeding. A doctor who has personal experience with these things may also be more open-minded. Certain parts of the country tend to be more progressive, such as Washington State, where home births approach 10 percent, New Mexico, where midwives attend 25 percent of births, or Chicago, where four clinics provide physician-attended home births. Most births in the United States, however, are attended by ob/gyns.

Family physicians. These are medical doctors who have three years of family practice residency, including a minimum of three months in the specialty of obstetrics and gynecology. While most of these doctors attend births in hospital settings, the American Academy of Family Physicians has issued a statement encouraging birthing as a family event that can be safely experienced in a variety of settings, including the home. Your particular physician may or may not be open to nonhospital options. Again, their training may strongly influence their point of view on the childbirth experience.

Which One Is Best for Me?

There is no formula that can help a mother-to-be decide what type of care provider will be best for her. That is because every provider is different, even within such different categories as "obstetrician" and "midwife." Some obstetricians are very open to the idea of a birth with minimal or no interventions. Some midwives may practice in hospitals and be much more likely to rely on technology than others.

For this reason, it is necessary to interview several candidates before making a final decision. It also helps to know that no decision is absolutely final. While it may not be ideal to change birth attendants midstream, it is better than working with someone you find you are unhappy with.

To decide who to interview, consider these points:
- Check to see if this person is able or willing to attend a birth in the location you have chosen. Most doctors will not attend home births, so this will narrow your field automatically.
- If you want an attendant who will be with you throughout most of your labor, you should consider using a midwife. Obstetricians will generally only be with you during the final stages of labor, checking on you intermittently beforehand. You will be attended to by labor nurses for the most part.
- Know that midwives spend significantly longer on regular checkups than most doctors do, from twenty to forty minutes per visit. Again, there are always exceptions to this.
- Cesarean section rates, on average, are much lower for midwives than for medical doctors. In addition, rates of successful VBACs (vaginal births after a cesarean) are better for midwives. Certified nurse-midwives, for example, have a rate of 11.6 percent for C-sections and 68.9 percent for successful VBACs. The national average is, respectively, 23.3 percent and 24.9 percent.[5]
- Choosing a male ob/gyn, rather than a female,

increases your chances of ending up with a cesarean section by 40 percent.[6]

- Using a family practice physician can be advantageous if this is a person who is already very familiar with you and your family. Perhaps this will be the same person who is going to care for your newborn.

Questions to Ask

Once you've decided on the type of caregiver and chosen several good candidates, it is important to ask very detailed questions about their practices. First and foremost, though, ask yourself if you like this person. Is he too chatty? Or not chatty enough for your taste? Does she smile and make eye contact? In other words, what is your gut response to this person? Then ask her:

- If you are not available at the time of my labor and birth, who usually covers for you? If I want to meet that person ahead of time, will you facilitate that?
- Will you help me with nutritional guidelines or refer me to someone you trust who can? What are your views on weight gain during pregnancy?
- How are partners involved in prenatal visits, during labor, and at the birth?
- What sorts of prenatal testing do you normally recommend? (See chapter 5 for more information on prenatal testing.)
- For home births and birth centers: What backup hospital do you use? Under what conditions do you transport a patient to the hospital?
- What labor positions do you recommend to your clients? Do you encourage movement dur-

---

HIGHER GROUND

Pregnancy Affirmations

An affirmation is a positive thought that you consciously introduce into your thinking. You do this so that your thoughts will support you and not undermine your confidence. Here are some affirmations you can either write down, read or say aloud, or even tape and play back—note that these affirmations progress from pregnancy to birth.

- Pregnancy is a natural, normal, healthy, and vibrant state for my baby and me.
- My baby and I are loved and supported.
- It is safe for me to have my baby.
- There is nothing to fear.
- I am calm and relaxed. My baby feels my calmness and shares it.
- The baby and I are ready for our lives together to unfold.
- The baby is naturally doing what he or she should.
- The movements of my uterus are massaging and rocking my baby.
- The rhythm of my uterus as it expands and contracts brings me closer to my baby.
- The baby is descending naturally.
- The baby's head fits perfectly in my pelvis.
- My vagina expands easily as my baby's head crowns, and then emerges into my hands.

ing labor? How much fetal monitoring do you routinely use during labor?

- Approximately how many of your clients have unmedicated births? What is your rate of cesarean sections, and under what circumstances do you usually advise them? Your rate of episiotomies? Do you rupture the membranes to speed up labor?
- Under what circumstances are forceps or vacuum extraction (where a suction device on the baby's head pulls it out of the womb) used? How often?
- How long after birth is the umbilical cord cut?
- How often do you use pitocin or other labor-inducing drugs? Under what circumstances?
- What would be your routine for the baby and me directly after birth? Will I hold the baby immediately at birth?
- How do you feel about other children, friends, or a doula attending the birth?
- How much postnatal care do you do? If this is a home birth, how long would you stay in my home after the birth?

Communicating with Your Birth Attendant

It's a good idea to take a little time to consider how you would like to communicate with your new care provider. After all, you will be seeing this person regularly for the next few months, through all of your ups and downs. This person will help you through labor and usher your new baby into the world!

First consider what your past communications with doctors and other health practitioners have been like. There are three different types of relationships people tend to have with their care providers:

- *Activity-passivity.* In this relationship, the health provider is the actor and the patient is the person acted upon. This type of relationship is certainly appropriate at times, say, when a person is unconscious or otherwise unable to participate in their treatment.

- *Guidance-cooperation.* In this type of relationship the care provider is an authority figure, and the patient takes the given advice without question. This has historically tended to be the pattern for most doctor-patient relationships.

- *Mutual participation.* This is more like any other adult-peer relationship. The provider and the patient decide together what type of treatment is most appropriate under the circumstances.

While there's no need to actually sit down with your care provider and discuss the above three options (and all the possibilities in between), you should carefully consider which feels right to you and who can best fulfill that preference.

Here are a few tips to assist you in talking to your care provider:

- Shake hands at the beginning and end of each visit. This helps to establish your adult-to-adult relationship and reminds the provider of your personhood.
- Refrain from asking questions when the midwife or doctor are in the process of examining you. Ask them, instead, either before or after the examination. If you prefer to talk to them fully dressed, request that they meet with you after the exam is over and you have put your clothing back on.
- Do not hesitate to discuss things about your practitioner that bother you. This can be difficult—we are, after all, socialized to see medical professionals as authority figures. Keeping the things that bug you bottled up inside will only make you more anxious.
- Conversely, let your practitioner know what you like. This will help to reinforce it in your future relationship, and will benefit other patients as well.

- Don't be afraid to ask for all the clarification you need. It may help to ask the care provider to repeat what he or she is saying "in regular language."
- If a course of treatment makes you uncomfortable or you aren't sure you want or need it, say so. There may be other options, or perhaps the treatment is not strictly necessary. Don't forget that you can decline treatments you do not want.
- Try to get to your appointment with enough time to relax a bit before your care provider sees

you. Seeing health practitioners makes some people feel nervous. Bring a good book or magazine to read.

Using the techniques we have suggested throughout this section will help to ensure that you match yourself up with the right birth attendant for *you*. You can now begin a relationship unlike any other you will have in your lifetime. This person will be one of your guides on the journey to motherhood, both physically and spiritually.

PART TWO

The Second Trimester

What's Happening in My Body?

MONTH FOUR. During the fourth month, your appetite will begin to increase again, and you may find yourself craving certain foods. You may have to urinate more frequently during the night. Despite these changes, you feel a new calmness—you're becoming accustomed to pregnancy.

MONTH FIVE. At month five, it's finally safe to tell the world you're pregnant. The risk of miscarriage is past. Morning sickness subsides, and your appetite continues to increase. You may even have a decrease in your need to urinate as your body adapts to pregnancy.

MONTH SIX. You will now feel distinct fetal movements, especially after you palpate your abdomen, eat, drink a cold beverage, or walk for five minutes. You may even feel some achiness in your lower abdomen.

You will notice that your skin pigmentation darkens to form a line between your belly button and your pubic area. By the sixth month, you finally look pregnant. Your skin may itch as it stretches. You may feel sharp twinges on the sides of your belly as the ligaments that support your uterus expand.

Surprisingly, you may also take more pleasure in sex. Your breasts may begin to produce colostrum, the baby's first milk, though in the ninth month this will increase in anticipation of the baby's birth.

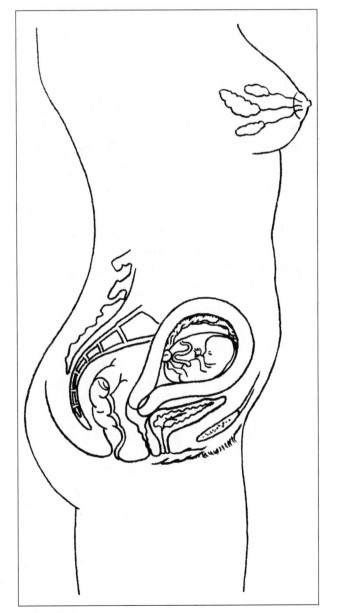

Months 3–4

What's Happening with My Baby?

MONTH FOUR. Your baby weighs about five ounces and is between two and three inches long, just about the size of the palm of your hand. The head is out of proportion to the body. And while it's not possible to tell yet if your baby is a boy or a girl, he or she does have ears and eyes now.

MONTH FIVE. The baby is about four inches long now. The growth of the baby's body is now catching up with the head. Fingers and toes are well defined. This is the month you may feel the first fetal movements and will be able to detect the baby's heartbeat.

MONTH SIX. The baby is very active now. He can turn head over heels and kick. He has periods of waking and sleeping. He hiccups, and can suck his thumb. His eyes open, close, and blink. Already, a baby girl's ovaries are completely formed and contain her lifetime supply of eggs. Hair has begun to grow on the baby's head, and white eyelashes have appeared. He is covered with a thick covering of vernix, a white, creamy substance that protects your baby's skin before birth. At six months, your baby is about eight to ten inches long and weighs between one and one and a half pounds.

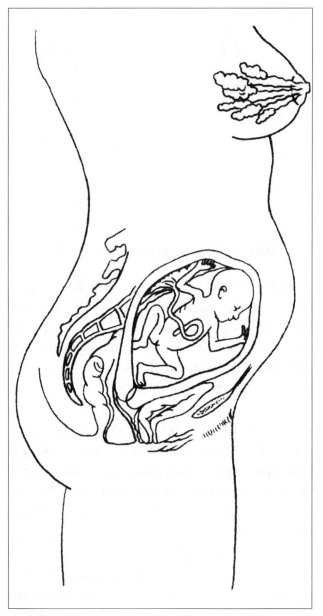

Months 5–6

CHAPTER 4 *Self-Awareness and Self-Appreciation*

To keep a lamp burning we have to keep putting oil in it.

—MOTHER TERESA, *Meditations from a Simple Path*

As the second trimester approaches, you may feel a dramatic change. The nausea, fatigue, and depression of the first trimester may disappear. Or the changes may feel much more subtle to you. Now that the newness of pregnancy has passed, you might feel like you are entering a never-ending period of waiting for the baby.

Because the newness has worn off, and pregnancy symptoms have become more familiar, many women are now able to notice, for the first time, an altogether new relationship with their own emotions.

Powerful Emotions

First you may feel like you can conquer the world, handle all your relationships with ease, or hike the entire Appalachian Trail. Then you may feel like a wet, wrung-out dishrag: large, incompetent, and vulnerable. While you might normally be easygoing, reading the news might now make you weep uncontrollably, and a stolen parking space might cause an outburst of rage. What's going on?

Even though it may feel like you are heading straight for a nervous breakdown, you aren't. You're pregnant and going through an unbelievably dramatic change, one driven by hormonal, physical, and psychological changes that affect every cell in your body and every iota of your spirit.

By the second trimester, many women begin to realize their emotions have become incredibly powerful. Once it was possible to hide the fact that things were bothering you. Now it seems impossible to moderate *any* emotions, either the uplifting ones or the difficult ones. You may have cried more in the last few weeks than since you were a child. You may find yourself revisiting very old issues, perhaps even from your childhood. Relationships with your partner and other peers suddenly become challenging.

All of this is difficult, but completely normal. You will most likely experience heightened feelings throughout your pregnancy and well into the postpartum period—a time that tends to come with its own set of challenging emotions.

Now is the perfect time to learn how to truly care for yourself. When your baby is born, you will need all the self-love and self-awareness you can gather. Here is your opportunity to do everything you can to smooth the pathway to motherhood.

WORKING THROUGH NEW EMOTIONS

It's easy to blame your heightened emotional state on hormones, but experts say that isn't the whole story. "Heightened hormonal levels are not *making* you have feelings, they are making you more aware of them," says Jennifer Louden in *The Pregnant*

Woman's Comfort Book.[1] She adds that being pregnant is like being injected with truth serum. For instance, you are suddenly unable to pretend you aren't mad when you feel criticized by your partner—because you *are* mad.

Many other feelings are heightened as well: fear, sadness, love, frustration, excitement, and a thousand others. A lot of women notice their tolerance for minor annoyances is practically gone, and the breaking point is quickly reached with long-winded friends, a neighbor's barking dog, or a partner's procrastination. You might be tempted to try to ignore all these powerful emotions at first. We all have our own ways of doing that—watching too much television, for example, or eating a whole boxful of cookies, or becoming as busy as we possibly can in order to avoid confronting these emotions.

Try instead to look upon this heightened awareness of your feelings as a gift. We live in a culture where we are often encouraged to hide strong emotions, even from ourselves. It's so much healthier to *know* what you feel and then decide what to do about it.

Keeping a pregnancy journal is a great way to explore your feelings and give them real credibility. Feel free to write whatever you like, with no restrictions. You might want to include landmarks like the first time you feel the baby's movements. You'll enjoy looking back at this record of your pregnancy later on, or you might want to view it as a temporary tool.

To help you get more in touch with your feelings, try this exercise. When you have a troubling experience or feeling, describe it in your journal using the following prompts:

- The situation that's bothering me is: You might reply, "my friend was late for our dinner date."
- I was feeling: "angry because she does this so often. Disrespected. Doesn't she value my time?"
- My body reacted by: "becoming exhausted. I started to feel incredibly tired, as though I needed to go home immediately and lie down."

Another good way to explore and express emotion is by writing a letter you don't intend to send. The letter can be to your boss or your partner, or even to your baby. You can say whatever you like and use any language you like to say it. When the letter is finished, you can throw it away or keep it in your journal.

Sometimes strong feelings can actually have physical roots, so it's important to keep that possibility in mind. If you haven't eaten well or you are overtired, you might react in ways you wouldn't normally. Don't, however, use physical symptoms to hide from your true feelings.

While occasional feelings of sadness are normal, seek help if you feel overwhelmed or deeply depressed. Don't wait and hope these feelings go away. Anxiety and depression can sometimes surface during pregnancy, and it's vital to get help if they become overwhelming.

DEALING WITH PAST HISTORY

It is normal to find yourself suddenly revisiting old issues. You are about to become a mother—many women find each stage of the journey reminds them of something from their own childhood. Having a baby can be tremendously healing in this respect. In a way, you really do have a second chance at childhood. As you travel through your baby's growth, you will learn a lot about yourself.

Some women find it very helpful to write down their own birth stories in as much detail as possible. Interview your parents, older siblings, or other relatives, if possible (and if you feel comfortable doing so). Try to learn as much as you can about your mother's pregnancy and labor, as well as your infancy and childhood.

You can now begin to make decisions about the things you really do want to do differently than your parents did. You can start to talk this over with your partner. If you like, you can even formalize the process and write out a pledge to your child, for example: "I promise to listen to your troubles at school and not try to downplay your feelings."[2]

Again, if you find your emotions are coming up with such intensity that you can't manage them, make sure to get some help. This is a great time to try therapy if you never have before. There are also good parenting classes and pregnancy support groups available. Check with a local mental health practitioner to see what's available in your area. If they are appropriate for your life, you may want to consider a twelve-step program like Al-Anon or Adult Children of Alcoholics (ACOA).

Creating a Strong Network of Other Women

We all need our friends, it's true, but friends are especially critical for new mothers. Build strong relationships with other women *now,* so that you have support when your baby is born, as well as while you are pregnant. Friends of both sexes can be supportive, but there is something about the company of women that is special. Another woman is most likely to understand what your mind and body are going through, particularly if she is also a mother or mother-to-be. If possible, a whole community of women close to your home is even better.

How can you meet other women in your area? Try:

- Pregnancy and motherhood support groups. Check with your childbirth educator to see if there is a group in your area—or start one yourself!
- La Leche League. This national organization offers information and support to breastfeeding mothers and mothers-to-be.
- Exercise classes. Check with local gyms to see if special classes for pregnancy are offered. If not, consider a prenatal or gentle hatha yoga class.
- Book discussion groups. Contact your local bookstore or library to find out what's available.
- Continuing education courses. Ask your local high school or community college to send you a course catalog. Choose a topic you enjoy, such as painting or cooking.

Don't forget to seek out the support of older women, too. Our culture tends to separate us from previous generations. You may live far away from your own mother, aunts, or grandmother. If you can find ways to see more of them and other older women, you may find a gold mine of support. Women who have already experienced motherhood can teach you a lot about coping. They may be able to help you with your pregnancy and your baby's birth, as well as some of the tricky parts of parenting like breastfeeding and colic.

Other Relationships

There's just no two ways about it, your relationships with everyone in your life will change. *You* are changing, and the circumstances of your life are shifting as well. It's bound to affect all of your relationships. Unrealistic expectations—both your own and others'—can complicate your relationships. Communication is the key to identifying these expectations and to understanding the people in your life.

You may find a number of new challenges in dealing with the people in your life. Perhaps your tolerance has diminished, and you can no longer cope with certain difficult people or situations. Some people might find your new behavior challenging, particularly if they are used to being cared for by *you.* Others might have trouble with your new emotional intensity.

It is particularly important for you and your partner to spend some time talking about your fears, concerns, and hopes for the future together. Try to touch base every day, even if only for a few minutes. Talk specifically about how you are feeling, not just about what you did during the day. And work at listening to your partner.

If you already have a child, you will need to spend extra time talking to her about how your family is changing. If you've had to deal with fatigue or morning sickness, your child may be worried about you and will need reassurance. See chapter 8 for suggestions on helping children through pregnancy and the birth of a sibling.

If your partner is also a woman, there will be special issues to discuss, such as how your family will be accepted by your local community. You need to be sure to develop support, particularly from other same-sex parents. See appendix 2 for the names of helpful organizations.

SEXUAL RELATIONSHIPS

As noted earlier, pregnancy is unpredictable. You may have an aversion to sex right now, you may notice no change in your sexual desire, or you may feel more passionate than ever before. If your expectations are not the same as those of your partner, it can be an emotional challenge.

Get to the bottom of whatever feelings you have. Are you embarrassed about your increased desire for sex? Do you feel guilty that sex is the last thing in the world you want right now? Do you have preconceived notions about sex during pregnancy? Are you worried that sex could harm your baby?

The pointers below may provide some insight on how to deal with your sex life during this time:

- It's okay to say no. If you're feeling fatigued or nauseous, explain this to your partner. Make it clear that it is not your partner's fault, but share your changing feelings and be willing to explore them.

- Consider devoting extra time and attention to pleasuring your partner in other ways. Try cuddling or sitting on the couch and holding hands.

- Explore the world of sensuality that is not related to sex. Try massage, light lovely candles, or create a feast of favorite foods.

- If your changing body has made you feel less desirable, or if you've become self-conscious about the weight you've gained, find ways to feel sexier—a new nightgown or a pedicure can make all the difference. Explore new sexual po-

sitions. You may find that a change is in order. In future months your expanding tummy will make this necessary, anyway. If you need some creative ideas, consider buying a good, illustrated guide (see appendix 2 for more information). If it feels like your sex drive is out of control, talk to your partner to find out how he feels about it.

Appreciating Yourself

The bottom line is this: you need to take very special care of yourself right now and do whatever you can to build your self-confidence. See yourself as both the athletic trainer and the athlete, and visualize success in all aspects of your pregnancy, both physical and emotional. Rehearse fearful situations in your mind, whether it is a confrontation with your partner over chores, shyness about meeting new people at an exercise class, or impending labor.

Take some time to treat yourself well and to reward yourself for dealing with situations and people who are difficult. Remember, though, you don't need any special justification for being good to yourself. You deserve it! Every day, find time to treat yourself to at least one of the following items:

- Take a bubble bath or an aromatherapy bath (keep the water warm, not hot).

- Meditate. Try to find ten minutes a day to sit quietly by yourself. Sit up straight and close your eyes. With your hands on your belly, pay attention to your breathing as you inhale and exhale. As you notice other thoughts, let them go and return your attention to your breathing again.

- Learn to say no more often. This can be tough because so many women are taught to say yes. It can be hard to say no to something, because you fear you won't be liked or understood.

- Try this journal technique: time yourself and write for ten minutes. Keep your pen moving, don't think about what you are writing, just

HIGHER GROUND

Toning

If you've heard Gregorian chants, you know how soothing sound can be. Sounds vibrate in the body when we make them, creating a feeling of peacefulness and balance.

Simply making vowel sounds can be relaxing. Stand comfortably in a private, open space, inside or outside. Let your arms hang slightly out from your sides with your palms up. One by one, recite or sing the following sounds gently and with vigor. Increase the volume, but do not force your voice.

AH ("mama")
EE ("see")
AY ("say")
OH ("toe")
OO ("too")

allow whatever comes up to appear on the page. When you are finished, put it away. Look at it again a few days later with fresh eyes and see if you can learn anything new.

- Screen your phone calls and return them only when and if you are ready.
- At the end of every day, write down three things you did well. It doesn't have to be big stuff. "I brushed my teeth after dinner," or "I listened compassionately to my best friend complain about her boss," are perfectly valid entries.
- Buy something nice for yourself—some new lipstick or a bouquet of flowers—or get a new haircut.

- Read a trashy romance novel and refuse to feel bad about it.
- Don't read a newspaper or watch the news on TV for a week, or if that feels like too much, start with twenty-four hours and work your way up to more time.
- Make up affirmations that work for different parts of your pregnancy. "I am already a good mother to my baby" is one that works anytime. "I am eating good food to help my baby grow" or "My body is growing in just the way it should to support my baby" are others. Make up your own!
- Splurge and get a massage. There are massage therapists who specialize in treating pregnant women—some even have tables with special round support holes for large tummies.
- Re-create a memory from your childhood: buy an ice cream cone, have a sleepover with some of your buddies (perhaps at a nice bed and breakfast), go to the movies, or go on a picnic.

Second Trimester Common Concerns

The second trimester brings new physical changes as well as emotional ones. These are not usually as dramatic as the symptoms of the first trimester. Some women will still feel remnants of early symptoms, such as morning sickness or fatigue. Generally speaking, though, the second trimester tends to be the most energetic part of pregnancy.

Baby's first kicks. One physical change that is also emotionally charged is the baby's first kicks. Many women begin to feel these around week fifteen. Others, especially second-time moms, feel them a bit earlier, and others don't feel anything until the twentieth week or later. At first, you might think you just have a little gas. Then it might feel like you have a butterfly fluttering around inside your abdomen.

Increase in appetite. Now that most of the nausea and morning sickness of the early weeks are gone, you may notice a dramatic change in your desire for food. This is normal, and necessary to the baby's development. Your cravings may still guide your food choices. Listen to what your body wants to eat and drink.

Stretch marks. You may have begun to notice stretch marks by the end of your first trimester. They can appear in your breasts, which may be much fuller than they were. You may begin to notice them in your lower abdomen, as well. The skin on your abdomen may by itchy. This is a normal result of the skin stretching from underneath as your belly begins to expand. Stretch marks will not disappear after you have given birth, but will fade with time. It can be very soothing to rub oil into these areas. There are a number of products on the market made specifically for relieving stretch marks, or try plain wheat germ or hazelnut oil.

Varicose veins. Your blood volume increases during pregnancy. The valves that direct this increased blood through your veins and back to your heart have softened, due to higher progesterone levels, and sometimes can't keep up with the flow. This causes blood to pool up and create varicose veins in the legs.[3] A few women will also get varicose veins in the vaginal area. For some, this condition can become quite uncomfortable. Your health care provider may suggest prescription support hose. These need to be put on first thing in the morning, before you even get out of bed.

It may also be helpful to avoid standing and to put your feet up as much as possible. Exercise may also reduce varicose veins by keeping your circulation moving. Ice packs and a diet rich in vitamin B6 can also relieve discomfort.

Hemorrhoids. These are actually another type of varicose veins that appear around the rectum. If you've been suffering from constipation, hemorrhoids can result from straining during bowel movements. Treat your constipation and avoid straining while on the toilet. (See page 13.) Elevating your legs and resting may offer some relief.

Soaking a pad with witch hazel and applying it to the affected area can also help. Try keeping the witch hazel in the refrigerator. The cold will help numb the

---

NATURAL SOOTHER
Your Beautiful Belly

To help prevent stretch marks and enhance the natural resilience of your skin, add essential oils to your skin-care preparations and massage yourself regularly. Lavender and neroli are particularly helpful in preventing stretch marks.

Don't forget that essential oils are concentrated and should not be applied undiluted to the skin. Always add essential oils to a carrier oil such as grapeseed oil, sweet almond oil, jojoba oil, or sesame oil.

Here is an excellent skin enhancer that may be massaged into your entire body or just on your abdomen:

Belly Butter

> 1 oz. vitamin E oil
>
> 3 oz. sweet almond oil or grapeseed oil
>
> 25 drops lavender essential oil
>
> 5 drops neroli essential oil
>
> 5 drops frankincense essential oil
>
> 5 drops lemongrass essential oil
>
> Combine the vitamin E and sweet almond oil in a clean glass or plastic container. Add essential oils one at a time, shaking or mixing gently. Apply as often as you like.

---

pain and constrict the swollen veins. Try taking a cool sitz bath with 7 drops of lemon essential oil added to the water.

Bleeding gums. Increased blood volume is the culprit behind this symptom—it increases pressure on the capillaries in your gums. Changes in your estrogen and progesterone levels also exaggerate your gums' response to plaque.

While you're more likely to have gum problems in the third trimester, it's wise to take extra care of your gums and teeth now. Be diligent (but gentle) about brushing and flossing, and visit your dentist twice during the course of your pregnancy.

Frequent nosebleeds. This is also caused by the increase in blood volume, which raises the pressure in your nasal capillaries. Get plenty of vitamin C in your diet—lack of it can cause even more nosebleeds. Put a little non-petroleum jelly into the nostril to help stop the bleeding. Avoid blowing your nose hard.

Urinary tract infection. Also called cystitis, this is a common complication of pregnancy.[4] You will notice a stinging or burning sensation when you urinate. It may feel as though you need to urinate constantly, even after you've just gone.

Any type of infection in pregnancy is serious. Your health care provider will most likely put you on a course of antibiotics to treat this. You can help things along by drinking lots of water and lots of cranberry, orange, or grapefruit juice. Marshmallow tea is also helpful.[5]

If you've gotten one infection, try to prevent another by avoiding tight pants and pantyhose. Wear only cotton underwear and pantyhose with cotton panels. Continue to drink a lot of fluids. Because UTIs are caused by *E. coli* bacteria contained in feces, it's important to wipe from front to back after using the toilet.

Vaginal discharge. You are likely to notice an increase in vaginal discharge during pregnancy. This is due to hormonal changes that increase your body's mucus production. As long as the discharge does not have a strong, unpleasant odor and is not accompanied by itching or redness, it is normal.

Yeast infections. Pregnant women are at greater risk for yeast infections and other types of vaginitis.[6] A yeast infection is usually marked by increased discharge, intense itching, irritation in the vaginal area, and possibly an odor. If you suspect that you have a yeast infection, consult your midwife or doctor. Oral drugs used to treat yeast infections and other forms

---

BODY WISE
Kegel, Kegel, Kegel

Kegel exercises are great for women not only during pregnancy, but at any time. They increase circulation to the perineum and tone the vaginal and pelvic floor muscles that support the uterus.

What's great about Kegels is that you can do them anytime, anywhere—and no one even knows what you're doing. You can do them sitting, standing, or lying down. They're great to do in the car at red lights or when you have to wait in line.

Tighten your pelvic floor muscles as you would to stop from urinating. You will feel a slight lifting of your pelvic floor and a tightening in your lower abdomen. Hold this for 10 seconds if you can. Then release. If 10 seconds is too long, don't worry—begin with holding for 3 seconds, then 5 seconds, and gradually work your way up to 10. If you feel your muscles loosening before the ten seconds, simply retighten them. See if you can eventually hold for 20 or more seconds, retightening as the time lengthens. Then relax and rest. Start with 5 Kegels a day and work up to 100—or set your own goal. You can do your Kegels in sets of 5 to 25 several times during the day.

---

of vaginitis have not been tested for safety in pregnancy.[7]

The most effective natural remedy for yeast infections is acidophilus, "good" bacteria that compete with the fungus that causes these infections. Acidophilus can be purchased fresh from the refrigerated section of your natural grocery store or as a supplement. Keep refrigerated. You can also combat yeast infections by eating yogurt, which contains acidophilus bacteria; by reducing the amount of sugar, white flour, and fruit in your diet, since they are high in the sugars that encourage bacterial growth; and by eating extra garlic, which is a natural antifungal.

Elevated blood pressure. Your blood pressure will be tested at every prenatal checkup. Your care practitioner wants to know what a normal blood pressure reading is for you, in order to check against high blood pressure in later pregnancy, and during labor.

You might have a higher-than-usual blood pressure reading at one of your visits. In some cases, blood pressure is only elevated in the doctor's office, a condition known as "white-coat hypertension," or in response to stress and psychological pressures, known as "transient hypertension." In early pregnancy, these rarely indicate a real problem.

Braxton-Hicks contractions. These might take you by surprise at first. Some women begin to have them toward the end of the second trimester, while others never have them at all. These contractions feel as though a wide, tight rubber band is squeezing your entire abdomen. If you place your hands on your belly during one of these contractions, your abdomen will feel hard.

Don't worry; these contractions are perfectly normal. They are your body's way of circulating extra blood to the placenta, and also serve as a "rehearsal" for the main event—labor. Just relax and practice your breathing exercises while you wait for the contraction to pass.

Backache. About three-quarters of all pregnant women suffer from backache that starts in the second trimester, and a third of them experience severe problems.[8] Backache during pregnancy is usually caused by a shift in posture, due to your growing ab-domen. Hormones that cause joints and ligaments to loosen up can also contribute to back strain. For many women, back problems are particularly acute at night.

Yoga may help relieve back problems. Yoga can help you to keep your posture in check, as well as stretch out the affected areas. The cat/cow stretch described on page 77 is particularly useful. You can also purchase special tummy/back support slings made just for pregnant women. It will probably be just as effective, however, to work on toning the muscles of the abdomen, which will help the back muscles in supporting your extra weight. Most yoga and Pilates classes for pregnant women address these issues.

Some women also feel pain in their buttocks, or running down the back of one or both of their legs. This type of pain is called sciatica, and is the result of the growing uterus's pressure on the sciatic nerve in your back.

To relieve general backache and sciatica:

- Apply warm compresses, hot water bottles, or a heating pad to the area that hurts.
- Have a professional massage. Try to choose a practitioner who has experience with pregnant women.
- Place your feet on a low stool when you are sitting. This will take strain off your lower back and sciatic nerve.
- Put a pillow between your knees while lying on your side in bed. This will help keep your hips and back in proper alignment.
- When you rise from a lying-down position, roll over onto your side and use your upper arm to push yourself up into a sitting position before you stand up.

Birth goes best if it is not intruded upon by strange people and strange events. It goes best when a woman feels safe enough and free enough to abandon herself to the process.

—PENNY ARMSTRONG AND SHERYL FELDMAN, *A Midwife's Story*

Even if you have not given birth before, you are probably already familiar with the terminology of prenatal testing. Words like *sonogram* and *amniocentesis* have become a familiar part of our general vocabulary.

There is a good reason for that familiarity. It is because many of these prenatal tests, originally created to test certain high-risk pregnancy situations, have become standard practice for all pregnant women. While you may think that these tests can do no harm, some of them have never been thoroughly studied for safety to mother and baby, and may present physical risks to both. Relying on prenatal tests to ease your concerns may also create an atmosphere of worry and anxiety, just what you had hoped to avoid by taking them. Results can sometimes be vague and, what's worse, misleading.

As long ago as 1974, the American College of Obstetricians and Gynecologists (ACOG) recommended that its members take great care to obtain informed consent from their patients before proceeding with any tests or treatments. ACOG was careful to distinguish between *consent* and *informed consent*. In other words, patients should fully understand what will happen to them and their unborn children before proceeding blindly with any type of testing or treatment. This is particularly important now, years later, since many tests are prescribed by physicians who assume that their patients understand what the tests are meant to assess, as well as their risks to mother and baby.

Informed Consent

Informed consent means much more than just showing up for a scheduled ultrasound or amniocentesis. You have the right to:

- Understand in detail how the procedure is administered.
- Understand all the risks associated with it.
- Know what the alternatives are: is there another test or procedure that poses less risk?
- Carefully consider the physical and emotional impacts.
- Feel free to say no to any tests you don't feel are necessary.

Before you can decide to give informed consent, you need to understand the tests and procedures that are routinely administered during pregnancy—ultrasound, the triple screen, amniocentesis, and chorionic villus sampling.

Ultrasound

Ultrasound, or sonogram, was originally developed during World War II to detect enemy submarines. This diagnostic technique has replaced X rays, now known to be dangerous, as the method of choice to view a baby inside the uterus. Ultrasound uses sound waves to create a two-dimensional image of the baby that is suitable for viewing.

WHY IS ULTRASOUND USED?

Ultrasound is used in two ways. One is to investigate a specific concern. If a woman has a family history of a medical condition, or if another test indicates risk, an ultrasound may be recommended. More commonly, however, ultrasound is used as a routine procedure performed on almost every pregnant woman to screen for potential problems, even if she is not at any particular risk.

HOW IS ULTRASOUND DONE?

During ultrasound, a device called a transducer that produces high-energy sound waves is either run across your belly or, in very early pregnancy, inserted into the vagina, where a heartbeat can be detected earlier. The sound waves then rebound and are converted into a visual image of the fetus.

Ultrasound may be done in your practitioner's office, or you may be sent to a hospital. You will usually be asked to have a full bladder for this procedure, depending on the reason for the ultrasound (checking for placenta previa, which we discuss later in this section, requires an empty bladder, for example). You will lie down on a table and will be asked to remove your pants and pull up your shirt or dress to expose your belly for an abdominal ultrasound. You will need to undress from the waist down or wear a gown for a vaginal ultrasound.

For an abdominal ultrasound, a gel will be squirted over your belly to facilitate the movement of the paddle-like transducer across it. For a transvaginal test, the lubricated wand will be gently inserted into your vagina. The transducer is then moved around until the operator or doctor finds the appropriate view.

Most ultrasound exams last only a few minutes. The procedure is painless, though your full bladder may cause you some discomfort. You will usually be able to see the monitor as the test is being done. How much information you are given during the procedure itself will depend on the operator. If your midwife or doctor is present, you will most likely be able to ask questions. Most technicians, though, have been trained to tell the patient nothing until your midwife or doctor reviews the results. Sometimes it is possible to have copies of the ultrasound pictures.

Other uses of ultrasound include the Doppler, or Doptone, a small hand-held device used to hear the baby's heartbeat after the tenth week, and electronic fetal monitors (EFMs), used by most hospital maternity wards to monitor the baby's heart rate during labor. See chapter 13 for a complete discussion of EFMs.

WHEN IS ULTRASOUND NECESSARY?

Ultrasound diagnosis has important uses in pregnancy:

- To quickly establish whether or not a fetus is still alive.
- When there is early bleeding, to predict if a miscarriage is happening.
- To confirm a suspected ectopic pregnancy (where the egg has implanted into a fallopian tube rather than the uterus), a blighted ovum (where a sac grows without an embryo inside it), or a molar pregnancy (where a "false" pregnancy grows inside the uterus), when used in conjunction with other tests.
- To determine the position of the baby during procedures such as amniocentesis and chorionic villus sampling (discussed later in this chapter).
- To establish whether or not levels of amniotic fluid are still adequate in the late weeks of pregnancy.
- To ascertain the position of the placenta at the time of birth if a low-lying placenta is suspected.

Generally speaking, ultrasound is more accurate to explore a specific situation such as those above than when used in a generalized, routine way, in part because highly trained technicians and better machines are used to detect suspected problems.

If an ultrasound is necessary, check on the experience of the operator. Choose someone who has a high level of skill and experience (about 750 scans per year), since a license is not required to operate an ultrasound machine.

WHEN IS ULTRASOUND UNNECESSARY?

According to the American College of Obstetricians and Gynecologists, the country's leading group of obstetrical experts, ultrasound is not necessary for every woman or in every pregnancy, and is not recommended for routine use. Despite this recommendation, ultrasound is used routinely in as many as 70 percent of pregnancies in the United States.[1] Here are the common reasons that ultrasound is used routinely:

- To estimate the baby's due date. Done prior to eighteen weeks, it is most accurate (after this, it is only accurate within a week either way).
- To look for physical abnormalities. Many major abnormalities, such as Down syndrome, cerebral palsy, and heart or kidney problems, most likely won't show up on an ultrasound.
- To confirm multiple fetuses. Ultrasound is only reliable in confirming multiple fetuses when other heartbeats have already been detected with a stethoscope.
- For verification of a breech position. This occurs when the baby is lying in a feet- or buttocks-first position near the end of pregnancy, rather than head down. A qualified midwife or doctor can diagnose this by simply palpating the mother's belly.
- To screen for intrauterine growth retardation (IUGR). IUGR is a condition where the baby is not growing in the womb as it should.
- Location of the placenta during pregnancy. A very low-lying placenta (a condition called placenta previa) puts the mother at risk of severe bleeding during labor, and usually necessitates

a cesarean section. However, nineteen out of twenty cases of placenta previa detected by ultrasound in the second trimester correct themselves as pregnancy progresses.

While routine screening for the above problems is not recommended, ultrasound may be necessary to

NATURAL SOOTHER

The Language of Flowers

Making decisions about prenatal testing can be nerve-racking. What better soothers than flower remedies to help you regain your presence of mind? In the 1930s, British homeopath and medical doctor Edward Bach began to treat the mental and emotional symptoms of his patients with the essences he derived from flowers. The use of flowers in healing has numerous historical precedents, but Bach was the first modern physician to use them. He developed a repertory of thirty-eight remedies from native or naturalized plants in rural England.

Flower remedies are safe and gentle, and can be used during pregnancy. Using them forces you to know yourself, because you have to identify your emotional state to choose the right remedy. There are remedies for feeling overwhelmed, for different kinds of fears, for grief, and for shock.

Two you can try in the second trimester are Aspen, for fears of the unknown, and Walnut, for times of transition. Aspen can help with the inevitable nervous anticipation that accompanies the birth of the first child. Walnut provides resiliency as you go through the various transitions of pregnancy.

Pour about 8 ounces of fresh water into a beautiful glass. Add 3 drops of Aspen and 3 drops of Walnut to the water. Sip slowly during a bath or while you sit quietly.

confirm a problem that has been detected by other tests.

HOW EFFECTIVE IS ULTRASOUND?

The effectiveness of ultrasound as a routine procedure has never been proven. In fact, a number of studies have shown definitively that there is no better outcome for women who have had one or more routine ultrasound examinations during their pregnancies, as compared to those who have had none.[2] It is, as well, a very expensive procedure, costing the United States more than a billion health care dollars per year.

According to Australian physician and ultrasound authority Sarah Buckley, M.D., there is no evidence that ultrasound is necessarily more accurate at estimating due date than hands-on palpation done in conjunction with a woman's own guesstimate of her due date, even if the woman is unsure of when she conceived. Palpating the mother's belly can also accurately diagnose a breech position, and a stethoscope can be used to detect multiple fetuses. In addition, a stethoscope or fetoscope is as effective as a Doppler in detecting fetal heart tones after sixteen weeks.

When used routinely, ultrasound also has a very high rate of false positives. In some instances, normal babies are aborted because of a false positive diagnosis. A United Kingdom study found that 1 in 200 babies (.5 percent) aborted for major abnormalities after a positive ultrasound result were, in fact, normal babies.[3]

In one Swedish study conducted at Uppsala University, ultrasound screening for intrauterine growth retardation (IUGR) was compared to a midwife's repeated measuring of the uterus in 581 pregnancies.[4] The report concluded that the midwife's measurements were more accurate than the ultrasound measurements. Dozens of additional studies in the United States, England, and Sweden have come to the same conclusion. According to Dr. Marsden Wagner, perinatal epidemiologist and former head of the Responsible Office for Maternal and Child Health for the European Office of the World Health Organization, more than 50 percent of ultrasound screenings for IUGR give false positive results.

A recent study at a major women's hospital in Brisbane, Australia (where 99 percent of women receive routine ultrasounds), showed that routine ultrasound missed about 40 percent of abnormalities.[5] A 1989 study conducted by the American College of Obstetricians and Gynecologists revealed that ultrasounds miss abnormalities just as often as they give false positive readings. In the ACOG study, 51 percent of ultrasounds failed to reveal a serious problem when it actually did exist.[6]

IS ULTRASOUND SAFE?

The National Institutes of Health cautions against routine use of ultrasound, noting that "the data on clinical efficacy and safety do not allow recommendation for routine screening at this time; there is a need for multidisciplinary randomized controlled clinical trials for an adequate assessment."[7]

Similarly, the World Health Organization (WHO) urges prudence: "Ultrasound screening during pregnancy is now in widespread use without sufficient evaluation. Research has demonstrated its efficacy for certain complications of pregnancy but the published material does not justify the routine use of ultrasound in pregnant women."[8]

According to perinatal epidemiologist Marsden Wagner, the safety of ultrasound has never been clinically proven. The editors of the Cochrane Database, a review of over 9,000 controlled trials from eighty-five different countries, note that "there has been surprisingly little well-organized research to evaluate possible adverse effects of ultrasound exposure on human fetuses."[9]

In a 1999 study, six scientists at University College Dublin found that ultrasound creates changes in cells. Patrick Brennan, the lead researcher, said, "It has been assumed for a long time that ultrasound had no effect on cells. We now have grounds to question that assumption."[10] Further evidence that ultrasound has an effect on cells is indicated in recent research that shows a higher-than-average rate of left-handedness in boys exposed to ultrasound in utero.[11]

The Triple Screen

This simple blood test measures the levels of three chemicals in the mother's blood: alpha-fetoprotein (AFP) and the hormones estriol and human chorionic gonadotropin (hCG). It does not identify the existence of any specific abnormality, only the presence of chemicals that can indicate risk.

WHY IS THE TRIPLE SCREEN USED?

The test is done to evaluate the risk of Down syndrome, spina bifida (a disorder where part of the spinal cord develops outside of the baby's body), anencephaly (where the skull fails to grow over the brain), and other abnormalities. If a fetus has Down syndrome, for example, the hCG levels in the mother's blood are often higher than normal, while estriol and AFP are often lower.[12] High levels of AFP, on the other hand, may indicate risk of a neural tube defect such as spina bifida or anencephaly.[13]

These levels are factored in with a woman's age to calculate the *likelihood* that one of these abnormalities may be present.

HOW IS THE TRIPLE SCREEN DONE?

If you have this test, you will have blood drawn either in your practitioner's office or in a lab, around week sixteen. Results are usually available within a couple of days.

Generally, if a woman receives a result indicating risk, she will be advised to take the test again. If she receives a second result indicating risk, further testing such as ultrasound and amniocentesis will be recommended, as will genetic counseling.

WHEN IS THE TRIPLE SCREEN NECESSARY?

The triple screen is an elective test. Some women over forty who are pregnant with their first child find it reassuring, but it is not medically necessary.

BODY WISE
Pelvic Rock

When questions about risk assail you, you can take refuge in your very normal, pregnant body. The Pelvic Rock is grounding and strengthening. It is a great exercise for relieving backache and gas, and for readjusting the baby's position later in pregnancy. It also improves posture and strengthens the abdominal muscles. There are several different ways to do it.

Lie on the floor on your back with your knees bent and your feet flat on the ground. Inhale as you contract your abdominal muscles and flatten the small of your back on the floor. Hold this for a count of five as you exhale. Repeat five times. To make sure you're doing it right, put your hand under the small of your back as you rock your pelvis. Repeat five times a day. Don't do this exercise if it makes you feel light-headed.

Get on your hands and knees with your back straight and your knees hip-width apart. As you exhale, tighten your abdominal muscles and arch your lower back. Let your head hang loose. Hold for five seconds. Inhale as you relax your back to the starting position. Repeat five times a day or whenever you feel gassy and uncomfortable.

WHEN IS THE TRIPLE SCREEN UNNECESSARY?

The triple screen is not necessary during pregnancy, but it has been used routinely, up until recently, for women under age thirty-five, while amniocentesis (described later in this section) has been routinely administered to women over thirty-five. The American College of Obstetricians and Gynecologists (ACOG) now recommends the triple screen for all pregnant women, since amniocentesis can cause miscarriage. It is not medically necessary, however, that you receive this test.

HOW EFFECTIVE IS THE TRIPLE SCREEN?

Because this test does not identify the existence of any specific abnormality, but only the presence of chemicals that may indicate risk, its results are inconclusive and open to interpretation. For example, while high levels of AFP are associated with spina bifida, they might also indicate the presence of more than one fetus. Low levels associated with risk of Down syndrome can simply mean that the fetus is younger than was previously thought.

IS THE TRIPLE SCREEN SAFE?

The triple screen is safe. It is a simple blood test. Although it is the least invasive of all prenatal tests, the triple screen has a high rate of false positives, which incorrectly indicate risk in healthy pregnancies, resulting in weeks of anxiety while further tests are evaluated. In fact, 96 to 98 percent of women who first receive a positive triple screen result will go on to have normal babies. The risk of this test is emotional rather than physical.

Amniocentesis

Amniocentesis is a procedure in which some of the amniotic fluid surrounding the baby is removed from the mother's uterus. The amniotic fluid has passed in and out of the baby's body, and therefore contains some of the baby's cells. These cells can be read to see if a disease such as Down syndrome, spina bifida, cystic fibrosis, Tay-Sachs, sickle cell anemia, or anencephaly is present.

WHY IS AMNIOCENTESIS USED?

This test is used to obtain information about the baby's genetic makeup and the potential for genetically inherited diseases. It can also determine the gender of the baby. In addition, if there are concerns that the baby will be born prematurely, amniocen-

tesis can determine if the baby's lungs are mature enough to breathe normally after birth.

HOW IS AMNIOCENTESIS DONE?

A hollow needle is inserted into the mother's uterus through her abdomen. A local anesthetic may be used, though discomfort might still be experienced. Ultrasound is conducted before the amniocentesis to determine the position of the baby and the placenta, to avoid hitting them with the needle. About half an ounce of amniotic fluid is removed for study. This test should take less than thirty minutes.

If you decide to have amniocentesis, you will need to take the day off. It is done either in a doctor's office or in a hospital. You will probably be advised to lie down at home after the test and rest. Some practitioners suggest their patients have a glass of wine to relax and reduce cramping. You will get results from the test in about two to three weeks. Your practitioner will not reveal the baby's sex to you unless you specifically ask for this information.

WHEN IS AMNIOCENTESIS NECESSARY?

As mentioned earlier, ACOG now recommends the less invasive triple screen in all pregnancies for women over thirty-five, following up with amniocentesis only if high risk is indicated.

WHEN IS AMNIOCENTESIS UNNECESSARY?

Genetic conditions happen to the babies of women of all ages, while genetic accidents, such as Down syndrome, occur more often in the children of older mothers. This is one reason amniocentesis was routinely prescribed for women over thirty-five, until recently. It may be, however, that other age-related factors such as diet, general health, exercise, and exposure to radiation and environmental toxins—rather than age alone—are the real causes of genetic anomalies. That's why age alone is not an absolute indicator of risk.[14] You can review questions regarding your own personal risks with your birth attendant.

HOW EFFECTIVE IS AMNIOCENTESIS?

While amniocentesis can diagnose hundreds of diseases and conditions, it is most effective when the laboratory is instructed to look for a specific condition. The procedure has two major disadvantages in terms of acting on the information. It can take two to three weeks for the results to become available, and the procedure is not usually done until the end of the fourth month, when sufficient fluid for testing is available. Culture failure, which occurs in 2 percent of test samples, can require a repeat sample and therefore prolong final results until well past the middle of the pregnancy.

IS AMNIOCENTESIS SAFE?

Amniocentesis carries a miscarriage risk of 1 to 3 percent (almost three times the miscarriage rate in a pregnancy where amniocentesis has not been performed).[15] With a more experienced practitioner, the risk may be slightly less. Studies also show a risk of low-birth-weight infants in about .5 percent of women who have undergone the test, and an increase in respiratory distress syndrome in their infants.[16]

Side effects of the procedure itself include cramping, bleeding, and leaking of amniotic fluid. These side effects may be quite minor, or severe. In addition, those women whose tests have to be readministered double their risk of miscarriage from 3 to 6 percent.

Chorionic Villus Sampling (CVS)

A small sample of the chorion, the outer sac that surrounds the embryo during the first two months of pregnancy, is gathered along with the villi, hairlike tissues that protrude from the chorion. These are studied to assess the fetal chromosomes for genetic abnormalities.

WHY IS CVS USED?

CVS was originally developed to detect chromosomal abnormalities early, at around week ten, because amniocentesis can't be effectively done until week sixteen. This allows a woman to terminate her pregnancy much earlier if the test confirms the presence of a severe problem.

HOW IS CVS DONE?

This test is done in a hospital setting. You will lie down and have an ultrasound examination to locate the baby's position in your womb. Then a hollow needle will be inserted through your abdomen (or vagina) into your uterus to gather a sample from the embryonic sac. The test is sometimes painful, but takes less than forty-five minutes. Results will be available in about ten days.

WHEN IS CVS NECESSARY?

This is an elective test and is not medically necessary. It is normally reserved for cases in which earlier knowledge is important to the patient and the practitioner due to a high genetic risk for certain diseases.

WHEN IS CVS UNNECESSARY?

Because of its risks, which are discussed below, CVS is not recommended for most pregnant women.

HOW EFFECTIVE IS CVS?

CVS sampling is not quite as accurate as amniocentesis in assessing the presence of Down syndrome, and is not capable of assessing the risk of neural tube defects such as spina bifida.

IS CVS SAFE?

Some studies show a miscarriage risk of 1 to 5 percent associated with CVS, much higher even than the rate of 1 to 3 percent for amniocentesis, and nearly six times the average miscarriage rate. If the needle is inserted through the abdomen (as is more common now), rather than through the vagina, the risk is reduced.

Other suspected problems associated with CVS include higher rates of preterm birth, limb and facial deformities, cervical lacerations, and maternal infection. These are more likely to occur if the test is conducted before ten weeks. There are also higher rates of false positives and failed tests, where the procedures must be repeated, than in amniocentesis.

Emotional Impact of Prenatal Tests

The emotional effects of these prenatal tests have not been well studied. This means you need to take responsibility for figuring this out for yourself and for your family.

One of the most obvious effects of all of this testing is that it serves to "medicalize" your pregnancy. Trying to turn a healthy pregnancy into a medical experience can cause unnecessary worry and a tendency to avoid bonding too soon with the developing baby until it is "certain" that everything is okay. Going through these tests can make it easy to forget that birth is a normal process and does not need to be frightening. And remember—none of these tests is foolproof.

In fact, being forced to worry about conditions that ultimately work themselves out (like early diagnosis of placenta previa, for example, picked up in a routine ultrasound) can have negative effects. It is hard to shake off the anxiety of wondering whether everything is okay. Waiting two weeks for the result of an amniocentesis can be very stressful, even if you

have every reason to believe that you and your baby are healthy.

Parents who are especially jittery, and think they might feel better after having these tests, need to consider this information even more carefully. You might think that prenatal tests will provide you with a sense of security, but unless there is a true indication of high risk, these tests can be misleading. You can find security by discussing your concerns with your health care provider, who will take the time to listen and explain, and by talking with your partner, doula, or friend.

Many women have testing done even though they have no intention of terminating an abnormal pregnancy. This is often because of pressure from family and friends to "find out" if everything is okay, even though these tests offer no guarantees. It can take great courage to say no under pressure. Remember that having prenatal tests done just to appease your family or partner will have consequences only for *you*. You must carefully think through each step of this decision, and review the possible consequences of prenatal tests before you decide if they are right for you.

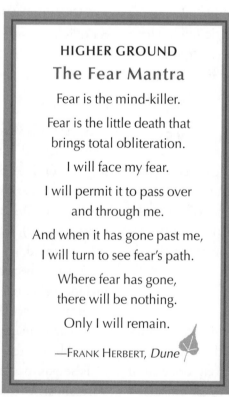

HIGHER GROUND

The Fear Mantra

Fear is the mind-killer.

Fear is the little death that
brings total obliteration.

I will face my fear.

I will permit it to pass over
and through me.

And when it has gone past me,
I will turn to see fear's path.

Where fear has gone,
there will be nothing.

Only I will remain.

—FRANK HERBERT, *Dune*

CHAPTER 6

Childbirth Education

Lessons in preparing for childbirth are really lessons in living.

—LYNN MOEN, *Around the Circle Gently*

When you think of childbirth education classes, you may automatically think about being taught how to cope with labor. You probably assume that you will learn about breathing techniques or how to control pain.

Most childbirth education courses offer much more than this. You will find a broad range of them with different focal points and philosophies. Before we go over the specific types of classes that are available, let's take a look at some things a childbirth class might offer. The range of possibilities may surprise you.

- *Nutrition.* You might be taught just a few basics about eating during pregnancy, or your class might go into a lot of detail about recommended minerals and vitamins, calorie requirements, and even recipe suggestions. Some teachers will know more about some eating habits— vegetarianism, for example—than others.

- *Body awareness and conditioning.* Many teachers will include Kegel exercises or yoga postures to help prepare your body for birth. Some may include conditioning or prenatal aerobics, for example, as a part of their package, or as an optional add-on.

- *Visualization and relaxation.* Your instructor may take you through one, or many, visualiza-

tions to help prepare you for labor and birth. Some may teach meditation techniques.

- *Communication and community.* Being in a group with other parents-to-be is an important part of most childbirth education classes. You benefit from listening to other people's questions and from the dialogue among parents. You can discuss issues ranging from worries about parenting to finding a pediatrician. You may develop friendships that will last for many years and give you a real community of fellow parents to enjoy.

- *Labor preparation.* You may learn breathing and other techniques that can help you manage (not control) pain and the other stressors of labor. Some classes will focus almost exclusively on potential complications and the stages of labor. You may watch births on videos and hear birth stories. Other classes may offer specific information on water birth or birthing at home.

- *Parenting/breastfeeding preparation.* Most teachers include preliminary instruction on breastfeeding and basics about newborn care.

- *How to be your own advocate.* You and your partner may learn how to ask questions and take appropriate steps to help ensure you will have the type of birth experience you want.

HIGHER GROUND
A Room of Your Own

In a way, meditation is like having a room of your own. It's a way to focus on your inner world and let the outer world go by. The focused calm that you gain through meditation can help you to handle the physical changes of pregnancy, the powerful experience of labor and birth, and the demanding early time with your new baby.

Like many people with busy schedules, you may have difficulty finding the time to meditate. Designate a special place for meditation that's uncluttered and quiet— a place where you can sit comfortably with your back straight. Choose a specific time of day to meditate. If you're a morning person, you may prefer to meditate upon rising; night owls may prefer to meditate after dinner.

Begin your meditation by closing your eyes and taking a deep breath. Imagine that your breath is pouring in from the top of your head and flooding your body. Pay attention to each inhalation and exhalation, and try to extend your exhalation longer and longer. Disregard intruding thoughts and return to your breathing.

In the beginning, meditate for a short time, perhaps ten minutes. As you become more accustomed to the practice, increase your sessions to twenty minutes, then thirty.

If you'd like, light a candle or a stick of incense as a small ritual to prepare for your meditation. Put it out after you finish. Prevent distractions while you meditate—take the phone off the hook and don't answer the doorbell. Take this time for yourself in "a room of your own."

Types of Childbirth Education Courses

This section will tell you about some of the organizations that certify childbirth educators. You may find instructors who are certified by one of these organizations, and teach only those methods, or you may find an instructor who incorporates a number of different philosophies. Some organizations encourage their members to broaden their horizons, while others insist that certified instructors of their method adhere very strictly to their outline for a class.

LAMAZE INTERNATIONAL

The breathing and muscle-control techniques that eventually came to be known as the Lamaze method were originated in France by obstetrician Fernand Lamaze during the 1950s. Lamaze's methods were introduced to this country in 1960 by renowned childbirth educator Elisabeth Bing and her colleague Marjorie Karmel well before anyone taught any kind of childbirth education at all. Today the word *Lamaze* has almost become a synonym for childbirth education classes, regardless of the philosophy.

All childbirth education is not created equal, however, and if Lamaze is what you want, you need to make sure you have selected someone who is really trained in the methods (see appendix for information on Lamaze International).

A Lamaze class will offer at least twelve hours of instruction with small class sizes (six to ten couples) and an emphasis on discussion. Training in breathing techniques and birth positions along with relaxation and massage will be taught for use during labor. Information about normal birth, medical procedures, healthy lifestyles, and breastfeeding is also taught.

BRADLEY METHOD

The Bradley Method promotes natural childbirth and attempts to achieve this goal with a very thorough and detailed course program for new parents. They teach avoidance of drugs during pregnancy, birth, and while breastfeeding unless absolutely necessary. A key part of the method is to train the husband as coach. Although some Bradley-trained parents also use a doula during their labor (see chapter 7 for more on doulas), the husband (or partner) is meant to take the major role.

The course includes information on nutrition, as well as relaxation and natural breathing as tools to use during labor. Parents are taught how to handle unexpected situations and how to be self-advocates. Classes are held over a period of twelve weeks. Of all the childbirth methods listed here, this one is the most strictly formulated: Bradley classes are taught in the same manner no matter where you go.

BIRTHING FROM WITHIN

"Through soul-searching and listening more deeply to the women I was working with, I finally understood that women have to prepare for birth in their heart and soul, not their head," says Pam England, the founder of Birthing from Within (BFW) and author of the book by the same name. England draws birthing wisdom from several different cultures. Parents are not forced to learn any one method—instead, they can draw on many different ideas from many sources to help them through labor and birth. The goal is to be present for your baby's birth, whatever that means for you. In general, classes tend to be experiential—incorporating active exercises for learning—rather than lecture-oriented.

A typical class is divided into three parts: (1) a multisensory activity, incorporating singing and

---

NATURAL SOOTHER
Pregnancy Massage

If you've never had a massage before, pregnancy is the perfect time to start. The deep breathing and relaxation that you can experience during massage are also effective tools to use during pregnancy and at your baby's birth. Massage can be both soothing and energizing. The deep manipulation of the muscles helps to reduce stress and fatigue while improving circulation. And when you're less stressed, your baby's environment is calmer.

Look for a massage therapist who has a good reputation and experience with massage during pregnancy. Some massage therapists have a special table with an opening to accommodate your belly. Others will massage you while you lie on your side. Direct the therapist to any parts of your body that are particularly sensitive. See appendix 2 for more information.

---

drumming, for example, which could be derived from art or music; (2) pain-coping practices such as Coyote Circle, where parents learn that vocalizing during labor is normal and helpful; and (3) practical information about specific topics such as "How to push your baby out."

Classes vary in length and size, depending on the instructor. Sign up during your second trimester.

BIRTHWORKS

Birthworks' major goal is to develop a woman's self-confidence and faith in her ability to give birth. Founded by physical therapist Cathy Daub in 1981, Birthworks' program is inspired by the work of the famous French obstetrician and advocate of midwifery Dr. Michel Odent. Odent teaches that women should give birth in any way that's comfortable for them, and Birthworks encourages women to use their intuition during the birth. Birthworks does not call its teaching a "method," because its teachers believe there is no "right" way to give birth. Birthworks encourages women and their partners to begin the course as early in pregnancy as possible, perhaps even before becoming pregnant. A large part of the course is meant to help parents learn how to communicate with care providers. Nutrition is also taught, as well as a method known as Pelvic Bodyworks, which teaches women how the pelvis moves and opens in different labor positions. Birthworks teaches deep slow breathing and working with contractions, rather than trying to use patterned breathing to resist the intensity of contractions.

The classes generally meet for two and a half hours each week for ten weeks. Women with any type of medical history are encouraged to attend, including women who are expecting twins or who have had previous cesarean sections.

INTERNATIONAL CHILDBIRTH EDUCATION ASSOCIATION (ICEA)

ICEA's philosophy encompasses the idea of birth as a major family/life event, rather than a medical procedure. ICEA encourages family-centered care, and believes that birth professionals should guide rather than direct women. ICEA-certified teachers are expected to know detailed information about pregnancy, labor, nutrition, and preparation for parenting.

A teacher certified by ICEA will devise her or his own curriculum, including class length, so this will vary from class to class. ICEA also offers certification in prenatal fitness and postnatal teaching (baby care and breastfeeding). If your instructor is certified in these areas as well, you will get the benefit of that extra knowledge.

ASSOCIATION OF LABOR ASSISTANTS AND CHILDBIRTH EDUCATORS (ALACE)

ALACE seeks to link women together to try to make up for the fact that most are no longer well connected to female relatives from previous generations. This organization feels that birth has come to resemble a mechanized medical emergency, and that this conjures images of fear and pain. ALACE's method views birth as a sacred passage and creative expression of love.

ALACE's training program for educators was developed by a midwife, Rahima Baldwin. Childbirth preparation is taught for women giving birth in a hospital, birth center, or at home. The principles of mind-body integration are taught, along with relaxation and coping tools to work with pain and discomfort. Women who have previously had cesarean sections are encouraged to attend ALACE programs.

ALACE-certified instructors will devise their own curriculums and class lengths, so you will need to check each one to find out this information.

HYPNOBIRTHING

While many childbirth educators seek to give their students tools to *manage* pain, Hypnobirthing's philosophy is that childbirth simply does not need to be painful. Pain is thought to stem directly from an expectation of it and from fear. Marie Mongan, who founded Hypnobirthing, based her philosophy on the work of Dr. Grantly Dick-Read, a well-known English obstetrician, who first began the natural childbirth movement in the 1920s.

This program uses hypnosis to help women through the process of labor and birth. Hypnosis is introduced as a naturally induced state of relaxed, focused concentration, similar to states we slip in and out of throughout the day as we watch television or focus on routine tasks. Hypnobirthing claims this method shortens labor considerably, resulting in reduced pain, less medication, healthier newborns, and reduced postpartum depression. Hypnobirthing also offers women suggestions on how to avoid overmedicalized birth experiences. Hypnobirthing is taught in four two-and-a-half-hour classes. You and your partner will be taught the basics of hypnosis techniques, prenatal bonding with your baby, relaxation and breathing techniques, and visualizations. You will also learn how to deal with birthing institutions.

Again, the courses in your area may not be advertised as any of the methods described above, but may incorporate techniques from all of them. Knowing about these philosophies will make it easier for you to talk to a specific instructor and figure out if the philosophy is right for you. You will want to make your decision based on a number of factors:

- Schedule and length of classes
- Convenience of location
- Number of participants
- Inclusion of subjects, such as nutrition or exercise, that are particularly important to you
- Instructor's experience with things you may be considering, such as water birth or home birth
- Your own personal beliefs about birth and pregnancy
- And last but not least, whether or not you like the instructor and feel you can learn effectively from her

Hospital Courses

Perhaps your hospital or birth center offers a course. Wouldn't that be the most convenient possibility? Perhaps, but you need to carefully review the particulars. Some hospitals offer a very shortened version of what most childbirth educators recommend. If the class only meets four times for an hour and a half, for example, that may not be enough to cover the subject in detail. Many hospitals devote the majority of class time to touring the facility in preparation for birth. While a hospital tour is a good idea, it does not replace childbirth education.

Generally speaking, it might be wisest to take a class not affiliated with any large medical or birth institution. This way you can be assured of the most objective possible picture of pregnancy and labor. After all, many of these classes devote time to teaching you just how to deal with these institutions to be sure your experience is the best it can be.

There is also something to be said for finding a class that is as close to your home as possible, since

BODY WISE
Going for a Swim

While you're concentrating on childbirth education, don't forget to concentrate on your body. Swimming is one of the best exercises for pregnancy and can be done right up until the birth. It provides aerobic exercise, strengthens and tones the entire body, and is at once both relaxing and invigorating. If you already have a swimming routine, you should still be able to use it during pregnancy. Just adjust to your new energy level. Here are some simple ways to relax in the pool. Use a flotation vest if you like.

Go to the deep end of the pool. Do flutter kicks as fast as you can for about 30 seconds. Then do them as slowly as you can for another 30 seconds. Repeat this three to five times.

"Run" in place in the water for 30 seconds. Repeat three times.

Follow these exercises by just playing in the water. Bob up and down. Float aimlessly. Get to know your new body.

developing a community of fellow parents can be a very vital part of your experience. Same-sex partners may find it helpful to try to find a childbirth educator who teaches other same-sex partners in order to increase their support base and sense of community once the baby is born.

Other Options

While the best choice is to take a local class taught by a live instructor, childbirth education courses are also available on video and even online. Courses are occasionally offered in vacation settings, such as a mountain or seaside resort. You can also learn more about childbirth through videos and books (see suggestions in appendix 2).

A doula provides support consisting of praise, reassurance, measures to improve the comfort
of the mother, physical contact such as rubbing the mother's back and holding her hands,
explanation of what is going on during labour and delivery and a constant friendly presence.

—WORLD HEALTH ORGANIZATION, *Care in Normal Birth: A Practical Guide*

The second trimester is the perfect time to line up support for your upcoming labor and birth. By now, you've chosen a birth location where you'll feel physically and emotionally safe, as well as a practitioner with whom you'll feel comfortable. You've probably also signed up for a childbirth education course, so you'll know what to expect when your baby is born. And you may be thinking about the other people you'd like to have around, such as your partner, your mother, or a best friend.

But there's one more important person to include in your support team—someone who could:

- Reduce your labor time by 25 percent
- Reduce your chances of having a cesarean by 50 percent
- Reduce the likelihood that you will need medical interventions such as pitocin, forceps, or vacuum extraction by up to 40 percent
- Reduce the likelihood that you will ask for pain medication or an epidural by as much as 60 percent
- Increase your chance that labor will progress normally
- Increase the chances that you will feel satisfied with your birth experience
- Decrease the likelihood that you will experience postpartum depression

- Improve your bonding experience with your baby
- Help you to breastfeed with greater ease

If that sounds good to you—and it's hard to imagine that it wouldn't sound good to any woman—consider hiring a doula.

What Is a Doula?

The word *doula* is derived from ancient Greece, and it means "woman caregiver of another woman." The word was revived by author Dana Raphael in her book *The Tender Gift*, about the positive impact of women helping women give birth. Today, *doula* signifies a woman, hired by the expectant mother and her partner, to "mother the mother." Other names for a doula include labor coach, monitrice, labor assistant, birth assistant, and labor companion.

Doulas, or their equivalents, are common in many other countries, such as Holland, where they are considered a necessity. Here in the United States, we are just beginning to appreciate what doulas can do for us.

Doulas can be broken down into two categories: postpartum doulas and birth doulas. A postpartum doula can help you adjust to your new baby and learn how to breastfeed. She can give you advice on new-

NATURAL SOOTHER

Feeding Your Face

Your doula will encourage you to take care of yourself in many ways. Here's something you can do for yourself at home that is easy and leaves your skin feeling like silk. It also uses ingredients that you're likely to have in your own kitchen. Purchase some powdered cosmetic clay (French green, red, or white) to use in this recipe. You can find it at your natural foods store.

Using a clean washcloth, clean your face well with a nonsoap facial cleanser and warm water. Rinse your face with cool water and pat dry.

Boil a deep pot of water on the stove. When it comes to a boil, remove it to a table and set it on a hot pad. If you'd like, add 1 or 2 drops of lavender or rose essential oil, or sprinkle in a handful of dried rose petals. Let the water cool until you can comfortably hold your face over the pot, forming a tent with a large towel.

Remain as long as you're comfortable, taking breaks if needed. The steam will open and cleanse your pores as well as moisturizing your tissues. When the water cools completely, pat your face dry with a clean towel.

Mix 1 to 2 tablespoons of cosmetic clay with enough water or egg white to make a paste.

Apply the paste to your face. Sit comfortably with your feet up for at least 10 minutes. If you'd like, sip a cool glass of water with lemon. When the mask feels dry and tight, rinse it off with warm water and a washcloth. Follow up with a cool-water rinse and pat dry.

Combine 2 tablespoons plain yogurt and 1 tablespoon honey. Apply the mixture to your face for 10 to 20 minutes. Rinse it off with warm water and a washcloth, followed by a cool rinse. Pat your skin dry with a clean towel.

born care, cook or run errands, and much more. She might be the same woman who served as your birth doula. We'll talk more about postpartum doulas in chapter 21.

A birth doula, as the name implies, helps a woman through the process of labor and birth in any setting: at home, in a birth center, or in a hospital. She is not a midwife, although she has probably witnessed many births and is very knowledgeable about how to cope with pain during labor. A doula is there just for *you*—she will be your best advocate and greatest source of comfort throughout your birth experience. A doula serves as the link between the physical, emotional, and spiritual parts of labor and birth.

Among the services doulas provide are:

- Meeting with you before your due date to plan for the birth and to discuss any questions you might have. If you are nervous about any part of it, she will consider it her job to reassure you.
- Giving you prenatal tips on exercise, nutrition, and relaxation techniques.
- Helping you at home until it is time to send for the midwife or go to the birth center or hospital.
- Transporting you and your partner to the birth center.
- Attending you throughout your labor, from beginning to end. Half of all hospitals are short-staffed, and doctors, nurses, midwives—even friends and relatives—may come and go during the labor. Not your doula—she is there continuously, a calm, focused, and experienced presence.
- Recognizing where you are in the labor process by observing your facial expressions and speech,[1] as well as acting as your ally and communicating your needs to health care personnel.
- Helping labor to progress more quickly if necessary.
- Helping you to cope with pain using natural techniques such as massage and acupressure.
- Explaining what is happening to you during

each step of the birthing process and preparing you for what is to come.
- Helping you breastfeed your newborn.
- Explaining newborn tests.

The benefits of doulas have been shown in fourteen controlled trials in several countries,[2] and the results reported in highly respected publications such as the *New England Journal of Medicine* and the *Journal of the American Medical Association*. Most of these trials noted that touch and words of encouragement were particularly effective tools used by doulas. Women reported more positive evaluations of the birth experience and felt more relaxed during labor when they received continuous and experienced woman-to-woman support.

Why Can't My Partner or My Best Friend Be My Birth Doula?

In some cases, a friend or partner can be an effective doula. The problem is that, until you have occasion to see them in a birthing situation, neither you nor they will know if they can provide the support you need.

Additionally, partners may have difficulty during the birth and may need their own support. No matter how much a partner loves you, he may end up feeling overwhelmed, squeamish, or exhausted by the experience. The very fact that this person loves you so much might make it impossible for him to relax and think objectively about what the current situation calls for. Additionally, your partner or friend will most likely not have anywhere near the experience and knowledge that a competent doula will.

Your partner can still be an essential part of the baby's birth. Author Mayri Sagady reports that having a doula relieves most families "of the pressure to 'be the experts' and frees them to feel and express their own emotions as they themselves witness the miraculous and challenging process of labor and birth."[3] In fact, it's family and friends who can best

---

BODY WISE
Learning to Squat

Having a doula reminds you of the importance of woman-to-woman support. In traditional societies, women did everything together; often, when you see photos of tribal women, they are squatting while cooking a meal or grinding grain.

As modern women, we're not used to squatting for long periods, but it increases the mobility of the pelvic joints and strengthens the muscles of the inner thighs and Achilles tendons. Squatting is also a great position in which to give birth, but it can be uncomfortable unless you get some practice.

Stand with your feet about hip width apart and your heels on the floor. Keeping your back straight and your weight equally distributed between your heels and toes, squat slowly as you exhale. If you need support, hold on to a secure piece of furniture, a doorknob, or your partner's hand. You can also lean back against a wall or between your partner's knees.

Do not bounce. Stay in the squatting position for at least 30 seconds, then inhale and return to a standing position. Repeat 5 times a day. Work up to squatting for 90 seconds.

If your heels do not lie flat while you squat, your Achilles tendons may be tight or short. You can compensate by spreading your feet farther apart, wearing shoes with heels, or placing a book under each heel. You can also hold on to something. Of course, if squatting causes pain or if you have hip, knee, or ankle problems, check with your birth attendant before trying this exercise.

appreciate a doula's expertise, since she can guide them to be as effective as possible in helping the birthing mother.

How Doulas Are Trained

A number of different organizations train and certify doulas. If you choose a doula who has undergone such training, you can be assured that she has the knowledge and experience she should have to give you the help you need. The organizations below are most commonly used by women who would like to become certified doulas:

- *Doulas of North America (DONA):* DONA certification requires attendance at a fourteen-hour training course; training in childbirth education, midwifery, or labor nursing; three client evaluations; and documentation of three birth experiences.

- *Birthworks:* The Birthworks certification program includes attendance at a three-day workshop, two client evaluations, and tours of two birthing facilities.

- *Association of Labor Assistants and Childbirth Educators (ALACE):* ALACE requires that prospective doulas attend a two-and-a-half-day workshop, have infant CPR certification, take a written exam, write self-evaluations of six births they have attended, and have three client evaluations.

- *International Childbirth Education Association, Inc. (ICEA):* ICEA certification requires attendance at an eighteen-hour workshop and verification of practical experience in childbirth education, labor, and postpartum support.

This profession is still relatively new, and many excellent doulas are not certified. Because doulas are not licensed, anyone can call herself a doula,

even if she has had no previous experience. Do your homework and check out the candidates thoroughly.

If you have someone in mind, you like her, and you've received positive references about her, you can feel comfortable using her services even if she isn't certified.

How to Find a Doula

- Contact one of the certification groups mentioned earlier (see appendix 2 for contact information).
- Check with local childbirth educators.
- Look at bulletin boards in local pediatricians' offices.
- Get a referral from a friend who has recently given birth and who has used a doula.
- Ask your midwife or obstetrician.
- Call local birth centers.
- Go to a La Leche League meeting and ask members for referrals.

The following list of questions might come in handy as you interview a potential doula. Remember, your doula should be someone you like, since she will be with you during one of the most intense experiences you will ever have.

- Are you certified? By what organization? What kind of training have you had?
- How long have you been in practice as a doula? How many births have you attended?
- What care providers have you worked with? How many home births have you attended? In what hospitals have you attended births?
- Tell me about some of the births you've attended.
- What is your philosophy about childbirth? How do you support women and their partners throughout labor?
- May I meet with you to discuss our birth plans and the role you will play in supporting me?

- May I call you with questions or concerns before and after the birth? How can I contact you in an emergency?
- Do you work with one or more backup doulas (for times when you are not available)? May I meet them?
- When do you join women in labor? Would you come to our home or meet us at the birth center or hospital?
- Can you drive us to the birth center or hospital if necessary?
- Will you meet with us after the birth to review the labor and answer questions?
- What is your fee? Is any part of your fee refundable if, for some unexpected reason, you do not attend the birth?
- Can you provide references?

Paying a Doula

It's a good idea to check with certification organizations or friends who have used doulas to learn the going rates in your area.

As more and more published studies show the advantages of doula support during delivery, some hospitals are beginning to offer in-house doula services as part of their regular maternity package. Insurance companies are also beginning to recognize that the services of a doula can save a lot in health care dollars and are covering some, or all, of their fees. Some companies offer incentives to women who have short hospital stays; for example, if you leave within twenty-four hours after a normal vaginal birth, they may pay for some hours of home care. Check with your company to see if they offer such an incentive.

HIGHER GROUND
Creation

My baby quivers inside my belly
and my world stops.
Around me, clouded and fuzzy,
Computers whirr,
Errand boys run,
Telephones ring.
Hustling and bustling,
the office carries on.

But I sit, seat pushed back
from my desk
with my hand on the future.

—MARLENE ANNE BUMGARNER,
Mother Poet

CHAPTER 8   *Children and the Birth of a New Sibling*

At every step the child should be allowed to meet the real experiences of life;
the thorns should never be plucked from the roses.

—ELLEN KEY, *The Century of the Child*

If you already have children, you may be wondering how involved they should be with your pregnancy in the months to come and how best to prepare them for the birth of a new sibling. They will most likely have many questions, and finding answers can be difficult. Keep in mind that there are no correct answers to these questions. You must decide what is appropriate for your child. Most child psychologists believe that sheltering children from intense life events is not necessary, and that children do best when adults talk with them honestly about difficult situations like death, divorce, bankruptcy, and war. That also holds true for happy life events such as falling in love, marriage, and of course, birth.

Like adults, children have a tendency to fantasize about things they don't fully understand. When human beings "fill in the blanks," they don't tend to be optimistic, and those fantasies can become quite alarming. For example, if your partner goes into the hospital for minor surgery, you are likely to imagine the worst-case scenario, even if only for a moment.

Children are no different. The late Dr. Lee Salk, pediatric psychologist and professor of psychology and pediatrics at Cornell University, noted that children's fantasies are almost universally more alarming than reality. Your child may already have some preconceived notions about childbirth, even if she is very young. Children are notoriously good at picking up tidbits of conversation we do not know they have even heard. "She was in labor for two days! Can you imagine?" you may have said to a friend in a horrified voice, while your curious daughter was playing in the next room.

That's why it's important to discuss pregnancy and childbirth with your children. If you're comfortable, offer to let your child accompany you during visits to the doctor or midwife to provide reassurance that you are doing fine and in good hands.

When deciding if your children should attend the birth, the location will be a consideration. More and more hospitals are allowing siblings to attend births, especially if it is within an alternative birthing center. Freestanding birthing centers generally welcome kids—and if you are going to birth at home, you are free to decide whether your children will be present. Many people choose to birth at home so that their families can fully participate.

Your child's age and emotional state will also affect your decision. If you feel that your child will be overwhelmed by the situation, you may decide that it would be better for her to stay with a friend or relative until after her new baby brother or sister has arrived. If so, talk to your child in advance about where the birth will be, who will care for her, and when she will be able to see the new baby.

NATURAL SOOTHER

Rescue Remedy

You'll be talking to your older child about your pregnancy and the upcoming birth and including her in ways that seem comfortable and appropriate to you and your family. During your pregnancy and especially at the birth, you may want to help soothe your child's excited emotions. Bach flower remedies are safe, very mild, and especially well suited for children. The all-purpose Rescue Remedy can be used, as its name implies, in all kinds of situations. Keep some Rescue Remedy in your purse to use after a challenging appointment, when the day falls apart on you, or any time you feel off balance. You can also give Rescue Remedy to your child in similar situations. You child's birth companion can give it to her during the birth, as well.

Put 3 drops of Rescue Remedy in a six-ounce glass of water and sip slowly. You can also place the drops directly on your tongue, but the taste may be too strong for a child.

Advantages of Involving Children Fully

If you feel that your child would benefit from attending the birth, there are many advantages:

- When children witness the birth of a sibling, there may be less rivalry and jealousy afterward. While this has not been documented in any controlled studies, many parents agree that children witnessing the birth bonded more intensely with their new sibling.

- Involving children in birth can strengthen family bonds.

- Because we no longer live close to our extended families, we lose a sense of connection. Being present at the birth can help your child to feel more connected to his family. Even very young children can retain memories of a sibling's birth.

- Teenage children can benefit from birth; it can become a "real" experience that can help to guide their decisions regarding sexual behavior.

PREPARING YOUR CHILD

If you decide your child would benefit from being present at the birth, talk to him about it. Ask if he wants to participate. You can start off by asking simple, age-appropriate questions such as: "Do you want to keep me company at the doctor's office today?" You may have to make decisions for toddlers—watch to see how they react during trips to the doctor's office, or while watching videos that describe birth to young children.

While you should never force a child to watch or read anything that distresses them, there is little reason to expect that this will happen. When parents are frank and reassuring in their discussions with children, the children are usually comfortable expressing their wishes.

Older children may initially say they do not want to attend the birth, but would like to help out by cooking or cleaning. Respect their wishes, but leave the door open for them to change their minds. Without forcing the issue, see if you can find out why they do not want to be there for the actual birth. Perhaps they are feeling frightened or confused.

As your due date gets closer, you can ask your child more detailed questions, such as: "Do you want us to wake you up if the birth happens in the middle of the night? Do you want us to take you out of school if it happens while you are there?" This will help them to feel in charge of their part in the birth.

There are other things you can do to prepare your child for both the months ahead and for the birth itself:

- Share children's books and videos about childbirth and becoming a big sister or brother (see appendix 2 for some suggestions).

- If you have been struggling with fatigue or nausea, reassure your child that you are okay and that this is temporary. Explain that you may not be able to give him as much time and attention as you would like to because you aren't feeling well. Make sure that he gets attention at other times, or from someone else.

- For a home birth, explain what room you will be in and which friends and family will be there. If the birth will not take place at home, take your child on a tour of the facility you will use. Show your child what is all right to touch and what is not. Have your child meet your care provider at least once.

- Check to see if your childbirth educator, midwife, or birthing facility gives a sibling class to prepare for birth.

- Identify a close adult friend or relative who will be your child's support person during labor and birth. This person must be able to be there for the entire birth and be dedicated only to the care of your child, which might include meal preparation, trips to the playground, and diaper changing. This person should practice answering questions ahead of time in simple language like, "Mommy is making those sounds because it helps her to push the baby out." She or he must also be willing to leave the birth if your child wants to leave. This should be someone your child is very comfortable with, someone who would not frighten her if she were the one to wake your child up. If you have more than one older child, consider providing each one with his own support person.

- Role-play with your children. Rehearse some of the sounds you may make during labor with them. Try describing events in terms of things they might understand. For example, you can describe the opening of the cervix as like a flower slowly unfolding from a bud.

- Ask your child to help you, both before and during labor, by washing sheets for the home birth, helping you pick out or make massage oil for the birth, helping you pack, bringing you a drink of water, or putting a damp cloth on your forehead. Let them practice these steps as well.

- Encourage them to express their feelings about the birth process artistically, in drawings or paintings.

BODY WISE
Yoga Together

Prenatal exercises and yoga are wonderful ways to spend time with your child. Children can do their own version of your exercises, and they'll enjoy being a part of your self-care routine.

Here are a few fun yoga exercises geared just for kids that you can do together:

Cat and Cow. Get onto your hands and knees. Keep your back straight. Breathe in. Stretch your head back as your back curves. Moo! Now breathe out and stretch your head down so your chin is tucked into your chest. Let your back arch up. Meow! Keep stretching and arching back and forth between Cat and Cow positions. After ten repetitions, stretch back one last time into Cow. Let's hear a big Moo!

Beautiful Bird. Sit on your heels. Bring your arms straight out to each side, touch your fingertips to the ground, and begin flying with your "wings." Let the backs of your hands touch above your head. Inhale up and exhale down. Fly high to find that special cloud!

Lion's Roar. Sit on your heels. Take a big breath, then scrunch up your face as tight as you can and close your eyes. Raise your chest up into the air, open your mouth and eyes wide, and as you exhale, stretch your tongue out as long as you can and roar like a lion! You are the king of the forest!

- A child over four might like to create his or her own plan of special activities for the baby's birth. Remind the child that the plan is subject to change, as birth itself is unpredictable. You can help the child to make and write down a flexible plan with plenty of options. These might include things like: "I want to take a picture of the baby," or "I want to rub Mommy's back when she is waiting."
- Tell your child the story of *her* birth. Children usually love to hear about their entrance into the world, and this is a way to give them extra attention while reassuring them that birth is safe and natural.
- Questions about reproduction are likely to come up, so be prepared to discuss where the baby came from in the first place (see appendix 2 for helpful materials).

Preparing for a New Sibling

Think carefully about ways you can prepare your child for a new sibling. It may be helpful, especially for a younger child, to "borrow" a friend's baby a few times and let your child see what it is like. Show your child how to hold the baby properly and to practice using a gentle touch.

Ask for your child's input on choosing a name for the new baby. Your child can also help you to fix up the baby's room or to shop for a new car seat. Talk about where the baby will sleep and where you will sit to nurse the new baby. In fact, it's wise to set up the car seat, crib, and other items ahead of time so that your child will get used to seeing them.

Try to make changes several months before the new baby arrives. For example, if your child will be moving into a new room, do it early to avoid creating the impression that it is the baby's fault. And after the birth, avoid springing any big changes on your child for a couple of months.

Encourage your child to talk to the new baby, even though it is still in your womb. Your child can read,

sing, or tell stories to the baby. Let her feel your abdomen when the baby kicks.

During the Birth

During labor and birth, women tend to vacillate between an inward focus and a need for social interaction. You may feel like interacting with your child more during certain times in your labor, especially nearer the beginning.

Your child's special support person will be his most consistent source of contact. That person should follow your child's lead at all times. If the child expresses a wish to leave the room at any time, this should be respected. Your child's support person should be on the lookout for signs of fatigue, sensory overload, or distress, and should suggest a play or rest break. Your child will express distress in his own unique way—crankiness, unusual clinginess, and hyperactivity are good signs that a break is in order.

With your child's support person, plan out some special activities to keep your child busy during these breaks, as well as reviewing your child's birth plan discussed earlier. Baking a birthday cake for the new baby is a popular activity. Your child can also make a Welcome Home sign for the new baby. Choose a few familiar activities too, such as a favorite art project or a comforting book. You and your child can also choose a thank-you gift for the support person ahead of time.

Prepare your child for the fact that the birth may take place at night, however, and ask her if she wants to be awakened. Let her know that her birth plan, like your plans for the birth, can change.

Emergencies are not a part of most births, but they do happen occasionally. There are also moments of drama and tension in birthing situations. You can prepare your child ahead of time with a book or video. In addition, talk to her about how things are done in hospitals: people move and speak quickly sometimes, for example. Explain that children are sometimes not allowed into certain rooms in hospitals. Since the purpose is to prepare your child—not

> **HIGHER GROUND**
> ## Birth Is Normal
>
> Fear of birth is often rooted in childhood experiences. Your pregnancy is an opportunity to help your child see birth as a normal, natural part of family life rather than a medical emergency.
>
> These are ways you can help your child learn more about birth:
>
> - Take your child to a farm or zoo to witness birth firsthand. Get a stethoscope and let your child listen to the unborn baby's heartbeat, as well as her own.
> - Watch for opportunities for your child to hold friends' babies.
> - Let your child hold the new baby right away.

to frighten her—be matter-of-fact about this and explain that everything will work out fine.

Make sure your child's companion is someone who is not likely to lose her head if an emergency does occur. That person's job is to remain calm and reassure your child.

After the Birth

Your child may have unanswered questions about the birth. If so, or if the experience turned out unexpectedly and frightened or upset your child, you can try one of the following exercises that help children understand their feelings:

- *Artistic expression.* Ask her to draw the birth scene. Children tend to draw as they perceive, not necessarily as life presents itself. Allow yourself to respond emotionally, not in an analytical way, to understand what she has created and what it reveals about her. Ask questions about her creation, rather than immediately commenting on it. Notice how different colors, shapes, and textures make you—the viewer—feel. Then try to describe those feelings to your child. This will give her the nonjudgmental recognition she needs.

- *Recall processing.* Recall processing is a technique that allows a child to safely remember a scene and discharge any emotions connected to it. Have your family sit in a circle, or on a bed. Ask the children, either one at a time or altogether, to close their eyes and "see" the birth scene. Ask them to tell the story as though it is unfolding now ("Mommy is leaning on Daddy and breathing hard and moaning"). When they're done, ask them to share their feelings further: what they liked, what they didn't like, what worried or frightened them. All feelings are okay. You can end by talking about the birth the way they *wished* it would have happened.

- *Role-playing.* Most children love to role-play. If yours does, then set up a birth scenario. You can use yourselves as the actors, or a doll family and building blocks to set the scene. Allow your child to take the lead. This will help whatever thoughts and feelings she has to come out. Do not worry if what they create does not resemble what actually happened. Play is usually symbolic.

- *Gifts.* Ask everyone in your family to describe the gift they received from attending the birth.

For example, a child might say they learned how much their parents love all of them. You can also choose to symbolize these "gifts" with something tangible, like a framed picture of the whole family or by planting a tree.

Since children learn by repetition, you may wish to repeat an exercise that is helpful. Even a child who witnessed a calm and orderly birth might need to retell it in order to understand what happened. There's no need to force your child to talk if she does not feel the need to do so.

If you talk openly about what happened, and give your child lots of opportunities for self-expression, then there is little reason to be concerned. If, however, your child shows signs of distress such as withdrawal, big changes in appetite, or extreme irritability, consider seeking outside help from a child therapist. This is particularly helpful in extreme cases, such as a stillbirth. See chapter 27 for more information.

Your entire family will be starting a new journey together, no matter how many children you've already had. As you grow and adapt, keep all lines of communication open. This will make it easier for your new family to move ahead—together.

CHAPTER 9

Preparing for Breastfeeding

She broke the bread into two fragments and gave them to the children, who ate with avidity.
"She hath kept none for herself," grumbled the Sergeant. "Because she is not hungry,"
said a soldier. "Because she is a mother," said the Sergeant.

—VICTOR HUGO, *Les Misérables*

Until the early part of this century, mothers didn't give a thought as to how to feed their babies. All babies were breastfed, if not by the mother herself, then by a wet nurse, a lactating woman who breastfed the child instead. Then along came formula, which provided a viable feeding alternative to women and babies physically incapable of breastfeeding and infants without a mother. Yet the availability of formula has created a complex dilemma for women all over the world.

Experts today are unanimous in their support of breastfeeding as the hands-down best way to feed a human infant. In 1998 the American Academy of Pediatrics (AAP) released a landmark statement that babies should be fed breastmilk exclusively until the age of six months and continue to breastfeed, after the introduction of solid foods, until age one and beyond. The AAP recommended that breastfeeding should begin immediately, within the first hour of birth. Many years before, the World Health Organization had already proclaimed that breastfeeding a baby until age two is ideal. Just why is it that respected institutions like the AAP and WHO recommend breastfeeding so strongly?

In chapter 23, we'll go into more detail on the how-tos of breastfeeding your newborn. In this chapter, you will find the information you need to make

an informed decision about whether to breastfeed your baby.

The Advantages of Breastfeeding

The advantages of breastfeeding are so numerous that it is difficult to name them all. Researchers are continually finding more and more information that show long-lasting health benefits of nursing. Here are some of the highlights of breastfeeding's benefits to the baby:

- Breastmilk is the perfect nutrient for each human baby. Like breastmilk in all mammals, it is species-specific. For example, while cow's milk contains far more iron than human milk, the iron is in a form that is not easily absorbed by humans. When human babies drink their mother's milk, they absorb most of the iron present.[1] Human milk contains dozens of other ingredients, including amino acids, vitamins, minerals, salts, and sugars, in proportions that are just right for human babies.[2] As babies change, breastmilk changes to match the different stages of development. For example, fats in more digestible forms are present in greater proportions when the baby's digestive system is still immature.[3] Fat proportions continue to change as the baby's needs change.

- Breastmilk protects infants against a wide range of diseases, including respiratory infections, bacterial meningitis, diarrhea, pneumonia, botulism, and middle ear and urinary tract infections. Studies also suggest breastmilk may protect against sudden infant death syndrome (SIDS), allergies, insulin-dependent diabetes, Crohn's disease, lymphoma, and several digestive diseases.[4]
- Children who are breastfed are ill much less often than those who are not. The cost to the nation as a result of this may be as much as $2 to $4 billion annually.[5] The health care cost to an individual family may be almost $1,000 a year.
- Children are never allergic to mother's milk. By contrast, some babies do develop allergies to cow's milk, soy, or other ingredients contained in infant formula.
- Breastmilk may protect your baby's future health in ways you may not realize. For example, though researchers aren't sure why, an adult requiring a kidney transplant has a much better chance of a good result if he was breastfed as a child. The result will be even better if the substitute organ is from a sibling who was also breastfed, rather than one who was formula-fed.[6]
- Unlike formula, breastmilk is not subject to the risk of contamination. Formula, like any other canned product, carries a potential for salmonella, glass particles, insect parts, and a number of other possible contaminants. Contamination from improperly sterilized bottles and nipples is also possible and does happen here, not only in Third World countries.[7]

Most important of all, nursing strengthens the bond between mother and child. Something special passes between an infant and its mother while they are breastfeeding together. Nursing makes infants feel safe and secure the way nothing else can. Bottles and pacifiers are no substitute for the warmth of human contact through nursing.

There are also numerous benefits to you, the mother, for breastfeeding. They include:

- A rise in oxytocin levels. This feel-good hormone helps reduce the postpartum bleeding[8] and postpartum depression that sometimes accompany new motherhood.
- Continuous breastfeeding is a natural birth control and child spacer. If you breastfeed exclusively, using little or no formula, your chances of getting pregnant are less than 1 percent during the first six months (as long as your menstrual period has not returned).[9]
- Studies indicate that breastfeeding your baby exclusively for a year or more may protect against ovarian and breast cancer. Other studies suggest it may reduce the number of urinary tract infections and protect against osteoporosis.[10] Pregnancy depletes your bones of some of their mineral content. Breastfeeding women get those mineral levels back more quickly than women who feed their babies with formula.[11]
- Breastfeeding is much less expensive than formula feeding. In fact, other than the added cost of the good nutritious food that all breastfeeding women need, it's free! It costs at least $900 per year to feed one infant with formula.
- Studies show that breastfeeding can help you get back to your prepregnancy weight more quickly.[12] Once you begin to breastfeed, more than 30 percent of the calories you take in will be used in the production of milk.
- Breastmilk is the perfect convenience food. You don't need to own a full retinue of bottle-feeding devices such as bottles, nipples, cans of formula, bottle brushes, sterilizers, and bottle racks. You don't need to refrigerate breastmilk (unless you are pumping it for later use), mix it with water, or heat it up to the right temperature. When you leave the house, you take with you all you need to feed your baby, without packing a thing.

BODY WISE
Watch Your Back

Breastfeeding is all about posture. If you can get comfortably situated in a cozy rocking chair with a big glass of water nearby, you can nurse all day. If you're not comfortable, however, you won't enjoy the experience. These exercises stretch your pregnant back and strengthen it for breastfeeding.

Stand upright with your feet hip width apart. Extend your arms above your head. Slowly stretch your upper body as you reach up and forward. Move your arms gently from side to side.

Next, tighten the muscles in your buttocks as you lower your arms and place your palms against the small of your back with your fingers pointing downward.

Exhale as you arch backward. Look up at the ceiling if you can. Hold for 5 seconds. Come up gradually while keeping your back straight.

Variation

Stand with your feet hip width apart, knees slightly bent, and place your hands on your waist. Gently twist your upper torso from side to side, exhaling as you rotate away from your center, inhaling on your return.

- It feels good to know you're providing your baby with all the nutrition and comfort he needs to survive.
- Nursing your baby helps you to bond with her. This is important for both of you, but will particularly help you while you make the transition to early motherhood. Loving your baby, and feeling close to her, makes it all worthwhile.

Last, but not least, formula production is harmful to the environment. In their book *Milk, Money, and Madness: The Culture and Politics of Breastfeeding,* Naomi Baumslag and Dia Michels illustrate that commercial milk production is a very uneconomical use of land. They note, "It would take 135 million lactating cows to substitute for the breastmilk of the women of India. This number of cows would require 43 percent of the surface area of India for pasture."[13] Cans need to be manufactured to contain the formula, paper produced to make labels, energy consumed to process the milk and transport the finished product to stores. These are only a few of the environmental costs of formula.

Overcoming Obstacles

Given all of these overwhelming advantages, why do some women choose not to breastfeed? Why do some of them start nursing and then quit after only a few weeks or days? The reasons are varied and complex.

Perhaps the biggest reason women choose not to breastfeed is because of cultural bias against it. The trend is changing, fortunately, but in some parts of the country breastfeeding is considered unsanitary and inappropriate.

Ideas about discipline and child-rearing philosophies also explain why some women choose not to nurse. Breastfeeding means holding your baby for many hours each day. Because breastmilk is far more digestible than formula, most breastfed infants need to be fed more frequently. This can be difficult for many people in our independence-fixated society, where some mothers fear they will "spoil" their infant by "giving in" too often. If the infant is wakeful at night, breastfeeding is often deemed the cause of the problem.

Successful breastfeeding demands a flexible, baby-centered mothering style, especially during the first two to three months. This type of mothering style clashes starkly with some parents' emphasis on early independence, arm's-length parenting, and incentives to help babies be content alone, sleep through

Visualizing Breastfeeding Success

Visualization is just a fancy word for something we do all the time. We are always making mental pictures of what's to come. To visualize, you do not have to create an actual mental picture, just an impression or feeling. Try this simple visualization:

Sit upright in a chair, on a cushion or in your bed. Close your eyes.

Breathe gently for a few minutes until you feel relaxed. Imagine yourself sitting in a rocking chair, holding and breastfeeding your baby. Hear the contented coos of the baby. Notice the gentle sighs of your breathing. See the soft smiles on each of your faces. Just enjoy the scene for a few minutes as you rock back and forth and breathe deeply.

If other thoughts intrude, gently bring your attention back to your visualization.

To end, bring your attention back to your own breathing and then to the room. Slowly open your eyes.

the night as early as possible, and follow a rigid schedule of activities.

Mother-centered considerations are also a cause for a decision to formula-feed. Many women do not want to put in the time to make breastfeeding work. At first, nursing may entail sore nipples, leaking breasts, and frequent feedings, both day and night. It

may be very difficult to leave the baby with someone else at all for the first two months. Some new moms think, erroneously, that they don't have enough milk for the baby because he wants to nurse so often: they begin to supplement with formula to ease their concerns.

With support, you can make it through this initial period of difficulty. Once breastfeeding is established, it is far easier than bottle feeding. It takes great self-confidence and conviction to overcome negative attitudes against breastfeeding and do what you think is healthiest for your baby. If you want to nurse your new baby but feel intimidated by social pressures against it, try to find support from other nursing mothers, perhaps at a La Leche League meeting.

One of the biggest deterrents to breastfeeding is the workplace. Women who will be returning to work in six weeks or three months might hesitate to begin breastfeeding. In fact, experts say that breastfeeding for even a short time is better than not breastfeeding at all. In addition, it may not be necessary to stop when you return to work. Here are a few things to think about now, before your baby arrives, so that you can plan ahead:

- Look around at the options in breast pumps and consider either purchasing one, borrowing one from a friend, or renting one. With preparation and practice, it is possible to pump enough milk to feed the baby while you are gone.

- Find a space at work where you could pump your breasts a couple of times each day, if needed. Comfort and privacy matter, so try to avoid using a bathroom. Once you've found a location, talk this over with your supervisor. Discuss when pumping might be allowed. Do you already have scheduled break times? Can you use some of your lunch break at other times of the day?

- Consider changing your hours. Is it possible to work part-time for a while? Or could you work out of your home, some or all of the time? Some women have had luck with job sharing, a situation in which two persons perform one job, each on a part-time basis. Perhaps you could compress your hours by reducing or skipping your lunch hour. Conversely, maybe you could lengthen your lunch hour and nurse the baby during it, then stay a bit later to make up for the extra time. Is it possible to bring the baby to work with you some or all of the time?

• Begin to think about your child-care options in terms of nursing. Is it possible for the baby to be close by, if you are going to use a day care? If you have a sitter, can she bring the baby to you at work once or twice a day to nurse? Or are you close enough to go home for lunch?

• To convince your supervisors of the importance of nursing-friendly working conditions, explain that women who nurse tend to return to work sooner, that women who continue to breastfeed after returning to work miss less time because of baby-related illnesses, and that when breast-fed babies do get ill, it tends to be of shorter duration.

The Importance of Mother-to-Mother Support

In the past, mothers had the support of plenty of other women who already knew how to breastfeed. Women tended to live near, or even with, their mothers, aunts, and mothers-in-law. Not only do very few modern mothers have that proximity to their elders, they probably couldn't have taught us anyway—when our mothers were having babies, very few women breastfed.

Breastfeeding is natural, yes, but learning how to do it doesn't just happen. It takes practice! The first few days can be challenging. You need to be around other women who have breastfeeding experience or who are learning, just like you. These women can assure you that, with a little time, nursing does become a snap. They can tell you what to do to relieve en-

gorgement or sore nipples. (See chapter 23 for more on the how-tos of breastfeeding.)

It is possible to get this kind of mother-to-mother support from friends and relatives. Perhaps you can start a mother's group once the baby is born. It may be best to join a breastfeeding support group. You can find these groups through your midwife, pediatrician, or childbirth educator (also see appendix 2).

The best known breastfeeding support group of all is La Leche League, a nonprofit, nonsectarian group formed in 1956, when breastfeeding rates were down to 20 percent in the United States.[14] Today postpartum breastfeeding rates are up to 60 percent, largely due to the efforts of La Leche League, whose prime mission is to support breastfeeding

NATURAL SOOTHER
Breast Preparation

Experts disagree about the need to condition your nipples for breastfeeding. Some suggest that you rub your nipples with a clean, dry washcloth from time to time during pregnancy to condition them. You can also gently pinch your nipples and extend them. Here is a breast massage oil that can be used to soothe your changing breasts and soften your nipples:

Breast Massage Oil

2 teaspoons sweet almond or grapeseed oil

1 drop rose essential oil

Mix together and apply gently to nipples. Massage oil into breasts.

Nipple Conditioner

To soothe sore nipples at the beginning of breastfeeding, apply a small amount of buttermilk, thick honey, comfrey, calendula or chickweed ointment, or wheat germ oil.

mothers. There are chapters in every state, and all over the world.

La Leche League has come on strong in their activism for breastfeeding women. They support women who want to stay at home with their babies, women who want to breastfeed while working, and women who want to nurse in public without harassment.

In fact, La Leche League supports nursing moms in all types of situations: working, stay-at-home, single, and lesbian. If you attend a La Leche meeting, you will meet dozens of women who are nursing their babies. You can receive both group and one-on-one support from mothers who can answer your questions. Additionally, these meetings can be a wonderful way to strengthen your community ties. You may meet people who will end up being a permanent part of your life and your baby's life.

The meetings are designed for you to attend before your baby is born, and are helpful afterward. They will help to prepare you for breastfeeding, and will establish a support system so that it will be right at your fingertips when the need for it arises.

Concerns about Your Ability to Breastfeed

You may really want to breastfeed, but be concerned that you will not be physically able to do so.

Some women have inverted nipples, in which the nipple, rather than protruding from the areola, dimples in. Women used to be directed by their physicians to wear breast shells, plastic discs worn under the bra to encourage the nipples to protrude, during pregnancy, or to perform nipple-stretching exercises. Neither of these have been shown to be particularly effective, though trying them is probably harmless.[15]

Don't worry—you can still breastfeed with inverted nipples. True, the initial latching-on process may be a bit more challenging, but once you and the baby have accomplished this, everything will be fine.

Women who have had breast implants wonder if they will be able to breastfeed. Breastfeeding success depends completely on the type of implant and surgery you have. Generally speaking, implants placed behind the milk ducts do not impair breastfeeding at all, as long as the nerves to the nipple and areola and the milk ducts themselves have not been severed. Implants that were attached from the front may present a problem, however, if the area around the areola was cut. You will need to discuss this with your care provider.

There is also concern about whether or not silicone leakage from breast implants can contaminate breastmilk. The bad news is that no one really knows. Studies need to be done to determine whether or not this is a real problem. The good news is that there have not been any recorded cases of a baby being harmed by breastfeeding with silicone implants.[16]

Breast-reduction surgery may also present a problem. This surgery usually impairs a woman's milk supply to some degree, although that is not always the case. It is suggested that you try to breastfeed and monitor the baby's weight gain carefully. Many women who have had reduction surgery use some type of supplemental feeding system, such as Lact-Aid, in conjunction with breastfeeding, or use a breast pump to try to increase their milk supplies.

If you have any special conditions such as these, line up support ahead of time. Discuss your situation with your health care provider and consider meeting with a lactation consultant (see chapter 23 and appendix 2 for more information). Even if you are not able to breastfeed exactly as you might like, you can still have a satisfactory experience and provide your baby with the skin-to-skin nurturing she needs.

Finding a Breastfeeding-Friendly Birth Setting

Research has shown that information and support are essential to successful breastfeeding. While it is likely that midwives at home and in birth centers will recommend and support breastfeeding, if you are giving birth at a hospital, look for one that is breastfeeding-friendly. An international health initiative, the Baby-Friendly Hospital Initiative (BFHI), will help you to recognize such hospitals and birth centers.

The BFHI was created in 1991 as a joint project of the World Health Organization (WHO) and the United Nations Children's Fund (UNICEF). To be certified by BFHI, a facility must follow the Ten Steps to Successful Breastfeeding. They are:

1. Have a written breastfeeding policy that is routinely communicated to all health care staff.
2. Train all health care staff in skills necessary to implement this policy.
3. Inform all pregnant women about the benefits and management of breastfeeding.
4. Help mothers initiate breastfeeding within an hour of birth.
5. Show mothers how to breastfeed and how to maintain lactation, even if they should be separated from their infants.
6. Give newborn infants no food or drink other than breastmilk, unless medically indicated.
7. Practice "rooming in" by allowing mothers and infants to remain together twenty-four hours a day.
8. Encourage breastfeeding on demand.
9. Give no artificial teats, pacifiers, dummies, or soothers to breastfeeding infants.
10. Foster the establishment of breastfeeding support groups and refer mothers to them on discharge from the hospital or birthing center.

You might think that there would be plenty of Baby-Friendly Hospitals in the United States. In fact, while 15,000 hospitals have been certified worldwide due to the health benefits of breastfeeding, less than 100 of these are in the United States. Even though studies show that early exposure to formula undermines a mother's breastfeeding success, most American hospitals routinely give free formula samples

and formula literature to new mothers. Hospitals are offered incentives to do this by companies that manufacture formula. BFHI certification prohibits hospitals from accepting or offering these free or low-cost substitutes for human milk, and from giving out literature or other items bearing the name of formula products.

Choosing a BFHI hospital or birth center will help to ensure that you and your baby will start out breastfeeding with greater ease. Knowing the guidelines will help you, no matter where you give birth. Implement as many of these steps as possible in your birth experience.

If You Can't Breastfeed

It can be heartbreaking not to be able to breastfeed when you had looked forward to doing so. La Leche League leaders, lactation consultants, and your doctor or midwife should be able to give you the advice you need for success. But sometimes things beyond your control make breastfeeding impossible, such as some breast reduction surgeries, double mastectomies, some birth defects, and hormonal problems caused by severe hemorrhaging at birth.

When this happens, you will naturally wonder what to feed your baby. Ask your midwife or doctor for a recommendation. If you don't want to use commercially prepared formulas, you can find acceptable substitutes. There is one organic toddler formula, Nature's One, that may be appropriate for certain infants. Check at your local natural grocery store.

The book *Nourishing Traditions* by Sally Fallon contains recipes for infant breastmilk substitutes. Some mothers use fresh or powdered goat's milk either alone or with supplemental ingredients. Look for organic or at least GMO-free products.

Remember not to use honey in any preparations for babies under one year of age because honey can carry botulism. Seek the advice of a qualified infant nutritionist or a health care professional to ensure that any recipe you use is nutritionally sound.

PART THREE

The Third Trimester

What's Happening in My Body?

MONTH SEVEN. You feel good during this month. You have a hearty appetite, and may feel less moody and more in the groove of your pregnancy. Your baby will be moving around a lot, and you may notice that your belly itches. You may also have breast tenderness, and leg cramps that wake you from sleep.

MONTH EIGHT. During month eight, you may experience shortness of breath as your uterus presses on your diaphragm or ribs. You may have heartburn and indigestion as your uterus puts pressure on your stomach. As the baby grows larger, you may have a hard time finding a comfortable position in which to sleep. Pressure on your bladder may make urination more frequent.

MONTH NINE. By month nine, you're wondering if your pregnancy will ever be over. You may have a few Braxton-Hicks contractions, light contractions in which the top of your uterus tightens and releases in preparation for labor. These may happen more after you have been sitting for a while or if you overdo it. You will be feeling the baby's strong, regular movements, but he may become quieter as the birth approaches. Your ankles may swell due to the increased pressure within your abdomen, the decreased blood return from your legs and feet, and the effect of the hormone progesterone, which relaxes the walls of the blood vessels. Your lower back may ache from the increased weight of your uterus.

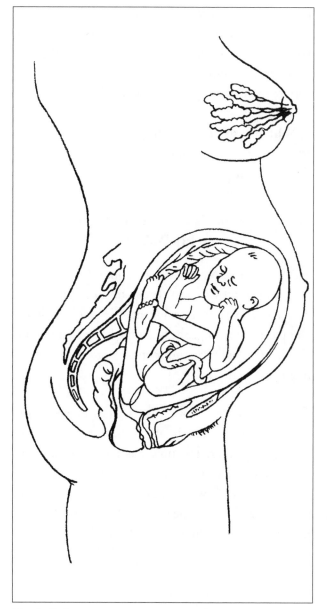

Months 7–8

By this time, the top of your uterus is right under your rib cage and presses against your lungs, while the bottom of your uterus puts pressure on your cervix as the uterine muscle begins to soften. Hormone production in the placenta prepares the uterus for labor contractions and also ripens the cervix. During the last weeks of pregnancy, there will be less amniotic fluid, and the placenta will grow less efficient in anticipation of the upcoming birth.

At thirty-five weeks, the baby fills all of the space in your uterus and has usually settled into a head-down position. The baby will move down into your pelvis about two weeks before birth. You may be able to breathe easier, as there is less pressure on your lungs and stomach, but there will be greater pressure on your bladder. You'll need to urinate very frequently, and sleeping will be even more challenging.

Your breasts increase their production of colostrum, the early milk for the baby, and the connecting tissue in your pelvis relaxes.

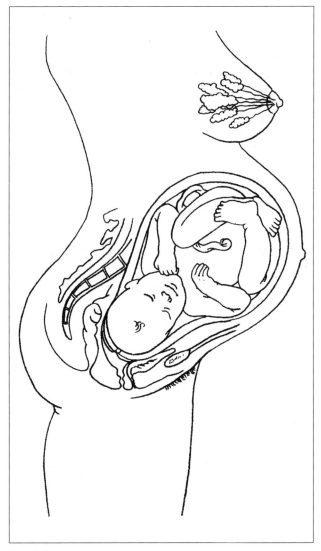

Month 9

What's Happening with My Baby?

MONTH SEVEN. The baby is about thirteen inches long and weighs two to three pounds. The baby is covered with thin, translucent skin and has hands about one inch long. She is adding body fat and is beginning to practice rudimentary breathing movements in the uterus.

MONTH EIGHT. Your baby weighs between four and six pounds and is about sixteen to eighteen inches long. Her skin now has fat stores, and her liver is storing iron. However, her lungs, digestive, and heat control systems have not yet matured. The bones of your baby's head are soft and flexible. She may respond to pain, light, and sound.

MONTH NINE. Your baby is now about eighteen inches long and five to seven pounds, with hands about two inches long. His sucking reflex is mature, and his lungs and heart are almost ready to function outside the womb. Brain growth accelerates, and the baby can see and hear. He has lost most of the lanugo, the downy hair covering his body, and is now covered by a thick, creamy protective coating called vernix. He is less active and is gaining immunities from the mother to protect him after he's born.

Your fear is a measure of your courage.

—JACK JOHNSTON, Psychotherapist

You are now entering the third and final trimester of your pregnancy. For many women this time is marked by impatience. It seems like pregnancy takes forever! For others it is a dreamy time that seems to float peacefully by. No matter how you're feeling, this is an excellent time to take stock of your choices up until now and to look deep inside yourself to inventory your mental state and emotions.

In this chapter, we will examine one very common emotion that comes up during pregnancy, especially toward the end. That emotion is fear. Later in the chapter, we'll take a look at other common concerns of the third trimester.

Dealing with Fear

It has been shown that fear can profoundly affect childbirth. Fear causes the body to release the fight-or-flight hormones, catecholamines. These hormones are in direct conflict with those that cause labor to progress smoothly, including endorphins, the body's natural pain-reducing hormones, and oxytocin, which causes the uterus to contract in a smooth, powerful, and coordinated way, urging the baby into the world.

But don't panic! Before you add "fear of having fear slow down your upcoming labor" to the list of things you are already afraid of, know that it is really the inability to *express* fear that is the problem. *Feeling* fear is completely normal. In fact, the good news is that even women who are extremely fearful and nervous often have totally normal births, perhaps because they have been honest about their worries.

You don't need to completely resolve all your concerns. No one enters the experience of pregnancy and childbirth fear-free. What is important is to try to understand yourself as best you can and find ways to give your feelings of fear legitimate outlets.

WHAT IS THERE TO BE AFRAID OF, ANYWAY?

Every woman is different. Each brings her unique history, attitudes, and beliefs to the pregnancy table. Here are a few common fears:

- Labor will be too painful for me to bear.
- Something awful will happen to me or to the baby during labor.
- The baby will be born with a horrible defect.
- I will end up having a cesarean section.
- I will find myself connected to tubes and taking painkillers even though I wanted a natural birth.
- I will suddenly find myself in the midst of an emergency during my home birth, and won't be able to make it to the hospital in time.

- I will not be capable of taking care of a small baby.
- My life will change too much after the baby is born, and I will lose myself.
- My relationship with my partner will never be the same again after the baby is born.
- I will never lose weight after the baby is born, and my partner will no longer be attracted to me.

There are countless others besides these. Many women create scenarios in their minds that feel very real. It is not uncommon, for example, to worry about whether the baby is moving around enough, whether the pain relievers you took unknowingly in early pregnancy harmed your baby, or whether or not you'll want to return to work once the baby is born. Though it would be possible to try to discount each of these fears and tell you why you don't need to worry, we aren't going to do that. You don't need any more reasons to try to *suppress* your worries. In fact, the best thing you can do is to explore your emotions and get to the root of your concerns.

HOLDING FEAR IN

Women harbor secret fears about childbirth and don't express them for a number of reasons:

- They feel an almost superstitious concern that naming their fears out loud will make them come true.
- They don't want to worry their partners or friends.
- They may not know exactly what they are afraid of and don't know how to put it into words.
- They think that allowing their fear to come out might somehow harm the baby growing inside them.

Although it might seem as though voicing your fears will give them greater strength, it's holding fear in that gives it such tremendous power. Acknowledging fear is very hard, but once done, it can provide re-lief from anxiety, and this will help send you down a smoother path toward labor.

Ultimately, no one is successful at trying to keep feelings inside. They have a way of coming out, albeit indirectly. You may find yourself having nightmares or strange, troubling dreams. Or you may wake up feeling disoriented or troubled, but unable to remember any specific dreams. Perhaps you are tired all the time, or grouchy. People have hundreds of ways of expressing emotions indirectly. Think about your own ways of doing this and see if something feels off to you.

PUT A NAME ON IT

The first thing to do is to try to get as clear as possible about *what* frightens you. You want to be as precise as you can and avoid generalizing. Talking to a trusted companion and writing about it are good ways to start out. The Birth Inventory,[1] below, helps to uncover ideas you may have about pregnancy and birth that you are not even consciously aware of by exploring influences from your past.

BIRTH INVENTORY

Answer each question as truthfully as you can. You need not be concerned about accuracy. Remember, there are no right answers—only what is true for you. You may want to give several answers for each question. It may be helpful to do this exercise with your partner, or with another friend who is pregnant.

- What do you believe about your own personal birth (not your child's)?
- What does your mother believe about your birth?
- What does your father believe about your birth?
- What do you believe about women?
- What does your mother believe about women?
- What does your father believe about women?
- How would a group of women from your family (aunts, sisters, grandmothers, etc.) fill in this statement: The women in our family are _____ .

- How would a group of women from your family fill this statement: Childbirth is _____ .
- What did you believe about sex at age sixteen?
- What does your mother believe about sex?
- What does your father believe about sex?
- What do you believe about pregnancy?
- What does your mother believe about pregnancy?
- What does your father believe about pregnancy?
- How do you feel when talking to a midwife or physician?
- What have your friends told you about pregnancy?
- What have your friends told you about childbirth?
- What three words do you associate with "pain"?
- What three words do you associate with "hospital"?
- What do you believe about your siblings' birth (if relevant)?
- What does your mother believe about your siblings' births?
- What does your father believe about your siblings' births?
- What did/does your religion teach you about birth?
- What did/does your religion teach you about sex?
- What are your three most secret thoughts about childbirth?
- What do you fear the most?

Once you have completed the questions, take some time to look over your answers. You may want to wait a day or two before doing this. Then analyze your answers to see what preconceived notions you may have about birth. For example, you may discover that you are feeling as though you have to live up to the expectations of an important family member, such as your mother, and you have a bit of "performance anxiety." Someone in your family may have had a cesarean section because they had a "small pelvis" (which rarely requires a cesarean sec-

tion), and you may fear that your pelvis is too small as well.

By identifying the fears that your answers reveal, you can then begin to address them. Read on to learn ways that you can reassure yourself.

How to Cope

Here are a few ideas on getting in touch with yourself and dealing with fear and anxiety:

- If you haven't yet signed up for a childbirth education class, do so now. This will help you get familiar with what is to come both during the birth and afterward.
- If your worries center around labor and the baby's health, talk to your health care provider. Be honest—don't be afraid of looking like a hypochondriac. They've seen and heard it all, and they know that expectant mothers often experience anxiety. Ask for a reality check.
- See a therapist or make an appointment to speak to a childbirth education teacher one-on-one.
- Talk. Then talk some more. Talk with your partner, or if your partner feels too close to the situation, try a friend who is good at listening. Although you want reassurance, you also want someone who will let you vent and not try to talk you out of your worries.
- Write in a journal. Try to write continuously for a set amount of time, say ten minutes to start with. To let your thoughts flow freely, keep your pen moving the whole time and try not to edit your words before they've even hit the page.
- Daily meditation, even for just a few minutes, can really help to center you. If you are able, try extending the time to twenty minutes, or meditating twice, first thing in the morning and right before bed. See "Making Time for Yourself" in chapter 1 for more on meditation.
- Make a list of affirmations to repeat to yourself. Write them down on an index card and carry it

HIGHER GROUND

Painting Your Fears Away

Late pregnancy is a time when fears may resurface, and art is the perfect medium to address challenging emotions. Gather together five small sheets of paper, an envelope to hold them, some inexpensive finger paints, and several large pieces of finger painting paper.

Choose some open-ended time when you won't be interrupted for a while. On the small pieces of paper, write down five things that you are afraid of at this time in your pregnancy. Use just a few words or a title that signifies the fear, then fold the papers and place them into an envelope.

When you're ready to paint, draw a slip of paper at random from the envelope. Paint your interpretation of this fear with the finger paints, using a large piece of finger painting paper. Hang it to dry. Paint another. Paint as many as you like.

Let the paintings dry for three days. Look at them as they dry. Then take them down. Place them in a fireplace, a woodstove, or a pit outside, and burn them. Don't stand and watch them burn. Turn and walk away as soon as they are in flames.

Come back later and gather some of the ashes in a small container. In early labor, throw the ashes to the wind. As you do, consciously throw your fears away and surrender to the birth as it comes.

around in your wallet. Good ones to start out with are:

I am at peace.

I am safe and my baby is safe.

I am being cared for by a higher power who wants the best for me and my baby.

My body knows how to have a baby.

- Create a fear box or basket. Decorate it, if you like, or choose something that pleases you or symbolizes something important to you, such as your grandmother's old jewelry box. Whenever a fear overwhelms you, write it down on a piece of paper. Fold it and place it in the box, releasing it into a safe space.

- If you are inexperienced at baby care and feel anxious about this, try to gain a little experience. Visit a friend with a new baby and change a diaper. Take a class on infant care from your local hospital or birth center. Begin a library of baby care and child development books so you'll know you have resources at hand when you need them.

- If your fears are centered around your relationship with your partner, talk to him or her. Express your concerns using "I" statements. "I am scared that you will be disgusted by the extra fat on my body after the baby is born and that you won't be attracted to me."

Fear can be a powerful emotion—it can either make you helpless, or it can be harnessed to spur you on to success. Tame your fears by using tools like childbirth education, open communication with your health care provider, and honestly conveying your feelings to your partner. Also, check out some of the ideas in chapter 4, which is full of suggestions on how to work through powerful emotions.

Third Trimester Common Concerns

Sleep issues. One of the most common problems for women in their third trimester of pregnancy is sleep, or lack of it, to be precise! It is reported that a full 97 percent of pregnant women fail to sleep through the night, according to one study done by researchers at St. Joseph's University in Philadelphia, Pennsylvania.[2] It gets harder and harder to get a solid night of uninterrupted rest. Your body is becoming more unwieldy, and your sleep positions have probably become limited to your side. The baby's movements might wake you up or you may feel pressure on your bladder, causing you to use the bathroom more frequently during the night.

You may also find yourself plagued with restless dreams and fears in the night hours. Some say this sleeplessness is good practice for when the baby arrives, but that is not much comfort right now. You want to sleep!

Try these ideas:

- Try to get a little extra exercise during the day, especially in the late afternoon or early evening, but not within two hours before you retire. Exercising too close to sleep time can actually make sleep more difficult.
- Use pillows to help support you in bed. Put one between your knees and others around your shoulders or back, or wherever they feel good. Some women find a soft wool mattress pad makes them more comfortable and promotes sleep. You can also purchase a "body pillow," an extra-long rectangular pillow you can mold around your whole body as support.
- Try aromatherapy. Sprinkle neroli blossom or sandalwood around your bed, or place a drop or two on a tissue and put it under your pillow. Lavender works also. For nightmares and anxiety, use frankincense instead. You can also put these oils in a warm bath before bedtime. A

good bath blend is lavender, chamomile, and neroli.

- Have a cup of herbal tea. Skullcap relieves nervousness and contains calcium, which can also promote sleep. Oat tea also contains calcium. You can also try chamomile tea, an old sleep-inducing standby.
- Place chamomile and lavender blossoms into a thin cotton bag and add it to the bathtub for a soothing soak.
- Try a good old-fashioned cup of hot milk. Milk contains both calcium and the amino acid tryptophan, which promote sleep. Any cup of warm liquid will raise your body temperature slightly, making it easier to slow down and relax.

BODY WISE
Get Moving

Exercise, especially walking and swimming, stimulates circulation, strengthens your body during late pregnancy, and gains you precious sleep. If you haven't incorporated walking or swimming into your pregnant life yet, it's not too late. Walking is a great exercise for the last trimester, and even during early labor.

Choose a beautiful place for your walk—a park or a natural setting near your home or office. Make a ritual out of your walk—consider it a time to be with yourself during these last few months before the baby joins you.

Start with a small goal. Go to this special place once a week for thirty minutes, then increase the time to two to three times a week for forty-five minutes each. Perhaps you can walk for an hour once each week. Wear comfortable clothes and shoes and take your time. Amble. Stroll. Once you get in the habit of walking, it will become easy to find the time.

- Homeopathic treatments good for insomnia include *Coffea cruda, Pulsatilla, Arnica,* and *Chamomilla.* You can find a premade remedy at a health food store, or see a homeopath.

Leg cramps. Half of all women report problems with leg cramps toward the end of pregnancy. This seems to happen primarily at night and can be quite uncomfortable. The reasons for this phenomenon are still not understood, though many studies have attempted to figure it out. Calcium, magnesium, and sodium tablets are sometimes recommended. Although these are harmless if their use is supervised by a health care provider, studies have not actually proven them to be effective.[3]

While there is no definite link between leg cramps and good nutrition, it makes sense to get enough vitamin B6 and vitamin E, as both these nutrients aid circulation. Use extra garlic in your cooking to cleanse your circulatory system and make sure you're getting enough salt, calcium, and magnesium in your diet, as a lack of these minerals can contribute to leg cramps.

Massage, calf stretches, and keeping your calves warm are probably the most helpful thing you can do to relieve leg cramps. Dry brush the affected area, then massage a little arnica ointment, a homeopathic remedy that may offer some additional relief. Taking the homeopathic remedy *Chamomilla* may also help.

Here's a good calf-stretching exercise you can do when leg cramps are bothering you (see illustration above). Stand in front of a wall or closed door and place your hands on it, directly in front of you. Move your right foot back several inches. Bend your left leg, keeping both feet flat on the ground. Lean forward slightly. You should feel a stretch in the calf of your right leg. Repeat this on the other side.

Edema. Swelling of the legs and ankles is also common toward the end of pregnancy, and can be quite uncomfortable. However, it has not been shown to have any negative effects on the baby. Do not try to decrease your fluid intake in the hopes that you will

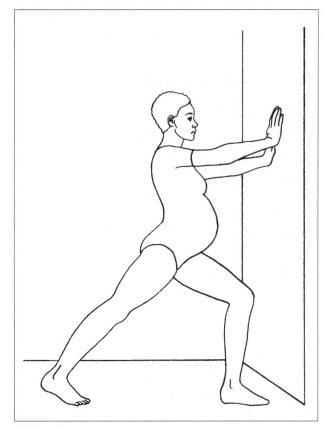

Calf stretch

reduce the swelling. It won't work. Besides, your body needs plenty of water during pregnancy.

Exercise, such as walking or swimming, may help to relieve this condition by increasing circulation. Try sleeping with your legs elevated on a pillow and also put your feet up frequently during the day. Support hose may also give relief.

Try tepid-to-cool footbaths to relieve swelling. Put 3 drops of geranium or lemon oil and 3 drops of lavender in the water and soak your feet as long as you can.

Changes in fetal movements. The baby's movements will change throughout pregnancy. In the beginning of the third trimester, they will feel strong and vigorous at times. You will most likely find that when you lie down or sit still, these movements will become more intense. If you get up and start walking around, the baby is rocked to sleep and moves less. As you get closer to the end of pregnancy, however, there is less and less room for the baby to move around.

NATURAL SOOTHER

Leg Relief

Your legs do extra duty during pregnancy. Take special care of them, especially during the last trimester, when you may be prone to edema, varicose veins, and other leg problems that are aggravated by increased blood volume, hormonal changes, and nutritional deficiencies.

Edema of the ankles and legs responds to lavender, geranium, and rosemary oils, all of which stimulate the lymphatic system to drain excess fluids from the body. Add 1 drop each of lavender, geranium, and rosemary essential oil to 1 teaspoon of grapeseed or sweet almond oil. Mix gently with your fingers. Using upward strokes, gently massage this blend of oils into your feet and ankles.

In addition, put 3 drops of lemon, mandarin, or other citrus oils in your bath for a mild diuretic effect.

You will continue to feel regular movements, but they will most likely feel less dramatic, and may be for shorter periods of time.

Hiccupping. This refers to the baby's hiccups, not yours! Many women experience the feeling of their baby's rhythmic hiccupping toward the end of pregnancy. Some babies seem to do it at about the same time every day, perhaps in the morning while you are still lying in bed. There is no cause for concern whatsoever, and those sweet little twitches may be the source of a good laugh or two!

Incontinence. Your growing uterus is expanding into new territory! Sometimes it presses against your bladder, causing occasional leaks. While annoying, it is normal. Daily Kegel exercises will help prevent incontinence (see page 55 for instructions).

Breast secretions. Some women begin to notice small amounts of a clear, or yellowish, liquid secret-

ing from their nipples during the third trimester. This is the first sign of colostrum, which is the first milk your newborn will drink. It may start to look white or opaque in the last weeks of pregnancy.

Air travel. Travel is no problem for the normal pregnancy during the early months. You can do what feels comfortable for you. Do keep in mind, though, that poor air circulation on airplanes does seem to bring on higher chances of contacting germs and catching colds or the flu. Make sure you drink plenty of liquids when you fly to avoid dehydration.

Check with your airline ahead of time about meal options. You may find that a special option, such as a vegetarian meal, for example, will provide you with healthier food choices than the standard meal.

As you move into the third trimester, however, you need to discuss your travel plans with your doctor or midwife. Your practitioner may want you to avoid traveling in smaller planes that are not pressurized, as this can reduce oxygen supply to the fetus. As your due date approaches, your practitioner will most likely recommend that you stay reasonably close to home.

If you need to fly during your third trimester, check with your airline, as some do not allow pregnant women to fly after a certain time, such as after the eighth month. Others may require you to provide a letter from your practitioner giving you permission to fly.

Feeling full. Most women notice that they feel fullness much more quickly in the third trimester. The baby, as it grows, begins to push on your organs, causing breathlessness at times and making you feel like you just can't eat. Of course it is important to keep taking in good, nutritious food. Try to eat small meals more frequently. Keep nutritious nibbling snacks handy so you can eat a bit throughout the day.

Shortness of breath. This is common and perfectly normal. The baby is taking up more and more room inside your belly, leaving you less room to breathe. At times, it may feel as though the baby is pressing directly against your diaphragm.

If you feel short of breath, don't push yourself.

Take your time with stairs in particular. Try to keep exercising, but make sure you can maintain a comfortable conversation throughout.

Dizziness and feeling faint. This is also common. It may be a result of low blood sugar, or a momentary drop in blood pressure. It is probably not a cause for concern, but check with your health care provider if you do feel dizzy or have a fainting spell. Try to carry snacks with you as a future preventative. Dried fruit and nuts are good choices. Avoid sitting or standing up too quickly. If you feel faint, lie down with your feet up, or sit down and place your head between your knees until you feel better.

Bleeding. If you find a small amount of blood right after having intercourse or a vaginal examination, there is probably nothing to worry about. Check with your health care provider for peace of mind.

If you have blood-tinged mucus that looks like the beginning of your period, you may have a "bloody show," which means that your mucous plug has released in anticipation of labor. This should also be reported to your practitioner, who may ask you to come in for a quick checkup.

Any bright red bleeding that appears heavy could constitute an emergency, perhaps indicating placenta previa or placenta abruptio (described next). Call your doctor right away.

Placenta abruptio. In this condition, a part of the placenta separates from the uterine wall, causing hemorrhage. The seriousness of this condition depends on how much of the placenta has torn away. There may also be accompanying abdominal pain. You will most likely be hospitalized until the bleeding has stopped and advised to take it easy and avoid sex until after the baby is born.

Diagnostic Tests of the Third Trimester

Testing for glucose tolerance. Throughout your pregnancy, your urine has most likely been tested for the presence of sugar. If high sugar levels are detected in your urine, you may be given follow-up tests to determine whether you are at risk for gestational dia-

betes, a temporary condition that will disappear after the baby is born.

Some practitioners believe that gestational diabetes can increase the risk of fetal macrosomia, or a larger-than-average baby. To prevent the baby from growing too large, and to avoid the need for cesarean section, women deemed at risk for gestational diabetes are often placed under careful dietary restrictions, monitored using blood tests and ultrasound scans, and occasionally given insulin. In some cases labor is induced early, or elective cesarean section is performed.

Gestational diabetes has been the cause of a great deal of controversy. Many experts question its very existence, calling it "a diagnosis in search of a disease." In addition, many birth practitioners believe that elevated blood sugar levels actually represent a healthy response to the inherent dynamics of pregnancy. Glucose may remain in the blood for longer periods so that it is more accessible to the developing baby. These experts add that pregnant women should not be tested using the same standards as nonpregnant women, since the pregnant metabolic condition is not being taken into account.

Only 30 percent of women with an abnormal glucose tolerance test will have larger than average babies. It is just as easy, however, to predict the likelihood of a large baby by assessing prepregnant weight, weight gain during pregnancy, and gestational age.[4] In fact, most large babies will be born to mothers with normal glucose tests. The glucose tolerance tests themselves are unreliable and can only be duplicated 30 to 50 percent of the time.[5]

No controlled studies have proven that high blood sugar leads to problematic or high-risk pregnancy. In fact, one clinical trial that studied the outcomes of women who had elective cesarean sections because of gestational diabetes showed a significantly higher incidence of mortality for the babies, with no better outcomes than the control group.[6] Further, Murray Enkin, M.D., and his colleagues, who compiled data from 9,000 controlled trials from 400 medical journals in eighteen different languages for the Cochrane

Database, found that labeling patients "high-risk" due to gestational diabetes subjected them to many expensive and time-consuming tests and interventions that have no proven benefits.[7]

Gestational diabetes should not be confused with a preexisting diabetic condition. Women who have been diagnosed with some variation of diabetes prior to pregnancy, or who have a family history of diabetes, are obese, or who have previously delivered a baby that weighs more than nine pounds,[8] are more likely to have true glucose intolerance during pregnancy. They may require close monitoring throughout their pregnancies to prevent stillbirth and congenital defects.

Testing for Group B streptococcus (GBS). Unlike the bacteria that causes strep throat, GBS causes blood and skin infections and pneumonia. In pregnant women, GBS can cause bladder and womb infections and stillbirth. Before prevention methods began to be used, about 8,000 babies in the United States contracted GBS infections every year, and about 5 percent would die.

Between 5 and 35 percent of pregnant women temporarily carry GBS in their bodies, often in the vagina or rectum, although they do not develop symptoms. When a baby moves down the birth canal, it can become infected by the bacteria, which can lead within a few hours to pneumonia, sepsis (infections of the blood or tissues), or meningitis. As infants don't handle infection well, the disease can spread quickly, and some can die before it is even detected.

It is now routine practice to test pregnant women for the presence of GBS in late pregnancy, around week thirty-seven. This is done by swabbing the rectum and vagina. A culture then takes a few days to give results.

A positive test (indicating that you have GBS) does not necessarily mean that you will transmit it to your baby. Actual transmission of GBS involves other risk factors, including:

- The presence of fever during labor
- A urinary tract infection due to GBS

- Rupture of membranes (water breaking) eighteen hours or more prior to delivery
- Rupture of membranes prior to week thirty-seven
- A previous baby with GBS

If you test positive for GBS, antibiotics will be offered to you intravenously during labor. Taking a course of antibiotics *prior* to labor, however, does not protect the baby. If you decide to have intravenous antibiotic treatment, ask for a heparin lock on your intravenous line, which allows it to be unhooked so you have freedom to get up and move around during labor.

Testing for preeclampsia. Preeclampsia, also called toxemia, is a condition that affects 5 to 10 percent of pregnancies, usually in the third trimester.[9] Preeclampsia is pregnancy-induced hypertension characterized by elevated blood pressure, excessive retention of fluids, especially in the hands and face, rapid weight gain, double or blurred vision, growth retardation in the fetus, and protein in the urine. Having any of these symptoms may not necessarily indicate preeclampsia, however. As well, some women with preeclampsia have no symptoms at all other than a feeling that "something is not right."

No one knows what causes preeclampsia. You are more likely to have it if you have diabetes, are less than five-three in height, or have had a previous history of high blood pressure. New research indicates that a previous history of preeclampsia in either the mother or the father's family is a risk factor. The risk is also higher for first-time pregnancies and for women who have new partners for their second pregnancies. This suggests an immunologic contribution that is, as of yet, not well understood. It is also thought that nutrition may play a part in preeclampsia.

If left untreated, preeclampsia can develop into the more severe eclampsia, characterized by convulsions, coma, and even maternal or fetal death. This condition is quite rare, because most women receive treatment before it reaches this stage. In the more severe stages, symptoms can include abdominal pain, severe headaches, nausea, vomiting, and convulsions. Left untreated, failure of the placenta can occur, causing premature labor.

Preeclampsia is usually diagnosed during routine urine examinations that screen for high levels of protein. If it is determined that you have preeclampsia, you may be advised to get bed rest for most of the rest of your pregnancy, either at home or in a hospital. There is not, as of yet, conclusive evidence that complete bed rest is helpful for women with mild to moderate preeclampsia,[10] and it is not an easy thing to do. You will need to decide if this is right for you. You will most likely be given antihypertensive medication to keep your blood pressure down. Diuretics were commonly given in the past to treat preeclampsia, but are now generally thought to be effective only in reducing the symptom of water retention. Diuretics will not prevent preeclampsia's potential negative effects on the baby.

Promising recent studies suggest that using fish oils, evening primrose oil, and calcium in early pregnancy may help prevent preeclampsia in the future.[11] For many women, increasing their protein intake will reduce the symptoms of preeclampsia.

Testing for rhesus incompatibility. Rhesus incompatibility occurs when the mother's blood is Rh-negative and the fetus has inherited Rh-positive blood from the father.

If fetal blood enters the mother's bloodstream (for example, during delivery, miscarriage, abortion, amniocentesis, or fetal blood sampling), her body will produce antibodies to fight it. Although this condition rarely presents a problem in the first pregnancy, the antibodies remain in the mother's blood and in subsequent pregnancies may attempt to destroy the blood supply of the new fetus. This can result in severe anemia, jaundice, brain damage, or death to the baby.

Your blood will be tested in early pregnancy to see if you are Rh-negative. If you are Rh-negative and your partner is Rh-positive, you will be tested frequently throughout pregnancy to see if you have developed any antibodies. During your third trimester or soon after delivery, you will be given a vaccine (known as Rhogam) to prevent antibodies from developing and endangering future pregnancies.

In the past, Rhogam, like many vaccines, contained a preservative known as thimerosol, or mercury. The safety of this is now being questioned, and the use of mercury is being phased out.

CHAPTER 11 *Review Your Birth Choices*

Being pregnant is like getting on a train that whisks you down the track
to a destination not precisely known.

—RAHIMA BALDWIN AND TERRA PALMARINI RICHARDSON, *Pregnant Feelings: Developing Trust in Birth*

You have already spent a great deal of time making decisions about your pregnancy and upcoming delivery. You have chosen a health care provider and a childbirth education class, and decided whether or not you're opting for a doula. You have made decisions about what foods to eat and where to give birth.

The fabric of our lives changes constantly, how-ever, and many women find themselves questioning some of these decisions later in their pregnancies. Whether or not you have doubts about any of the choices you've made up until this point, it's a great idea to think it all through again and be sure you are really comfortable with all the different decisions you've made.

HIGHER GROUND
Taking Stock

As pregnancy draws to an end, you will be full of thoughts. Find a time and place where you will be able to relax and let your mind travel freely. Write your thoughts down in your journal if you like. Ask yourself these questions:

- How can I savor my pregnancy, my new life? How can I embrace the changes?
- What do I need to do to keep in touch with my friends and relatives before and after the baby is born?
- Will my interests and avocations change after the baby is born?
- How can I create a vibrant support system in my community that will help me to feel competent as a new mother?
- Where do I get my self-awareness? My personal equilibrium? My self-possession? My independence?
- How can I best prepare myself for the next season of my life?

Creating a Birth Plan

The concept of a birth plan may be familiar to you already. Many childbirth educators and doulas suggest that you create a birth plan to become clearer about your birth preferences. Doing this will help you to review the decisions you've made, and will prepare you for labor and delivery.

A birth plan states, in writing, your vision of the upcoming labor and delivery. It crystallizes your beliefs, states your preferences, and outlines any procedures you would like to avoid. It can be written in any format you prefer—there are no hard and fast rules. For example, you might write your birth plan in chronological order, from early labor to the postpartum period, or you might prefer to list your preferences in order of their importance to you, starting with what matters the most. You can use bullet points, or write your thoughts out in paragraph form. It's up to you.

A birth plan is not meant to be a script. By its very nature, birth is unpredictable. It is not possible to decide ahead of time how long you'll be in labor or what complications might occur. Give yourself options so that you do not set yourself up for frustration and disappointment if things do not go exactly the way you'd like.

You'll find a sample birth plan below. Remember, this format is not etched in stone, but it will give you an idea of things you'll want to include, such as a statement of purpose, your preferences, and things you'd like to avoid. You may find descriptions of procedures and terms that are unfamiliar to you—these will be discussed later in this book. Although some of the concepts may be unfamiliar to you now, you should review this plan several times throughout your pregnancy to review your birth choices.

Sample Birth Plan

My partner and I have planned and prepared for a peaceful and natural childbirth. We would like to allow our labor and delivery to unfold naturally, with as few interventions as possible. We would like to be informed about all procedures and tests before they are performed. We want to be aware and informed of all of our options in the event of an unexpected emergency.

OUR PREFERENCES

- Labor and delivery will take place: at home, in a freestanding birth center, in an alternative birthing center within a hospital, in a small hospital, in a teaching/large hospital
- Partner or labor coach, doula, and midwife present throughout labor and birth
- Children present throughout labor and birth
- Freedom to walk, move, and change positions as desired throughout labor and birth
- Freedom to eat and drink throughout labor and birth
- Use of the shower or a tub as desired
- Ability to use relaxation and pain relief methods as desired, including herbal therapy, homeopathy, and aromatherapy
- Ability to control the environment, including temperature, lighting, and music
- Use of gentle, controlled pushing
- Use of an upright labor position
- Massage and support of the perineum to avoid tearing
- Natural methods of strengthening labor, if needed, such as walking and nipple stimulation
- After the birth, immediate contact between mother and baby: baby placed on mother's chest, breastfeeding encouraged, mother and baby left undisturbed for one hour following birth, and any newborn procedures performed afterward
- Delay of clamping and cutting umbilical cord until blood stops pulsing
- Placenta delivered spontaneously
- Full informed choice regarding all newborn procedures, including eye ointment, vitamin K injection, and PKU test

- All baby examinations done with the permission, and in the presence, of a parent

WHAT WE WISH TO AVOID

- Medications
- Shaving
- Enemas or IV
- Electronic fetal monitoring
- Stripping of membranes or breaking of bag of waters
- Use of pitocin or other drugs to induce, speed up, or strengthen labor
- Supine (lying down) position for pushing stage
- Episiotomy
- Use of forceps or vacuum extraction
- Supplemental bottle feedings
- Unnecessary medical tests and procedures, such as medical circumcision

While some practitioners view a birth plan as a dialogue between parents and care providers, it is not a guarantee that your wishes will be honored. To be sure that your caregivers will be compatible with your preferences, you must carefully choose your place of birth ahead of time.

A birth plan is best used as a tool to clarify your preferences and to help you choose your ideal place of birth and convey your preferences to your health care providers.

Visualizing the Birth

Another good way to plan for birth is to learn how to have a relationship with the unpredictable. Birth, as the ultimate creative process, cannot be controlled. The birth may challenge you in ways you do not expect, or perhaps parts of it will be much smoother than you had anticipated. Things may turn out even better than you'd planned. You need to remind yourself that while you do not know exactly how it will go, you *will* be able to meet the challenge of a new experience.

Visualizing the birth, rather than just planning it

out, can be very helpful. Try to imagine a successful, satisfying birth. Keep the image of success in your mind. Spend a few minutes daydreaming about it every day. It may work better for you to write down these images, including lots of details such as the atmosphere of the room, the smells around you, and who is with you to provide support.

As you imagine the birth, try to match your visions with the birth environment you have chosen and the people you have picked out as your support team. Do they go together? Is there anything or anyone you want to change or reconsider?

Include, in your visualizations, a few alternate scenarios. Ask yourself how you might meet the challenge of something that doesn't go just as you'd imagined. This is not to suggest you visualize awful birth and labor scenarios, but simply that you prepare yourself for the unknown. Try to imagine actions you can take if some aspect of your ideal birth does not happen just as you'd like it to. For example, if your water breaks and your labor doesn't progress, what would you want to do?

You may not know what your options are—you may need more information. As you read the rest of this book, speak with your health care provider about specific scenarios to determine how you'd like to handle these situations if they arise. In the example just mentioned, you might want to consult a homeopathic practitioner.

You Are Allowed to Change Your Mind

Here you are, going into your third trimester, and you find yourself having doubts about some things. Perhaps you are not clicking with your midwife in the way you'd hoped to. Maybe you are finding out that your doctor is not as open-minded as you'd hoped he would be, and now you wish you had chosen a midwife to begin with. Maybe you've heard stories about the hospital you planned to use, and now you have doubts about it. Perhaps new health issues have come up that are causing you to

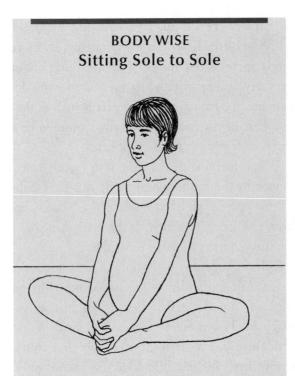

BODY WISE
Sitting Sole to Sole

This simple exercise can be done shortly after eating, so it won't interfere with your digestion—and it's very good for limbering inner thigh muscles.

1. Sit on the floor with your spine straight, fitting the soles of your feet together. Grasp the upper part of your feet with your hands.

2. Look straight ahead and inhale. As you inhale, pull up on your feet as far as is comfortable.

3. As you exhale, keep the pull on your feet, but relax the inner thigh muscles so that you can feel your knees drop.

4. Repeat four times. Relax by sitting cross-legged or by lying on the floor on your back.

reevaluate either your practitioner or your place of birth.

It can be very hard to allow yourself to explore the feelings of dissatisfaction you may be having. For one thing, many of us are socialized to view health care practitioners as authority figures, and to believe that it is not appropriate to challenge authority. So if you have doubts about your physician, for example, it may be very difficult to ask for changes, or to choose another practitioner.

Because you are different, emotionally, in pregnancy, it may not be easy to trust yourself. You may be afraid that changing to a different hospital seems capricious, especially at this late date.

You are allowed to change your mind. You don't need to justify your decisions to anyone but yourself and your partner. This is a time to let intuition guide you, even if your head tells you to just go with the flow.

CHANGING YOUR HEALTH CARE PROVIDER

If you are unhappy, for any reason, with your midwife or doctor, try first of all to understand as clearly as you can what is bothering you. It could be a personality clash. Maybe you've been kept sitting for hours in the waiting room every time you have an appointment, and this has left you with residual feelings of anger. Maybe you are finding that you and your health care provider do not agree on the amount of medical intervention appropriate to pregnancy. Any reason is good enough, even the seemingly small ones, but it helps to lay it out. You might want to write your thoughts down or discuss them with an objective party such as a childbirth educator, a doula, or a trusted friend.

Next, consider talking it out with the care provider. You may not be comfortable doing this, and you don't absolutely have to. Even if you are already sure you want to leave, though, it can help to discuss your feelings. You may then be able to leave the situation with less anger and stress.

It may also help to interview other midwives and doctors before actually leaving the first one. This can help you to learn a bit more about what you want. Also, you will feel much safer if you know there is someone out there to take care of you that you really like.

Starting up with a new midwife or doctor late in

pregnancy may not seem perfectly ideal. It is not uncommon, however, for women to change their minds about what is best for them, and it is certainly much better than going through the process of labor and delivery with someone who no longer fits your needs or who you have realized you don't really like. The fact is that sometimes, through no one's fault, a woman's needs can change.

CHANGING THE BIRTH ENVIRONMENT

Deciding you aren't so sure about the choice of birth environment you made earlier can also be difficult. Again, you need to get very clear about what precisely is giving you doubts. Are you worried about the safety of your planned home birth? Perhaps a friend gave birth at the hospital you were planning to use and was unhappy with her experience there. Are you having fears about the birth process in general that you may be ascribing to the place?

Again, no feeling is wrong, and you don't need to justify your choices to anyone. Start by trying to understand what your concerns are, without judgment. Take your time with this. After becoming clear about what is worrying you, think things over for a few days before you take any action.

If you are planning a home birth and feel doubtful or scared about your decision, it can help to talk about those concerns with your midwife or a childbirth educator. They may be able to help you connect with other women who have had home births. (Also see chapter 10 for more information about handling fear.)

If you have heard negative stories about your planned birth facility, it is certainly important to find out more. Maybe this particular institution has policies against allowing laboring women to walk around, and you just learned about it. This might cause you to reconsider your choice. Remember, though, every person's experience is different—while one woman may have a negative experience at a particular birthing center, another may have a positive experience.

NATURAL SOOTHER
Raspberry Leaf Tea

As you tone your mind in preparation for childbirth and fine-tune your birth plans, you can tone your body as well. Raspberry leaf tea is the most popular herb used during pregnancy, and is particularly useful during the third trimester. Its astringent and stimulating properties strengthen and tone the uterine and pelvic muscles, while its soothing properties relax the uterus. Raspberry leaf tea also tones the mucous membranes, soothes the kidneys, allays diarrhea, stops hemorrhage, quells nausea, sedates, and relaxes.

Raspberry leaves have been used throughout history to encourage safe, easy childbirth, to speed recovery from birth, and to stimulate milk production afterward. The tonic and relaxing action of the leaves reduces the pain of uterine contractions and makes them more effective and productive, thereby easing and shortening the duration of childbirth.

To make the tea

1. Fill a kettle with cold water and bring to a boil.

2. Meanwhile, fill a clean teapot with hot water from the tap. Let it sit until the water boils, then empty the teapot.

3. Place 2 tablespoons dried raspberry leaves or 4 tablespoons fresh raspberry leaves into the teapot.

4. Add 1 pint of boiling water to teapot.

5. Steep for 10 minutes.

6. Strain, pour into a cup and sip slowly.

To make a cup of tea, use half the amount of leaves and water. Drink one cup a day during your second trimester, and three cups a day during your third trimester.

If it will help to allay your fears, ask for another tour of the birth facility to see how you feel there now that you are further along in your pregnancy and know a bit more. You can ask more questions, if you like, or even ask the same questions over again. Perhaps you can ask for specific information about any negative stories you may have heard.

You may wish to reconsider other parts of the birth environment as well. Maybe you'd thought about having a water birth, for example, but now think you may only use the tub for labor and not the actual delivery. Perhaps you have doubts about having certain people in the room with you during the birth, such as your other children, your mother, or certain friends.

Change or Growth?

Somehow, in our culture, the idea of changing one's mind has gotten a bad rap. Perhaps it is better to think of it as *growth*. As you make the journey to motherhood, you grow in many ways: physically, emotionally, and spiritually. You need to feel comfortable in the real world, and sometimes this requires you to alter your plans. This is a wonderful way for you to nurture and respect yourself.

Please think of the children first. If you ever have anything to do with their entertainment, their food, their toys, their custody, their child care, their health care, their education— listen to the children, learn about them, learn from them. Think of the children first.

—FRED ROGERS, *Mr. Rogers Talks to Parents*

During the third trimester, you may begin to feel a strong urge to get ready for the baby. Your body and your mind know that it's almost time to welcome her into the world.

This is the ideal time to begin to give practical consideration to decisions about the baby's care and your own care, too, in the first days after the birth. There are things you will need to buy, or ask to be given for a shower, though you'll find you don't really need as much as advertisers might like you to believe. Still, you will want to do all you can to make the first few weeks of your baby's life smooth for the whole family.

The Baby's Room

In our parents' generation, getting ready for the baby might have followed a certain stereotypical pattern. The baby would have its own room. They would have it freshly painted, or paint it themselves in a bright color. Maybe they would add some kind of multicolored wallpaper border around the top of it. There would be a soft carpet installed on the floor in preparation for those early crawling days, and a number of pieces of furniture would be purchased: a crib, a changing table, a dresser, and a rocking chair. They would buy, or be given, an army of brightly colored toys and stuffed animals.

Many of us will follow a similar scenario today, or

at least some part of it. There are other ways of doing it, though. For one thing, many of us will do something most of our parents wouldn't have dreamed of: sleep with our babies.

THE FAMILY BED

One of the main reasons for this shift toward cosleeping (defined as the baby being in the same room, or in a sidecar-style crib), or the family bed (where infant and parents share a bed), has to do with breastfeeding. More and more women are breastfeeding their babies now, and they find that it is easier to do this if the baby is right there next to them during the night. If you bottle-feed, you need to fully wake up to feed your infant. You need to get the bottle and heat up the formula, and stay awake as long as the baby is still drinking. Many women who breastfeed, on the other hand, report that it is possible to doze off while doing so.

Women who sleep with their babies are following a well-established practice. In 67 percent of cultures around the world, babies and children sleep either in the same bed as their mother or both parents, or in a separate bed in the same room, until they are at least a year old. In many other cultures, infants spend significant amounts of time sleeping with their mothers and fathers. The United States has consistently stood out against these statistics.[1] Here infants are usually given their own beds and their own rooms right from the start.

It seems there are good reasons for cosleeping:

- Cosleeping reinforces the practice of breastfeeding and all the benefits that go along with it.

- Babies' brains are not fully developed, and they are not adept at managing the shift between conscious, controlled breathing and unconscious, automatic breathing until they are three or four months old.[2] Cosleeping seems to help babies with this, at least in part because of the influence of the sound of parental breathing and the external stimulation of being right next to another body. When babies and mothers are monitored while cosleeping, their brain-wave activity, heart rates, muscle movements, and breathing align.[3]

- Research suggests that infants who sleep in the same room with their mothers have significantly lower rates of sudden infant death syndrome (SIDS).[4] Japan, for example, where cosleeping is the cultural norm, has the lowest rates of SIDS in the world.

- Cosleeping is reassuring to both baby and parents and may help secure their bond. Parents who work all day find this to be particularly helpful in having that feeling of closeness.

- Most children seem to grow out of the family bed arrangement entirely on their own. At some point, children feel they would like to have their own space and are ready to sleep alone (the age at which this happens will vary with each child). This may be reassuring to parents who would like to try cosleeping but fear their children will never want to leave their beds.

The practice of cosleeping with your newborn is discussed in more detail in chapter 22.

PAINT

Regardless of the type of sleeping arrangements you and your family eventually decide upon, you may feel you want to do some work on your home.

Perhaps you'd like to repaint *your* bedroom, or create a special playroom for the baby. But many of the things we commonly use to fix up our homes have negative effects on our health and that of our unborn children. While you are pregnant, you need to be doubly cautious about exposing yourself to these things. Soon you will be bringing a new baby into your home—one who is very vulnerable to toxic chemicals and materials.

It is best to avoid doing the painting yourself while you are still pregnant. Many types of toxins, including paint fumes, can cross the placenta, exposing your baby to their effects.

First and foremost, be aware of the hazards of lead contamination. If you live in a home built prior to 1978, there is a good chance that underlying paint layers contain lead. If you sand the walls, and particularly the decorative moldings, you will breathe in lead dust. Have your home tested before you do anything (see appendix 2), or buy a lead test kit at the hardware store.

Once you are ready to proceed with painting, there are a few things to watch out for. Avoid using oil-based paints if you possibly can. All paints contain solvents, but those in oil-based paints are particularly dangerous. Latex-based paints can also contain hazardous chemicals that off-gas, or create fumes, which you can breathe in.

Your best bet is to look for paints that are labeled VOC-free and are low-biocide. Volatile organic compounds, or VOCs, are in paint and vaporize into the air we breathe. Low-biocide paints are 90 to 95 percent free of preservatives and fungicides. If you live in a humid area, though, where mildew is common, you do need to use a paint that contains a fungicide. Paints that are low-biocide and VOC-free do tend to be more expensive.

No matter what type of paint is used, try to keep the space that is being worked on well ventilated and sealed off from the rest of your home. It is best to try to stay away as long as you can smell fumes. Try to have all the paint work done at least a month before the baby's due date.

WALLPAPER

If wallpapers were truly made of paper, they might be a good alternative to painting. These days, however, most of them are made from vinyl, which can off-gas and may contain hormone-disrupting substances. The adhesives that are used to apply them can be even worse. Look for nontoxic alternatives.

FLOOR COVERINGS

To begin with, carpets harbor dust, and lots of it. A wall-to-wall carpet may not be the best choice for a room where the baby will spend a lot of time. Before you know it, your baby will be a toddler and will become intimately acquainted with the floor. Think carefully about what will be on it.

Carpeting, the adhesives used to attach it, and the padding underneath it can continue to off-gas for up to five years. In 1988 the Environmental Protection Agency (EPA) itself had to remove 27,000 square feet of new carpeting from its headquarters after the staff reported that it made them ill. If you must purchase new wall-to-wall carpeting, ask that it be attached to the floor with tacks rather than glue. Keep windows open in the room for at least seventy-two hours after installation to air the carpet out.

You can probably keep your older carpeting in place, but do keep the dust factor in mind, especially if your family has any history of allergy problems.

Area rugs are a good alternative. Stick to natural fibers such as organically grown wool, cotton, hemp, jute, ramie, or goat hair. Avoid carpets that are made from synthetic materials or backed with synthetics. Check to see if the rug has undergone any type of chemical treatment to make it stain- or mothproof; many people are sensitive to the fumes these chemicals emit, and it is not known whether or not they are safe to breathe in. Air new area rugs out for seventy-two hours (preferably outdoors) before putting them in place.

If you decide to have your wooden floor refinished, ask about using water-based urethanes instead of the usual polyurethane. Your flooring contractor may not want to use them because they are consid-ered less durable. In balance, though, they are so much less toxic that it may be worth it. After the floor has been refinished, air the room out for seventy-two hours before using it again.

BABY FURNITURE

Those antique cribs and old-fashioned rocking chairs are tempting and often seem to be so much better crafted than their modern equivalents. We know a lot more about furniture safety for infants, however, than we did in the past.

First of all, any crib manufactured before 1990 is not subject to the current safety standards. Those standards ensure that crib bars, for example, must be no more two and three-eights inches apart to keep the baby's head from going between them, a strangulation hazard. Used furniture may also be in weakened condition.

Another problem with antique baby furniture has to do, once again, with lead paint. Most paints used on furniture prior to 1988 contained lead. Therefore you must make sure that these pieces are completely stripped and refinished before you use them. Check "Paint," (page 108), for information on paint safety.

When buying a new crib, try to avoid those made of laminated wood, pressed wood, chipboard, plywood, particleboard, or synthetic veneers, all of which use formaldehyde-based glues. Also try to avoid plastics, especially polyvinyl chloride (PVC) and plastic coatings. There are companies that manufacture environmentally safe baby furniture. See appendix 2.

Consider purchasing a rocker. A rocking chair is a good investment that you will use well into your child's toddler years, and maybe longer. Rocking your infant will be soothing both to her and to you in the early months and can be the perfect place to nurse. There are many different types available, so shop around and try them out. You might like to find an antique rocker, or you might prefer a brand-new one that glides. You will probably find that a rocker with arms is most comfortable, especially for nursing. Cushions or padding are essential.

BEDDING AND MATTRESSES

It is also best to look for bedding and mattresses made from natural and untreated fabric, like cotton and wool. Certified organic cotton sheets are made of cotton grown without the use of synthetic pesticides and fertilizers. Green cotton is cotton that has been conventionally grown, but is unbleached and has not been processed with chemicals. If you want color, look for labels that say "natural" or "vegetable dye."

If you purchase nonorganic sheets and bedding, they will probably have been treated with finishes such as flame retardants and stain guards. Some people are sensitive to these fumes that are emitted by these chemical treatments, resulting in headaches, skin rashes, allergies, and asthma. Before using them, fill a washing machine with water, add one cup of baking soda, and soak the fabric overnight, agitating the machine a few times. Then wash and dry at least three times, adding 1/4 cup of baking soda to the detergent in the first two washes and 1/2 cup white vinegar to the final wash. After three cycles, if water soaks into the dry fabric, most of the finish has been removed. If it beads up, wash and dry it again.

Mattresses for cribs need to be quite firm, and they should fit very tightly into the crib itself, leaving no large gaps around the perimeter where the baby could get stuck. Avoid pillows and "cushy" quilts. These have been associated with a risk of suffocation and SIDS. Bumper pads for cribs may reduce the airflow in the crib and increase the risk of SIDS, and the bumper ties can pose a strangulation risk. For these reasons, bumper pads are no longer recommended and, fortunately, are not really necessary.

CURTAINS AND DRAPES

Concerns about bedding and the fumes released by synthetic fabrics also hold true for curtains. If you are going to use them, try to stick to natural fabrics. Also be aware that they will need to be washed very frequently to keep down the dust and dust mites that fabrics harbor.

BODY WISE
Baby Carriers

Instead of investing a lot of money in accessories like baby swings or bouncy infant seats, purchase one or two types of baby carriers that can do double duty: keep your baby amused and soothed *and* help you get back into shape. Exercise is also a great way to get out of the house, and is invigorating for both you and the baby.

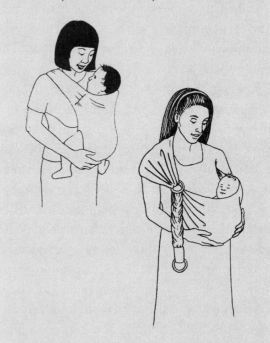

There are many different types of baby carriers. Many mothers like slings, the unstructured carriers that hang loosely in front with the baby cradled inside. There are also front pack carriers in which the baby sits vertically in a cloth seat within a carrier that is attached to your body.

As the baby gets older, many mothers like to use a backpack or stroller to walk the baby. Many strollers are specially designed for jogging, or have heavy tread on the tires. Be on the lookout for mother/baby exercise classes, baby swim classes, and yoga or dance classes that welcome new mothers.

Consider using blinds, which can be vacuumed. Avoid vinyl or other synthetic blinds. Instead choose steel, aluminum, bamboo, or wood. If they have been painted or given a wood finish, hang them outside to air out for several days before installation.

Be careful about pull cords for blinds and curtains. There are child-safe brackets you can install to keep the cords high off the floor. They can present a strangulation risk for your baby once he reaches the crawling stage.

LIGHTING

Consider using a dimmable light source in the room where your baby will sleep. This might come in handy when you want just a little light, but don't want it to be too bright. Make sure any floor lamps you have nearby are wide-based enough that they cannot be toppled over by grasping toddler hands. Place table lamps on furniture in such a way that the furniture blocks both the cord and the outlet.

Diapers

Back in the early 1990s, when environmental awareness was at its peak, many states were considering taxing the sale of disposable diapers, or perhaps banning them altogether.

The use of disposable diapers is now so prevalent that many parts of the country no longer have diaper services. Many parents believe that the processes used to clean cloth diapers are just as bad for the environment as using disposables. What happened during that time to cause such a remarkable shift in thinking?

In 1990 Proctor & Gamble, the nation's largest manufacturer of disposable diapers, commissioned a study on the environmental impact of disposable diapers. The results of this study were used to create an advertising campaign showing tree roots planted in compost with the caption, "90 days ago this was a disposable diaper." The ad was pulled after several lawsuits challenged its misleading message. The fact is, no composting facilities in the country could handle disposable diapers—a situation that has not changed over the past decade.

In response to this ad, the National Association of Diaper Services (NADS) issued several reports showing the strong environmental advantages of cloth diapers—but it was too late. Public opinion had been swayed, and the damage was done. Unfortunately, NADS did not have the financial resources to challenge the disposable diaper manufacturers who spend billions of dollars a year on advertising.

ADVANTAGES TO THE ENVIRONMENT

However, many parents who do their homework learn that cloth diapers are better for the environment. Here are a few facts to consider:

- Eighteen billion disposable diapers are placed in landfills each year. They take as long as 500 years to decompose.

- Disposable diapers make up the third largest source of solid waste in landfills, after newspapers and food and beverage containers.

- It would take more than 82,000 tons of plastic and 1.3 million tons of wood pulp (a quarter of a million trees) to manufacture the disposable diapers that cover all the babies in the United States right now.

- The wastewater produced from washing diapers is benign, while the wastewater from the manufacture of the pulp, paper, and plastics used in disposable diapers is toxic, containing dioxins, solvents, sludge, and heavy metals.

- The Landbank Report, an independent review and evaluation done by a London environmental agency, concluded that compared to cloth diapers, throwaway diapers use twenty times more raw materials, three times more energy, two times more water, and generate sixty times more waste.

ADVANTAGES TO YOUR BABY

While it's enormous, the damage done to our environment is only one factor in your choice between disposables, cloth, or a combination of the two. Another factor is the health and comfort of your baby. Consider these points:

- Superabsorbent disposable diapers contain a substance called sodium polyacrylate that absorbs up to 100 times its weight in water. When you change a baby that has worn one of these diapers, you may notice clear beads of this gel on her genitals and bottom. No studies have been conducted on the effects of sodium polyacrylate on infants, many of whom are exposed to it twenty-four hours a day for years.
- Dioxin, a by-product of the paper bleaching process used in making disposable diapers, is present in them.
- Recent research has indicated that disposables may be a trigger for asthma, due to the release of chemical fumes. This can affect asthmatic mothers as well as babies. No similar response occurred in cloth diapers tested.[5]
- A German study found a possible link between plastic diapers and male infertility. Plastic diapers undermine the body's natural ability to keep the scrotum and testicles cool. Temperature of the testicles is known to have a significant effect on fertility. Further studies are needed to see if these effects are long-term.[6]
- Disposable diapers seem to cause more skin problems in babies. Cotton seems to "breathe" better. Disposables are so well sealed that a baby can go for hours without a leak—but that same seal gives bacteria a fabulous breeding atmosphere, and the ammonia that develops in the bacterial breakdown of urine has nowhere to go.
- Babies in cloth diapers tend to be changed more frequently, whereas the sense of dryness that a disposable diaper gives may cause the parents to leave it on the baby for hours.[7]

- Cotton feels so much better on the skin than paper or plastic.

OTHER ADVANTAGES

Cost is another reason many parents choose cloth diapers over disposables. Disposable diapers cost between 14 and 32 cents per use. Cloth diapers can cost as little as 5 cents per use, if you launder them yourself, or between 8 and 15 cents per use, if you use a service. Over the course of three years, that can add up to a significant savings.

If you use a diaper service, you do not need to rinse diapers or shake out the fecal matter. On the other hand, you *should* shake fecal matter out of a disposable diaper before sending it off to a landfill. If you check the instructions on a package of disposables, you will see this written clearly, although almost no one does it. Leakage in a landfill could create a disastrous problem for a community's water supply because of the viruses that can be present in human waste.

Potty-training experts tend to agree that toddlers who use cloth diapers potty-train earlier than those that use disposables. There is a very good reason for this. Children that wear disposables cannot feel the dampness of their diapers. Why should they want to do anything about it or even pay attention to the fact that they need to go? When they wet a cotton diaper, they know it, and it helps them to monitor their own urges.

What Your Baby Will Need

You may be wondering what to have on hand before your baby arrives. Here are some of the items you'll need:

- Three to five dozen cloth diapers and five diaper covers (or five dozen all-in-ones, diapers with built-in covers).
- Diaper pins, clips, or Snappis (pinless clips).
- Two to three dozen cotton washcloths.

- One to three washable, waterproof bags for carrying soiled diapers while traveling.
- Diaper rash cream, lotion, or powder of your choice (don't buy talcum powder, which is dangerous to breathe in).
- A variety of outfits for different temperatures (including hats and gloves, if the weather will be cold).
- A diaper bag or backpack that you really like. You might find one with a changing pad and a place for your wallet, as well.

Getting Ready for Labor

Now is the time to stock up on things you might need during labor. If you are giving birth away from home, you can begin to pack your suitcase. Here are things you might consider having handy at home, or packing up to take with you:

- A couple of your favorite nightgowns or long pajama tops. You can choose one that is made for nursing, if you prefer.
- Something comfortable for your feet such as slippers or socks, or maybe a pair of slipper socks with rubberized bottoms.
- Hot water bottles, heating pads, and icepacks.
- A tennis ball for massaging the back or other massage devices, such as a back roller.
- Massage oil.
- Essential oils, such as lavender.
- Lip balm.
- Lollipops. Some women report that sucking on lollipops is helpful during labor. Try one of the sour varieties.
- Nourishing snacks for you and your partner.
- Herbal teas.
- A swimsuit for your partner so they can go in the shower or tub with you, if you like.
- Music that you love, and a CD or tape player.
- Candles and matches.

NATURAL SOOTHER
Baby Powder

Talcum powder can be irritating to a baby's respiratory system. You can make your own powder out of any combination of these ingredients found at your natural foods store:

Powdered orrisroot

Finely ground oatmeal

Finely ground rice flour

White cosmetic clay

Experiment to see which consistency and ingredients you like. You may add a small amount of finely crushed lavender flowers or rose petals for a mild scent, but make sure their texture is compatible with that of the powder. You could also keep a small lavender or rose sachet inside the powder container. Look for an interesting shaker with small holes at a kitchen store.

- Large sanitary pads (though birth facilities will have these on hand).
- Witch hazel or a witch hazel/aloe combo for soothing the perineal area.
- Hair accessories, particularly hair bands, if you have longer hair.
- A journal.
- Inspirational quotes.
- Any photograph, mandala, or other object that inspires you and could be used to focus on during labor.
- A camera or video camera.
- A list of phone numbers or address book so that you can easily place calls after the birth.
- Nursing pads.
- An outfit for your baby to wear.
- An infant car seat.

PREPARING THE HOUSE FOR A HOME BIRTH

This is a good time to get everything together that you will need, if you plan to birth at home. In the first stages of labor you will have ample time to set it all up:

- A firm mattress. You can put a board under the one you've already got if it seems too soft. A waterbed may be comfortable for the earlier stages of labor, but is definitely not recommended for the actual birth, as it is not supportive enough.
- A plastic sheet or shower curtain to place over the mattress to protect it.
- An old set of sheets that you don't mind getting stained.
- Disposable bed pads. You should be able to find these at a pharmacy or medical supply store. Large disposal diapers can work if you can't find anything else.
- Several towels and washcloths. These may get stained.
- Antiseptic soap, such as pHisoderm, for scrubbing up with.
- Rubbing alcohol.
- A large bowl to catch the placenta.
- Newspaper to lay out on the floor to soak up any liquids.
- A fleet enema. Discuss this with your midwife.
- A work area near the bed, such as a table or a dresser top, for the midwife's supplies.
- A place where the midwife can lie down and rest, if necessary.
- Snacks and drinks for the birth attendants.

You need to wash all the sheets, towels, and washcloths that you've set aside for the birth in hot water with chlorine bleach. Dry them in the hottest setting on the dryer, then fold them while they are still hot. Put them in unused plastic bags and seal them with tape until it is time to use them.

Your midwife will have other specific items she wants you to set up or purchase. She may also have very specific ideas on sterilization procedures. This is a good time to speak to her about this, if you haven't done so already.

Preparing for the First Few Weeks

Try to do all you can to prepare ahead of time for a smooth transition from the birth to your new life.

This will mean something different to everyone. Try to think ahead about the basics of life—food, laundry, and emotional support—and see what you can do now to cover your bases. Here are a few suggestions to get you started:

- Cook some dishes ahead of time and store them in your freezer. Choose your favorite dishes and think in terms of "comfort food," whatever that means to you. If homemade macaroni and cheese makes you feel good, then that's what you need.
- Consider using a postpartum doula (see chapter 21 for more information on postpartum doulas), meant to take care of the mom, so the mom can take care of the baby. A doula will be able to help you with breastfeeding, do laundry, pick up groceries, screen phone calls, and much more.
- Ask your best buddy to organize other friends to come over with a meal, or to straighten up and do laundry. You can also ask for these things for your shower instead of baby gifts. Try to arrange for about two weeks' worth of these visits. Don't be afraid to ask for help!
- Call around to see if there is a food delivery service in your area. Some offer meal packages for several days. You may be able to find one that specializes in the food you like: vegetarian, vegan, ethnic, etc.
- You may not normally use paper napkins and plates, for ecological reasons. You might want to purchase some made from recycled paper for the postpartum period, though. It will cut down on the amount of cleanup that needs to be done.
- Pick out birth announcements and thank-you

cards now. You can even begin to address the envelopes.

- Consider hiring someone to clean house for the first month or two (or more, if you can afford it).
- Have at least one set of nice clean sheets ready to put on the bed when you get home after the birth, or to change to after your home birth. Treat yourself to a new nursing nightie or pajamas, as well.

As you read the rest of this book, especially part 5, you'll think of more things you can do to prepare that suit your unique situation. Remember, as you do this, that your life doesn't have to be perfectly organized. While you can anticipate certain things about the postpartum time, there is much that will be unexpected. The friends, family, and other help you've lined up ahead of time can help you with the details.

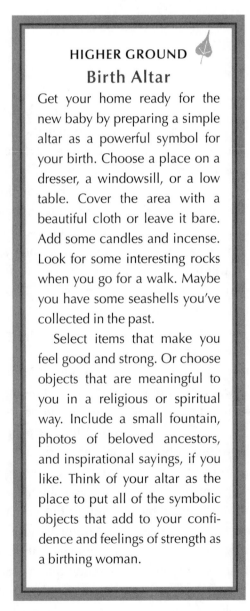

HIGHER GROUND
Birth Altar

Get your home ready for the new baby by preparing a simple altar as a powerful symbol for your birth. Choose a place on a dresser, a windowsill, or a low table. Cover the area with a beautiful cloth or leave it bare. Add some candles and incense. Look for some interesting rocks when you go for a walk. Maybe you have some seashells you've collected in the past.

Select items that make you feel good and strong. Or choose objects that are meaningful to you in a religious or spiritual way. Include a small fountain, photos of beloved ancestors, and inspirational sayings, if you like. Think of your altar as the place to put all of the symbolic objects that add to your confidence and feelings of strength as a birthing woman.

Rain, after all, is only rain; it is not bad weather.
So also, pain is only pain, unless we resist it, when it becomes torment.

—*I Ching*

Bring up the subject of pain in childbirth in a room full of women, and you'll start a conversation that could go on for hours. Everyone has something to say on this topic—even people who have never experienced labor themselves have a story to tell about their mother's, sister's, or friend's experience with pain.

Women are given very mixed messages about pain in childbirth. They are told it will be tremendously painful. They are advised to use drugs to avoid the pain. They are told that different women have different pain thresholds. They are also told that pain is all in the mind, and that they should be able to control the amount of pain they feel. Women are even told that with the right attitude and the right type of preparation, it is possible to have pain-*free* labor.

Here's the truth: labor is usually painful. Studies have shown that pain is registered the same by everyone. If you subject a wide variety of people to a pinprick, they will all physiologically feel the same amount of pain. What varies is how each person decides, consciously and unconsciously, to respond to it. The ability to respond less intensely to painful stimuli makes it *feel* like less pain.

The level of perceived pain is also affected by factors that are not necessarily under the control of the woman in labor. These factors include the baby's position, the labor environment, who is with the mother, whether or not she has given birth before, and how tired she is.

While pain is a definite part of the experience of giving birth, you do have some control over your relationship to that pain. We can work on the feelings we have in relation to pain. Before we get to that, though, and some specific techniques you can begin to practice now, let's find out why labor hurts to begin with.

Why Does Labor Hurt?

Try squeezing a muscle in your calf or arm very tightly and holding it there for some time. After a while, it will begin to hurt, and maybe even cramp up. While the pain of a squeezing uterus has its own sensation, the idea is the same. During labor, the uterus begins to squeeze very tightly, more than it ever has before, in order to move the baby down toward the birth canal.

Contractions of the uterus come in waves. In the beginning of labor, they are further apart and shorter in duration. As labor progresses, they go on for longer, and there is less time between them.

Some women liken the pain of uterine contractions to strong menstrual cramps. Others say it feels like an incredibly powerful elastic band is squeezing their lower abdomens. If you've experienced any Braxton-Hicks contractions during pregnancy, you may have a mild sense of what that squeezing feels like. Labor does not start out as gripping pain right from the very beginning, the way it is usually depicted in the movies. It generally begins as a mild tightening, slowly building up in strength and intensifying to an almost tingling, burning sensation. Some women report that the muscle stretches they have experienced in deep-tissue massage or Rolfing are similar to the sensation of contractions.

As labor progresses, the cervix begins to open up so that the baby will be able to pass through, and that causes new sensations. It can feel sharper and lower than the initial contractions of your uterus. You may begin to feel pressure on the cervix, pelvic joints, and vagina, as well. Sometimes this pressure can feel almost needle-like.

Sometimes babies are not curled up in the neat balls that make for easier births. Their heads, instead of being tucked in, can press into the small of the back of the mother. This is known as "back labor." The sensation is felt very strongly as an ache in the lower back and can, at times, be quite intense.

Another type of sensation is the stretching of the vulva in the final stages of labor, when the baby is passing through it. If you take your fingers and try to stretch your mouth open as wide as it can go, and then just a bit beyond that, you can get an idea of how that can feel. There is a stretching, burning quality to this type of pain.

Greeting Pain

As noted earlier, many women are given the message that having a natural, low-pain birth is entirely up to them, a "state of mind," or a matter of willpower. Buying into this notion can make for a lot of guilty feelings when labor gets intense. "I should be able to manage this," they tell themselves. Yet approaching labor as Superwoman does not take reality into account—labor hurts.

Still, thousands upon thousands of women throughout the ages and in the present day do have childbirth without drugs and would do it that way again if they had it to do over. Why is that?

One study compared a group of pregnant American women with a similar group of women from the Netherlands.[1] Each group was given the same information ahead of time about the risks of pain medication during labor. Labor was induced in the same percentage of women from each group. Yet only about 33 percent of the Dutch women asked for medication during labor, whereas 83 percent of the American women requested it. Interviewed forty-eight hours after the birth, the American women revealed that they generally anticipated a painful birth and the need for drugs, whereas the Dutch women anticipated less pain and less likelihood for the need for drugs. These results were repeated in several other trials, using subjects from different countries to compare.

A wide range of factors influences how pain is perceived by a woman who is in labor, including preconceived notions about pain and her ability to manage pain. Another factor is what we are told about childbirth in our culture. Other factors include the birth environment, the skill of the persons attending the woman, and the attention they pay to the details of her labor, from the lighting in the labor room to whether or not she is allowed to eat as she likes.

Dutch women, like those in the study mentioned above, are socialized to believe that birth is safe, so they have less anxiety about it at the outset. In the Netherlands, births usually occur at home, and women are given a great deal of support. They have not been socialized to associate pain in birth with danger.

We've already discussed the importance of choosing a birth environment that will suit you and finding the right kind of labor support. Let's explore the history of pain medications and then talk about some drug-free alternatives that can help you through labor and delivery.

The Use of Pain Medications in Childbirth

Around the 1920s, as medical advances began to accelerate, it became fashionable to give birth in the hospital. One of the main selling points of hospital birth was the new availability of "painless birth," which could only be obtained by having your baby in the hospital, under a doctor's supervision.

"Twilight sleep," originally created in Germany, was actually a series of treatments designed to eliminate pain, even the memory of pain, during labor and birth. Women were first given a shot of morphine, which dulled the pain of contractions. Next, they were given scopolamine, an amnesiac that removed memories of pain afterward. Finally they were given ether or chloroform to make them unconscious during the actual delivery.

Needless to say, by this time the woman was in no condition to help with the birth process in any way. She had to lie flat on her back, the position known to be the least effective during birth. Her arms and legs usually needed to be restrained to keep her from flailing them about. She was completely unable to push, once the baby began to move down the birth canal. Therefore, doctors needed to rely upon episiotomies to widen the vaginal opening enough, and forceps to pull the baby out.

Meanwhile, the baby moving down the birth canal was equally drugged by these medications and arrived in sluggish and sleepy condition. Mother and child would finally meet for the first time hours later, after both had a chance to recover from this traumatic experience.

Thankfully, the dangerous medications used back then, such as morphine, are no longer a part of the birth experience. Rare is the woman who is unconscious during the birth of her baby.

Today's Pain Medications

Today, there are two major techniques used for women seeking drugs for pain relief during labor: narcotic analgesics, which reduce pain and promote sleep, and epidural anesthetics, which are injected into the spinal area to actually numb parts of the body.

NARCOTIC ANALGESICS

The most commonly used narcotic pain relief is Demerol. Other choices include Nubain and Stadol. Sometimes another drug, known as an antagonist, is added to the narcotic to decrease some of its negative side effects (such as nausea and dizziness).

Why are narcotic pain relievers used? While they do not completely alleviate pain, narcotics can either reduce pain or make it seem more tolerable by virtue of their relaxation effect. They are sometimes also used to lower high blood pressure during labor.

How are narcotic pain relievers given? Narcotic pain relief is administered either by an intramuscular injection (usually in the buttocks) or via an intravenous (IV) line. IVs can be set up so you can self-dose as needed; in addition, a "heparin lock" can be used, allowing you to disconnect the IV to get up and walk. Results from injection take about thirty minutes, and the dose lasts for three or four hours. Results from IV usually take effect more quickly, but last for a shorter period of time.

It is usually best to avoid taking these drugs in very early labor, when they can slow things down. Once you have reached the pushing stage, they can affect the baby's respiration. See more on this below.

When is narcotic pain relief necessary? The only time the use of narcotics is medically indicated is to reduce high blood pressure, or to calm a woman who is experiencing severe anxiety.

When is narcotic pain relief unnecessary? Other than the uses described above, the use of these drugs is not medically necessary.

How effective are narcotic pain relievers? This question highlights one of the major problems with using narcotics during labor. Every woman reacts differently to these drugs, making it hard to predict what the outcome will be. While some women find that the relaxation effects of these drugs make it easier for them to carry on, others find that they end up feeling fuzzy-headed and out of touch with their labor. Some women may take these drugs hoping for a reduction in pain, only to find that they are now feeling "spacey," while hurting just as much as they did before.

Are narcotic pain relievers safe? When you take these drugs, so does your baby. The placenta reduces the effects on the baby, but about 70 percent of the medication reaches him.[2] Narcotics slow down the baby's heart rate and affect his respiratory system while he is still in the womb, and if given too close to birth can also impact respiration after birth. Babies of mothers receiving narcotics show general sluggishness and sometimes have trouble feeding in the early days. Remnants of the narcotics stay in their bloodstream for weeks. Long-term consequences to the baby's health after receiving narcotics are still unknown.

One thing is certain—narcotics can interfere with postbirth bonding. Both mothers and babies are often too dazed to respond well to each other after being given narcotic drugs. This can make breast-feeding a difficult challenge, at first.

For the mother, side effects can sometimes include nausea, vomiting, and dizziness. Some women are unable to walk around once they have taken narcotics because they feel unstable. Some find they can't push effectively during the second stage of labor, or respond well to direction from their labor coaches. All of this can slow labor down tremendously.

EPIDURAL ANESTHESIA

Epidural anesthesia, also known as epidural, epidural block, epidural analgesia, and walking epidural, has become the most popular form of chemical pain relief during labor. Unlike narcotic analgesia, epidurals leave women clearheaded and provide the most effective pain relief.

Why are epidurals used? For a woman who requires a cesarean section, epidural anesthetic is a godsend. She can stay awake for her baby's birth without feeling the pain of surgery.

How are epidurals given? A local anesthetic is used to numb your back, followed by a needle that is inserted into the epidural area of your spine, where all of the nerves that register pain are located. The anesthesiologist will then thread a tiny catheter into this space, which is hooked up to a bag of medication. This medication might be an anesthetic, an analgesic, or a combination of several of these, and can either be fed into the catheter continuously or in measured, timed doses.

The effects of this treatment on your pain levels, and on your ability to move about, will depend on how much and what type has been used. Effects are not immediate, and are usually felt somewhere between a half hour and ninety minutes later.

A walking epidural is one in which low doses of medication are mixed with narcotics so that you don't lose all of the sensation in your lower body. Its name is a bit misleading because most women are still not able to walk around much. They are usually able to feel their contractions, however, and can sometimes squat, kneel, or stand during labor.

You will be given intravenous fluids to hydrate you before you receive the epidural in order to prevent a drop in blood pressure that often occurs. Your blood pressure will require frequent monitoring. Since your body is numbed from the waist down, you will not be able to tell when you need to urinate. For this reason, a catheter will be inserted into your urethra. You will also need to be hooked up to an electronic fetal monitor (EFM) to be sure the baby is handling the epidural well. It isn't a good idea to have an epidural before your cervix is dilated to 4 or 5 centimeters, because the drugs can slow your labor down significantly, or right before the second stage of labor, since it may not take effect in time and can prevent you from pushing effectively. Epidurals are most effective between 5 and 8 centimeters of dilation. How quickly your labor is moving along will affect your decision.

When are epidurals necessary? An epidural, or another form of anesthesia, is necessary if a cesarean section is going to be performed. Epidurals are preferred because they allow the mother to be conscious during the birth of her baby. A woman who has preeclampsia or high blood pressure might also benefit from an epidural, as it can keep her stress levels low enough to keep blood pressure in a manageable range. This could allow her to have a vaginal birth rather than a cesarean section.

If labor is chemically induced, an epidural may be necessary simply because of the intensity of the contractions. It may simply be too much to bear.

When are epidurals unnecessary? For normal vaginal pregnancy, elective use of an epidural to relieve pain is not supported by medical evidence.

How effective are epidurals? Epidurals are typically very effective in their ability to reduce the pain of labor, although their use can weaken contractions and slow labor considerably, as discussed further in the next section.

Occasional problems with epidurals include failure to eliminate pain for no discernible reason, eliminating pain in only half of the body, and problems locating the appropriate injection site, which can require the procedure to be repeated or can result in numbing of the entire spine and headache for several days afterward.

Are epidurals safe? Unfortunately, familiarity with this technique and the prevalence with which it is used has left the general public with the impression that there is no price for its use. Nothing could be further from the truth. The most serious side effect of epidurals is that they interfere with oxytocin production, which typically slows labor down and decreases the strength of contractions. This can also cause the baby to shift from an ideal position or fail to descend into the pelvic cavity. Finally, women under the influence of an epidural may not be able to feel their pelvic floor and therefore will not be able to bear down as effectively during the pushing stage of labor.

These side effects present an increased chance that one or all of the following procedures will be needed if an epidural is used:

- Three times the chance of augmentation of labor with drugs such as pitocin or Cytotec
- Three times the chance of a forceps or vacuum-extraction birth, procedures that typically require an episiotomy
- A 50 percent higher chance of having a cesarean section, if the epidural was given toward the beginning of labor

Other possible side effects to the mother include:

- Loss of mobility, in many cases making it impossible for a woman to do anything but lie flat on her back. This has been shown to be one of the least effective positions for helping labor to progress.
- A toxic or allergic reaction to the drug or drugs used.
- Itching or nausea caused by certain drugs such as Sufentanil, Demerol, Duramorph, Fentanyl, and Stadol in about 1 out of 4 cases. Sometimes this is so severe the woman will need an antihistamine, which will make her drowsy.
- Fever, which becomes increasingly likely if the epidural has been in for four hours or more
- Decrease in maternal blood pressure
- Serious headache or breathing difficulties, which can result when the anesthesiologist inserts the needle into a blood vessel or the spinal canal instead of the epidural space. In extremely rare cases this can also result in meningitis, cardiac arrest, or even death.

While little is known about the effects of epidurals on infants, potential complications include:

- Heart rate deceleration and a drop in oxygen supply as a result of the mother's reduced blood pressure
- Rapid heart rate and fever, often requiring antibiotic treatment
- Subtle changes in newborn reflexes and neurobehavior, including suckling ability
- Difficulty in self-soothing or being consoled

African Dance and Childbirth

How about some African dance to get in the spirit of the last trimester and to prepare for labor? African dance is particularly grounding during pregnancy—it allows you to be present in the moment and to forget about everything else. You learn to focus your thoughts, a technique that has been proven to be helpful in labor and in dealing with pain. You also learn to follow the rhythms of the drum as you dance improvisationally—in much the same way that you will follow the rhythm of the contractions during labor.

African dance instructors encourage the class to relax and learn to "hear with the body," to breathe deeply and follow the movements with the feet, not the rational mind.

A special trademark of classes in African dance is the sense of community. They often begin by forming a circle and doing warm-ups. A pregnant woman has a special, honorable place in class and is supported to move along at her own pace.

After warm-ups, the dancers usually move across the floor in lines of four or five and progress to more complex dance steps. These steps are then presented in a dance combination that gives a taste of village life. For example, a dance may reenact winnowing, pounding and preparing food, picking fruit, bathing in a river, shoveling, carrying a baby on the back, or using a shuffling motion to soothe the baby.

Most of the dances taught in the United States derive from central and western Africa, Brazil, Haiti, Trinidad, and Tobago. The rhythms are wonderfully complex. For African dance classes in your area, check the newspaper, or call libraries, music stores, YWCA, bookstores, and musical venues. Also check the Web for resources.

Other links still being studied include increased rates of hypoglycemia in infants exposed to epidurals,[3] and increased addiction rates in children who are exposed to pain-relieving drugs during labor.[4]

Preparing for Pain in Labor

The efficiency of pain relief methods during labor has been more studied than any other medical aspect of pregnancy—yet the adverse effects on mother and baby is one of the least studied.[5] That's one reason why so many women are turning to natural ways to reduce and cope with pain—methods that do not involve the use of drugs. If you become familiar with these techniques, you can minimize the chance that you will need to rely on medication during labor.

There are a number of ways to approach preparation for pain in labor, ways to mentally prepare yourself and also specific pain relief techniques that you can begin to practice now to prepare for birth:

- One-on-one continuous labor support has been shown to be one of the most effective methods for reducing pain in labor in a number of well-conducted studies. One study reported a 30 percent reduction in requests for pain relief medication by women who used a doula for labor support.[6] Consider hiring a doula if you have not done so already. See chapter 7 for more information about doulas.
- Studies have shown that women who take a childbirth education course use significantly less pain medication than those who do not. If you have not done so yet, consider taking such a course now. Read chapter 6 for more information.
- Preparing a birth plan and visualizing the labor can help you to prepare. See chapters 10 and 11 to learn more. Imagine each stage of labor, and picture the baby moving out of your uterus, down the birth canal, and out into the world. Visualize the way the uterus squeezes the baby into position. Imagine the cervix opening up like a flower so that the baby can pass through.

- Begin to get used to the idea of going *with* the pain, rather than fighting against it. A study of marathon runners found that the best ones flowed with their sensations, allowing them to exist, rather than fighting against them by trying to focus their thoughts elsewhere. Women who report painless labors describe their favorite techniques in the same way: they picture what is happening in their bodies, then they relax and let it happen.[7]
- Continue to raise your own awareness of any fears you have. See chapter 10 for more about facing your fears. Holding on to unexpressed fears may increase the sensation of pain and make it harder to cope with.

Nondrug Pain-Relief Techniques

There are a number of highly effective natural pain-relief techniques that may be useful during your labor and delivery. Many of them involve relaxation. Relaxation reduces the sensation of pain by raising endorphin levels and reducing stressful messages you give yourself about what pain means. Practice these ahead of time and purchase any materials you may need:

- Bathing or showering in warm water is an amazing labor tool for pain relief that has been well studied.[8] Choose a temperature that feels comfortable and soothing, but not too hot. If you are having a home birth, it is possible to rent large hot tubs that can be set up in your home. You can use your bathtub as well, but a larger tub will give you more room and allow your partner to come in and help you. Many birthing centers and hospitals now have Jacuzzi tubs available. The jets can be soothing as a massage tool, but just being in the warm water seems to soothe and help labor to progress. The force of gravity is relieved when you are in the water, offering further relief. You need to check with your health care provider before adding anything to the water, such as oils or bubble bath.

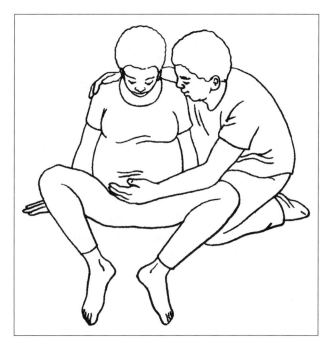

Effleurage

Showers can help, as well. You may want to find a low, stable stool that you can put into the tub so that you don't have to stand the whole time.

- Effleurage (shown above) is a light, rhythmic stroking of the abdomen, back, or thighs, usually done on bare skin with the tips of the fingers. You can do this yourself, or better, have a partner or doula do it for you. You can ask your partner to practice it now and learn, together, what feels right to you. Hold your fingers in an outstretched but relaxed posture. Run the tips of the fingers lightly over the chosen area. The abdomen, lower back, and forehead are good areas, but touching any part of the body can help you to relax. Try different motions, circular or up and down, for example. Experiment with different amounts of pressure. Maybe it feels better to you with one hand, or maybe two. Use a little cornstarch or lightly scented powder on your fingers first, to reduce friction.
- Massage is another way to relax and to help tired muscles keep working. Again, it is helpful to have your partner practice massage now in order to find out what works best. Try these techniques: Have your partner place his hands

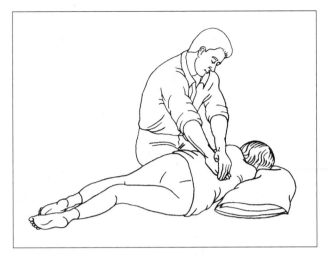

Massage

on your inner thighs and sweep them firmly down toward your knees as you release your pelvic floor muscles, as you would in a Kegel exercise. Or try kneading the buttock muscles deeply, both at the same time. For lower back pain or back labor, have your partner use the fist or the heel of the hand to firmly massage the area (see above). Some people also report relief by massaging the lower back with a tennis ball.

- You may want to purchase or make a soothing massage oil. Mix sweet almond oil with your favorite essential oils. Good oils include: lavender, chamomile, sweet geranium, jasmine, neroli, rosewood, melissa, mandarin, or cedarwood.[9] These oils are all relaxing; they increase endorphins, the body's natural pain relievers, and reduce sensations of pain. Try some of these ahead of time to see which appeals to you.

- Essential oils also smell wonderful. These smells can also evoke pleasant pictures in your mind, as well as help to cover up unpleasant hospital smells. You can put drops of oil on a napkin and keep it nearby, or on a damp washcloth for your forehead. You can also place them into an aromatherapy diffuser or add them to your bathwater (check with your health care provider first). Different labor positions work at different times during the labor process to relieve pain and discomfort. For example, getting on your

NATURAL SOOTHER

Labor Oils

These oil blends can be used to alleviate pain during labor.

Sweet Lavender Relief

2 ounces sweet almond, grapeseed, or pure vegetable oil

10 drops lavender essential oil

6 drops clary sage essential oil

4 drops geranium essential oil

2 drops jasmine essential oil

3 drops rose essential oil

Heaven and Earth

4 ounces sweet almond, grapeseed, or pure vegetable oil

8 drops spikenard essential oil

7 drops jasmine essential oil

3 drops lemon verbena essential oil

Mix the oils together in a plastic bottle with a pouring spout. Massage into abdomen during pregnancy and labor.

hands and knees and rocking back and forth often helps with the discomfort of back labor. Walking around can reduce the sensation of pain, as well. Plenty of variety in your positions can be extremely helpful in reducing pain. You will be taught some positions during your childbirth education classes, and also check chapter 17 for ideas. It's good to become familiar with these positions ahead of time in order to be prepared for labor, since you won't know which ones work until you are actually in labor.

- Have hot and cold packs available for use during labor. You can use a good old-fashioned hot water bottle, or an electric heating pad. Pads filled with hemp are also available that can be heated in the microwave or chilled in the fridge. Place the hot or cold pack anywhere that you feel pain, tension, or cramps. They are especially useful on the small of the back and on the neck and shoulders, areas where many people tend to hold tension.

- Most childbirth education courses teach helpful breathing techniques specifically geared toward working through pain in labor. The discipline of yoga also teaches both calming and invigorating types of breath exercises. Try this calming one, known as "alternate nostril breathing": place your right pinkie finger over your left nostril. Breathe in through your right nostril for a count of four; then place your right thumb over that nostril too. Hold your breath for a count of four; then release your pinkie from your left nostril and exhale for a count of eight. Now, keeping your thumb on your right nostril, breathe in fully through your left nostril for a count of four; cover it with your pinkie, then hold your breath for a count of four; then release your thumb and exhale through your right nostril for a count of eight. Continue like this as long as you like.

- Studies have shown that regular exercise during pregnancy increases endorphin levels in the blood.[10] Women who worked out regularly during pregnancy reported less pain during labor. Even if you have not exercised until this point in your pregnancy, it's not too late to gain some benefits and help to reduce pain in your labor. Try taking daily walks to begin with, and look for other ways to incorporate exercise into your pregnancy.

- Hypnosis is one type of childbirth education class that is available. You may want to consider this option, or consider seeing a private hypnotherapist who can train you to use autohypnosis or posthypnotic suggestion to prepare you

to react to pain in a different way. People vary in their reactions to hypnosis, but for some women it is extremely effective—some even claim to feel no pain whatsoever. See chapter 6 for more about childbirth education, and appendix 2 to find hypnotherapists.

- In China, acupuncture is used during cesarean sections instead of epidural anesthesia in 98 percent of cases.[11] While its use for surgery is not yet practiced here in the United States, it can be very effective for use during labor. It has no negative effects on the baby and is instantly reversible by simply removing the needles. If you are interested in this option, you need to find an acupuncturist willing to attend your birth, and you need to be sure your chosen birth environment can accommodate this.

- Acupressure may also be helpful, and it is possible that your partner or other birth companion can learn enough about it ahead of time to use during the delivery. Try these techniques: Apply pressure to the Ho-ku point on the back of the hand, right on top of the joint that connects the thumb and the forefinger. Press firmly into the bone of the forefinger near this spot for 10 to 15 seconds, three times, with a brief rest between each. The Spleen 6 point is about two inches above the ankle bone, on the inside of the leg. Press your thumb into the bone at this point for about a minute at a time. Apply pressure to both of these points as often as you like.

- Bach flower remedies can be extremely soothing during childbirth, especially the highly popular Rescue Remedy. You can also check out the other flower essences, each of which is intended to relieve a specific emotion or fear. See *The Language of Flowers,* page 59, for more information.

- Homeopathy is useful throughout pregnancy and during labor and delivery. *Arnica* is one homeopathic remedy that is particularly good for labor. It can reduce pain when taken internally, and helps with bruising and pain externally as well. Other pain remedies are both blue and black cohosh and *Chamomilla.* A birth practitioner trained in homeopathy can help you with correct dosage amounts.

- Music can be soothing and distracting for some women, whereas other women may find they want silence for some or all of the labor process. There have only been a few small studies done on the effects of music in helping to reduce labor pain, but those few have shown positive effects.[12] If you think music might help you, choose some favorites ahead of time and set them aside for labor. You may need to bring your own CD or tape player with you if you are going to a birth center or hospital.

Pain with Purpose

Studies show that women do not need to have pain completely eliminated in order to report satisfaction with the birth experience.[13] The pain of childbirth is not like the pain of injury, because it has a purpose and is productive. Of course, women also don't want pain to overwhelm and incapacitate them, and many are afraid, ahead of time, that this will happen.

Women receive little in the way of cultural messages that reassure them. Our culture teaches us to be fearful of losing control, and birth is a big unknown for most women, even those who have gone through it before. Preparing yourself with an arsenal of non-drug pain-relief techniques can empower you and boost your courage as you approach the upcoming delivery.

HIGHER GROUND
Soul Day

As you prepare for your baby's birth, the third trimester is a good time to start observing a Soul Day, a holy day for your family. In the Jewish tradition, the Sabbath is a day in which things are to be left as they are, a day for being—not doing. Follow this tradition or embellish your own.

Choose one day of the week to be your family's Soul Day. Do whatever you feel like doing. Stay in your pajamas all day. Don't answer the phone or go anywhere. Turn off the television. Putter around the house and eat small meals all day long. Take a long nap. Enjoy a bubble bath. Read, draw, and listen to the radio.

These days are so deeply relaxing that you will feel ready to rejoin the world after one of them. Make them a regular part of your week.

CHAPTER 14   *Avoiding the Cascade of Medical Interventions*

The more pregnancy is lived like an illness, the more it becomes in itself a cause of illness.

—DR. MICHEL ODENT, *Birth Reborn*

This book has focused on the tendency in our culture to turn pregnancy and childbirth into medical experiences. One intervention can lead to another in a cascading sequence of questionable procedures, many made necessary only because of a previous intervention. In chapter 13, for example, we explained how the use of chemical pain relief has been shown to increase the chances that you will end up having other medical interventions, such as a cesarean section.

We are indeed lucky to live in a time when medical aids to labor and delivery exist, but medical interventions such as labor induction, pain relief, and cesarean sections—measures that have saved many lives—have been overused.

This chapter will familiarize you with the most common tests in late pregnancy as well as the medical interventions associated with childbirth, and will explain when they are warranted and when they should be avoided.

Tests in Late Pregnancy

As you approach, or pass, your projected due date, your practitioner may suggest that you have one or more tests to assess the well-being of your baby.

WHY ARE LATE PREGNANCY TESTS USED?

These tests are conducted to try to assess the health of the baby inside your womb, if there is any reason to believe his health might be compromised. One of the most common reasons practitioners tend to think health might be compromised is postmaturity, when a baby remains in the womb past the time of his projected due date. Postmature babies can sometimes receive inadequate nourishment, due to placental failure. Many doctors automatically give women one or more of these tests as soon as they reach their due date.

Women who have been designated "high-risk" for any reason—whether because they have health problems such as diabetes, or because of a history of miscarriages—are likely to be given these tests one or more times as her due date approaches.

HOW ARE LATE PREGNANCY TESTS DONE?

Here is a list of the most common tests that are done in late pregnancy and how they are conducted:

• *Fetal movement counting, or "the kick test."* This is a do-it-yourself test. You set aside a several-minute block of time at the same time each day to do the test. Your practitioner will instruct you to begin timing with the first movement you feel, recording how long it takes to feel ten movements (the amount of time this takes is highly variable). The idea behind this test is that a healthy baby will move frequently, with more or less the same frequency, over time. You are asked to contact your practitioner if you notice that it is taking longer for the baby to move ten times, if the baby hasn't moved at all for twelve hours, or if there is a sudden and marked increase in kicks.

- *The non-stress test (NST).* The NST will be conducted in your practitioner's office, or in a hospital. You will sit in a chair, and an ultrasound transducer will be placed on your abdomen. You will be asked to signal every time you feel the baby move. The change in the baby's heart rate as a result of these movements will be observed. When two increases in the heart rate are observed during a twenty-minute test, or thereabouts (practitioners each have their own time frame for this test), the results are considered to be normal. If no big changes are observed, the result is abnormal, and the test might be repeated or further tests could be suggested.

- *Biophysical profile (BPP).* This test combines the non-stress test (described above) with other evaluations of the fetus, all using the ultrasound to obtain results. Fetal movement, heart rate, breathing movements, muscle tone, and amniotic fluid levels are each assessed. The fetus is given a score from 0 to 2 for each element, rather like the Apgar score a baby is given directly after birth. A score of 8 or higher suggests the baby is doing well. A score of less than 6 is of concern.

- *Contraction stress test (CST) or oxytocin-challenge test.* During the CST, the baby is subjected to minor contractions in order to see how she reacts. This will help determine how the baby is doing in the womb, as well as how she may react to the real contractions of the upcoming labor.

Because this test can bring on actual labor, it cannot be administered to women who have had preterm labor, placenta previa, multiple fetuses, or ruptured membranes. The test is normally conducted in a hospital. Ultrasound will be used to detect the baby's heart rate, probably with an electronic fetal monitor. The mother will be given a small dose of pitocin to stimulate minor contractions. It is also possible to do this test by using nipple stimulation to induce contractions. You can place a warm towel on the nipples for five minutes, or massage one or both nipples for about ten minutes. Most hospitals do not use nipple stimulation, however. If the baby is doing well, her heart rate will not change significantly during contractions, and will return to normal quickly after each one. This test may take several hours to complete.

WHEN ARE LATE PREGNANCY TESTS NECESSARY?

Tests that assess the well-being of a fetus are only necessary when there is a definite reason to believe that there could be a problem. One reason for worry might be that the mother has noticed a sharp and sudden reduction in fetal movement. Women categorized as high-risk because of serious health concerns that can impact the fetus, such as preeclampsia, high blood pressure, or insulin-dependent diabetes may need these tests, depending on the severity of their condition.

As we will see in the following sections, these tests are not absolutely reliable, however, and this needs to be taken into account when assessing results. Many experts believe that these tests do not routinely benefit even high-risk women.

WHEN ARE LATE PREGNANCY TESTS UNNECESSARY?

Late pregnancy testing is often used routinely by practitioners the moment a woman either comes close to, or passes, her due date. Studies have not shown that routine use of these tests results in better outcomes for babies—and, as discussed in the following section, the opposite is sometimes true.

It is important to remember that "due date" is only a loose estimate of the baby's birth date, and that birth either two weeks before or two weeks after that date is common. In fact, the American College of Obstetricians and Gynecologists (ACOG) defines true postmaturity as a pregnancy that lasts beyond forty-two weeks. The American Academy of Family Physicians suggests that it is perfectly normal for 80 percent of healthy babies to spend anywhere from thirty-eight to forty-two weeks in the womb.[1]

HOW EFFECTIVE ARE LATE PREGNANCY TESTS?

None of the tests discussed here has been shown to statistically improve outcomes for either the mother or the baby. Let's take a look at each of them to assess their effectiveness in greater detail:

- *Fetal movement counting, or "the kick test."* This test is only effective as a rough screening device. It has not been shown to be effective as a routine test in predicting the possibility of problems.[2] This is because the test is extremely subjective: fetuses, like adults, are highly variable. You might choose a time to measure movements that coincides with a nice long nap, for example, resulting in very little movement.

- *The non-stress test (NST).* The non-stress may cause false alarms, where the baby seems to be nonreactive as much as 75 percent of the time.[3] There also seems to be no improvement in outcome when this test is used to screen high-risk pregnancies. This rate of ineffectiveness causes one esteemed source of information, *A Guide to Effective Care in Pregnancy and Childbirth,* to remark, "One can only speculate as to why the [non-stress test] continues to be used in such an extensive way . . . and why the results from the only four randomized trials that have been published are so widely disregarded by many obstetricians."

- *Biophysical profile (BPP).* This test is more accurate when it detects either high- or low-range scores. Scores in the mid-range are less accurate.[4] Most experts think this test is more accurate in predicting abnormalities than the non-stress test alone.[5] However, studies testing the effectiveness of the BPP on women in high-risk categories did not show an improvement in birth outcomes.[6]

- *Contraction stress test (CST) or oxytocin-challenge test.* This test has a high incidence of false positives, where the results erroneously indicate that the baby is not doing well. It is not an accurate indicator of an acute emergency situation, where a baby should be delivered via cesarean right away. However, it can effectively alert a practitioner to keep a closer eye on a baby during labor.

ARE LATE PREGNANCY TESTS SAFE?

From a physical point of view, the only test discussed here with the potential to directly harm a baby is the contraction stress test (CST). One study on the CST actually showed a significantly higher death rate in women who had been given this test.[7] Because contractions are being induced, there is the potential to start real labor. This may not be in the baby's best interest if labor is not imminent, and other interventions may become necessary to keep the labor going. If pitocin is used to start the contractions, there are additional risks to the baby's health (see "Labor Induction" on page 129 for more about pitocin). Some practitioners who wish to avoid chemicals use nipple stimulation to start contractions during CST. Some studies, however, have shown that more fetal heart irregularities are reported with nipple stimulation, and that it takes longer to achieve results.[8]

Another danger of late pregnancy tests is that false positive results (erroneously indicating problems in a healthy baby) could motivate practitioners to recommend emergency cesarean section, unnecessarily subjecting mother and baby to the dangers of major surgery. Studies show that this is most likely to happen when women are given these tests routinely, rather than because of a specific concern.[9]

THE EMOTIONAL IMPACT OF LATE PREGNANCY TESTS

Since late pregnancy tests have such a poor track record of predicting trouble even in high-risk pregnancies, and render so many false positive results, taking them may set a woman up for unnecessary worry at a time when she needs to rest, relax, and prepare for the birth ahead.

Labor Induction

A decision to begin labor at a given time, rather than leaving it to nature, is referred to as labor induction. Various methods of induction have been used for hundreds of years by midwives. Nowadays, one-third or more of all labors are induced in hospitals, using drugs that stimulate the body to begin contractions.

WHY IS LABOR INDUCTION USED?

Labor is induced for a variety of reasons, ranging from medical necessity to convenience. Some physicians are very concerned about the consequences of babies who are still in the womb past their due date, and think it may be best to get labor going so that the baby will be born. Others worry about the possibility of infection in a woman whose water has broken, but who has not yet gone into labor. Sometimes it is the woman herself who is impatient and decides to try a little natural stimulation, such as taking a long walk, to get things going.

Additionally, many of the methods of induction, which we will outline in the next section, can be used to *augment* labor. Labor augmentation is meant to speed things up, either because it seems as though labor has come to a halt, or because the woman or her health care provider want things to go faster. Today, a large number of women have their labor augmented with some type of drug, despite the fact that both the American College of Obstetricians and Gynecologists and the Food and Drug Administration do not approve of the use of induction drugs for this procedure.

Another time that labor induction is used is during a contraction stress test, near the end of pregnancy. This test is meant to see whether or not the baby is able to tolerate the stress of labor by giving him a trial run.

HOW IS LABOR INDUCTION DONE?

Labor induction is done in a variety of ways, from mechanical to chemical to herbal. Here is a rundown of induction methods commonly used in hospitals:

- *Stripping the membrane.* The birth attendant inserts a finger between the cervix and the membranes of the amniotic sac to separate it from the uterine wall. This will sometimes cause labor to begin. This method is known to be generally safe, though not always effective. It is used by midwives as well as doctors. You may experience some discomfort during the procedure.

- *Prostaglandin creams or gels.* These are applied to a woman's cervix to help soften or ripen it. Before the cervix can begin to open, it must first be ripe. Think of this as the difference between pursing the lips of your mouth tightly and relaxing them and allowing them to soften. Sometimes cervical ripening begins to happen weeks before labor begins. In other cases it happens right before labor. If a woman has gone beyond her due date and her cervix is still not ripe, she may be offered a prostaglandin cream in her practitioner's office. It is also used in hospitals prior to chemical induction, if the cervix is not yet ripe. Sometimes an application of cream will also get contractions going. The application itself is painless.

- *Breaking the amniotic sac.* The practitioner uses a hook-shaped instrument to pierce the amniotic sac and release the fluid, which sometimes causes labor to begin or speed up. It has become routine for a woman to undergo this procedure, called amniotomy, prior to chemical induction. Some women report that they feel a sharp pain when their sac is broken.

- *Chemical induction.* The most commonly used chemical induction method is pitocin, a synthetic hormone that mimics the natural hormone oxytocin, produced by both the mother and the fetus during labor. Pitocin is made from pituitary extracts from various mammals and is usually administered intravenously. Pitocin is also used to augment labor that has stopped or slowed down, or is not proceeding as quickly as the practitioner would like. Pitocin cannot be used if the woman's cervix is not yet ripe, so a prostaglandin cream is sometimes applied to it to make it become ripe. Another, newer type of chemical used to induce labor is misoprostol, commonly known by its brand name Cytotec and made by Searle. This comes in the form of a pill that is taken orally, or placed inside the uterus or rectum.

WHEN IS LABOR INDUCTION NECESSARY?

Experts vary in their estimates, but most agree that only 5 percent of labors require chemical induction. Listed below are the conditions that might indicate a medical necessity to induce:

- The amniotic sac has broken or is leaking, labor is not starting, and the woman has a fever, which may indicate infection. More conservative practitioners generally tend to want labor to begin within twenty-four hours. Some are willing to give it more time.
- Certain maternal medical problems, such as severe preeclampsia (which sometimes results in placental failure), might indicate it is best for the baby to be born earlier. Other problems such as high blood pressure or diabetes are sometimes cited as reasons to induce labor, but

the diagnosis of these is controversial (see "Third Trimester Common Concerns" in chapter 10 for more about gestational diabetes and preeclampsia).

- Severe blood incompatibility between the mother and baby. If antibodies are detected, it is likely that labor will be induced in order to keep the mother's antibodies from harming the baby.
- When a woman is simply too exhausted to continue because labor has gone on for many hours or days. In this case, a dose of pitocin might actually help prevent a cesarean section. In most cases, though, a woman is able to work through the exhaustion if given proper support and encouragement.
- Postdate pregnancy, where there is a proven danger to the baby. In a few cases, a pregnancy can go on for too long, and the placenta becomes unable to provide adequate nutrition. In this case, inducing labor may be necessary.
- Fetal death.

Unfortunately, few of these situations are clear-cut. For example, sometimes a postdate pregnancy does not constitute a dire situation at all, and it is safe to wait for the baby to be born on her own. Inducing labor has been the center of great controversy, since it is often difficult to determine whether it is done out of medical necessity or as a preventive measure.

WHEN IS LABOR INDUCTION UNNECESSARY?

Unfortunately, chemical induction of labor has become a routine procedure in many maternity hospitals. Here are some of the reasons labor is unnecessarily induced:

- To speed labor up because a practitioner, or the woman herself, feels that labor is taking too long, or because contractions have slowed down. This is known as labor augmentation. Labor has natural ebbs and flows, but many practitioners do not wait to see if things will speed up on their own. In fact, neither the Food and Drug Administration (FDA) nor the American College of Obstetricians and Gynecologists (ACOG) has ever approved the use of chemicals (such as pitocin) to augment labor.

- To get labor started once a woman's water has broken, even though there is no sign of infection.

- Because a woman seems tired during labor. Labor is exhausting, but women's bodies are built to handle the work. Most need encouragement to get past the rough spots. It is rare that a woman is so exhausted that she absolutely cannot go on without chemical induction.

- To avoid larger-than-average birth size associated with gestational diabetes. As we discuss in "Third Trimester Common Concerns" in chapter 10, this diagnosis is highly controversial.

- Because a woman has gone past her due date. Many doctors begin to suggest induction once a woman has gone three or four days past her due date. As we discussed in chapter 1, determining exact due date is very tricky unless you happen to know exactly when conception occurred. For this reason, many a supposedly postmature pregnancy has been induced, only to result in the birth of a premature infant. Even when the exact date of conception is known, 80 percent of healthy babies spend anywhere from thirty-eight to forty-two weeks in the womb.[10] The American College of Obstetricians and Gynecologists (ACOG) defines postmaturity as a pregnancy that lasts beyond forty-two weeks.

- Because a woman, or her physician, has decided she would like her baby to be born on a certain date for convenience's sake. This type of elective induction is not approved by the FDA or ACOG.

HOW EFFECTIVE IS LABOR INDUCTION?

Despite its widespread use, the chemical pitocin has a failure rate of 40 to 50 percent. When this happens, contractions are not brought on as desired. If pitocin doesn't work effectively, the physician might increase the dosage.

Even when strong contractions are produced, pitocin may not be effective in making labor progress. Potential problems associated with labor induction include:

- The need to be hooked up to an electronic fetal monitor (EFM). Chemical induction can produce contractions that can begin suddenly and are much stronger than natural contractions. Because these can put the baby in a state of distress, the baby's heart rate and respiration must be continuously monitored. Being hooked up to an EFM increases the chances of surgical intervention, which we will discuss in the next section.

- The need for epidural anesthesia, since the contractions produced by pitocin are almost always too painful for a woman to manage without medications. Epidural anesthesia requires an IV line for hydration, and a urinary catheter.

- Reduced mobility due to the IV, catheter, anesthesia line, and EFM. A woman whose labor is induced usually cannot move around or change labor positions. She is typically lying flat on her back, the position that is least effective in helping labor to progress. If she has had an epidural, her lower extremities are probably too numb to allow her to stand up, anyway.

- Increased chance of cesarean section. Distress to the baby caused by high levels of pitocin, combined with slowed labor and the mother's exhaustion, often results in the need for a cesarean.

IS LABOR INDUCTION SAFE?

In 1998, the U.S. induction rate was 19.4 percent.[11] Augmentation rates for births attended by obstetricians are 17 percent, according to one study.[12] Other studies have shown overall rates of 60 to 80 percent in certain areas of the country. Yet Roberto Caldeyro-Barcia, M.D., former president of the International Federation of Obstetricians and Gynecologists, estimates that in only 3 percent of pregnancies is induction medically necessary.[13] The

World Health Organization has called for an upper limit of 10 percent induction rate in any given region.

The safety of using misoprostol, marketed under the brand name Cytotec, to induce labor is the subject of tremendous controversy. This chemical has never been approved for use during labor by the FDA, yet it has become a favorite of many practitioners and is growing in popularity every year. It was originally created for the treatment of peptic ulcers—and its manufacturers insist that it is only recommended for that purpose. The drug's package insert specifically states, "Cytotec may cause the uterus to rupture during pregnancy if it is used to bring on labor."

One of the reasons for Cytotec's popularity is that it induces labor before a woman's cervix has ripened. There is no need to use prostaglandin creams first. Cytotec is also much easier to administer. It comes in the form of a pill that can be swallowed or inserted into the vagina or rectum.

The use of Cytotec has had negative consequences for many women. Studies of its use have shown significant problems, including hemorrhages, emergency hysterectomies after birth, brain-damaged babies, stillbirths, and even some maternal deaths. Pitocin, while less potentially dangerous than Cytotec, also has a history of problems. It can occasionally create contractions strong enough to cause uterine rupture, although this is rare. Another potential risk of pitocin, particularly when used in early labor, is dangerous amounts of water retention in the mother, which can occasionally result in coma, convulsions, or even death. Some recent research also indicates a possible link between the use of pitocin and autism.[14]

As mentioned earlier, both Cytotec and pitocin tend to create a domino effect of increasingly aggressive medical interventions.

Even the less invasive practices of membrane stripping and breaking the waters are not without potential risks, including more painful contractions or the accidental breaking of the amniotic sac during the procedure of membrane stripping. If labor does not begin shortly afterward, the mother is at risk of infection. This puts a time limit on how long labor can continue—once the sac is broken, there is no turning back. In this case, more serious methods of induction might be needed.

Avoiding postmaturity is often the reason for induction. True postmaturity can be dangerous, with an increasing chance of fetal distress and mortality, as well as meconium aspiration, a condition where the baby breathes in amniotic fluid that contains fecal matter, and dysmaturity syndrome, where a baby's overall health is threatened by being in a declining environment in the uterus.

In most cases, though, it is simply not known whether a postmature pregnancy is the actual cause of increased risk to a baby, or whether babies who are inherently at higher risk are more likely to be overdue. More research needs to be done in this area. However, even when true postmaturity occurs, most of these babies overcome problems after birth and go on to be healthy.[15] In fact, while ACOG estimates that 95 percent of postterm babies are born safely between forty-two and forty-four weeks,[16] very few practitioners ever allow a woman to go past week forty, although midwives tend to be more patient in this area.

The biggest problem with labor induction is its very concept. Why do we think we know better than Mother Nature when a baby should leave the womb? The forces that trigger birth are still poorly understood. No one really knows what causes labor to start. Some think that birth is initially triggered by the brain of the soon-to-be-born infant, when it has developed enough to leave the womb. Although much about the initiation of labor is mysterious, we do know that the mechanism is complex, with far more triggering it than the simple release of a hormone such as oxytocin.

Unfortunately, many practitioners are driven by a desire to control the birth process. Induction is often viewed as a means to prevent pain and discomfort in their patients. Because many practitioners believe chemical induction is harmless, they use it to schedule labor so that it fits within an orderly time frame, rather than allowing nature to take its course. However, ACOG does not condone induction without medical necessity, and neither ACOG nor the FDA approves of induction for speeding up labor that has already started.

It isn't just medical personnel who contribute to overuse of induction methods. In our speed-oriented culture, we are not typically encouraged to be patient. In addition, we tend to view medical providers as authority figures, so we hesitate to question their opinions. However, childbirth is one area of our lives that does not happen on a medical timetable. Birth is proven to be safest when allowed to happen in its own time.

Natural Induction Methods

Natural methods of induction have been used for many years by women all over the world—they are considerably less invasive than modern medical interventions, and far less likely to trigger the cascade of unnecessary medical procedures. If you are working with a midwife, she may suggest natural induction methods to you as your due date approaches. These approaches are likely to get labor going only if your body, and the baby's body, are ready to begin anyway.

No matter what method of induction you are considering, it is imperative that you work in conjunction with your health care provider to ensure a safe experience. Before blindly agreeing to any in-

---

HIGHER GROUND
My Baby Knows

Remember that your due date is just an estimate. Nine months is an average. Each baby has her own length of gestation. Try to set a range rather than a date as the time to expect the baby. Instead of "the baby is due on December 20," say, "The baby is due in late December." Add a couple of weeks to your due date so you can relax and not be inundated by well-meaning phone calls toward the end of your pregnancy.

Here's a visualization exercise you can use if you're worried about the due date of your baby.

Find a place where you can sit quietly for fifteen to thirty minutes. Take a few deep breaths and bring your attention to your breathing. Place your hands on your abdomen as you slow your breathing by letting your breaths get longer and longer.

Begin to imagine your baby. Silently say to yourself:

My body has everything my baby needs.

My body knows how to give birth.

My baby knows when to be born.

Repeat these phrases a few times as you breathe deeply with your hands on your abdomen. Turn them into a song if you like.

Finish with a few moments of silent breathing.

133

duction method, both you and your provider need to be sure that induction is in the best interest of the baby.

Before deciding to induce your labor, consider your reasons carefully. While many of the natural methods discussed in this section are relatively benign—such as going for a walk—make sure your motivation isn't simply impatience, and don't allow other people—whether they're doctors or friends—to put pressure on you because they feel you've been pregnant too long.

While nature has reasons for keeping your baby in your womb for the time being, here are descriptions of some of the time-honored methods of natural induction:

NIPPLE STIMULATION

Nipple stimulation has been long used by midwives to either ripen the cervix or start labor. In fact, breastfeeding produces natural oxytocin, which makes the uterus contract and promotes healing after childbirth. For the same reason, nipple stimulation can trigger labor.

One study compared nipple stimulation with a breast pump to chemical induction with oxytocin. There was no difference in the amount of time it took for labor to begin in both groups. However, the time it took to reach the active phase of labor was significantly shorter in the women who had used nipple stimulation.[17]

You may find that having a partner perform the stimulation or doing it yourself is much more effective than using a pump to do it. While there is no absolute prescribed length of time, you might try the stimulation three times per day for up to an hour.

SEXUAL INTERCOURSE

It is believed that this helps to induce labor because male sperm is high in prostaglandins. These cause the woman's cervix to begin to ripen. As well, the contractions of the uterus during orgasm may help to stimulate labor, and nipple stimulation during lovemaking may also contribute.

If you decide to try this, it may be best to choose a man-on-top position so that the sperm has the best chance of doing its job.

WALKING AND EXERCISE

Moving around during labor can help speed things up. It is also thought that going for a long walk may help bring labor on. Proceed at whatever pace is most comfortable for you, but don't walk until you are utterly exhausted.

HERBS

Although there is a long history of herbal induction by midwives, studies on the use of herbal preparations to induce labor have not been conducted. Here are several time-tested methods; consult your midwife or health care provider about trying these.

- 3 capsules of evening primrose oil daily for up to a week.
- 10 drops of black cohosh tincture under the tongue each hour. Continue until your practitioner says your cervix is soft and ripe.
- 3 to 8 drops of blue cohosh tincture in warm water or tea. Take every half-hour for several hours; this only works if your cervix is already ripe. If, after four hours, labor does not begin, put a dropperful of the tincture under your tongue every hour for up to four hours.
- Red raspberry leaf tea can help to strengthen contractions that have already started.

HOMEOPATHY

Consult a homeopath to find the correct remedy for you. *Caulophyllum 30* is often used six times a day to stimulate labor.[18]

ENEMAS

No one really knows why enemas stimulate labor. There is no research to back up its effectiveness, though it has been used by midwives for generations. Check with your practitioner.

NATURAL SOOTHER

Blue and Black Cohosh

Along with raspberry leaves, blue and black cohosh have been used in later pregnancy for hundreds of years to prepare women's bodies for childbirth. They are not safe to use during early pregnancy, but can be safely consumed in tea form during the last four to six weeks of pregnancy.

Like raspberry leaves, blue and black cohosh have both stimulating and relaxing properties that facilitate childbirth. Blue cohosh tones the uterus and promotes regular and effective contractions. Black cohosh is a powerful painkiller specifically for nerve and muscle pain. It is one of the best remedies for ovarian and uterine pain. Drinking blue and black cohosh in tea form during the last month of pregnancy helps to prepare the uterus for birth.

1. Fill a teapot with cold water and bring to a boil.

2. Meanwhile, fill a clean teapot with hot water from the tap. Let it sit until the water boils, then empty the teapot.

3. Place 2 tablespoons dried black cohosh and 2 tablespoons dried blue cohosh into the teapot.

7. Add 1 pint of boiling water to teapot.

8. Steep for 10 minutes.

9. Strain, pour into a cup, and sip slowly.

To make a cup of tea, use half the amount of leaves and water. Drink 1 to 3 cups of this tea a day during the last month of pregnancy.

ACUPUNCTURE

The use of acupuncture for inducing labor is well accepted in Asia and Europe, and it is becoming more common in this country. It is known to be effective in stimulating labor.[19]

Acupuncture is performed with dles or electrical stimulation at the body. You need to see a trained a acupuncturist in order to have this procedure Some midwives are trained in using acupressure, where the hands are used to stimulate the correct points on the body, rather than needles.

Electronic Fetal Monitoring (EFM)

Prior to the 1970s the baby's heart rate was checked intermittently, every fifteen minutes or so, by a maternity nurse using a fetal stethoscope or a hand-held Doppler ultrasound monitor on the laboring mother's belly. When the electronic fetal monitor (EFM) was first invented, it was heralded as an incredible time-saving device that could free the nurse up to minister to her patients in other ways. It was also a more accurate method of checking on the baby's well-being continuously, rather than just every few minutes. By the 1980s, the use of EFMs had become routine practice in most hospitals.

WHY IS AN EFM USED?

An EFM is used to assess the baby's heart rate and respiration levels during labor, to ensure both are staying within a safe range. In some cases, a fetus can become overly stressed by labor. If that happens, steps will be taken to help the baby, such as giving the mother oxygen to increase the baby's oxygen levels or performing a cesarean section.

The idea behind continuous monitoring, rather than intermittent stethoscope monitoring, is that care providers receive immediate notification if there are any serious changes in the baby's heart rate. It is also meant to monitor gradual changes to the baseline heart rate.

EFM monitoring is also used during late pregnancy tests that assess the well-being of a fetus that is postdate.

HOW IS AN EFM USED?

There are two types of EFMs: external and internal. When the external type is used, two large straps or wide elastic bands are placed around your belly. One of them has a Doppler device on it that uses ultrasound to measure the baby's heart rate. The other strap has a pressure-sensitive device that detects your contractions.

The internal type of monitor, which is more accurate, requires that your waters be broken. A wire is placed inside your vagina and attached to the baby's scalp with electrode clips. A catheter is put inside your uterus to measure your contractions.

Whichever method is used, the information gathered by the monitor is sent to a small box by the side of your bed. This box displays and records information on a screen or paper tape.

If the baby is handling labor well, the heart rate accelerates during contractions due to oxygen deprivation, then returns to normal once the contraction is over. If there is an irregularity in the baby's heart rate, the EFM sounds alarm.

WHEN IS THE USE OF AN EFM NECESSARY?

Experts are divided on this issue: some see EFMs as a help, others as a detriment. Most professionals believe that continuous EFM is essential during chemical induction or epidural anesthesia, because the chemicals used can cause sudden changes in the baby's heart rate. As discussed in the section on labor induction, the intense contractions resulting from induction can stress the fetus by depriving him of oxygen during contractions. The EFM might show that, over a period of several contractions, the baby is in distress. Other experts believe that intermittent monitoring with a stethoscope is just as effective, even during induction and epidural.

WHEN IS THE USE OF AN EFM UNNECESSARY?

In many hospitals, it is standard practice to use an EFM from the moment a woman enters the door, regardless of any other aspect of her labor. Some hospitals are very rigid in this policy, and will allow no exceptions. Such routine use of EFM is not necessary, and has not been shown to be more effec-

tive than the use of intermittent monitoring with a stethoscope.

HOW EFFECTIVE IS THE USE OF AN EFM?

Several well-conducted studies have not been able to show a benefit in using a constant EFM rather than intermittent monitoring, such as with a stethoscope, for a normal-risk pregnancy. There was no improvement in death rates or Apgar scores for infants who were continuously monitored. The American College of Obstetricians and Gynecologists now supports a policy of using intermittent monitoring. Despite this fact, many hospitals continue to use continuous EFM. One reason for this may be that nurses and doctors are no longer well trained in interpreting intermittent monitoring.[20]

Hospitals have also become dependent upon EFM in terms of manpower allocation. It takes more time to check a woman every fifteen minutes by hand than to use EFM. The obvious benefit to the woman is that intermittent monitoring guarantees her personal attention every fifteen minutes.

Despite this, electronic fetal monitors are notoriously unreliable and require constant repositioning as the woman or baby move around. If she shifts from side to side, the straps will shift as well, often causing an alarm to go off because no heartbeat is being detected. It is also possible to confuse the mother's heart rate with the baby's, causing panic if the practitioners believe that the baby's heart rate has suddenly dropped.

Another big problem with EFMs is that they often malfunction, causing an alarm to go off for no reason. When this happens, it causes a moment of panic for both the care provider and the mother, adding to the stress of the situation.

IS IT SAFE TO USE AN EFM?

The biggest problem with the safety of constant fetal monitoring is in the interpretation of results. Babies' heart rates do change significantly during contractions. Sometimes babies even fall asleep, causing doctors to worry that fetal distress is happening when it is not.[21] Studies have shown that when EFMs are used, C-section rates increase.[22] If the diagnosis of fetal distress is followed up by blood tests to confirm distress, C-section rates are not as high, but these tests are often not performed. There is also concern that EFM may prolong labor, perhaps because it restricts women's movement. The ability to walk around and change position has been shown to help labor progress.

Another potential side effect of EFM is infection or abscess in the baby's scalp if an internal monitor is attached to his scalp. Because EFM works with ultrasound, all of the concerns about the safety of ultrasound that were discussed in chapter 5 apply. You and your baby are exposed to ultrasound waves for several hours.

If you must use a hospital where EFM is used routinely, try to work out a compromise. If the doctor is unwilling to allow intermittent monitoring with a stethoscope, perhaps he will consent to intermittent monitoring with the EFM. Some EFMs use telemetry, which transmits information from the sensors to the box via remote. Since no wires are used, you can move about more easily. If you are concerned about the effect of EFMs on your baby, check out your birth location's policy ahead of time, and consider using a facility where the use of EFM is not mandatory.

Cesarean Sections

The cesarean section, perhaps more than any other major surgical procedure, has enormous life-saving potential. According to popular legend, Julius Caesar was born this way, and this is how the name "Cesarean section" was created. For hundreds of years, however, a successful cesarean birth meant death to the mother. Since history shows that Caesar's mother was still alive when he was an adult, it is unlikely that he was actually birthed this way.

We are fortunate to live in a time when this procedure usually means that both infant and mother will survive. In the unlikely event that something goes wrong, cesareans are a blessing indeed.

Cesarean sections are now so commonly practiced that we even have a nickname for them—"C-sections." Since one in four babies in the United States is now born via surgery, most of us probably know several people who have undergone this procedure.

WHY ARE CESAREAN SECTIONS USED?

In theory, a cesarean section is used to remove a baby from the mother's womb surgically when, for some reason, a vaginal birth cannot happen or would endanger the life or health of the mother or child.

In practice, however, cesarean sections are often used before the possibility of vaginal birth has been completely ruled out. To understand why this is true, we need to look carefully at how this surgery is performed and the specific reasons it is done.

HOW ARE CESAREAN SECTIONS DONE?

Because a small percentage of women truly require surgical intervention during labor, it is a good idea to learn about C-sections. This can alleviate your fears if cesarean becomes necessary for you. First, a nurse will shave your upper pubic area and abdomen to remove hair. You will be given intravenous liquids to keep you hydrated, and a catheter will be inserted to collect your urine while you are under the effects of anesthesia.

Epidural anesthesia is most commonly used during cesarean sections. This will allow you to be awake during the procedure, and to see your baby right away. In a serious emergency, there is not always time to wait for an epidural to take effect, requiring the use of general anesthesia, given in the form of an inhaled gas that will put you to sleep completely. Because it can impair your baby's health, general anesthesia is typically avoided.

In the operating room, a surgical nurse will wash your belly to make it sterile. A drape will be put up that will mask your view of your lower body. You can ask to have it lowered so that you can witness the moment the baby is pulled out of your body.

Cesareans can be very frightening. In addition to the stress created by worries over your baby's health and fear associated with surgery, you will be surrounded by strange people, unfamiliar equipment, and a sterile environment. Fortunately, your partner can almost always be with you during a cesarean. Once the anesthetic has taken effect, the surgeon will make a small horizontal incision just above your pubic bone. You may feel tugging or pressure, though you will feel no pain, as the baby is pulled from your uterus. In many cases, babies born this way need a little help to begin breathing (such as a bit of oxygen or a rubdown), since they didn't experience the stimulation provided by moving down the birth canal.

The baby will most likely be handed to your partner. You might be able to cuddle with the baby against your shoulder with a bit of assistance. While this is happening, your placenta will be removed, and you will be sutured. The birth itself takes less than ten minutes. The stitching will take fifteen to thirty minutes more.

WHEN ARE CESAREAN SECTIONS NECESSARY?

As with many medical procedures, especially those involving birth, clear-cut definitions of necessity are difficult. These situations always require cesarean surgery:

- *Placenta previa.* For unknown reasons, the placenta sometimes grows partially or completely over the cervical opening. A vaginal birth could tear the placenta, depriving the baby of oxygen and nourishment. It is sometimes possible to deliver vaginally if there is only partial placenta previa, but otherwise a cesarean section will definitely be necessary. Keep in mind that diagnosis of placenta previa early in pregnancy via ultrasound is unreliable, as the large majority of cases will resolve themselves naturally.

- *Prolapsed umbilical cord.* When the umbilical cord comes out of the cervical opening before the baby does, there is a danger that the baby's oxygen supply could be cut off. This condition also calls for an emergency C-section.

The conditions below might require cesarean section, although surgery may not be necessary depending on the circumstances:

- *Active herpes at the time of labor.* While this usually indicates surgery, the amount and exact position of the lesions should be taken into account. Sometimes lesions can be covered with bandages, and vaginal delivery is possible.
- *Transverse lie.* In this condition, the baby is positioned sideways in the mother's belly. If the baby cannot be moved into a viable birthing position, transverse lie almost always indicates a cesarean section.
- *Cephalopelvic disproportion.* This is when the baby's head is simply too large to pass through the pelvis. Although physicians often schedule a cesarean section ahead of time for a baby they believe has cephalopelvic disproportion, the condition is rare, and can only be determined when you are actually in labor.[23]
- *Decision to end pregnancy early.* This might be done if the baby has a medical condition that can be better treated outside the womb.
- *Severe preeclampsia or uncontrolled diabetes.* Although these conditions often require cesarean section, sometimes even before the due date in order to protect the health of the baby and mother, each situation should be assessed individually.

WHEN ARE CESAREAN SECTIONS UNNECESSARY?

Many experts are concerned and outraged that the United States' rate of cesarean section is among the highest in the developed world. The World Health Organization has called for a cap of 10 to 15 percent of C-sections worldwide. At 25 percent, the United

States has some work to do to measure up to that goal.

One reason that experts know cesarean rates are too high is demographics: increased surgery rates are often attributed to place and provider, rather than to specific medical conditions. For example:

- A woman has a 40 percent higher chance of having a C-section if her birth is attended by a male ob/gyn, rather than a female ob/gyn.[24]

- Midwives have a cesarean section rate of only 11.6 percent in the United States,[25] compared with 18.4 percent in large teaching hospitals, 21.2 percent in community hospitals, and 24.3 percent in community teaching hospitals.[26]

- The Netherlands' C-section rates are less than 10 percent. In most of Europe, the C-section rates hover around 5 percent. In some parts of Latin America, the rates are as high as 85 percent!

- Research shows that women who are white, married, and have private health insurance giving birth in private hospitals have higher surgery rates.[27]

These facts suggest a huge disparity between real necessity for surgery and other factors, such as doctor's beliefs about birth, financial considerations, convenience, and the overuse of medical interventions that tend to lead to cesareans, such as pitocin and epidurals.

Just why are so many unnecessary cesareans performed? Consider these points:

- *Failure to progress.* Doctors often perform cesareans because labor goes on for too long and is not progressing. To determine whether cesarean is warranted, it's important to define whether "too long" indicates a risk of health problems to mother and baby, or whether it simply means labor is not adhering to a predetermined timetable.

- *Fetal distress.* If your baby is having a hard time with the delivery, the fear is that his or her health might be compromised. This does hap-

pen to some babies, and surgery can save their lives. Many experts, however, believe this is done too frequently without good medical cause. Fear of litigation is, without a doubt, a big factor in a physician's decision to opt for surgery when he is not sure. Electronic fetal monitors have been the main culprit in causing physicians to incorrectly believe that the infant is experiencing distress.

- *Breech position.* Most infants in the breech position, where the baby comes out legs or buttocks first instead of headfirst, are delivered via cesarean section automatically. This accounts for about 4 to 5 percent of all cesarean procedures. Sometimes the cesarean is even scheduled by doctors before the woman goes into labor. There is no conclusive evidence that cesarean delivery of breech babies is safer than vaginal birth. At one time, there was a belief that breech babies showed signs of higher IQ and less cerebral palsy when they were delivered with cesarean section. This theory has since been disproved.[28] Some experts see this use of C-sections as a self-fulfilling prophecy. The more surgery is used for the breech position, in the belief that it is safer, the less skilled our health care providers become in delivering breech babies vaginally.[29] There are doctors and midwives who are skilled in this type of delivery, although they are hard to find. It pays to ask about this when you are choosing your health care provider. (See "Breech Births" later in this chapter for more ideas on how to deal with breech position.)

- *Twins.* Studies have not shown that automatic delivery of twins via C-section is statistically safer. There may be good reasons to deliver twins through surgery, if one or both of them is in distress, is very underweight, or has a health problem that needs to be immediately addressed. Vaginal delivery of twins is rapidly turning into another "lost art," much like breech delivery.

- *Large baby.* Some physicians will schedule a cesarean just because the baby looks too big to them. This is not a legitimate reason for surgery.[30] As mentioned earlier, true cephalopelvic disproportion, when an infant's head is too large to pass through the birth canal, is quite rare and can only be determined once labor has begun.
- *Health problems in the mother.* Hypertension, diabetes, and other conditions don't necessarily require C-sections, but many physicians perform them just to be on the "safe side."
- *Previous cesarean section.* Vaginal birth after a cesarean (VBAC) is a subject of ongoing debate. In fact, previous cesarean sections are one of the primary causes of our current high cesarean rates. While a second C-section is not necessarily medically indicated, it is commonplace. We'll talk more about VBACs later in this chapter.
- *Convenience.* Some women plan to have a cesarean delivery even when there is no indication that it is necessary. This might be done to ensure the baby is born at a specific, convenient time—or to avoid the experience of labor altogether. Some women believe they are too small to deliver vaginally. This is rarely true. C-sections are major surgery and carry with them all the potential complications and discomforts of such surgery. Perhaps most importantly, babies who are born vaginally are immediately more alert and better functioning. This is also true of babies who experience labor, even when a C-section is the ultimate result.

HOW EFFECTIVE ARE CESAREAN SECTIONS?

As noted earlier, cesarean sections are one of the best examples of the wonders of modern medicine. Not only is this surgery potentially life-saving, but you end up with a baby after it's all over! Cesarean sections do indeed accomplish what they set out to do: deliver a baby that might otherwise not have survived, or might have survived with severely compromised health.

As a routine method for birthing babies, cesareans are not quite as effective. Despite escalating rates of cesarean sections (only 5 percent in 1970 compared with 25 percent in the late 1990s), birth outcomes have not improved—mortality rates have not gone down, and the general health of mothers and newborns has not changed.

ARE CESAREAN SECTIONS SAFE?

It bears repeating: a cesarean section is major surgery. Like any other surgical procedure, it involves a number of risks and consequences, both physical and emotional. As it is for all mothers, your primary concern will be the health of your baby. During vaginal birth, natural hormones are released that contribute to the well-being of the baby. Some of these, called catecholamines, the so-called "fight-or-flight" hormones, help the baby to breathe, retain body heat, remain alert, and control pupil dilation to see the mother better. Babies who are born via cesarean miss out on these health benefits, although babies who are born surgically seem to do better if the mother has been in labor prior to the surgery.[31] Babies born through elective cesareans often have breathing difficulties. Anesthesia administered during the surgery contributes to this problem.

In terms of the mother's health, current statistics show that the risk of death to the mother from a C-section is approximately one in 1,000, two to four times that of vaginal birth.[32] Contributing factors to maternal death include reactions to anesthesia, infection, and hemorrhage. Many women who have cesareans require rehospitalization for various reasons, including infection, gallbladder disease, urinary tract conditions, and appendicitis. Women who have had cesarean sections seem to be at increased risk for ectopic pregnancy, placenta abruptio, and placenta previa in future pregnancies.[33]

Also of great importance is the psychological effect that a cesarean section can have on a woman. Most women who have cesarean sections reported that the experience was traumatic. One study of women who underwent emergency C-sections showed that 52 percent of them had various forms of post-traumatic stress disorder one to two months after the baby was born.[34] Other women leave their birth experience feeling disappointed, and perhaps even angry with themselves for not being able to have the birth they'd hoped for.

It is not just doctors who are to blame for the increasing rates of cesareans. Unfortunately, our litigation-conscious society has also helped C-section rates to soar. With malpractice cases skyrocketing, it's not difficult to understand why the slightest sign of fetal distress may cause physicians to head straight for the operating room.

Vaginal Birth after a Cesarean (VBAC)

"Once a cesarean, always a cesarean." The reasoning behind this outdated cliché was that a woman who had undergone a previous cesarean section had a scarred, weakened uterus that could more easily rupture during the stress of another labor and delivery.

Fortunately, cesarean surgery has changed and improved over the years. Once upon a time, a woman having a C-section would receive a long vertical scar from her navel to her pubic bone. Now, a cesarean can be performed with a low horizontal cut popularly referred to as a "bikini cut," only three or four inches wide. This horizontal type of incision is much more stable for future deliveries. For most women, a vaginal birth, even though they have had a cesarean section in the past, is a realistic possibility.

WHY IS VBAC USED?

The reason is simple: vaginal birth is safer than surgery. As noted in the section on cesarean surgery, there is a 1 in 1,000 mortality rate for women who have C-sections. This is two to four times the rate for vaginal birth. Most women want to have a trauma-free birth experience and postpartum period. As well, most women want to feel in control of their experience. Vaginal birth is the best way to achieve this. With vaginal birth, you can enter the postpartum period in good shape for the weeks to come.

WHEN IS VBAC UNSAFE?

This is the subject of controversy in the medical world. Many doctors and midwives recommend strongly against attempting VBAC if you had a "classic" cesarean incision—a long vertical cut that increases the chance that the uterus might rupture during labor. Other practitioners feel that it is safe to attempt VBAC, no matter what type of scar you have.

Resolving this disagreement is difficult. Since women with classic incisions are now rare, and since most have been prohibited from trying a VBAC in recent years, there are no statistics available to support either point of view.

The most clear-cut indications that a woman should not attempt VBAC are health conditions such as placenta previa and abruptio placenta, which call for emergency cesareans. If a baby is clearly in distress, cesarean will be performed regardless of the mother's previous birth history. One very common reason for elective repeat cesareans is small body size. Many petite women are convinced that they can't handle vaginal birth. In fact, there is no evidence to back this up. Small women can give birth to very large babies, even if they've had a previous cesarean. Only in cases of true cephalopelvic disproportion (where the baby's head is too large to fit through the birth canal) is this true, although this rare condition cannot be identified until labor has begun. Yet many small women are given cesareans because of this concern. When it comes to the second baby, many do not even bother attempting VBAC, and opt for a scheduled, elective C-section. Yet research has shown that going into labor, even if it later leads to a C-section, is beneficial to the baby. Hormones that come into place only after labor has begun improve the baby's respiratory system and state of alertness at birth.

HOW EFFECTIVE IS VBAC?

Current statistics show that the success of a VBAC is strongly influenced by environment. The current nationwide rate for VBACs is 24.9 percent. However, certified nurse-midwives have a successful VBAC rate of 68.9 percent overall.[35] In some practices, the rate is as high as 80 to 90 percent—the rate recommended by the World Health Organization. One reason for this might be that women who have had cesareans are generally treated as high-risk patients by practitioners, who typically require electronic fetal monitors and IV lines as precautionary measures. As discussed earlier, these and other routine procedures tend to necessitate chemical induction, pain relief, and ultimately, another cesarean section.

If you would like to try VBAC, your best bet is to carefully research the practitioner and facility you want to use. Select a practitioner with at least a 70 percent success rate with VBACs, one who feels that you are a good candidate and who will actively encourage you through the rough spots of labor and delivery.

When you tour the facility you are considering, listen carefully to your intuition about the place. Aside from asking about their success rate with VBACs, talk to the staff and listen for encouragement about VBAC. If you don't feel that the staff is enthusiastic about this concept, consider using another facility, such as a birth center, or having a home birth attended by a midwife with lots of experience with VBACs. VBAC is a terrific example of how one-on-one, woman-to-woman support by a doula is the number-one aid to a smooth delivery. If you're having a VBAC, a doula is even more essential. She can act as an intermediary between you and medical personnel, which will improve your chances of success.

Learn all that you can about VBACs, and consider contacting a support group such as the International Cesarean Awareness Network (ICAN), which can guide you through the experience (See appendix 2 for contact information on this group.).

IS VBAC SAFE?

As noted earlier, the main safety concern of VBAC is the risk of uterine rupture. However, a woman attempting VBAC has a 99.8 percent chance of birthing without a uterine rupture.[36] In addition, most studies show that no woman or baby has ever died from a uterine rupture, no matter what type of incision the women had. On the other hand, women *have* died from complications of cesareans, and the death rates are higher in repeat cesareans.

In any event, the words "uterine rupture" evoke terrifying images of the uterus tearing in two. In truth, the uterus typically tears slowly, not all at once, and is accompanied by noticeable symptoms. Uterine rupture can happen to any woman in any pregnancy. It can even happen before labor begins, although this is not common.

Breech Births

As noted earlier, breech babies are frequently delivered by cesarean. In fact, breeches account for about 4 to 5 percent of all cesarean births. In many parts of the country, cesarean sections are automatically performed without even giving vaginal birth a try, although no conclusive evidence exists that cesarean delivery of breech babies is safer than vaginal birth.

By thirty-two weeks, most babies are in a head-down position in the mother's womb. This is the ideal birth position. About 3 to 4 percent of babies, however, remain in what is known as a breech position as birth approaches. In a complete breech position, the baby is curled up in the standard fetal pose, with her head up in the womb and her bottom facing the cervical opening. In a frank breech position, the small of the baby's back is facing the cervical opening, and in a footling breech position, the baby's feet are facing the cervical opening.

Sadly, fewer and fewer physicians are even being trained to deliver breech babies vaginally. Many new ob/gyns never even see one example of this in their training. However, there are midwives and doctors who are skilled in birthing breech babies. It is important to seek them out if you find yourself with a baby in the breech position toward the end of your pregnancy. If you'll be delivering a breech baby vaginally, a doula will be even more vital for a successful experience.

In the meantime, there are a number of methods you can use to try to turn your baby, so she is in a better birth position:

- *Breech tilt.* This exercise can successfully turn a breech baby, sometimes within a single week. It can safely be done during the third trimester, but only if your birth attendant has confirmed

that your baby is in the breech position and you want the baby to turn head-down to avoid a cesarean. For maximum effectiveness, the breech tilt should be started between the thirtieth and thirty-fourth weeks of pregnancy.

- *Moxibustion.* Usually performed by an experienced acupuncturist, this technique involves burning Chinese herbs on sticks to stimulate certain acupuncture points. This technique has

BODY WISE
Breech Tilt

Prepare a surface where you can lie down comfortably on the floor. Have several pillows ready.

Get on your hands and knees and breathe deeply for a few minutes.

Sit up.

Lie down on your back on a hard surface for ten minutes with enough pillows under your pelvis to raise it to a height of 9 to 12 inches above your head.

Lie in this posture with your pelvis raised as described above twice daily for 10 minutes at a time.

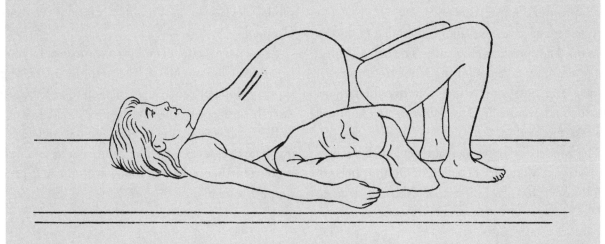

Perform the breech tilt on an empty stomach. Wear loose clothing or do the posture nude. Do not wear a leotard or constrict your abdomen in any way.

This position can be effective as long as the baby has not dropped too deeply into the pelvis. Practice the posture for four to six weeks or until the baby turns head-down. Ask your birth attendant to check the baby's position frequently, as he could turn within a week. Once the baby has turned head-down, discontinue the breech tilt at once and begin walking frequently to help the baby snuggle down into your pelvis.

been shown to be effective in getting some breech babies to turn to a head-down position.

- *External version.* This technique is usually done around the thirty-seventh week of pregnancy. Using ultrasound and an electronic fetal monitor, the doctor or midwife will attempt to turn the baby with external manipulation of the mother's abdomen. This is usually done in an office setting, but might take place in a hospital. It can be quite uncomfortable for the woman. The majority of babies stay in the head-down position after this is done, but some do turn back into a breech position. If that happens, one more attempt may be tried before labor begins.

Active Management of Labor

You will most likely never hear the term *active management of labor* while you are in a hospital. Nonetheless, it is a real medical philosophy that can have a profound impact on you.

Active management of labor is intended to make a woman's labor progress efficiently. The belief behind this philosophy is that allowing labor to progress at its own rate puts some women at risk for fatigue, which could eventually cause labor to stall and lead to a cesarean section.

The model for active management of labor was the National Maternity Hospital in Dublin, Ireland, well known for its support of laboring women and low rates of cesarean. At National Maternity Hospital, women underwent a thorough course in childbirth education and were assigned a labor nurse-midwife who remained with them constantly during labor, providing expert one-on-one support from a sympathetic woman. A woman's labor was expected to keep pace with the set criteria (1 to 2 centimeters' dilation per hour). If that did not happen, then techniques such as induction would be used to speed things along. In fact, National Maternity Hospital's rates of C-section were quite low.

Studies of this philosophy have shown that the reason behind its success is the one-on-one support women receive during birth. This kind of continuous attention has been definitively shown to shorten labor and reduce the necessity for C-sections, forceps deliveries, and other interventions.

Unfortunately, hospitals that espouse active management of labor have tended to focus on using machinery and chemicals to control and speed up the process of birth. Sadly, active management of labor has come to exemplify the opposite of the original model developed at Dublin's National Maternity Hospital.

As we have seen, reliance on one medical intervention during labor tends to lead to the next, creating a slippery slope of procedures that, all too often, leads directly to the operating room.

Birth, however, is safest when left to progress at its own rate in its own way. The baby has a timetable for his own birth, one we can follow with the help of our support team and birth attendant.

PART FOUR

Labor and Delivery

What makes a good birth experience [depends on] how we discover that energy
and enthusiasm that carry us through any challenging situation in life.

—SUZANNE ARMS, *Immaculate Deception*

Chapter 11 covered the concept of learning to have a relationship with the unexpected. The reason why this is such an important skill to develop is because labor and birth can't really be predicted. There are as many unique birth stories as there are people to tell them.

To give you an idea of how true this really is, we have compiled a selection of diverse birth stories for you to read. You will see, after reading these tales, how very difficult it is to really summarize the birth experience, and how richly varied labor and birth can be.

A Home Birth: Lisa's Story

Our second child, a boy, was born on a Saturday afternoon last fall. The sky was blue, a gentle breeze rustled the leaves, and the clouds floated along as I labored. The midwife arrived at our home at 2:30 P.M. I was dilated 2.5 centimeters, very excited, and a little scared.

I went for a long walk in the neighborhood with my midwife, Shelly, my doula, Anna, and my husband, Stephen. I was keenly aware of my surroundings. I walked with my arm around Shelly's shoulders, and with each contraction I would gently squeeze her. Just as I reached my street, I truly fell into labor. It was a downward force that pulled me toward the center of the earth, a drawing down that took my legs with it. I grabbed for Stephen's hand and fell into the three of them. "How the hell am I going to make it across the street and down the last block?" I remember saying to Stephen. "Get the ?*&% car!" I was being sucked into the very ground.

Home, in bed, I just wanted to rest, to sleep. Shelly had checked me when we returned from the walk. I was hovering around 7 centimeters. It hurt. My back. My front. I asked Stephen to call Eliot, my acupuncturist, and shortly he arrived, bearing roses. The baby was moving through me, and I was spreading out across the room. I was being pulled in every direction, up, down, sideways, lengthwise, and it hurt. The pain of countertension. The force of pulling apart. The quiet fullness between contractions when the baby and I were still one, rocking and waiting to pull again.

Then I felt a transfer of energy. "Lisa, how do you want to do this? Your side, sitting?" Shelly asked. I chose to sit. Stephen massaged my belly. Up, up, up, I was now feeling. I was deep under this child, and we were rising. I felt the head between my legs, the full, tight, stuck feeling. I could actually feel him moving inside me. It was very sensual and exciting, but he did not want to linger. He wanted out. And then one howling push, and the baby was free.

Everything moves quickly now. There are tears in

everyone's eyes. I deliver the placenta, we cut the cord, I receive a single stitch. I breastfeed. The midwife and my doula move about, working efficiently. The storm has passed, and now we clean up. But, oh, how good everything feels. I get up and am escorted to the shower. Eliot passes the soap. Shelly combs my hair.

I am back in my bed, and my little man lies naked across my chest. Having spent the day at the carnival with friends, my daughter, Isadora, arrives home. "Mommy, he has a penis. He's a boy." I am so tired. It is dark out now, and the candles in my room throw off a comforting light. I pass my son to my friend and fall into a deep sleep.

Home Birth after a Cesarean: Ginny's Story

Being a midwife and an obstetrical nurse, I felt home to be the safest place for a healthy mother and baby to give birth. But my past birth experiences were not normal ones. So when I became pregnant with Amber Rose, where to give birth presented a problem.

My first child, Doug, was born at a hospital where the promise of a "natural" birth was, in reality, a birth with routine interferences such as the breaking of the water bag, labor in bed, a shave and enema, and the labor unattended by the father himself. He was sent out to breakfast without my knowledge while I was in mid-labor. Before I even realized what was happening, delivery was "assisted" with forceps and a spinal block. I did get to watch in a mirror when the doctor's back wasn't in the way, and I held my new son at once, because I was so vocal about it!

Three years later, I became pregnant with twins, Jonathan and Denise, who I'd planned to give birth to at home. My water broke at the crack of dawn. As I felt my belly and told my babies I'd be seeing them soon, the cord and a tiny foot slid out of my vagina! A prolapsed cord! We went to the hospital forty minutes away with me in a knee-chest position, praying that this would keep the babies off the cord. My

NATURAL SOOTHER
Your Birth Altar

Whether you give birth at home, in a birth center, or in a hospital, collect a few items to surround yourself with during labor. Keep them simple but personal. If your inner concentration will not be distracted by music, choose some selections to have on hand for the birth. Think about the lighting. If the birth is at night, do you want soft lighting, candles, or lamps? Have different choices on hand and see what appeals to you at the time.

Your birth altar can be within view if that is convenient. You may want some affirming mantras that you've written and hung about the room, or on cards you can pick up to look at if you like. Consider having flowers in the room. Roses in bloom provide a lovely visual parallel to birth, and the scent is relaxing.

You might want to use an aromatherapy diffuser. Look for one in your local natural foods store. Add 3 or 4 drops of your favorite oil or one of the selections below to the diffuser. You can do this in early labor and ask your doula to do it later. If you don't want to bother with a diffuser, just have the bottle of oil on hand to sniff from time to time. Or you can add 2 to 4 drops of your choice of oils to a small spray bottle of water. Mist this on yourself during labor.

The following oils can relieve anxiety and fear, and help you to relax between contractions while your body's endorphins provide natural pain relief:

Neroli

Bergamot

Rose

Frankincense

babies were born by C-section, weighing five pounds each.

Now, I secretly hoped for a home birth for Amber Rose. This hope was nearly shattered by an ob/gyn who quoted horrid statistics of my chances of scar rupture and subsequent death, as well as my child's death.

It seems the statistical data the doctor gave was not too accurate. Most women, 99.8 percent, are able to have a vaginal birth without a ruptured scar. And ruptures, it turns out, sound scary but are usually more like tears that do not present a danger to the mother or child.

The doctor's warning only added fuel to my fire! I did my research. My diet was aimed at creating a healthy scar. I did a lot of visualization of my uterus as a strong, safe place to grow a baby. I exercised daily, and I listened to my body and my intuition. My baby was head down and healthy. My uterine scar was low and horizontal, and my partner, Danny, was supportive of any decision I would make.

I saw Abby, my midwife, and she felt good about a home birth, if that was my choice. I saw a doctor for medical backup. He also felt I was a very good candidate for a vaginal birth—in the hospital. Fearing he would not help me if I said I wanted to try a home

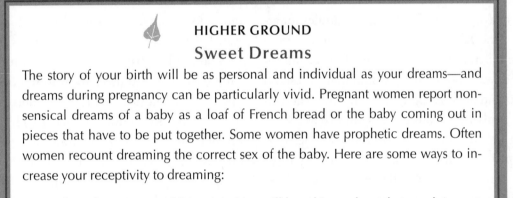

HIGHER GROUND
Sweet Dreams

The story of your birth will be as personal and individual as your dreams—and dreams during pregnancy can be particularly vivid. Pregnant women report nonsensical dreams of a baby as a loaf of French bread or the baby coming out in pieces that have to be put together. Some women have prophetic dreams. Often women recount dreaming the correct sex of the baby. Here are some ways to increase your receptivity to dreaming:

- Take at least 25 mg of B6 a day. (You will be taking at least that much in your prenatal supplement.)
- Sleep on a regular schedule.
- Have no intoxicants.
- Put a blank piece of paper or tablet and a pen or pencil near your bed. Look at the blank piece of paper before you turn off the light.
- Allow yourself to awaken slowly.
- Don't jump out of bed right away.
- Loud noises and large motor movements dissipate the dream.
- Write down whatever snatches of dream you can remember, then read them back to yourself like a story. Some dream experts say that all of the characters in the dream are some aspect of you. The characters you recognize represent qualities you associate with them. The characters you don't know represent unknown parts of yourself. Tell yourself the dream as if it is a metaphor. Trust the first ideas that come into your mind. Don't force it. And don't be afraid of "negative" elements. Everything in the dream is for your growth, so try to understand it in that light.

birth, I felt it necessary to let him think I was having a hospital birth.

One Saturday morning, I awoke with the usual Braxton-Hicks contractions. They had become stronger the last few evenings, and this day they came every five minutes, but were not painful at all. Danny and I went on a drive in the mountains where we live. The contractions continued all day. I ate high-protein foods and drank a lot of raspberry leaf tea to help strengthen the contractions. As evening came, the feeling of the contractions changed.

At 8:30 P.M., I had my first true contractions. They came every three minutes and lasted sixty seconds. We put the kids to bed and promised to wake them when the baby was here. I showered. Danny and I burned sage to purify the air, lit candles for atmosphere, and felt very secure at home. I labored a lot on the toilet, as the "chair" seemed to accommodate me perfectly. Sometimes I would walk and stand a bit. Four and one-half hours after my first real contractions, Amber Rose was born in our bed as I knelt on it and held Danny's shoulders to push her out. Abby helped catch her. The kids all heard my birth song and came in just as she slid out. She cleared her throat with a quiet sound and lay in a wet, warm puddle on the bed.

Once labor began, I forgot all about my uterine scar. There was only trust in my body and God that all would be fine. Amber Rose weighed over ten pounds and was twenty-two inches long.

Alternative Birth Center in a Hospital: Karen's Story

I chose to have my baby in the alternative birth center (ABC) of a metropolitan-area hospital. I attended Bradley classes in preparation and was seen regularly by my doctor. We were escorted through the birth center to view the birthing room beforehand. The nurse-midwives also showed us the "traditional" labor and delivery rooms, let us hold forceps, and told us what situations would require our being moved from the alternative birth center.

On September 27, my contractions progressed steadily from ten minutes apart at 6:00 A.M. to five minutes apart at 11:00 P.M. At that time we drove to the ABC. We had filled out forms in advance, so we went directly to the large and dimly lit birthing room. My doctor met me there, checked me, and went for a snooze. I lay down on the queen-size mattress and prepared for contractions. The nurse-midwife, Debbie, helped me time them and relax. I showered in the private bathroom, letting the water rush over my skin. I spent a lot of time in the shower because the water was soothing and sensual.

Transition set in around 3:00 A.M. I let fly a few profanities this way and that, but Debbie never left our side, or interrupted Mark's coaching. At 4:00 P.M. I felt the urge to push. My doc woke up, and they all put beanbag chairs in the bed for support. I sunk into them and used my arms to hold my knees open. When I heard "push," I did—and twenty minutes later out slid beautiful Zachary. He was laid on my heaving, excited chest immediately. No crying, no fussing. He was mellow from the first minute. My husband was able to cut the cord.

Although I had prepared my perineum with oil, I had a small episiotomy. While that was stitched, I called my folks. The atmosphere was at our discretion. I left the next day and was visited by a nurse-midwife two days later at our home.

Even though we gave birth in a hospital, you never would have guessed it by the atmosphere—total joy. I feel I got the best of two worlds—freedom and security.

The Glorious Pelvic Thrust: Maria's Story

My first labor was a disaster. When my water broke, I went to the hospital, where my labor was induced, and spent the next thirty hours hooked up to every imaginable type of monitor. Too encumbered by the infernal gadgets to walk, I became incredibly frustrated, because I knew I *should* be walking. Finally, in disgust, I succumbed to the nurse and had two doses of Demerol *and* an epidural. All I remember is a constant stream of faces—doctors, nurses, janitors—and the enormous Macy's Thanksgiving Day Parade balloons that I hallucinated. Ultimately I had a healthy baby boy.

Pregnant for a second time, I was too chicken to have a home birth, yet I was determined to avoid an overly medical experience. I met with a midwife and was immensely relieved. She assured me that as long as things were going well, I could get by without the equipment.

On Friday, October 15, immediately after a dinner of pasta and cheese and vegetables, I was overcome by a throbbing backache. At 11 P.M., with contractions coming every twenty minutes or so, I fell asleep until 12:45.

I knew that hard labor had started when I woke up with the song "Walking on Broken Glass" running through my head, and extreme pain radiating across my back and down my legs. Deciding not to wake my husband, Michael, and son, Wolf, I went to the kitchen and turned on the radio. It felt good to walk around in between contractions.

I went to visit our downstairs boarders, Stella and Deborah, who were still awake. I told them about an article I had read, explaining that belly dancing originated as a way to prepare women for labor. I did a belly dance as a joke and instantly realized it was no joke—the movements felt really good.

I returned upstairs with some of their dance tapes. Belly dancing to the music, I found that the contractions were much more bearable. Basically, I step-touched around the kitchen until I felt a wave of pain coming, then I would step in place until I could only sway, then I would sway and bop and thrust my pelvis back and forth until the pain subsided. Oddly enough, the more obscenely I thrust my pelvis back and forth, the less it hurt. I was amazed! Why hadn't I known that these movements were linked to the act of birthing? I wondered. How come no one ever mentioned it in childbirth class?

Most of the night I was happy to be alone. After all, I was big as a house and thrusting my pelvis like a maniac—hardly a seemly occupation for a Woman Great with Child. As the hours passed, I began to understand why pelvic-thrust movements are not heralded in birthing classes: everyone is just too damned embarrassed about them!

Moments later I discovered that all the pelvic thrusting I had been doing in my life—dancing to get a date, making love, and now, giving birth—was integrally connected.

Later, when Michael dropped me off at the emergency room entrance and went to park the car, the nurses thought I had already been admitted because I was so calm. In the birthing room I immediately turned on the B-52s. The nurses came in and laughed. One of them swayed beside me, holding the fetal monitor up to my belly. Honoring my wishes, the nurses never hooked me up to anything and only intermittently took stats.

Eventually, I felt the urge to push. It came on so fast that I thought for sure the baby was tumbling down the birth canal like a bowling ball down the alley. I was howling an incredible howl. My midwife let me birth in the position I had somehow assumed. I was on my knees, holding on to the back of the bed. From behind me, she guided the baby out. My husband was thrilled to see the head emerging! Then I heard someone ask me what the baby's gender was. "It's a girl," I answered, pleased that she let me discover this on my own.

An Emergency C-section: Dee's Story

Like so many other women, I had read all the books I could find on childbirth. With my partner, Bill, I had carefully plotted how we would bring this baby of ours into the world. At first, we had planned to have her at home. The midwife told us to visit a doctor early in my pregnancy so we would be familiar with him in case of emergency at the time of the delivery. Emergency? Why should there be one? I was healthy and in good shape. I ran five miles a day, and

I ate a good, wholesome diet. This birth would be fast and easy.

Dr. Miller was warm, friendly, and enthusiastic about working toward the perfect birth for us. He suggested we investigate the alternative birth center (ABC). The ABC had a double bed, a tiny cradle, two rocking chairs, and sunlight streaming through the window. We could leave the hospital sixteen hours after delivery. We decided it would be a good idea to be there. Of course, we wouldn't need the emergency services available, but it was nice to know they were there.

Labor began at 9:00 P.M. on a Saturday night. We gathered our necessities and went to the hospital. By 10:00 A.M. on Sunday, I was fully dilated and ready to push. For the next six hours I pushed—leaning against Bill on the bed, squatting on the floor, sitting in the wheelchair on the way for a sonogram, lying in the labor room strapped to a fetal monitor, wheeling down the hall in a gurney on my way to surgery.

Samantha was wedged firmly in my pelvis. She stayed there until Dr. Miller pulled her through the opening in my abdomen. The cesarean was not as bad as I had expected. Bill stayed with me, assuring me that everything was fine. The mood in the surgery room was festive. A baby had been born.

The physical recovery was easy compared to the mental anguish I felt. I had been so prepared for a natural delivery. It had been the only way to have a baby. I was a failure at childbirth!

I asked myself a lot of questions in those months following Samantha's birth. Did Dr. Miller do this to me because it was Sunday and he wanted to spend time with his family? Did I do this to myself because I didn't try hard enough?

Slowly, I became more rational about Samantha's birth. I realized that our doctor would never have done a cesarean to please himself. He had patiently sat and answered our questions, sometimes for an hour at a time, during the whole pregnancy. He had allowed me to push far beyond the recommended two-hour limit before suggesting cesarean. At my six-week postnatal checkup, he explained the deliv-

ery in detail. Apparently my cervix had swollen because I'd pushed for so long. This, plus Samantha's position, had prevented her from descending into the birth canal. I was relieved to know that due to circumstances beyond anyone's control, I had a cesarean.

Sometimes in our quest for the perfect birth, we forget that there is no such thing. Our minds fantasize about a beautiful, romantic childbirth, but our bodies can't always deliver it. By refusing to look at all the possibilities, we are limiting ourselves. Now I realize that the only perfect birth is the miracle of a healthy child.

Sudden Birth: Maxcie's Story

We had just moved into our new apartment. Our anxiety and excitement had much less to do with that, however, than with the fact that our first baby was due to be born. Neither my wife, Maxcie, nor I had a clue about what to expect. Sure, we had gone to Lamaze classes. We were well versed in breathing techniques. Yet no class on earth could have prepared us for the next seventy-two hours.

Not normally a light sleeper, I had slowly become one over the previous few weeks in my role as principal hot-towel presser, remedy fetcher, and help-me-roll-over-to-my-other-side facilitator. It was a little after 1:30 A.M., and Maxcie was clearly having another bout with her lower back. Within three minutes I had a hot compress on her back. This time, though, things were different. The hot, stabbing pains she described continued and were coming at regular intervals. In fact, they were only about three to four minutes apart—active labor!

I quickly called our doctor. "You're about twelve hours from delivering. Believe me, if you were in labor, you'd know it," he said. "Go on down to the hospital and have them examine you if you want. I'll see you there later."

I threw on some clothes, grabbed our bag, and dashed out into the freezing rain to get the car while Max struggled into her sweats. "I've got to go to the bathroom one more time before we leave," she said. I mulled over the fastest way to the hospital.

My thoughts were interrupted by strange guttural sounds coming from the bathroom. Racing through the bathroom door, I found my wife half standing above the toilet, her pants around her ankles, her eyes fixed on me with confusion, shock, and pain. She gasped and locked her hands around my forearm in a white-knuckled vise grip. Then she screamed. "Something's happening," she said, pushing my hand down. "Feel." I felt a strange, smooth lump— like a water balloon stretched taut. It was the baby's head!

We were both frozen in shock, not sure what to do. I moved in a daze to the living room phone and dialed 911. While desperately trying to explain our situation to the operator, I was stopped cold by a second electrifying scream from my wife, followed by, "Baby . . . baby . . . baby, baby!"

This time, through the bathroom door, I was greeted by an image that I know will be imprinted on my memory forever. My wife was sitting on the floor, and there at her feet, in a pool of blood and amniotic fluid, was my firstborn child! He was big and beautiful, with a full head of hair, ten fingers, and ten toes.

I calmly yet quickly scooped him up and flipped him over facedown across Maxcie's lap. Together we massaged his throat and his nose to remove the fluid. He sputtered, coughed, and started to cry. I covered mother and child with towels for warmth and ran back to the phone, where an elated 911 operator was waiting, having "witnessed" the entire event. I was at last able to give her our address.

Later, as I watched him lying under the heat lamp at the hospital, my heart swelled again and tears flowed down my face. Actually, two champions were born that morning: my son, certainly, and in my eyes, Maxcie as well. With pregnancy, she had changed from a fun-loving schoolgirl to a radiant mother-in-waiting to—in one glorious moment—a superwoman managing to heroically handle a dangerous, frightening situation while coping with her own indescribable pain.

BODY WISE
Roll, Roll, Roll Your Neck

In late pregnancy, tension can settle in your neck. To relieve neck pain, stand or sit comfortably upright. Let your arms hang easily at your sides. Relax your shoulders and imagine that a string holds up your head. Begin by lowering your head slightly to the front and bend forward from the neck until it is no longer comfortable. Slowly move your head to the left in a circle. Breathe slowly as you roll your head. Slowly roll your head to the back and all the way around until you come back to the front. Repeat on the right side. Roll your neck each way three times.

Past My Due Date:
Madeleine's Story

My husband, Ted, was outside with the neighbor's children while I lay lopsided in bed, a pillow under my leg propping up my huge belly. I was deeply engrossed in a novel—resigned to being pregnant forever, as my due date had passed three weeks before.

Just the day before, I had been to see Joan, my midwife, who we visited weekly. She had stopped charging me for my visits three weeks ago.

"Well, this baby is ready to come out. More than ready!" she told me. "Do you think perhaps you are holding it in? Are you afraid of motherhood or labor?"

"No," I answered. "I can finally say that I am tired of being pregnant, and I want it to be over."

"Well," Joan said, handing me a bag, "I would suggest that tomorrow morning when you wake up, make yourself a pot of this tea. Drink one cup an hour, and if you're ready, it'll start things moving. If you haven't started labor by the evening, wait until the next day and try again."

I reflected upon this as I lay in bed, ten cups later. I drifted back to my novel and left my swollen body behind once again. Suddenly, a gush of liquid rushed from between my legs. "Oh, God, it's happening!" I yelled, stumbling to my feet and rushing to the bathroom for a towel, which I crammed between my thighs.

I yelled out the front door to Ted. My mind went into overdrive, ticking off a mental list of things I had to do in preparation. First call Joan? Then my parents? Make up the bed? Have something to eat? I hobbled around the house, doing four things at once, while water spurted from my womb with alarming force. At this rate, I thought, I will use up all my towels, and then what?

Joan told me when I called her, that she would be there when I wanted her. I got my first labor pain a half-hour later. It stopped me cold. I sank into a chair, struggling to assimilate this pain. Within one hour the contractions were five minutes apart and one-half to one minute long.

All my preconceptions of the labor—what I would do, and how it would be—were invalid. I had imagined walking around my circular driveway to speed things along, or sitting in a warm tub to lessen the intensity of the contractions. As I could barely walk from kitchen to bedroom, the idea of doing laps around my driveway seemed ludicrous. Two hours after the water broke, I was in my bed, which would be my world until labor was over.

Joan arrived with Erin and Constance, her assistants. She brought with her an air of competency and professionalism.

"Okay, Madeleine, when you feel the next contraction, blow out of your mouth as hard as you can. It's too soon to push, you need to open up more first."

This method worked, but was hard to do. Ted helped more than anything. At this point, I was fading out between contractions for a minute or two,

gathering my strength for the next onslaught. When I could focus on my surroundings, the room was rosy around the edges, and everyone's faces were soft.

I had begun to feel a change in the rhythms of my body. Joan checked my cervix and said, "You're completely dilated. Let's try to push with the next contraction." When it was time, instead of blowing air out, as I had been doing for five hours, I pushed. Out of my mouth came a primal grunt. I surprised myself, not knowing I was capable of such sounds.

I pushed and groaned and grunted for over an hour. It felt good to now be an active participant in this primal dance. I tried many positions to push from. I tried on my hands and knees. I also pushed lying on my back, propped up by pillows, and finally by squatting over a mirror. In this last position I saw the baby's head for the first time, blue and spongy, as warm to the touch as my own body.

My legs began cramping, so I returned to my pillows on the bed. I pushed until I felt the baby's head crowning, fully stretching my perineum. I didn't think it possible to open that far, but open I did. Joan reached a gloved hand inside me to feel the baby's shoulders. One more push, and my child was born.

"It's a boy!" I exclaimed. Joan made sure he was breathing, and within seconds my son lay in my arms. He was confused as to where he was. He cried his first rusty cries, then found my eyes with his own and slowly calmed.

Joan had to remind me to push out the placenta, which I did as if an afterthought.

As the baby found my nipple with his tiny mouth, I locked eyes with Ted, who radiated love and wonder to me. We lay together, touching and loving each other as we welcomed our son, this brand-new person, into our world, into our life. I thought to myself, "It's over." But in fact it had all just begun.

There is no way out of the experience except through it, because it is not really your experience at all, but the baby's. Your body is the child's instrument of birth.

—PENELOPE LEACH, *Your Baby and Child*

You are, step by step, working your way up to labor, though you may not even realize it. You may feel quite different now. Perhaps it seems as though the baby's head is pressing against your pelvic floor more than it did before. You might begin to have more frequent Braxton-Hicks contractions. Your midwife or doctor may tell you that your cervix is ripe, or even that it is slightly dilated.

A woman is not considered to be in true labor, though, until she is dilated to around 3 centimeters and is having contractions that are regularly spaced apart. Labor itself is generally divided into three stages. During stage one, regular contractions are slowly opening the cervix. In stage two, the cervix is fully dilated, and the contractions are pushing the baby down the birth canal until it is born. In stage three, the placenta and other membranes are expelled.

The Signs of Early Labor

Before labor begins in earnest, you may experience some, or all, of these early signs that it is likely to happen soon:

- *The "nesting instinct."* You may find yourself compulsively cleaning the house. You may feel a real urgency to make sure that everything is prepared and ready for the baby.

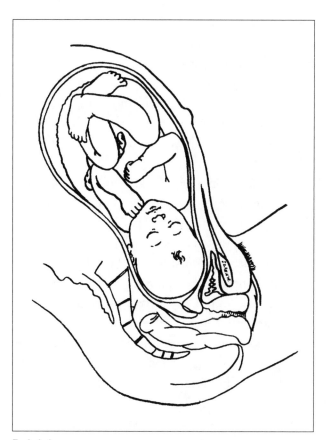

Early Labor

- *"Lightening" or "engagement."* As the baby's position changes, you might find it easier to breathe, but the head's contact with your pelvic floor will bring new sensations. You may need to urinate more frequently. Some people also say that the baby has engaged or "dropped" into a position that prepares him for birth.

- *Weight loss.* Women will sometimes lose two or three pounds right before they are going to go into labor.

- *Malar flush.* This is a rosy-colored flush over the cheeks and chin that often happens shortly before a woman goes into labor.

- *Light contractions.* You may have experienced Braxton-Hicks contractions throughout your third trimester, or you may not have felt any at all, until now. These contractions generally feel like a thick elastic band is stretching around your midsection and pulling tight for a few seconds. They are not usually strong enough to interfere with your daily life, though you may pause for a moment while you are actually having one. They may become more and more frequent as time goes by, or you may have them for a couple of days and then stop altogether. Some women never experience them at all. These contractions are helping your cervix to ripen.

- *Cervical ripening.* This sometimes happens gradually over a period of several days, or it can happen quite quickly. The ripening, or effacement, of the cervix is often likened to the difference between pursing your lips of your mouth up tight and then allowing them to relax and become soft. The cervix must become soft so that it can begin to dilate.

- *Cervical dilation* (see figures at right). When your cervix has dilated 1 or 2 centimeters, labor may be close, or it could still be many days away.

- *A bloody show.* The mucus plug that has sealed your cervix off until now is expelled. It will look like a bit of bloodstained mucus. This often means labor is imminent.

- *Cramps.* You may feel a low, indefinite crampy sensation. It may feel like you are about to have a menstrual period.

- *Low backache.* The crampy sensation described

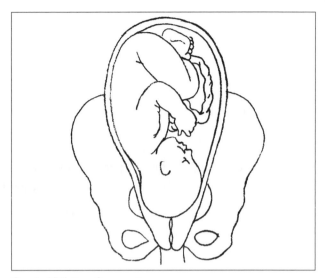

Cervical Dilation: 0 percent

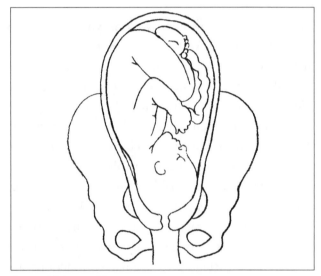

Cervical Dilation: 50 percent

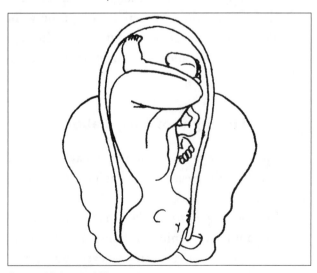

Cervical Dilation: 100 percent

above may be more centered in the area of your lower back.

- *Breaking or leaking of the bag of water.* This may happen all at once. You'll find yourself, all of a sudden, standing over a small puddle of clear liquid. Or you may notice just a bit of it in your underwear. If you are leaking, and your due date is three weeks or less away, try to just go about your business, but call your physician or midwife and let him or her know. If the water bag breaks all at once, you should let your care provider know, but you are still not in active labor until you are having regular contractions.

If your water has broken, there is an increased chance of infection as time goes by. For this reason, many physicians and midwives do not want you to wait for more than twenty-four hours after broken waters without going into labor. Some are less strict about this policy and will wait longer to try to give you the chance to go into labor on your own before they use chemical induction methods. They may ask you to take your temperature regularly because a fever could indicate the beginnings of an infection. You have about an 85 percent chance of going into labor on your own.[1] Try some of the suggestions in chapter 14 to get labor started.

Revisit Your Birth Intentions

You have some signs of early labor, and you know that your baby will be born soon. You may be nervous in anticipation of what is to come. Now is an excellent time to take a few minutes to ground yourself and review everything you have set in place previously.

The day your baby is born will be one you will never forget. The details will be with you for the rest of your life. Your upcoming labor may be fast and smooth, or it may hold surprises and present challenges. Either way, the most important thing to do is to stay connected to the present moment and to take care of yourself. Avoid trying to anxiously anticipate what the next few hours will hold.

Here are some suggestions for ways to think about the challenge of the coming hours:

- Think of the process of birth and labor as an initiation. You will pass through this initiation and come out transformed: you will be a mother and you will have experienced an event that is one of life's major rites of passage.

- Concentrate on the sensuous and sexual nature of the birth experience. There are many parallels between lovemaking and birth. The senses become acute in both experiences. Both processes are marked by intense emotions, vulnerability, and a lessening of social inhibitions. The same hormone, oxytocin, is released during both lovemaking and labor. Your body already knows how to handle this experience.

- Labor is a time when most mammals seek privacy and protection. You can do this for yourself, starting now. Find a place to get comfortable for the beginning of your labor. Create a nest for yourself.

This is a good time to reread some of the previous chapters and look ahead to the chapters that follow. Review the information on preparing for pain in labor in chapter 13. Also review chapter 10, about dealing with fear.

There may be quite a bit of time before you go into active labor. You may not want to do anything in particular, or you may want some quiet activities to keep you occupied while your body and mind work to go into labor. Try these:

- Short bouts of meditation, periodically. This can really help you to focus more inwardly and to relax.

- Have a professional massage or an acupuncture session for relaxation.

- Take a walk. Walking is known to help labor progress, but it can also be a kind of meditation if done slowly and thoughtfully.

- Find a task that does not require too much mental energy. This might not be the ideal time for bill paying, for example, but it could be a good time to mount photos in an album or knit. Some people might find satisfaction in cooking and setting food by for later.

- Take naps if you feel the urge. It's good to get as much rest as you can before real labor sets in. If you have trouble resting, try some lavender, neroli, geranium, or chamomile oils on a warm compress or aromatherapy diffuser.

- Don't forget to eat and drink plenty of liquids to keep up your strength.

- Ask a friend to come over and keep you company, rather than relying solely on your partner. Choose someone who you feel safe and comfortable with. Companionship is an important labor tool, even in these early hours when it seems like not much is happening.

Final Home Birth Preparations

Earlier, this book discussed the preparations you needed to make for your home birth. Now is the time to make your final touches.

Start by getting the bed ready. Make it up as you normally would with fresh sheets. Over this, place your plastic mattress pad or tablecloth. On top of this will go your sterilized sheets, once you get a little closer to true labor. After the birth you will be able to just remove the top layers and have, underneath, a freshly made bed on which to rest.

Go through your checklist of items, such as rubbing alcohol and antibacterial hand cleaner, and begin to place these items in their designated spots.

Clear off the tabletop or dresser that you have decided will be the worktable where your midwife can place her tools. Get a cot or couch ready for the mid-

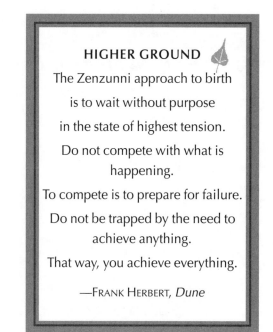

The Zenzunni approach to birth
is to wait without purpose
in the state of highest tension.
Do not compete with what is
happening.
To compete is to prepare for failure.
Do not be trapped by the need to
achieve anything.
That way, you achieve everything.

—FRANK HERBERT, *Dune*

wife to lie down on in case she needs to rest during the labor.

Place newspaper or brown paper on the floor where you want to protect it from drips. The pathway from the bed to the bathroom is particularly important.

Be sure your car is easily accessible and has a full tank of gas, in case you need to make a transfer to the hospital.

Don't feel you must do all of this on your own, unless you find it helpful as a distraction. Otherwise, get some help and try to rest as much as you can.

Leaving for a Birth Center or Hospital

If you are using a birth center or hospital for your birth, don't be in too much of a hurry to get there. You will be generally more comfortable at home, and there may be many hours of labor ahead, so stay there as long as you can. Even if you're having a home birth, however, it is a good idea to have the car nearby and ready to go with a full tank of gas so that when you're ready, you don't need to wait. The last thing in the world you will want to do is sit in a car in a gas station while you are having contractions!

A good rule of thumb is to leave when the contractions are between fifty-five and sixty-five seconds long and are less than five minutes apart. You might want to take a pillow with you for support in the car.

Except for being hung up by the feet, the supine position is the
worst conceivable position for labor and delivery.

—DR. ROBERTO CALDEYRO-BARCIA, past president of the International Federation of
Obstetricians and Gynecologists, in *NAPSAC News*

Once you are having regular contractions, you
are considered to be in true (or *active*) labor.
The duration and distance between contractions will
differ from labor to labor, but they may be around
five minutes apart or less. Your cervix will, at this
point, probably be dilated to about 3 or 4 centimeters. You are entering the first stage of labor. The first
stage of labor continues until it is time to push the
baby out, which is the second stage of labor.

Birth in Art and Culture

Throughout history, women have given birth in
upright postures: sitting, standing, and mostly squatting. We know this is true because we see it over and
over again in artworks from every civilization and
every era. Statues from Greece and paintings from
ancient Peru all depict the same scene: a woman in a
squatting position held up from behind by another
woman, while a midwife is in front, delivering the
baby. Margaret Mead said that whenever we see the
same custom being used by many different peoples,
it probably is based on some "very stubborn species-
characteristic element that is worth following up."[1]

In the Renaissance, however, with the rise of science, the flat-on-your-back, or supine, position
began to be used by doctors for difficult births. The
reasons for this were simple: it was more convenient

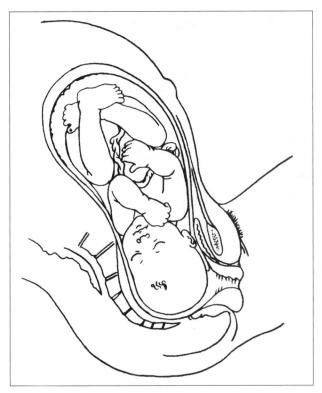

Active Labor

for the physician. In time, this position began to be
used more and more commonly, even for normal,
low-risk births.

Today the flat-on-your-back position is standard
procedure in most American hospitals. Fortunately,
the growing movement to return birth to a more natural process is slowly changing this. More and more

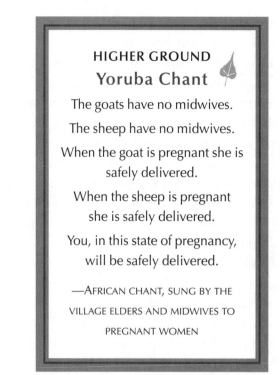

HIGHER GROUND

Yoruba Chant

The goats have no midwives.

The sheep have no midwives.

When the goat is pregnant she is
safely delivered.

When the sheep is pregnant
she is safely delivered.

You, in this state of pregnancy,
will be safely delivered.

—AFRICAN CHANT, SUNG BY THE
VILLAGE ELDERS AND MIDWIVES TO
PREGNANT WOMEN

- Labor is, on average, 36 percent shorter when a woman works in an upright position instead of lying on her back. This is because contractions are stronger and more efficient.[2]
- In an upright position, labor is less painful, with less need for painkilling drugs.[3]
- There is less chance a woman will need an episiotomy or that a perineal tear will happen.[4]
- Women who are not confined to their backs on a table will naturally change positions and try new ones. This freedom to decide where they want to be may contribute more to shorter labors than anything else.[5]
- Being upright encourages better drainage of liquids and tissues from the uterus.
- Pregnant women are advised not to lie on their backs for extended amounts of time in later pregnancy. That is because this position can reduce blood flow and oxygen to the uterus and the baby. This is also true during labor itself.[6] An upright posture eliminates this concern.

There is also a strong psychological component to take into account when thinking about birth positions. Human beings tend to feel more vulnerable and less in control when they lie on their backs. They tend to become the "subject," while their birth attendants, who are standing all around them, are the "authority." When women lie on their backs on a table to give birth, there is a tendency for attendants to focus on their genitals. When women are squatting or in a birthing chair, there is more of a tendency for attendants to focus on their faces.

hospitals now have birthing chairs or birthing beds in their labor rooms, and women are being taught alternative labor positions in childbirth education classes.

Why Upright Is Best

What are the reasons why upright is still the preferred position by women all over the rest of the world?

- The force of gravity assists the baby in coming straight down and out of the birth canal. There is less need for forceps. In cases of cephalopelvic disproportion, where the baby's head is too big for the mother's pelvis, this position creates a little extra room for birth, thus decreasing the risk of eventual cesarean delivery.
- The mother is better able to use her abdominal muscles to assist her uterus in pushing the baby out. Imagine trying to have a bowel movement while lying flat on your back with your legs in the air! This is a difficult childbirth position for the same reason.

A Potpourri of Birth Positions

Here is a sample of the birth positions most commonly used around the world. It may be helpful to have a variety of pillows available that can be used to support you in different positions. Some women also like using a beanbag chair because it can be molded into different supportive shapes.

- *Squatting.* This is the classic, time-honored position for women all over the world and is a favorite of first-time mothers. We are not accustomed to squatting in our day-to-day life, however, and you may find this position difficult to sustain. Try a supported squat (see below), squatting with your back against a wall for support, or squatting with your partner or doula sitting in a chair behind you. Position yourself between his open knees and rest your forearms on his thighs for support. If a full squat is just too hard to manage even with support, try placing pillows between your thighs and calves to take some of the pressure off your legs.

- *Kneeling.* You can kneel on a pillow or soft rug

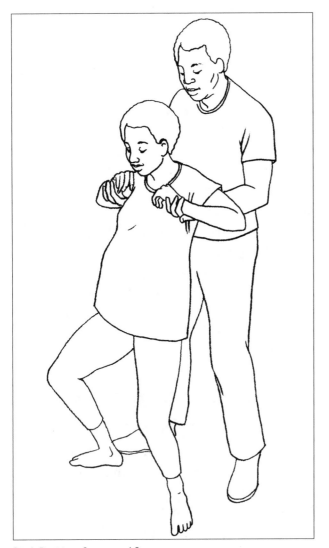

Birth Position: Supported Squat

and support yourself by leaning over onto a chair or into someone's lap.

- *Standing and walking.* You can use your partner for support. Some women like to have their partner supporting them from behind while they stand in place or slowly move about. You can also stand with one foot up on a stool.

- *Pelvic rocking.* You may find it very helpful in labor to slowly rock your pelvis, like a belly dancer, during contractions. See the birth story "The Glorious Pelvic Thrust: Maria's Story" in chapter 15 for more on this.

- *Bending forward.* Stand and lean over onto a tall table or counter. You can cushion your arms with a pillow if you like.

- *Sitting.* You can sit in a comfortable chair, in a birthing chair, or upright in bed. Try sitting backward on a straight-backed chair, with your legs open to either side, and support your upper body on the chair's back. In this position your partner can massage your back comfortably. You might like sitting in a cross-legged position on the floor, or on the bed. These positions will give you variety during labor, and some, such as the birthing chair and the floor position, may also be useful as birth positions.

- *On the toilet.* Many women report that laboring on the toilet was good for them. This is probably because the toilet is a place where women are used to relaxing their pelvic floors.

- *Semireclining.* This position involves sitting up at a 45-degree angle by propping yourself up with pillows or adjusting the angle of your hospital bed.

- *Hands and knees.* This position (shown at right) is especially favored by second-time mothers. This is a good one for back labor because it takes the weight off your spinal area. You can rock back and forth in this position during contractions. A variation of the hands-and-knees position is to rest on your elbows and knees, with your buttocks straight up in the air.

- *Lying on the left side.* Contractions will be

stronger in this position than lying flat on the back[7] (but still not as strong as when squatting). This position takes the weight off the main blood supply to the baby and reduces tension on the perineum. During the second stage of labor you will need someone to hold up your right leg for you while you push. This position is restful, but doesn't have the other advantages that upright positions have.

Back Labor

While most women experience at least a bit of back discomfort during labor, for some it can be acute. This is especially true if the baby is in a posterior presentation, with the back of his head pressing against your spine. Most babies will rotate at the end of the first stage of labor, though about 5 percent do not.[8] You will probably also experience backache if the baby is in a breech position.

Try these tips to help relieve the discomfort of back labor:

- Change positions frequently. Lying on your back will be the most uncomfortable position because gravity will cause the baby's head to press even more against your spine. Try the hands-and-knees position or any upright one.

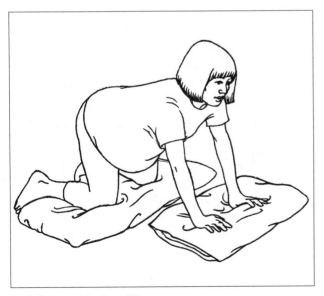

Birth Position: Hands and Knees

- Ask that your membranes not be artificially ruptured. Once the waters are broken the baby may sink into the pelvis in that same posterior position. As long as your water is still intact, the baby may move her head about and give you some relief.
- Use massage as a pain aid. Counterpressure against the back using the heel of the hand or a tennis ball can be very helpful. You may find that a great deal of pressure is what's called for, or a good old-fashioned back rub may be just right.
- Acupressure may offer relief, even though the points you press are not anywhere near the back.[9] Try applying pressure just below the center of the ball of your foot. Also try the fleshy pads under the big toe and the one next to it. Ask your partner to use strong pressure on those points with a thumb or finger.
- Apply heat to the area. This is where the hot water bottle or electric heating pad can come in handy. Electric heat is unsafe in the first trimester, when there is risk of miscarriage, but it is safe to use during labor as described here because there is no long-term exposure.
- Take a hot shower and let the water cascade onto your back area. Or soak in warm water and try some different positions in the tub.
- Ask a homeopathic practitioner ahead of time about remedies for back labor, which may include *Kali carbonicum*, *Pulsatilla*, *Causticum*, *Nux vomica*, *Chamomilla*, or *Coffea cruda*.

Signs of an Emergency in Early Labor

It isn't likely that you will experience an emergency situation at this point in your labor, but it's good to know the signs, just in case:

- More than a tablespoon of bright red blood. *If you are bleeding, do not allow anyone, under any circumstances, to give you a vaginal or rectal ex-*

NATURAL SOOTHER
Labor Massage Oil

Here's a massage oil made from relaxing essential oils. Ask your partner or doula to use this oil to massage your back, feet, or legs during early labor.

Into 4 ounces of sweet almond, olive, or grapeseed oil, mix:

15 drops of lavender essential oil

5 drops of neroli essential oil

2 drops of rose essential oil

800 IU vitamin E oil

BODY WISE
Practice Breathing

There are three kinds of breathing exercises that you will want to practice during the last weeks of pregnancy and use during the first stage of labor. These are variations on the classic Lamaze-prepared childbirth breathing.

1. *The deep cleansing breath.* This is a simple breath. Sit with your spine comfortably straight. Put your hands on your abdomen. Slowly inhale as you watch your belly rise. Slowly exhale. Let out a sound as you exhale. Use this deep cleansing breath at the beginning of each contraction to help focus you and then begin the chu-chu or moan-pant.

2. *The chu-chu breath.* This breath begins to sound like a steam engine chugging along. Inhale and exhale slowly, then quicker and quicker. Breathe at a pace that parallels your contraction. Use this breath with early contractions. Some women prefer to go directly to the moan-pant.

3. *The moan-pant.* Begin using this breathing technique when you're afraid you can't stay on top of the contractions—when the big waves come and you just need to stay in the present moment—and use through the delivery, if you like. The moan-pant consists of three or four rhythmic pants followed by one blow, which can be a real release. As labor progresses and you get more focused, you can turn the pants into moans, and even into sounds that feel like singing.

amination unless you are in a hospital. Bleeding can indicate a serious condition, which could be aggravated by an examination. Do not risk an examination until you are in a facility that can handle emergencies.

- A greenish or discolored discharge

- An abdomen that remains hard and tense *between* contractions

- Any sign of the umbilical cord coming out of your vagina. *If this happens, get into a hands-and-knees position with your head down and your bottom in the air immediately.* Call 911 and try to stay in this position on the way to the hospital in order to avoid putting any pressure on the cord and cutting off the baby's oxygen supply.

If you experience any of these symptoms, call your practitioner immediately.

While you can still *ask* if you *should* push, you are not *ready* to push.

—SHEILA KITZINGER, *The Complete Book of Pregnancy and Childbirth*

According to popular belief, a woman reaches her second stage of labor at a definable moment, and she is told that it is now "time to push." She then starts the hard work of bearing down at every contraction, and after some time, maybe half an hour or maybe two hours, the baby is finally born.

In reality, few women experience such a clear-cut transition to the second stage of labor. Technically speaking, the second stage begins when the cervix is fully dilated at 10 centimeters. The transition into the second stage, however, begins somewhere between 8 and 10 centimeters of dilation.

Transition into the Second Stage

For many women, transition is marked by a sudden intensity of contractions that begin to follow each other quite rapidly. The contractions may become erratic and don't seem to follow the neater wave pattern they had before. Other signs of transition might include:

- Irregular or more shallow breathing. It may become difficult to do breathing exercises. Some women start to make grunting noises.
- Extreme irritability and a general "out-of-control" feeling. Feeling as though you do not want to be touched.

- Discouragement, feeling as though you just can't manage labor anymore.
- Disorientation or dizziness.
- Shaking and shivering. Some women find their legs shaking.
- Prickly skin.
- Hot and cold flashes.
- Nausea or even vomiting.
- Hiccups.
- Sleepiness in between contractions.

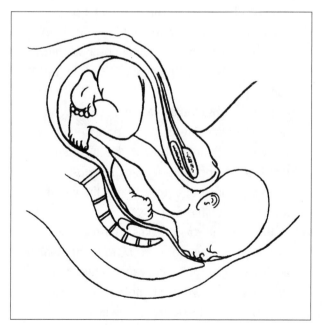

Pushing

- Feeling like you are going to have a bowel movement, or that there is pressure against your anus.

You may have just one or two of these symptoms, or you may not have any of them. Every woman's transition will be different. This is when many women begin to feel as though everything is going haywire. It is at this point that some women are tempted to ask for medication, and yet, the pain is almost past.

This is the time when you will need support most of all. You *can* manage this transition, and your labor partners can help you through this phase. Refer to chapter 13 for reminders of all the drug-free methods of pain relief that can help you at this critical time. Once you get past this hump, you will find it easier to carry on.

If you are experiencing fear or anger, or feeling overwhelmed, ask your birth attendant about these aids:

NATURAL SOOTHER

Water: A Natural Relaxant

Water can be very relaxing during labor. Some women like to take a bath in early labor. Others will get into a warm tub during active contractions. With the water almost body temperature, about 100 degrees, it feels very soothing.

French obstetrician Michel Odent pioneered the offering of warm pools of water to women during labor at the hospital in Pithiviers, France. He found that most used them for labor, not birth, and that the women found them comforting.

Being in the water makes it easier to squat as the water supports you. You can lean against your partner in the water between contractions. Some women believe that the warm water replaces the desire for medication.

- *Chamomilla* is a homeopathic remedy that can help with unproductive labor pains, irritability, and an inability to relax. *Aconitum napellus* can also soothe a fearful woman who is hot and restless.

- *Gelsemium* is another homeopathic remedy good for fear, especially for women whose symptoms include trembling and chattering teeth.

- Rescue Remedy is a blend of five Bach flower essences. Add a few drops to a glass of water and sip as needed. This is good for labor attendants too!

- Try some essential oils in a diffuser or on a warm compress for your forehead or abdomen. Lavender is always a good choice.

Sliding the Baby Out

The trend in labor and delivery in recent years is to begin pushing the moment a woman is fully dilated, whether or not she feels a particular urge to do so. Women are directed to "bear down" with all their might, holding their breath for as much as ten to thirty seconds and straining until each contraction is over. Some women actually break blood vessels around their eyes and cheeks from straining and holding their breath so intensively!

In fact, there is no evidence that pushing right from the very start is particularly effective in speeding labor along.[1] It may actually have the opposite effect, or might put the baby into transverse arrest, where he gets "stuck."

There is also evidence that holding your breath for long periods of time might be harmful to both mother and baby. Holding the breath and sustained bearing-down efforts may seriously reduce the amount of oxygen the baby receives, and can affect maternal blood pressure. This is particularly true if the woman is in a flat-on-the-back position.[2]

Birthing doesn't have to be so rough and tough. In

tended to hold their breath for no more than six seconds at a time and bore down briefly two or three times during each contraction. Average length of second-stage labor was only forty-five minutes for these women, and none of them went longer than ninety-five minutes.[3]

Many women will not feel an instant urge to push once they are fully dilated. Some may experience a kind of holding pattern, or plateau, at the beginning of the second stage, taking a bit of a break before their bodies are ready to begin to push the baby down the birth canal. Some women, particularly second-time moms, may not *ever* feel a strong pushing urge during their whole labor. And for others, the urge to bear down will come and go.

Occasionally, a woman will feel a very strong urge to push before her cervix is dilated enough. In this case it can help to pant softly, focusing on the breath and trying to avoid bearing down. You can also get on your hands and knees or lie down on your left side for a moment to try to slow things down a bit. Lying on your left side helps facilitate more comfortable breathing because less pressure is placed on major blood vessels than when lying on the right. Bearing down before full dilation can bruise or tear the cervix. Too much of this might cause it to swell, causing it to close up again.

Here are a few tips to help you through the second stage of labor and get you to the moment when your baby will slide out and be placed into your arms:

- As you begin to reach the second stage, think of your body as opening up like a flower. You will do this most effectively by trying to relax, not by getting ready to "work hard."
- Think of relaxing your pelvic floor. This is where doing Kegel exercises and yoga may really pay back. Do a Kegel, then release it and think of continuing to release. When you do feel the urge to bear down, allow the release to continue, otherwise you are working against yourself. Renowned British childbirth educator Sheila Kitzinger suggests that you allow your pelvic floor muscles to bulge out, like a heavy

one study, women were allowed to bear down spontaneously during the second stage and were given no directions on how or when to do so. The women

As mentioned in the text, squatting and hands and knees are particularly helpful during the pushing stage. Birthing in an upright position allows gravity to assist you during delivery. Some women, however, choose a semi-reclined position during labor and birth.

For this position, you will sit upright, slightly bent forward and with your legs apart. Gather a lot of pillows to put behind you for support so that you can sit upright more easily, or ask your support person to sit behind you. It is comforting to rest against someone during delivery.

Choose either a bed with a firm mattress or a floor with a rug. Sit with your torso erect, your back straight, and your shoulders directly above your hips. Open your legs wide with your knees bent and your hands resting on your thighs. Put your feet either flat on the floor or place your soles together on the bed.

Practice this position during pregnancy.

sack of apples. Sitting on a toilet for a few minutes can help you to get this feeling of release.

- Your position is most important at this stage. It has been shown that squatting, kneeling, or standing are the ideal positions for pushing and delivery.[4] At the least, you should be sitting up at a 45-degree angle. You may want to change positions frequently during this phase. Follow your body's cues.
- Push at will. You don't need to bear down at every contraction. Take a rest if you feel like it. You may want to push only during the peak of your contraction. Speak to your caregiver ahead of time and let them know you'd like to take the lead during this time.

- Hold your breath if it feels appropriate. Try not to do so for longer than three to six seconds. Otherwise, think of slowly releasing air as you bear down. Many women find it helpful to *grunt* the air out.
- Making other noises, such as moaning or singing, may be very helpful. Allow yourself to do this if it feels good.
- Take a couple of deep cleansing breaths between contractions.

Episiotomies

An episiotomy is a surgical enlargement of the vagina by means of an incision in the perineum, which is the skin and muscles between the rectum and the vagina. An episiotomy is done with either scissors or a scalpel. There are two types: midline (straight) or mediolateral (diagonal). A "pressure episiotomy" is an episiotomy done at the last minute, as the baby's head is crowning.

Medical literature first described episiotomies in 1741 as a surgical technique performed to enlarge the vagina so that forceps could be inserted high into the pelvis, thereby assisting in difficult births. By the 1930s episiotomies had become routine in hospital births. It was around this time that women began to deliver under the influence of "twilight sleep." Knocked out completely, women were unable to assist in birthing their babies at all, making the use of forceps and episiotomy a foregone conclusion in almost every case.

Doctors believed that episiotomies prevented perineal tearing, damage to the pelvic floor muscles, urinary incontinence, future uterine prolapse, and injury to the fetus's head, perhaps even mental retardation or cerebral palsy. One well-known doctor even claimed that it would be "irresponsible for a physician to allow the child's head to be used as a battering ram against a woman's perineum!"[5]

Today, episiotomies may be the most common surgical procedure performed. Around 89 percent of all births are accompanied by an episiotomy.[6] Many doctors still perform them automatically, in the belief that it will make the birth go more smoothly and prevent a woman from having a torn perineum.

There is no medical evidence that routine episiotomy is necessary. After all, women's bodies are designed to give birth without this procedure. None of the reasons why episiotomy was thought to be beneficial to begin with have proven to be true.[7] The American College of Obstetrics and Gynecology does not advise the routine use of this procedure, and the World Health Organization (WHO) strongly concurs, noting that alternative methods of perineal protection (described in the next section) should become the norm. WHO claims that the evidence only supports episiotomy rates of between 5 and 20 percent.[8]

What matters most to women who undergo this procedure is how they feel afterward and the risks that go along with it:

- Recovering from an episiotomy is painful! Some women report the pain to be so strong that they feel they need pain medication to deal with it. Just plain sitting down can be excruciating at first, making breastfeeding rather challenging.
- Episiotomies can become infected. As many as 25 percent of women experience some infection at the site of their episiotomy. A few develop abscesses.
- Some women will experience excessive blood loss with an episiotomy.
- Vaginal swelling is common.
- Some women experience problems with sex for months after the surgery.
- Having an episiotomy may actually increase your chances of tearing further.
- Some women feel mutilated by this routine procedure—and many others feel betrayed or violated by doctors who do not ask permission before performing episiotomy, even when their patients have specifically asked them ahead of time to avoid it. Those feelings of violation can do even more to put a damper on a woman's sex life after birth.

There are times, of course, when an episiotomy is absolutely necessary. If there is fetal distress or cord compression during the second stage of labor, or the presence of meconium (fecal matter from the baby's intestines) in the amniotic fluid has been observed, then episiotomy is appropriate. If the second stage of labor proceeds very rapidly, it may not have been possible to allow for gradual stretching. Other appropriate times include: premature birth (but even then it is usually unnecessary); certain breech births; cephalopelvic disproportion (when the baby's head is too large for the mother's pelvis); before a necessary forceps or vacuum extraction delivery; or if there are signs that tears are occurring near the woman's urethra.

HOW TO AVOID AN EPISIOTOMY

It really is possible to avoid an episiotomy. Statistics show that episiotomy rates are related to *who* assists in a birth and *where* it is done. This means that it is much more about practice and habit than it is about medical necessity. In some countries the episiotomy rates are a third of those in the United States.

Here's what you can do:

- Choose your health care practitioners carefully. In your very first interview, find out how they feel about episiotomy. Ask what percentage of their patients actually receive one—and why. Ask if they are experienced with perineal massage and support of the perineum (shown on page 170) during the second stage of labor.
- Find out how your health care provider feels about epidurals. Having an epidural increases your chances of having an episiotomy, since it may inhibit your ability to push your baby out.
- Practice good nutrition throughout your pregnancy to help keep your tissues supple. It is especially important to get enough vitamin E and fatty acids, especially omega-3s. Keep your protein intake up as well. Review chapter 2 on diet.
- Get plenty of exercise during your pregnancy. Being in good shape increases your body's abil-

ity to perform well during labor. One of the most important things to do is to practice Kegel exercises, as shown in the sidebar on page 55. Kegels will make your pelvic floor muscles strong. This increases your ability to bear down during the second stage and control your progress, slowing down when necessary to allow the perineum to stretch further. It isn't too late to start exercising and doing Kegels now, if you haven't been doing this already.

- Practice perineal massage during your pregnancy, especially in the last six weeks. First, wash your hands. Then lubricate your fingers with oil, such as vitamin E oil or a homemade blend of 1 ounce of wheat germ oil, 3 drops of lavender oil, and 1 drop of geranium oil. Insert both of your thumbs into the vagina and gradually stretch the perineum downward and out. Stretch only until you feel a slight tingling, then hold the stretch until the sensation subsides. You can also massage the perineal tissue between your thumbs and fingers. Think of relaxing during this process, which may help you to automatically relax when it is done while you are in labor. You can prelude massage by soaking in warm water with a little bit of lavender oil to soften the tissues beforehand. Incorporate perineal massage into your lovemaking, if you like.

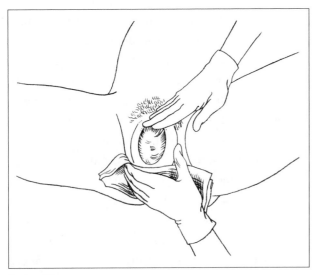

Perineal Support

- Massage and oil the perineum during delivery. If you do this, have a brand-new bottle of oil set aside for labor to help cut down on the possibilities of spreading bacteria around from an already opened one.
- Apply hot compresses during the second stage to help to soften the perineal tissues.
- Ask your midwife or doctor to perform perineal support (shown below) when they notice the perineum turning white from stretching. This means that your practitioner will apply light pressure with their fingers on the perineum. This is when they may also suggest you slow down and refrain from bearing down for a bit. Doctors who perform routine episiotomies will instead decide to perform surgery at this point.
- Take your time during the second stage. Many physicians try to make the second stage of labor happen as quickly as possible. Directed bearing down, as opposed to allowing the mother to push at will once her cervix is fully dilated, increases the necessity for an episiotomy because the perineum does not have adequate time to stretch out.
- Use a variety of birth positions, emphasizing those that take advantage of gravity. Being in an upright position, such as a squat or on hands and knees, reduces the chances that your perineum will tear.

WHAT IF I TEAR?

Tears do sometimes happen during normal birth, no matter how careful you and your practitioner are. Many care providers have observed that small, naturally occurring tears heal more quickly than the straight cuts of an episiotomy. Studies in Dublin, Montreal, and Argentina have shown that superficial tears are less painful than episiotomies, and that even larger tears are certainly no more painful than an episiotomy.[9] If you follow the guidelines above, your chances of tearing will be reduced. In most cases, natural tearing is very minimal. If this happens, you may not need any stitches at all, or you may need three to five of them to close the tear up. In chapter 21, you'll find ways of relieving the pain of tears and helping them to heal more quickly.

As Birth Approaches

When the second stage begins, optimize the environment in your birthing room in preparation for the baby's arrival. This is a good time to dim the lights, first of all. Bright glaring lights are not conducive to relaxation and are hard on the infant's eyes. You may have special candles you've saved for this moment, and you might want to use some fragrant essential oils.

This is also the time to make sure you are surrounded only by people who you are comfortable with. Hospitals, particularly, are notorious for having a constant flow of personnel in and out of patients' rooms. You can ask your midwife or doctor to kindly keep this to a minimum. Even at home you may find you now want privacy, even though you'd originally thought you'd like to be surrounded by loved ones. Do not hesitate to ask people to step outside for a time. Your partner and other birth attendants can handle this for you.

Years ago it was unheard of that a woman should wish to see the afterbirth. Today, nearly every mother who watches her baby born asks me to show her the placenta. This I do, and point out the bag in which the infant, now lying peacefully in her arms, developed and became a perfect little human being.

—GRANTLY DICK-READ, M.D., *Childbirth without Fear*

Your beautiful baby has just been born and been placed, slowly and gently, on your stomach. Flesh-to-flesh contact will probably feel just right to you, so if your gown or T-shirt are still on, you might want some help in removing them. Skin contact will feel good to your baby, too, and keep her warm. You may want to have a blanket placed over both of you and a hat put on your newborn's head to cut down on heat loss.

Now is your chance to touch and gaze at this amazing new life. Babies are incredibly alert directly after birth. You may find him staring at you with wide open eyes! Talk to your baby, if you like. He is already familiar with the sound of your voice from hearing you inside the womb.

If you place the baby on or near your breast, you will observe her beginning to root for the nipple. Some babies do this right away. Others take a bit longer, so be patient and follow the baby's lead. Once the baby begins to move her mouth or lick your nipple, try to get her to latch on (see chapter 23). If you feel unsure about this (and many new mothers do), ask your midwife to help you. If you are in a hospital, ask the nurse to call the lactation consultant for you.

Clamping the Umbilical Cord

In standard hospital births, the umbilical cord is clamped in two places right away, usually within one minute of birth, and then cut between the clamps. More recently, however, many practitioners have begun to perform later cord clamping.

You will notice, when the baby is born, that the umbilical cord is still pulsing with the movement of blood that is flowing to the baby. Proponents of late cord cutting think it best to wait until the cord is no longer pulsing, allowing all of this blood to go to the infant, and then to cut it. If this is something you'd like, discuss it with your midwife or doctor ahead of time.

Those who still prefer early cord clamping sometimes state that earlier clamping cuts down on an infant's blood bilirubin levels, thus reducing his chances of having newborn jaundice. In fact, studies show the difference in bilirubin levels between early- and late-cord-clamped infants is not significant.[1]

Sometimes later cord clamping is not possible, however. Some babies have a short cord, for example. Other babies are born with the cord wrapped around their necks, so that it is necessary to cut it right away.

If a mother is Rh-negative and has an Rh-positive baby, there is an especially good case for leaving the cord until blood has stopped pulsing. This will reduce chances that the Rh-positive baby's blood still in the placenta will backwash into the mother's bloodstream, causing her to develop anti-

Get Your Hormone Boost

Oxytocin and prolactin are two hormones that help you to feel and act like a mother.

Oxytocin is secreted during lovemaking, male and female orgasm, birth, and breastfeeding. It also causes the rhythmic uterine contractions of labor. High levels of oxytocin continue to be produced after birth, culminating with the birth of the placenta, and then gradually subside.

Ongoing oxytocin production is enhanced by skin-to-skin and eye-to-eye contact and by the baby's first suckling. That's another reason it's so important to look at, touch, and breastfeed your baby immediately after birth. These activities keep your contractions strong for delivering the placenta.

Oxytocin also mediates the letdown reflex of breastfeeding and is released in pulses as the baby suckles. During ongoing lactation, oxytocin continues to keep the mother relaxed and well nourished.

Prolactin, the "mothering hormone," produces the aggressive, protective instincts of motherhood, as well as the ability to surrender and submit to the needs of the baby. Levels of prolactin increase in pregnancy and during labor, and peak at birth. Prolactin is also the major hormone involved in breastmilk synthesis and production. In the breastfeeding relationship, prolactin activates the mother's vigilance and helps her to put her baby's needs first.

bodies that can complicate future pregnancies (see "Rhesus incompatibility," page 242).[2]

If your partner would like to be the one who cuts the cord, arrange for this with your birth attendant ahead of time. Cutting the cord is simple and satisfying.

Birthing the Placenta

Once the baby is born, your uterus continues to contract, although you may not feel it happening. The placenta separates from the uterine wall and is expelled. There are two ways of handling the birth of the placenta.

One is the practice of "active management." This means that the practitioner (usually a doctor in a hospital setting) takes a proactive stance and tries to hurry things along. The cord is cut immediately, and oxytocin, or another drug, is administered to create contractions that will expel the placenta, even though this will occur naturally. Sometimes the birth attendant will pull on the cord and ask you to bear down to help it out.

The other method is one of watchful waiting, allowing the placenta to come out naturally. Sometimes gravity can help with this, if the woman sits up or squats for a few moments. She can try to bear down at will and help the process. Nursing the baby can also help because breastfeeding encourages the production of the hormone oxytocin, which causes the uterus to contract. The cord is cut once the placenta is delivered.

Applying pressure to the top of the abdomen is sometimes used by both doctors and midwives to help the placenta to come out.

The average length of time for the third stage of labor in home births is about twenty minutes. In hospitals it is closer to five minutes.

THE AMAZING PLACENTA

The placenta is a most amazing organ—one that tends to get ignored in the rush of excitement over the baby's new arrival! Most of us think of it as a thing that looks like liver, or some other organ, that comes out after the baby is born.

The placenta and the fetus both arise from the same cell. The placenta grows as the baby grows. Blood from the mother is fed to the baby via the placenta. It acts as a filter, allowing some things in and others not. When you hear of certain things, such as

BODY WISE
The Tree of Life

Disposal of the placenta takes on a ritualistic significance in some cultures. In New Zealand, for example, the Maoris believe that the placenta must be buried in ancestral land soon after birth. In the United States, some parents plant their child's placenta under a special tree or in the garden.

In other cultures, the placenta is considered too potent and powerful a medicine to waste, and is reputed for its tonifying effects. In Chinese medicine, for example, the placenta is dried and taken in powdered form as a medicine. Today, it is used worldwide in the healing of burn patients and as a rejuvenating ingredient in cosmetic preparations.

You will want to give some thought as to how you would like to dispose of your baby's afterbirth. Ask if the hospital uses the placenta for burn victims, for example, or tell your attendant ahead of time what you would like to do with the placenta.

medication, "crossing the placenta," it means this is something the placenta does not filter out.

Many cultures around the world attach ritual significance to the disposal of the placenta. In Malaysia, the child and placenta are considered to be siblings. Since it is thought that the two are reunited at death, the *kampong bidan* (midwife) carefully washes the placenta, cord, and membranes and wraps them in a white cloth to be buried. In some cultures the placenta is eaten, just as many animals do. The Maori, from New Zealand, on the other hand, consider cooking the placenta to be taboo. Instead, it is customarily buried on ancestral land.

Generally speaking, midwives have been the keepers of these traditions, passing them on to the next generation of birth attendants. In our culture, where birth has become highly medicalized, there is no sin-

gle tradition. In hospitals, the placenta is sometimes used to help burn victims to recover, but some hospitals simply discard or incinerate it.

Proponents of a practice known as Lotus Birth suggest that it is better not to cut the umbilical cord after birth at all. They wash and pat dry the placenta after birth and keep it attached to the cord and the baby for several days, until the cord falls off by itself. Those who practice Lotus Birth say that it seems as though the baby can feel when the placenta is touched. Lotus Birth practitioners promote keeping the baby quiet and secluded for a time, while the placenta is still attached. They feel this is beneficial to both baby and the family.

Creating some kind of ceremonial treatment for the placenta can be a wonderful way to give thanks for the process of nurturing that has been so much a part of your life for the past nine months. You might bury the placenta under a favorite tree, or in your garden. For some women it is enough to just say a silent prayer of gratitude, or reflect, for a moment, about the amazing journey she has been on.

The Moments after Birth

Breastfeeding and skin-to-skin and eye-to-eye contact with your baby (see page 175) enhance the production of oxytocin, a hormone that wards off postpartum depression and ensures continued uterine contractions that prevent hemorrhage and speed healing. Beta-endorphins, neurotransmitters that accelerate the intense bonding experience between mother and baby, peak in the mother twenty minutes after the birth and are present in breastmilk.

Right after birth, your uterus will be about the size of a grapefruit. You will experience several strong contractions for the first twenty-four hours after birth as your uterus contracts. Over the next six weeks, your uterus will return to its normal, pearlike size. The place where the placenta was attached to the uterus will heal completely, leaving no scar tissue. As your uterus heals over the next six weeks, you will have a bloody discharge that is bright red in the be-

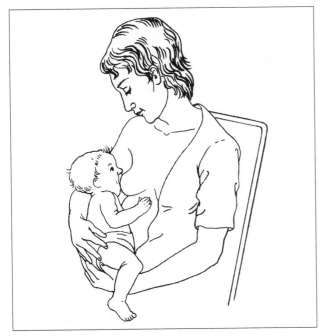

Contact with Your Newborn

ginning and then becomes a pink, brownish, and almost clear or yellowish fluid.

At birth, your breasts contain colostrum, a precursor to breastmilk that contains vital nutrients. Your "true" breastmilk will come in within twenty-four to forty-eight hours after the birth, depending on how soon you begin to nurse your baby. When your milk first comes in, your breasts may feel swollen and tender for a few days.

It may sting at first when you urinate after birth. It may also take a couple of days before your bowel movements become regular again. You may feel sore and bruised.

At birth, your new baby already has a highly developed sense of taste and can distinguish between different flavors in your breastmilk. He can see objects about eight to ten inches away—which is exactly the distance between your face and his when you're breastfeeding. He is already accustomed to hearing your voice and will respond to it when you talk or sing. Within just a few days, your baby will know you by smell alone.

Touch is especially essential to newborns. Your baby needs to be held in order to feel secure and uses touch to learn about his environment. You may be surprised how much your baby wants to be held, but it is just what he needs.

Your baby may lose a little weight right after birth if you do not breastfeed immediately, but otherwise he should gain steadily. He should soak six to eight diapers daily.

At first, your baby will sleep most of the time. Gradually over the course of her first two weeks her periods of wakefulness will increase. It will take a couple of weeks before your baby begins to establish her own schedule.

HIGHER GROUND

Here's a simple breathing meditation adapted from the meditations of monk and author Thich Nhat Hanh. You can use this exercise to refresh yourself as a new mother, even while you're breastfeeding:

- Inhale for 4 to 6 seconds.
- As you slowly inhale, say silently to yourself, "Breathing in, I calm my body."
- Hold your breath for 1 second.
- Exhale for 8 seconds.
- As you slowly exhale, say to yourself, "Breathing out, I smile."
- Hold your breath for 4 seconds.

Repeat as often as necessary.

Among the most important of the newborn infant's needs are the signals it receives through the skin, its first medium of communication with the outside world.

—ASHLEY MONTAGU, *Touching: The Human Significance of Skin*

As discussed in the previous chapter, during the moments directly after the birth, you need plenty of time to rest quietly with your baby. Don't let anything stand in the way of that. If you give birth in a hospital, there may be some pressure from nurses who have a routine to follow. They may want to take the baby to a warming bed in the nursery, or to an examination. You are the best warmer a newborn baby can have, especially if you can hold him skin-to-skin, not wrapped up in a tight bundle. If for some reason you are not able to hold your baby, then your partner can, instead. As long as your baby is not sick, you have the right to insist on time to hold him and begin to breastfeed.

Your midwife or doctor will want to see that your baby is in generally good health. It should be possible to do all that is necessary while you are holding the baby. These factors will be checked:

- The baby's weight and length at birth.
- The baby's air passages. Many birth attendants routinely suction the airways, while others feel it best to leave the baby to do this on her own and only intervene if necessary.
- The baby's heart rate.
- The baby's tummy, to see if the liver and spleen seem to be all right.
- The baby's skull.

- The roof of the baby's mouth, to check for cleft palate.
- The genitals, if it is a boy, to see whether both testes are present.

Newborn Testing and Treatment

APGAR RATING

Your baby will be tested at one minute after birth, and again at five minutes, using the standard Apgar scoring system. This checks five points:

- **A**ppearance (skin tone)
- **P**ulse (heart rate)
- **G**rimace (response to stimulation)
- **A**ctivity (muscle tone)
- **R**espiration (breathing effort)

A baby can get 0, 1, or 2 points for each category, with a maximum score of 10 for all the points together. Most babies score a 7 or higher. Many infants score in the low range on the first test, but then score much higher on the second one, after they've had a few minutes to adjust to their surroundings. It should be possible to conduct this test right at your side, so the baby does not need to be taken away from you.

Keep in mind that the Apgar rating is subjective. It

> ## BODY WISE
> ## Hold Your Baby
>
> Holding your baby for the first hour after birth activates nature's hormonal blueprints for the brain and nervous system of both mother and baby.
>
> Mothers in all cultures instinctively cradle their babies at their left breast. When the baby is in contact with the mother's heart rhythm through this skin-to-skin contact, the mother's senses, instincts, and intelligence are flooded with the supportive, confirmative, instinctual information that she needs for this radical change in environment. The mother instinctively knows what to do, and begins to communicate with her baby on a nonverbal level.
>
> This awakening of maternal capabilities is well known among animal researchers, who link it to the action of pregnancy and birth hormones on the brains of mothers who have recently delivered.

is an evaluation done only with a visual check, and one person may tend to score very differently than another.

VITAMIN K SHOTS

Babies are born with extremely low levels of vitamin K—in fact, most mammals are born with low levels of this vitamin. Scientists are not sure just how vitamin K is metabolized in the body, but it is known to promote coagulation of the blood, although it is not a clotting agent in and of itself.

A few infants get newborn hemorrhagic disease soon after birth, a potentially life-threatening disorder that causes severe bleeding. Other infants, about 1 in 17,000,[1] get this same disease later, between two and twelve weeks of life. Because of this risk, it has become general practice to give *all* newborn infants a vitamin K injection shortly after birth, whether or not that infant is in a high-risk category for hemorrhagic disease. The hope is that increasing vitamin K levels in the baby's body will boost his ability to coagulate blood. Indeed, this treatment has proven to be a deterrent, cutting the rate of late-onset hemorrhagic disease down considerably.

In many other countries, including Canada, Sweden, and Britain, oral vitamin K is given instead, usually in three separate doses over the first few weeks of life. It is considered to be much more humane to give the supplement orally, rather than subject a newborn infant to the pain of a shot. As well, it reduces the slight chance of infection from having an injection at this early age. This approach has been shown to be effective, as long as parents are diligent about giving the follow-up doses—but unfortunately oral vitamin K is not always available in the United States.

The safety of vitamin K supplements is a matter of great controversy. There has been some speculation that they may increase risk for leukemia and other cancers in children after a study in Britain showed this possibility. While further studies have not backed up this concern so far, the potential for such serious illnesses warrants caution. More recent concerns focus on high percentages of newborn jaundice in infants who have been given this shot, perhaps because vitamin K is synthesized by the liver. In fact, some vitamin K packaging warns of this possibility and adds the disclaimer, "Little is known about the metabolic fate of Vitamin K."[2]

Some newborns *are* at higher risk for early hemorrhagic disease. If the mother has been treated with anticoagulants, antiseizure medications, or antibiotics during her pregnancy, for example, there is an increased chance of it. Women who have used extremely excessive amounts of vitamin E, aspirin, mineral oil, alcohol, or have been exposed to rat poison are also in a high-risk group. On the other hand, if you avoid these substances and eat a sensible diet with plenty of vitamin K–rich foods such as green vegetables, alfalfa, kelp, green tea, and dairy products, you will not be in this high-risk group and will reduce the chances that your infant will have hemorrhagic disease at birth.

There might be a good reason why most mammalian infants are born with low vitamin K levels—and we just haven't figured out why. Unfortunately, proponents of vitamin K injections suggest that breastfed babies are at higher risk for the later onset type of hemorrhagic disease. This is because human milk is naturally lower in vitamin K than cow's milk. This does not mean, however, that the levels in breastmilk are not enough. Colostrum, the first fluid a breastfeeding infant receives from his mother for three to four days, is quite rich in vitamin K.

In many states in the United States, having a vitamin K injection is mandatory. In New York State, for example, refusing the treatment can result in having Child Protection Services take your child away from you. In other states, it is possible to refuse the treatment without risk of intervention, but a great deal of pressure is put on parents to comply with it.

If you have a home birth or use a birth center, you will need to go to a hospital, clinic, or doctor's office to have the vitamin K injection or oral dose, as midwives are not generally licensed to give injections to newborns.

EYE TREATMENTS

Another routine newborn treatment is the application of antibiotics to the infant's eyes shortly after birth. This is done by midwives after home births, and in hospitals and birth centers to prevent gonorrhea, or other infections, from attacking the newborn's eyes and potentially causing blindness. About 5 percent of women who give birth do have gonorrhea. Most are not even aware of it. Unfortunately, tests for this disease are notoriously inaccurate—it is quite easy to test a false negative.

On the other hand, blindness from gonorrhea does not happen instantaneously. No tests have been conducted to see if having the eye drops as a preventative is any more effective than watching your baby for signs of trouble.[3] If you do choose to skip the antibiotic treatment, report any signs of irritation or infection, such as oozing or redness, to your baby's health care provider, explaining that she was not given antibiotic eyedrops at birth.

Hospitals used to apply a solution of silver nitrate to infants' eyes before the use of antibiotic ointments became common. A few still do use it, so be sure to ask. Avoid silver nitrate because it stings and appears to be quite painful to newborns. It causes puffiness and oozing in the eyes. It is also not effective in treating chlamydia, another sexually transmitted disease that can affect a newborn's eyesight.

If you decide to go ahead with the eye treatments (and, again, in some states, you have no choice), be sure to delay it for one hour. The ointment will temporarily blur your baby's vision—so take some time to bond and cuddle together first.

PKU SCREENING

Phenylketonuria, or PKU, is a rare error in the metabolism of an essential amino acid, phenylala-

---

NATURAL SOOTHER

Arnica, Oh, Arnica

As you are making decisions during the early minutes and hours of your baby's life, you will still want to take care of your own healing. *Arnica,* a homeopathic remedy associated with relieving sports injuries, bruises, and bumps, is a perfect remedy for this time.

Arnica montana (leopard's bane) provides both mental relief and physical comfort. It works internally and externally on bruised, traumatized tissue, helps to stop bleeding, prevents infection, helps to heal stitches, and soothes hemorrhoids.

Ask your homeopathic practitioner if *Arnica* is right for you. You'll find *Arnica* 30X in your natural products store. Take 3 to 5 pellets every fifteen minutes after birth until you feel comfortable.

nine. The bodies of afflicted infants are unable to process this amino acid, which is found in animal proteins, including dairy products. If your baby is born with this problem and it is left untreated, it will eventually result in some degree of mental retardation, possibly severe, and other physical problems, including hyperactivity, severe exzema, and convulsions. Although it is not curable, if it is caught early and dietary changes are put in place, it is possible to bypass most or all of these troubles. The problem is that these dietary changes, to be most effective, need to be started as soon as possible, hopefully before the age of three months.

In most states it is mandatory for all infants to have this screening within two to six days of age. The baby needs to eat for two to three days before the test can be effectively processed. If you have given birth in a hospital setting, you may not be permitted to leave until this has been completed. If you give birth at home, or in most birth centers, you will need to go to a hospital, doctor's office, or clinic to have the PKU screening done.

Blood samples to test for PKU are usually taken by pricking the baby's heel with a sharp lancet. The blood fills three quarter-size circles on an absorbent card. In most hospitals, protocol forbids the mother from holding the infant during this procedure, which is clearly a painful one.

One carefully conducted study in Stockholm, Sweden, compared the response between newborns who had blood taken in the standard way, via heel lancing, to infants that had blood drawn with venipuncture (a small needle inserted into a vein).[4] The result was quite dramatic. The infants who had blood drawn with venipuncture cried less vigorously and for a shorter period of time. It was also easier. With venipuncture it only took one try in 86 percent of the babies. With lancing it took one try in only 40 percent of babies.

Ask your institution to use venipuncture rather than heel lancing, or to allow you to hold your baby while the procedure is done, as these measures are obviously more humane. You might want to specifically ask for someone who has experience drawing

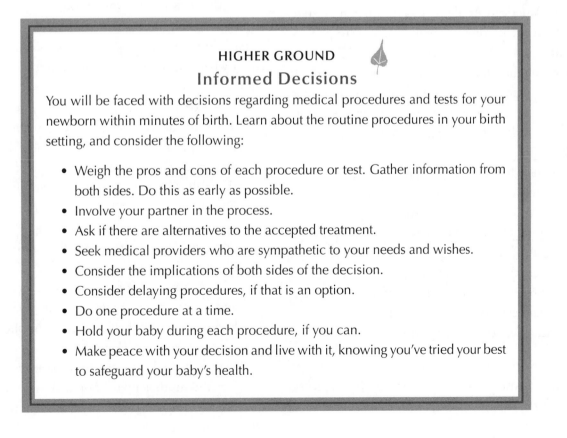

HIGHER GROUND
Informed Decisions

You will be faced with decisions regarding medical procedures and tests for your newborn within minutes of birth. Learn about the routine procedures in your birth setting, and consider the following:

- Weigh the pros and cons of each procedure or test. Gather information from both sides. Do this as early as possible.
- Involve your partner in the process.
- Ask if there are alternatives to the accepted treatment.
- Seek medical providers who are sympathetic to your needs and wishes.
- Consider the implications of both sides of the decision.
- Consider delaying procedures, if that is an option.
- Do one procedure at a time.
- Hold your baby during each procedure, if you can.
- Make peace with your decision and live with it, knowing you've tried your best to safeguard your baby's health.

blood from infants to do this, particularly if you gave birth at home and have come to the hospital just to have this test done. While this should not present a problem, hospitals and clinics do like to stick to their routines. It takes people asking for these changes over and over to finally make a difference.

Medical Circumcision

Circumcision is a surgical procedure in which the foreskin of a male is removed from the penis. It is done by some people, particularly those of the Jewish faith, for religious reasons. More commonly, in the United States, it has been done for medical reasons. It was thought, in the past, that circumcision prevented a huge range of problems from cancer to uncleanliness to compulsive masturbation.

During the Cold War era, circumcision became a part of routine hospital care after birth—so routine, in fact, that parents were usually not even consulted beforehand. In the 1970s, a series of lawsuits made parental consent mandatory.

The American Academy of Pediatrics now states that there are no proven medical reasons to perform circumcision. Despite this, in 1998, 57 percent of boys in the United States were circumcised.[5] In 1992, 64 percent of boys were circumcised, so there has been some improvement over the past few years, but the rates are still quite high compared to the rest of the world.

The male foreskin is a uniquely specialized organ. As an extension of the penile shaft skin, the foreskin covers and usually extends beyond the glans before folding under itself and reattaching around the edges of the glans. The foreskin is a double-layered organ. Its true length is twice the length of its external fold, comprising 80 percent or more of the penile skin covering.[6] Let's take a look at some of the purposes this "little piece of skin" performs:

- It protects the glans and keeps its surface soft, moist, and sensitive, just as your eyelids protect your eyes.

- It maintains optimal warmth, pH balance, and cleanliness. The foreskin produces oils that maintain proper health of the glans surface, which does not actually produce any oil of its own.

- The foreskin contains special cells and proteins that indicate it has an immunological and antiviral function.

- The foreskin is as sensitive as your fingertips or the lips of your mouth. It seems its presence may make subtle, but discernible, differences in how sex is experienced by both the man himself and his partner. Furthermore, without its protection, the glans itself becomes *less* sensitive.

- The foreskin provides extra skin for an erection. The foreskin, as mentioned before, actually makes up 80 percent of the skin on the penis. When a man has an erection, this skin stretches out to accommodate it. Men who have had circumcisions sometimes have a problem with the skin being too tight.

Here are some important factors to take into account when considering whether or not you will circumcise your boy:

- It is extremely painful. Until very recently, it was thought that newborns did not really register pain in the same way adults do. Boys were circumcised without any type of anesthesia at all. We now know that is simply untrue. Furthermore, the effects of experiencing this painful surgery may be long-lasting. One study done in Canada revealed that four-month-old baby boys who were circumcised at birth seemed to cry more often, be more cranky, and display signs of higher sensitivity.[7] No one knows how long this lower pain threshold may continue to affect boys.

- Going through this painful experience may affect the mother-infant bond. A study done at the Washington University School of Medicine showed that most babies would not nurse right after they were circumcised, and those who did would not look into their mothers' eyes.[8] This is significant because, in fact, most babies do gaze at their mothers' faces while nursing, if they are awake.

- Circumcision is surgery, and surgery is never risk-free. Circumcision has a surgical complication rate of 1 in 500.[9] Most of those complications are local infection and mild bleeding. However, there are also cases of very severe infection and gangrene. The operation leaves a large open wound on the penis, which various bacteria can easily enter. There are also cases of baby boys who have had some or all of the glans removed during the procedure by mistake, and there are also fatalities. Oddly, although circumcision rates have gone down a bit, fatalities from the surgery, or from the accompanying anesthesia, have gone up. In 1999, the National Center for Health Statistics reported 51 infant deaths as a result of this surgical procedure.[10]

- Circumcision does not help prevent penile cancer or transmission of sexually transmitted diseases, as it was once thought. It does not keep the penis cleaner—in fact, the result is quite the opposite. Without the protection of the foreskin, it is much easier for bacteria to enter the area.

- It pays to ask yourself whether you have the right to cut off a part of your child's genitals without his permission. In chapter 5 we discussed the concept of informed consent. That concept allows for parental permission to perform medical interventions only in the case of clear and immediate medical necessity, since, clearly, a child cannot give informed consent on his own. There are almost no situations where circumcision can be considered a medical necessity.

Fathers who are circumcised may have a great deal of trouble making a decision about not circumcising their baby sons. They may worry that their sons will wonder why their penises do not look the same. Exploring the issue may bring up a lot of emotions for a man. He may feel angry about his own circumcision, or may unknowingly want to justify his own circumcision by having it done to his child. Religious preferences may come into play as well, and that can increase conflicts between partners. Try to concentrate on what is best for your baby. In cases where parents disagree about circumcision, it may help to seek out some counseling.

Vaccinations

By the time your child is just a few days old, you will need to make some important decisions about the role vaccines will play in the life of your baby, whether you're still in the hospital or during your first visit to your pediatrician or family practitioner.

What are vaccines and how do they work? Vaccines are fragments of inert bacterial or viral material that fool the immune system into thinking that there is an ongoing infection. The immune system responds by producing the antibodies that would occur with an actual infection, thus vaccinating the recipient.

NATURAL IMMUNITY

Babies are born with some natural immunity, especially during the first year of life, which they have received from their mothers while in the womb. They have some inborn immunity, for example, against diseases like measles, rubella, and tetanus, if the mother had immunity. There may be less immunity to other diseases such as polio and pertussis.

Babies also receive some immunity from breastfeeding. Breastfed babies get sick less often than formula-fed babies. Breastfed children also develop higher levels of immunity after being vaccinated than do formula-fed babies.

THE PROS AND CONS OF VACCINES

There is no doubt that vaccines have greatly decreased the outbreak of many acute diseases, such as measles, and have helped to eliminate others, such as smallpox. As the rates of acute infectious childhood diseases decrease, however, there have been increases in the number of chronic diseases, such as autism, asthma, learning disabilities, attention deficit/hyperactivity disorders, diabetes, and more. Some experts now believe that vaccinations might play a role in the increase of these diseases.

J. Barthelow Classen, M.D., founder of Classen Immunotherapies, has published epidemiological data demonstrating a pattern of increased cases of insulin-dependent diabetes in children correlating with increases in the use of certain vaccines, specifically *Haemophilus influenza* and hepatitis B. Stephanie Cave, M.D., a professor at Louisiana State University with a private practice in Baton Rouge, specializes in allergies, attention deficit disorder, autism, and other neuroimmune dysfunction. She treats over 400 children with autism a year. "Family genetics, family socioeconomic conditions, family medical histories, and the children's individual biochemical makeup will impact the risk/benefit ratio of these vaccines," says Cave. "What we see coming through the parents' histories over and over again in our office is that the development delays began after the vaccines."[11]

ADDITIVES

One of the biggest concerns about the safety of all vaccines has to do with additives that they contain. Until recently, most vaccines contained the preservative thimerosal—better known as mercury. In fact, the FDA acknowledges that most children get more mercury in the first six months of life than is considered safe by the Environmental Protection Agency.

Mercury is generally considered to be unsafe in food products and over-the-counter-drugs, yet until recently it was used consistently in vaccines. Adults get rid of mercury by secreting bile, but infants' immature livers do not yet produce bile. They are subject to mercury poisoning, which has symptoms very similar to autism, including social withdrawal, hypersensitivity to noise and touch, and repetitive and

self-injurious behavior. A confidential report authored by the Centers for Disease Control was recently made public by a law firm investigating a case of vaccine reaction. This report suggests that mercury exposure may increase a child's risk of developing autism by 2.48 times.[12]

While most childhood vaccines are now thimerosal free, the flu vaccine is not available without thimerosal. Be sure to ask about this before your infant receives any shot.

Other ingredients of concern include aluminum, formaldehyde, antibiotics, DNA and RNA from animals, and many other chemicals. How these substances affect our children is not fully understood, and their impact may not be known for decades.

STRUGGLES FOR VACCINE SAFETY

In 1999 Lynn Redwood, a nurse and the mother of an autistic son, came across an FDA report mentioning that children who received vaccines containing thimerosal, a mercury preservative, might possibly exceed federal guidelines for mercury exposure. She had a lock of her son's hair tested, and it revealed levels of mercury and aluminum at almost five times the acceptable amounts.

Redwood and other parents whose children suffer from mercury-induced neurological disorders formed the organization SAFEMINDS (Sensible Action for Ending Mercury-Induced Neurological Disorders). SAFEMINDS is currently working with Congressman Dan Burton (R-Indiana) to obtain raw data from a CDC study on thimerosal and vaccine safety through the Freedom of Information Act.

Another organization formed by parents of autistic children is the MIND (Medical Investigation of Neurological Disorders) Institute at the University of California–Davis Medical Center. This organization has quickly become the largest autism research institute in the world and is awarding grants, for the first time in history, for independent research into the relationship between vaccines and autism. Up until now, there has been a lack of studies on the possible adverse effects of vaccine. The FDA only requires short-term studies by the vaccine manufacturers prior to approval, and these are not independently done.

Although nonprofit groups are making some headway in their cry for more research, it isn't easy to fight the economic power behind vaccines. Vaccine manufacturers are a powerful political group: the production of vaccines is a $7-billion-a-year industry in the United States. In one year, for example, the worldwide sales of hepatitis B vaccine totaled $2 billion. A single vaccine can cost anywhere from $50 to $250 or more.

MAKING INFORMED DECISIONS ABOUT VACCINATION

Within the next few weeks, you will need to make decisions about many vaccines. The American Academy of Pediatricians recommends that before age two, babies receive vaccinations for diphtheria, tetanus, pertussis, influenza, polio, measles, mumps, rubella, chicken pox, and, in most states, hepatitis B. You will have to make a decision about hepatitis B upon the birth of your infant, as it is routinely administered to newborns in most states.

Because the benefits and risks must be weighed carefully, it's a good idea to review the current research and the issues involved with each of these vaccines. For example, the hepatitis B vaccine is now mandatory for most newborns, yet hepatitis B is primarily a sexually transmitted disease. Current statistics indicate that there are ten times more negative reactions to this vaccine than to any other—in fact, the National Vaccine Information Center (NVIC) released figures in 1999 showing that vaccine-related adverse reactions and deaths in children under the age of fourteen far outweighed the reported cases of the disease in the same age group. The American Association of Physicians and Surgeons recommends a moratorium on giving the hepatitis B vaccine to infants until more research is done.

Some experts think that the number of vaccines infants receive at one time, or the early ages when vaccines are given to infants, may be problematic. Boyd Haley, Ph.D., head of the chemistry department at the University of Kentucky, says that "giving a ten-pound infant a single vaccine in a day is the equivalent of giving a 100-pound adult 40 vaccines in a day."

Discuss each of these vaccines with your baby's health care provider so that you can make an informed choice. While vaccines are mandatory in forty-two states, all states offer medical, religious, or philosophical exemptions. The resource section of this book lists a number of advocacy groups and Web sites that offer more information to help you with this complex decision.

PART FIVE

Postpartum

CHAPTER 21

Taking Care of Yourself as a New Mother

During the early days postpartum with our four kids, we always put a sign on our door
to remind people that our home was a special sanctuary with a newborn inside.

—AVIVA JILL ROMM, *Natural Health after Birth*

Around the world, the postpartum period is considered a special time—a time in which a mother is born, as well as a baby. Many cultures have special practices and customs that serve to recognize this very special time in the life of a woman: the postpartum period. In many cultures, women are not expected to carry on their usual lives, but are revered and recognized for the new journey they are beginning.

In the Indian Ayurvedic tradition, new mothers stay at home and are pampered for twenty-two days after birth. This period of rest is considered vital to protect the delicate nervous systems of both mother and infant. Few visitors are allowed, and mother and child are protected from wind and bad weather.

In Japan, a new mother is treated as if she were the baby—she's put to bed for thirty days, waited on, and indulged while she recuperates from the birth.

In parts of Southeast Asia, a father begins to collect wood during the pregnancy, stacking it in a special place and reserving it for a practice called "mother-warming." After the birth, the house is closed up and a sign on the front door announces the new arrival, letting the community know that the new family needs quiet time. The father lights a fire next to or beneath the mother's bed, and she and the new baby are wrapped in warm blankets. Mother and baby are kept inside this womblike environ-ment, removed from the demands of daily life, and kept safe from wind and rain for several days or weeks, depending on the culture.

While Western countries do not have ceremonies or rituals quite like these, many do pay special attention to a new mother's needs, particularly in Europe and Scandinavia. In Holland, for example, where many births take place at home, a specially trained live-in maternity nurse stays with the mother for the first eight to ten days. She reports directly to the midwife and keeps her posted as to the mother and baby's progress. She also cooks, cleans, and helps take care of other children in the family. Until recently, women in the United States were encouraged to remain in bed for at least ten days after giving birth. Even the poorest women had friends and family to help around the house during the postpartum period.

The Importance of the Postpartum Period

Today, we recognize that moderate exercise and fresh air are beneficial to women after birth, helping them to heal faster. Hospital stays for the postpartum period have been drastically reduced, and we're encouraged to believe that we should be on our feet and back to normal within just a few days of birth. There are many benefits to the extended period of rest that follows birth in many cultures, but ours has been too quick to discard those customs in favor of a rapid return to "normal" life. Why?

One reason is the modern trend toward living far from our extended families. You may not live near your mother, mother-in-law, sisters, or cousins—and even if you have family nearby, their own busy schedules and finances may prevent them from giving you a great deal of their time.

Our culture's emphasis on independence often makes it difficult for women to admit that we can't do everything without help, even immediately after giving birth. While the trend toward female independence has reaped tremendous benefits over the decades, it can backfire drastically during the postpartum period—a time when your greatest responsibility is to rest and recover.

Economics have also contributed to the modern belief that women should resume normal activities immediately following birth. Many women return to work after just six weeks of maternity leave—and often it's unpaid leave, placing additional financial and emotional burdens upon the new mother and her family. Economics also play a role in the ever-shortening hospital stays for women who give birth there, since insurance companies usually cover only one or two days of care. While most women can't wait to get home from the hospital, the trend toward shorter stays has contributed to the impression that they are fully recovered and should carry on as usual.

The postpartum period needs to be treated as a special time, a time when women deserve extra care. Your mind and body are engaging in important work right now, whether or not you are consciously aware of it, including:

- *Physical healing.* It takes your body approximately six weeks to heal. During that period, postpartum bleeding completely stops. This is a time of unparalleled change in your body as your reproductive tract returns to its non-pregnant state. In addition, your cardiovascular, respiratory, musculoskeletal, urologic, gastroin-

NATURAL SOOTHER
Sitz Bath

Sitz baths or full body baths can be wonderfully healing and comforting right after birth. Here are two great recipes, one for a sitz bath and one for a regular bath.

A sitz bath is a shallow bath in water just high enough to cover your hipbones. They're easier and safer than a full bath in the early days postpartum. You can enjoy one once or twice a day for three to five days after birth. They are safe as early as one hour after birth. Sitz baths are highly recommended if you have perineal soreness or tearing or had an episiotomy.

Run hot water for the sitz bath, and when the temperature is comfortable and it is deep enough, add 3 drops lavender oil and 3 drops cypress oil. Mix well with the warm bath water and sit down in the water at once. Lavender encourages new skin growth, while cypress has astringent properties and constricts the blood vessels.

You may prefer to add a tea of healing herbs to a sitz bath or a full body bath. For a sitz bath, reduce this recipe by half.

Bring 4 quarts of water to a boil. Take the pan off the stove and add one handful each of the following dried herbs (use two handfuls if the herbs are fresh):

Lavender flowers

Comfrey leaves

Sage leaves

Calendula flowers

Rosemary

To this mixture add good quality sea salt without iodine. Add 1/2 to 1 cup of salt, depending on the size of your tub.

Strain the liquid and add the tea to your bathwater. Soak and enjoy. Your baby can enjoy this bath with you, too.

testinal, endocrine, and nervous systems all also return to a nonpregnant state. If you experienced perineal tearing or had an episiotomy, you may be experiencing pain that makes it difficult to sit down. If you required a cesarean, you need additional time for muscular healing, and may be recovering from loss of blood. Some practitioners think of the postpartum period as a "fourth trimester." While some mothers feel "back to normal" at six weeks, others may require up to three months.

- *Learning to breastfeed.* If you're breastfeeding for the first time—or even if you've breast-fed several babies—it can take time to master this practice, and it can be emotionally frustrating.

- *Bonding.* Most people still believe that mother/infant bonding happens immediately and completely, right after birth. Some lucky women do experience "love at first sight." For others, bonding can take a week or more. In any case, bonding is an ongoing process that requires a tranquil postpartum period.

- *Hormonal changes.* While your hormones are hard at work helping every cell and organ in your body to return to their prepregnancy state, the fluctuating levels may leave you feeling vulnerable and fatigued. Until your body recovers, you may cry at the drop of a hat or feel an overwhelming sense of joy.

- *Dealing with new emotions.* Even if you have other children, you're now faced with a completely new experience. The new sense of responsibility, your protective love for your new baby, and your fears for his health and safety can seem overwhelming—and you need time to adjust to these new emotions.

- *Adjusting to relationships.* No matter how well you've planned things, your relationship with your partner will undergo changes. Until you both adjust to the new situation, it can be stressful. If you have other children, you may feel guilty for taking attention away from them, or you may mourn the loss of the exclusive relationship you once had with an older child.

- *Starting the process of separation.* For many months, you and your baby have been functioning as one. The postpartum period is the first step in a long and gradual process of separation that will carry on for many years. It may feel strange at first, and takes getting used to.

- *Learning new things.* While changing a diaper is not intrinsically difficult, it is new. So are a hundred other things about a new baby. How do you answer the telephone while breastfeeding? How do you bathe a baby? How can you schedule anything—even reading the newspaper—when you don't know when the baby will be sleeping? Unfortunately, you'll be learning these new skills "on the job," and it will take time to develop your own methods.

Postpartum Doulas

The benefits of hiring a doula to help you during labor and birth were discussed in chapter 7. As noted earlier, doulas can also help you in the critical postpartum period. If you used a labor doula, she might also be able to work with you after the birth—or you might decide to hire a specialized *postpartum doula* to complement the help of friends and families, or compensate for their lack of availability.

A postpartum doula is hired to care for the mother. She may change occasional diapers or give the baby a bath, if you need that kind of help (if you are recovering from a cesarean, for example), but her primary focus is to help you so that you can care for your new baby. Doulas vary in experience and skills, but here is a short list of the basics you can expect from one:

- Emotional support and encouragement
- Help with baby care and breastfeeding
- Advice on self-care, nutrition, and postpartum healing
- Screening calls and visitors

- Light housekeeping, laundry, meal preparation, and errands
- Help with older children (driving or entertaining them)

If your partner is taking time off, you may feel you don't need the services of a doula. While this may be true, partners may also need time to adapt to the new situation, and may not be experienced at caring for others while juggling the demands of a new baby.

It is best to line up the services of a doula ahead of time. However, if you realize that you need a doula during the postpartum period, don't hesitate to call a doula service (see appendix 2) or ask a friend for a reference. Try to find a doula with skills that match your needs—for example, familiarity with vegetarian cooking or knowledge of your neighborhood.

Doula services vary in their fee arrangements. Some offer a package of postpartum care, while others require that you pay for a minimum number of hours.

Easing the Postpartum Period

You may be on an adrenaline high right after the birth and may feel like you can conquer the world! This is not likely to last, however, and when your energy levels plummet, you may be discouraged. For this reason, it may help you to think of the first few days after the birth as your "lying-in" period, just as women did in olden times. Consider staying in bed for most of the first week. Dress in your pajamas to remind yourself to take it easy, and if you feel more energetic and are able to get up and do more, then you'll be pleasantly surprised.

Here is a potpourri of tips to consider during the postpartum period:

- *Keep visitors to a minimum.* Limit visitors to people who will help you or make you feel good, and set time limits on visits so you won't be tired out. This may not be easy—you may be worried that you will insult others. This is the time to put your own needs first. Ask your part-

> ### BODY WISE
> #### Mini-Situps
>
> You can begin these within days after birth. Lie on the bed or the floor with your legs straight and your hands crossed over your abdomen. Take a deep breath. As you exhale, raise your head while you gently press your abdominal muscles toward the center of your belly. Hold for three seconds, then slowly lower your head. Repeat 3 to 5 times each day.

ner or doula to screen calls and visitors if you're not up to the task.

- *Stock up on nutrient-dense food.* Good choices include yogurt, eggs, beans, tofu, fish, chicken, sweet potatoes, leafy green vegetables, avocados, sunflower seeds, nuts, butter, hard cheese, whole grains, and fresh fruits. You will need 500 to 700 calories more per day than when you were pregnant. Fat stored during pregnancy will provide for 200 to 300 calories daily for the first three months; the rest must come from your diet. You'll also need more fluids. Plan on drinking ten 8-ounce glasses of water each day. Leave a glass of water or water bottles near the areas where you are likely to nurse during the day.
- *Redefine time.* Jennifer Louden, author of *The Pregnant Woman's Comfort Book,* refers to this period as living in "baby time." This means that you're now on the baby's schedule, and will need to gradually relearn time management. You'll need to take life one moment at a time and set realistic expectations for what you can accomplish. Resist the temptation to get too much done until you've had time to adapt to your new life.
- *Move around.* While it's important to get adequate rest, it's also important to exercise once you feel ready. Exercise will speed healing and improve your mood. While you are still in the

lying-in period, you can start to do simple movements in bed that will get your circulation going. Try rolling your ankles and wrists around. Stretch long like a cat, and then stretch each limb out, one at a time. Sit up in bed and let your head drop forward, like a heavy ball. Gently roll it from side to side to stretch out your neck muscles.

- *Don't become isolated.* Isolation is a problem most new mothers face. Once the deluge of visitors and the household helpers are gone, many women find themselves virtually alone. If you've been accustomed to adult company, this can be difficult. This is the time when a support system is critical. Breastfeeding support groups, mothers' groups, and postpartum exercise classes can be terrific social outlets.
- *Communicate.* Communication with other people is critical. So talk—talk to your partner, your girlfriends, your mother, other mothers, or a therapist. There's a lot going on in your life now, and it's important to communicate with others.

Healing Your Body

It isn't just emotional changes that create postpartum strain and fatigue. Amazing physical changes have taken place as well. Your body went through an awesome transformation for nine months, culminating in the traumatic experience of birth. It will take some time for your body to return to its earlier state. In the meantime, you may experience the following symptoms:

BLEEDING

You will continue to bleed for two to six weeks after the birth. This bleeding, or lochia, is the shedding of the lining of the uterus that built up during pregnancy. Bleeding should be moderate to heavy during the first three to five days after birth. You may also pass a few clots, some as big as an egg. As you near the second week postpartum, the bleeding will

---

POSTPARTUM WARNING SIGNS

Your birth attendant will check on you several times during the postpartum period. Meanwhile, your doula can help you to understand what is normal. Here are some warning signs that indicate you should contact your birth attendant right away.

- You soak more than two pads in a half hour or four pads in four hours.
- You have any bright red bleeding after the fourth day postpartum.
- Your lochia has a strong, unpleasant odor.
- You have a fever of over 101 degrees (aside from the first twenty-four hours after birth).
- Your breasts are red, hot, and painful.
- You have pain, burning, or difficulty when urinating.
- You have swelling, redness, heat, or discharge from the site of a cesarean incision.
- You have depression that makes it difficult for you to care for your baby.

These situations require the help of a health care professional; call your birth attendant if you experience any of these symptoms, or if for any reason you don't feel that you are steadily recovering after your birth.

---

lighten to a watery brown color, and gradually over the next few weeks it will become lighter and eventually stop.

Use disposable, unbleached menstrual pads, as these are the most hygienic. Avoid tampons, cloth menstrual pads, or menstrual sponges during the first month.

Be cautious about doing any strenuous lifting, pushing or exercise, as these can cause bleeding to resume, and postpartum hemorrhage can occur up to thirty days after birth.

Eat iron-rich foods during the first few weeks postpartum to compensate for any blood loss. Include red meat, dark-meat turkey, red beans, lentils, kale, collards, broccoli, raisins, black mission figs, apricots, and cherries.

PERINEAL SORENESS

Whether or not you had an episiotomy or experienced tearing, your perineum will be sore from the stretching of the birth, and you may experience some stinging pain. Here are a few techniques that will encourage healing of the area:

- Sit on a doughnut- or half-moon-shaped pillow to avoid placing more pressure on the area.
- Apply an ice pack to the area as often as you like. Leave it on for no more than twenty minutes at a time, and take a break of at least twenty minutes.
- Prepare a convenient, soothing sitz bath. Run warm water until the bath is just deep enough to cover your hipbones. Add 3 drops lavender essential oil and 3 drops cypress oil, and mix vigorously. Sit and enjoy! You can also double the amounts in this formula for a regular bath.
- Keep some witch hazel or aloe, or a mixture of the two, in the refrigerator. Use a plastic squeeze bottle to apply to the perineal area as often as you like. This mixture will ease discomfort and encourage healing of the perineal tissues.
- Apply some tea tree oil to the perineal area with a cotton ball or swab. You can dilute the tea tree oil with 1/4 teaspoon almond or olive oil. Then sprinkle on a mixture of equal parts of goldenseal, comfrey, myrrh, and echinacea powders. Hold a warm washcloth on the area. This will help to reduce swelling and redness after a few applications.
- When wiping after urination, you may want to just rinse with water or your plastic squeeze-bottle solution, and dab or drip dry.

- Do Kegels. The Kegel muscles are the support system for the muscles of the lower pelvis. Contracting them tones the muscles that support your uterus. Put one hand on your abdomen and one hand on your perineum. Contract your Kegel muscles in the same way you do when you hold your urination. Contract these muscles carefully and slowly. Repeat three times a day the first week, adding two Kegels each week until you're up to fifteen. Don't force yourself, and do less if that feels better.

WEIGHT LOSS

The birth of the baby, as well as the loss of placenta and fluids, will result in immediate (though relatively small) weight loss. At first, you may be discouraged to learn you've only lost ten or twelve pounds, especially when your still-large belly, rather than being firm, as it was during pregnancy, is now soft and jellylike. Don't despair—you will begin to lose weight relatively quickly, especially if you are breastfeeding. Producing breastmilk will consume about 30 percent

> **HIGHER GROUND**
>
> As new mothers, it is easy to have a running stream of inner thoughts telling you that you're not doing enough, not doing things as well as other mothers, not being a good enough mother . . . there is always some more you must do or something you must do better. Mothers need to find ways to calm these inner voices and affirm for themselves what beautiful and dedicated mothers they are.
>
> —AVIVA JILL ROMM,
> *Natural Health after Birth*

of the calories you take in. In any case, it's healthiest to lose the weight gradually, just as you gained it gradually, and this will occur naturally over the first few months of your baby's life.

ENERGY LEVELS

Your body needs plenty of rest in the first few weeks after birth. Your energy levels will return gradually after the six-week mark. Until then, consider the fatigue a message from your body, saying, "Rest."

RECOVERING FROM A CESAREAN

After a cesarean, getting up and walking around helps to speed healing. It may be quite difficult at first, so start out slowly. Try to stand up straight, even though you feel like hunching over. It is best to avoid stairs for the first week or two, and to avoid lifting for the first four to six weeks. In the first few days, try to have someone hand the baby to you as much as possible, rather than lifting her yourself. For this reason alone it's best not to be by yourself for any extended period of time for the first week.

Ask your birth attendant or doula for help with positioning the baby for feeding in such a way so as not to cause you discomfort, and put a pillow under the baby when you lay her on your lap. Normal activities such as turning over, getting out of bed, walking, and breastfeeding the baby will aggravate the pain of the incision and the stitches, but they will hasten your recovery.

While ibuprofen and acetaminophen are considered safe for breastfeeding mothers, it is advisable to avoid unnecessary medication, especially during the first three months postpartum. Two herbal analgesics, California poppy and Jamaican dogwood, are effective painkillers, but should also be avoided during the early postpartum period. In the event of pain that is difficult to manage, contact your birth attendant for a recommendation.

When you roll from your back to your side, don't use your abdominal muscles. Instead, bend your knees so that your feet are flat on the bed. Then raise your hips and twist them to one side as you roll your shoulders to the side. Before you get out of bed the first few times, do five ankle-circling exercises and raise your arms above your head five times.

Check your incision each day for signs of redness, which could indicate the beginnings of an infection. If you see any redness, call your birth attendant. Your stiches, clamps, or clips will be removed two to three days after surgery, and your incision will feel less painful after that.

You will probably experience gas pains after about three days, and this may continue for a few days. This is a good sign that your intestines are recovering and beginning to function normally after the surgery. It is best to avoid gas-producing foods during this time, like greens, beans, foods in the cabbage family, and cold and carbonated beverages. If you are constipated, make sure you are getting plenty of fiber, and slowly increase your activities, especially walking. Drink plenty of water. Keep a pitcher of water by the side of your bed at all times. This will help to relieve constipation.

You will bleed for up to six weeks, just like women who give birth vaginally (see "Bleeding," on page 191).

Exercising after Birth

Within the first few days postpartum, you can begin to do Kegels and leg lifts, either lying on your side or on your back in bed. Don't lift anything heavy during the first two weeks. You can also begin to take short walks within the first two weeks postpartum.

If you do too much, your bleeding will increase, so use that as a gauge. If you begin to bleed after having stopped, or if the bleeding increases or changes to a brighter color, curtail your activities. It is normal to feel energetic initially but tire easily.

After three weeks to four weeks postpartum, you can begin to do gentle stretching exercises, increasingly long walks, and moderate yoga. Don't do any yoga inversions such as headstands and shoulder stands until your bleeding has completely stopped. You can also begin light aerobics at three to four months' postpartum, but avoid heavy jumping or pounding movements. By six weeks, you may want to try a gentle dance class.

Three months is the time when you can begin to exercise more regularly, and by six months postpartum you can exercise actively. Avoid lifting heavy objects from a standing position for at least the first six months postpartum, as this can cause uterine prolapse.

As soon as you can, begin to do Kegel exercises again, even while you're still in bed. They'll help your perineal tissue to heal and bring your uterus and pelvic floor muscles back into shape. Contract your vaginal and perineal muscles and hold for a count of 10. Release. Repeat 5 to 10 times.

At first, you will just walk to the bathroom, and then around your home. Try to avoid walking on stairs or hills in the first few days. When you are ready, you can venture outside for some fresh air. The key with walking, as well as all other exercise in the postpartum period, is to start out slowly and see how you feel. If something hurts, or you feel very tired, stop and rest. Then try it again later. Work your way up to your normal walking pace very gradually.

YOGA FOR POSTPARTUM HEALING

Yoga is a great healing exercise and is energizing as well. You can begin to do the poses below three to four weeks postpartum. If you had a cesarean, start out cautiously. Generally speaking, you should stop if you feel any pain; rest for a day and try again. And, as mentioned above, you should also stop if your bleeding increases.

All of these postures below can be done with baby on a blanket beside you.

Pelvic tilt. This pose is designed to strengthen the muscles in your abdomen, buttocks, and lower back and to increase circulation to these areas.

Lie down on your back with your knees bent and your feet flat on the floor.

Place your feet about hip width apart and your arms straight at your sides with your palms down.

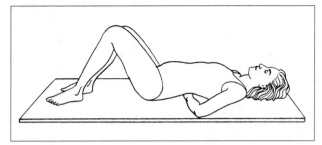
Pelvic Tilt

As you inhale, slowly lift your pelvis off the floor and keep your back straight and firm.

Hold this position for 10 to 20 seconds while you contract your buttocks.

Exhale slowly as you bring your pelvis back down to the floor. Try to bring your spine down one vertebra at a time. Imagine that you are pressing your belly button into the floor.

Leg stretches. This posture opens your chest and hips and gently stretches your spine.

Sit up straight on the floor with your legs as far apart as is comfortable.

Leg Stretches

Raise your arms above your ahead and stretch up toward the ceiling.

With your arms stretched out, lean forward toward the floor between your feet. Stretch as far as is comfortable.

Hold the stretch for 5 to 10 seconds, then return to center position.

Repeat 3 to 5 times.

Rock the Mama. This posture relieves tightness and tension in your lower back muscles.

Lie on your back on the floor with your arms and legs outstretched.

Bring your knees up to your chest and wrap your arms around your legs.

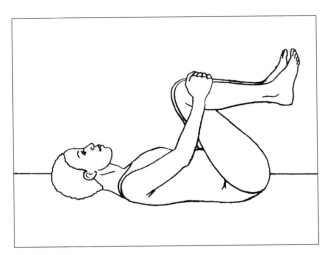

Rock the Mama

As you hold on to your legs, rock your back gently side to side.

Next, rock back and forth, massaging your spine. Rock as long as it feels good.

Slowly release your arms and lower them to the floor. Lower your legs to the floor.

AFTER SIX WEEKS

You will probably get the all-clear sign from your midwife or doctor after six weeks to begin regular exercise again. You should avoid strenuous or high-impact exercise until three months postpartum. Good exercises to consider at this time include dance, low-impact aerobics, swimming, and bicycling. An ideal choice is a mother/baby exercise class, which allows you to bring your baby, keep her next to you while you exercise, and even incorporate the baby into your workout. Mother-baby classes can also help you to meet other new moms in your area and cut down on the feeling of isolation that is common in the postpartum period. Ask your birth attendant or doula about where to find these classes in your community, or check the bulletin boards and family newspapers in your area.

Regular exercise classes may also be appropriate. Try a beginning Pilates course or a ballet or modern dance class. Let your instructor know that you have recently had a baby. Avoid salsa, kickboxing, or spinning classes until after six months postpartum. Whatever exercise program you choose, be sure to wear comfortable clothing and a good supportive athletic bra. Some companies make athletic nursing bras. Look for sources in parenting magazines and on breastfeeding Web sites.

CHAPTER 22 *Getting to Know Your Baby*

The child's hunger for his mother's presence is as great as his hunger for food,
and her absence generates a powerful sense of loss and anger.

—FRANK CAPLAN, *The First Twelve Months of Life*

Not so long ago, you and your baby were truly attached, functioning as a single biological unit. Although your baby now lives outside your womb, you and she are still interdependent. Unlike other animals that can function independently within hours of birth, human infants depend completely upon their parents for survival.

Interestingly, our large brains account for the helplessness of human infants. Meredith F. Small, anthropologist and author of *Our Babies, Ourselves,* says that "large brain size comes with a cost."[1] Small explains that babies are born with brains that are not fully developed, in part because after nine months, the placenta can no longer adequately nourish the growing brain. After the birth, additional nourishment, particularly in the form of fats, aids in brain development.

For this reason, experts also suggest that the ideal gestation period for a human baby is between eighteen and twenty-one months, but that as humans evolved and their brains became larger, babies had to be born earlier to allow their larger heads to fit through the birth canal.

Because babies are born in this helpless state, before their brain and nervous system are fully mature, they need more intensive care for a longer period than many animals. Human mothers know this instinctively, and have an overwhelming desire to protect and nurture their newborns.

Mother-Child Bonding

In most of the world's cultures, support for the process of bonding is built right in to the social structure, and carefully steers mothers on the right track. It is assumed that infants are completely helpless and need constant nurturing. Everything and everyone contributes to creating circumstances that will enable a woman to give that nurturing to her infant.

The hunter-gatherers of the Kalahari Desert are frequently used to illustrate the sacred bond between mother and child. In this culture, the mother carries the newborn in a sling throughout the day, and the baby nurses whenever he likes. The mother-baby bond is considered to be sacrosanct.[2]

In Bali, babies are revered as celestial beings, recently descended from the realm of the gods and goddesses. To preserve this divine nature, Balinese babies are literally not allowed to touch the earth. They are held continuously until they are six months old, at which time a ceremony heralds their first contact with the ground.

Most new mothers were raised in an age when mothers were warned about the dangers of "spoiling" children by giving them too much attention or responding too quickly to their needs. Best-selling author Dr. Benjamin Spock, for example, recommended letting babies "cry it out" in his early publications.

NATURAL SOOTHER
Miso Soup

Miso is a particularly hearty food for new mothers. This high-protein food typically combines soybeans, cultured grain, and sea salt, using a unique fermentation process. In Japan, the process has been elevated to a fine craft, much like wine making.

Miso is also a medicine. Unpasteurized miso, which can be found at natural food stores, is a living food containing natural digestive enzymes, lactobacillus, and other microorganisms that aid the digestive system. Regular use of miso is also believed to have anticancer, antiaging, cholesterol-lowering, blood-pressure-lowering, and stroke-preventing benefits. Miso also detoxifies the body by neutralizing the effects of harmful substances like tobacco smoke, atmospheric pollution, and radiation.

Quick Miso Soup

Mix 2 tablespoons of miso into a cup of hot water.

Ten-Minute Miso Soup

Add 2 to 6 pieces of kombu (seaweed), each about 4 inches long, to a pan containing 6 cups of water.

Heat the water until it just begins to boil.

Remove the kombu from the water and take the pan off the heat.

Add 1/3 cup of dried fish flakes (bonito) to the water. Let sit for 5 to 10 minutes.

Strain the liquid through a sieve. Pour all but 1 cup of the broth back into the pan; place over low heat.

Add 1 chopped scallion and 1 piece of tofu cut into small cubes to the broth.

Into the reserved liquid, add 5 to 8 tablespoons of miso, depending on your taste. Blend the miso into the liquid with a whisk. Add this mixture to the broth and stir. Increase the heat until the soup is hot, but do not boil. Serve at once.

Miso soup will keep fresh for about 24 hours.

While earlier generations feared that too much attention to infants would make later independence difficult, studies of cultures that encourage continuous attention to babies belie this belief. Hunter-gatherers of the Kalahari believe that the continuous contact and love they give their children cause them to be secure and better able to handle emotional stress.[3]

Modern researchers confirm the wisdom of these ancient cultures. Research by the distinguished developmental psychologist Mary Ainsworth, Ph.D., of the University of Virginia, confirms that the indulgence of early dependency needs leads to independence.[4] The responsiveness of the mother and close bodily contact are associated with increased self-reliance. The reduced anxiety levels that result when a child's attachment needs are met enable her to explore the environment.

Brain researcher and neurologist Richard Restak states that "physical holding and carrying of the infant turns out to be the most important factor responsible for the infant's normal mental and social development."[5]

Aside from creating a feeling of safety and making it easier for independence to develop, babies who are responded to and constantly touched feel loved and valued. What a gift to give anyone! Feeling loved will make it easier for an infant to grow into an empathic adult, capable of giving love to his or her future mate and children.

Attachment Parenting

Over the last ten years, the term *attachment parenting* has been popularly used to describe parenting that is responsive to and aware of the needs of children during the "attachment period"—the first three to five years of life. It is inspired by the seminal work of British psychoanalyst John Bowlby, whose distinguished research on the attachment needs of children underscores the critical importance of a responsive, nurturing, and more or less continually present caregiver. His research demonstrates that this early bond plays a crucial role throughout the child's life and that when children suffer disruptions in these attachments, they become more vulnerable as adults to depression, anxiety, and relationship problems.

In a landmark study of attachment parenting (defined as parenting that's "sensitive, cooperative, and accepting"), Steven Bell, Ph.D., studied the offspring of members of a Georgia La Leche League group. He analyzed and compared the results of several standard measures of adjustment and development in the adult offspring of the "responsively parented" group and a control group, most of whom grew up with less involved parents. Bell found that the offspring of the mothers involved in La Leche League scored significantly higher on a quality-of-life questionnaire, as well as on a standard psychological test of happiness.[6]

Current proponents of attachment parenting include nationally known pediatrician Dr. William Sears and his wife, Martha Sears, a nurse, childbirth educator, and breastfeeding consultant. They are the parents of eight children and coauthors of many books on the subject of parenting. According to this couple and other experts, attachment parenting contains the following components:

- *Babywearing.* This term, coined by the Searses, is the key to attachment parenting. It means using a sling, front carrier, or backpack to carry our babies with us during the first few months of life while we walk, shop, or do housework. Many cultures make use of slings, because they allow the baby to nurse. Baby carriers have become increasingly popular, and are available through parenting magazines and Web sites.

- *Breastfeeding "on demand."* This term means that the baby eats whenever she likes. If babies are held "in arms" or carried close to their mothers' bodies routinely, then their needs will be anticipated more quickly and they will seldom cry.

- *Avoiding separation.* Advocates of attachment parenting follow the lead of attachment theorists like John Bowlby and Mary Ainsworth, whose research supports the baby's need for his mother's presence in the early years of life. A baby under one year old has no capacity to understand that his mother is coming back, and can suffer distress if separated from her for too long. Babies need to know that their main caregiver is there and will continue to be there. According to the research of psychiatrist Elliott Barker, M.D., of the Canadian Society for the Prevention of Cruelty to Children, a child needs one consistent, loving caretaker up until five years of age in order to develop trust, empathy, dependency, optimism, and conscience.

- *Relying on instinct.* Parents who practice attachment parenting rely heavily on their own instincts when making decisions about what is best for their babies. They typically agree with the research of Australian physician Sarah Buckley, which illustrates that a dormant, instinctual, maternal intelligence is unlocked by the hormonal chemistry of natural birth. Attachment parenting encourages you to trust in this intelligence: As you spend more time with your baby, you'll get to know him better and gain more confidence in your own inherent expertise. You'll understand his expressions and anticipate his needs.

- *The family bed.* Advocates of attachment parenting also recommend that newborn babies sleep with their parents in a family bed. Also called cosleeping, this arrangement offers many benefits over keeping your infant in a separate room. Babies tend to sleep more soundly, parents don't need to get up several times each night for feedings, and if the baby is breastfeeding, the mother needn't even wake up completely to feed her baby. (More on the family bed appears later in this chapter and in chapter 12.)

- *Responding to the baby's cries.* Experts believe that babies have a language all their own, with many types of crying to indicate many different needs. By responding to the baby's cries quickly, parents can learn to distinguish the different cries that signify the need for food, comfort, diaper changes, and other cues.

- *Balance.* While experts recommend a close connection with children, they also realize that good parents must refuel by taking appropriate breaks from the baby to rest, to be alone, or to spend time with others.

THE ADVANTAGES OF BABYWEARING

This critical component of attachment parenting is a proven, age-old method of baby rearing. Its many benefits to parent and child include:

- *Conditioning the vestibular system responsible for maintaining balance.* This system is undeveloped in infants, and the parents' movements help to establish equilibrium. The rhythmic movement of being carried in the sling brings more oxygen to the brain and stimulates brain development.

- *Reducing crying.* Mothers who carry their babies in slings report that they don't cry very much. Carrying the baby in a sling creates a close proximity to the mother that allows her to know her baby more intimately and respond more quickly to her cries. Research shows that not responding to babies' cries in the first six months actually increases the frequency of crying and distress in the next six months and later.[7] Soothed babies do not cry as much. The energy a baby spends on prolonged crying is diverted from regular bodily and emotional functions. There is no research to back up the old wives' tale that crying develops babies' lungs. Crying is, in fact, the baby's only language.

- *Facilitating learning.* Babyworn babies show enhanced visual alertness and are more responsive to their environments. This is because being rocked or carried is essential for brain growth. Babies who are carried feel both more stimulated by the environment of constant contact with the mother and more secure and thus better able to interact with their surroundings.

- Wearing your baby allows you to do more. One of the greatest advantages of babywearing is that it makes it so much easier to incorporate your baby into your everyday life. It makes it possible for you to do your chores around the house with the baby happily attached to you. You can vacuum, do dishes, do laundry—just about anything—with your baby in a sling or a carrier. It's also easier to get out and about with baby in a sling than in a stroller. You can go for a walk with your baby in a sling. The sling frees your hands and body for other things at the same time that it allows you to stay close to your baby.

- Babywearing during the day seems to help babies to sleep better at night. It is also a good way to help your baby to fall asleep before bed- or naptime. A sling allows you to place the baby gently on the bed and slip the sling off your shoulder without waking her.

CRYING

Crying is the only mode of expression babies have. It can signify many things, including hunger, thirst, fatigue, loneliness, or overstimulation.

To understand how integral crying is to babies, it helps to examine the animal kingdom, where there are two types of infant-rearing: that practiced by *caching species* and that practiced by *carrying species.* Caching species, such as deer, leave their young hidden and alone for long periods while they forage for food. Young deer have internal mechanisms that control their body temperatures in their mothers' absence. The milk they drink from their mothers is high in protein and designed to be gulped down quickly, with long intervals between feedings. The survival of caching species depends on their absolute silence when mother is absent.

On the other hand, carrying species, such as orangutans and humans, require almost continuous contact with their mothers because their milk is comparatively low in fat and therefore must be consumed frequently. The survival of carrying species depends on their ability to cry in the mother's absence or to signify distress.

Crying can be overwhelming and perplexing for many new mothers, who have not yet learned to differentiate between different types of cries and are given conflicting messages about how to respond. Most experts now agree that infancy is not an appropriate time to teach limits or establish premature independence—it's the time to create trust and security. Infants use crying not to manipulate but to communicate. They cry because they need something. By responding to those needs quickly, you will be teaching your baby that his environment can be trusted and his needs will be met.

This does not mean, however, that a happy, cared-for baby will never cry. All babies cry to some extent—some more than others. Whereas you can release tension by taking a walk, talking to a friend, or going shopping, your baby has only one form of release: crying. If you've tried to console your baby in every way you can, and she still cries, she may simply need you to hold her and be a loving presence. This lays another solid foundation by giving your child the message that her feelings are legitimate, that it is acceptable to complain sometimes, and that you understand and recognize those feelings. By your example, you can help to teach her that crying is a normal release of feelings.

Over time you will learn to distinguish the difference between your baby's different cries. Here's a guide from Sandy Jones, author of *Crying Baby, Sleepless Nights,* to help you to get started. Remember that each infant is different, and your baby may have his own particular way of expression.

- *Hunger.* Rhythmic, brief cries that get more and more intense until they become full-blown cries of pain. The baby may root or suck her fingers. When you try to feed her, she will respond right away by hungrily sucking. Let the baby establish her own feeding schedule, and you will soon recognize her hunger cry.

- *Cold.* Crying accompanied by starting or shivering, especially when he is undressed or placed on a changing pad. Cover cold surfaces with warm towels or baby blankets. Use a warm, damp washcloth to wipe and bathe him. If the weather is cold, dress him in a hat and socks.

- *Heat.* Whining and fussy crying that is intermittent and not resolved by the usual measures. It is often accompanied by a rash, flushing, or sweating. In cold weather, dress your child as you would dress; overdressing simply makes babies cranky and uncomfortable. Check for fever if crying continues or if your child was vaccinated within the last twenty-four hours.

- *Tiredness or overstimulation.* Sporadic crying, sometimes accompanied by batting at ears or head. Overtired babies often rub their eyes, turn away from adults, and resist soothing. Take a long walk with the baby, try nursing him to sleep, or lie next to him while patting his back. If it happens at the same time each day, try to reduce stimulation in the hours preceding the crying.

BODY WISE
Infant Massage

Make a simple baby massage oil by adding 2 drops of lavender and 2 drops of rose oil to 1 ounce of sweet almond or grapeseed oil. If your baby has a fussy period in the day, massage her half an hour before that period; to aid her digestion, massage her half an hour after a feeding.

Get a soft towel and sit outside or near a sunny window. Lay the towel on the ground, or over your lap. Place your naked baby on the towel. Gently, but firmly, massage her stomach in a clockwise motion with your fingertips. Do this with baby's legs outstretched as well as with her knees bent. Then move to the baby's shoulders, head, face, hands, and feet. Turn your baby over and massage her back. Wrap your baby up in a big towel when you're done. Wipe off excess oil, and dress your baby warmly.

- *Loneliness or boredom.* Coos or gurgles that gradually turn into protests and wails, usually occurring after the baby is three months old. Boredom can sound like "fake" crying, with low, throaty noises followed by moans. Keep the baby nearby so he can see and hear what you are doing. Place him near a mobile, offer him toys, or take him for a walk.
- *Internal pain.* Usually the first cry of pain is loud and long, followed by a long pause that sounds as if the baby is holding her breath before another alarming scream. The baby's mouth is wide open, and her tongue is arched; her hands and feet may be drawn up against her body or may circle in agitation. This type of crying can indicate a digestive problem like colic, or could be a sign of teething, muscle aches, or an ear infection. Try soothing techniques first like breastfeeding, rocking, or getting into the tub together. If the crying intensifies, call your health care provider.
- *Difficult bowel movements or urination.* The baby may cry out in pain while he turns red, squirms, and seems to strain. This is unusual in breastfed babies. If you suspect this problem, contact your health care provider.
- *External pain.* Piercing screams or sudden, intense cries for no apparent reason. This could indicate pain caused by a diaper pin, irritating fabric, or tight elastic. Check to see if any hairs or threads may be wrapped around baby's toes or fingers. Check for diaper rash; if this is the cause, apply some protective ointment and let the baby air out without a diaper for as long as possible.

Colic and Fussing

Colic is a term that strikes terror into the hearts of new moms, yet it is an overused and misunderstood term. A fussing baby is often called "colicky" when in fact he does not actually have colic at all. In fact, only 10 to 20 percent of all infants experience true colic. Belinda J. Pinyerd, Ph.D., RNC, uses the following "rule of three" to identify true cases of colic. Crying must:

- begin during the first three months of life;
- last longer than three hours per day;
- occur more than three days in any one week; and
- continue for at least three weeks.

While colic can be extremely distressing to mother and child, babies with colic are in fact physically healthy.[8]

Just what is colic? While medical experts agree that the problem is digestive, the cause is not known. For this reason, colic is usually defined in terms of its symptoms (as noted above). An infant with colic cries a lot; she tends to stiffen her limbs and arch her back when you pick her up to try to comfort her, and often appears to have a tense and bloated abdomen.

The symptoms are dramatic, and nothing you do to comfort your baby seems to help.

Colic may be caused by gas or heartburn, or may be allergy-related. The baby might be reacting to foods in a breastfeeding mother's diet, such as cow's milk or wheat, or to lactose or protein in the formula he drinks. Some babies are much more sensitive than others and react more intensively to digestive upsets.

In years past, women were sometimes told that their baby's colic was due to the nervousness of being a first-time mom. This theory has no basis in fact, and trivializing colic or blaming the mother can create needless emotional pain.

Long-term colic can make bonding difficult. After weeks of screaming, many mothers may begin to lose self-esteem, believe that they are poor parents, or label their children "difficult" at a time when the emotional tie between mother and child is at its most critical. Many mothers begin to tune the crying out completely. This may be necessary as a short-term coping strategy, but there are steps you can take to soothe colic and ease bonding with your baby.

First, start a "colic log" to determine the trigger. If you're nursing, keep a log of foods you eat each day, paying special attention to cow's milk, wheat, eggs, citrus, corn, gas-forming foods like beans, cabbage, broccoli, and cauliflower, caffeine, artificial colors, and preservatives. If your baby begins crying a few hours after you've fed her, try to identify a trigger food you ate recently. Eliminate it from your diet for a week to see if your baby's colic is reduced. You might also try feeding your baby in a different position and keeping her upright for a half hour after feedings, as well as feeding her more often and more slowly. Some mothers find that nursing the baby on only one side at each feeding helps; this allows the baby to digest more slowly.

If your baby is formula-fed, watch for an escalation of pain within an hour after eating, spitting up right after eating, diarrhea or constipation, or a red, circular rash around the anus. Ask your health care provider about lactose-free, hypoallergenic infant formulas now available. As with breastfed babies, changing position and feeding more often and more slowly can relieve colic.

Pay attention to the baby's bowel movements, their condition, and when they occur. Does the baby seem bloated or gassy? This and green bowel movements can indicate digestive disturbance and perhaps give you a clue as to something you or your baby might have eaten recently.

Remedies for colic include swaddling the baby tightly in a soft blanket, rocking her gently in a rocking chair, changing her position, and using a hot water bottle wrapped in a warm cloth and placed against her abdomen. Many mothers have also found that rhythmical sounds or movements will often soothe a colicky baby and distract her from her discomfort and crying. Try putting the baby in a sling or front pack and going for a walk or dancing to music at home. The sound of vacuum cleaning can be surprisingly soothing to a colicky baby, as can a car ride. And many mothers find that simple skin-to-skin contact relieves the baby's distress.

Try a "colic hold" (shown below). Place the baby tummy-down on your forearm with his head nestled into the crook of your elbow and his legs on either side of your hand. Or try it the other way with his head nestled in your hand instead.

Apply pressure to baby's tummy in other ways. Place her tummy-down on a hot water bottle (water

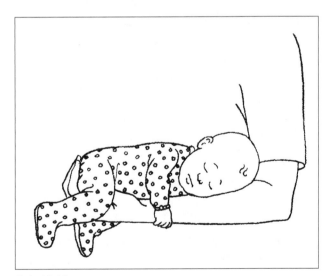

Colic Hold

warm, not hot) with a towel wrapped around it and allow her legs and upper torso to drape over the sides. This would also work with a pillow. If you have a large exercise ball or beach ball you can place her tummy-down on top of it and gently roll her from side to side, being careful to keep hold of her at all times.

If these don't seem to comfort your baby, you may want to try massaging his abdomen, using a rectal thermometer to help gas to pass from his system. You might also consider craniosacral therapy, a form of massage that focuses on the head and neck, since some experts believe that colic results from trauma to these areas. Traditionally, strained teas of fennel, dill, and catnip have been used for infants or breastfeeding mothers when colic is present. They can be given to baby with an eyedropper or sucked on from a clean washcloth. However, you should consult a qualified herbalist or homeopath for a remedy specially formulated for your baby's age and symptoms or for help in determining any sensitive foods in your diet or remedies you might safely take. Many people have reported success after taking their colicky infant to a chiropractor. A study in Denmark showed that spinal and joint disturbances, possibly caused by birth trauma, might account for some colic. Average crying time was reduced from 5.2 hours to 2.5 hours after the first treatment alone.[9] Look for a pediatric chiropractor. If nothing seems to work, contact your health care provider.

While it can be difficult to see your child suffering, it's a comfort to know that colic usually ends by the time the baby is three to six months old.

Nighttime Parenting

"Is she sleeping through the night yet?" You will probably be asked this question dozens of times in your baby's early months. In fact, it's rare for a newborn to sleep for more than three or four hours at a time.

Before your baby was born, he experienced con-

> ### HIGHER GROUND
> ## Lullabies
> Lullabies are perhaps as old as motherhood itself—the urge to soothe and comfort your baby translates perfectly into the language of song. Choose songs that you know by heart, and sing them while you are nursing or rocking your baby. If you sing them routinely at certain times of day, certain songs will signal that it's time to sleep, and they will help you and the baby to relax.

stant nourishment and the warm, comforting environment of your womb. His needs have not changed since birth. Babies have small stomachs and need mother's milk frequently because it is easily digested. Babies also have much shorter sleep cycles than adults, and are generally lighter sleepers.

There are good reasons for this. Nature designed your baby to wake frequently during the night for survival, ensuring that she would eat often, as well as wake easily if in danger (for example, of suffocation). For the first three months, most babies sleep in chunks of no more than four hours. After three months, sleeping time gradually increases to five- and six-hour stretches; with luck, this tends to occur at night. During this time, you may be tempted to blame your new baby's sleep habits for your own exhaustion, but in reality your sleep is actually less deep now—your hormones are working overtime to keep you alert to your baby's needs during the night.

Do not feel pressured by those who tell you that you must put your baby on a sleeping schedule. Your baby's sleep habits will depend on his particular temperament and biology. A baby who sleeps through the night is certainly convenient for new parents—but this is not typical. You shouldn't try to coax your baby onto such a schedule before he's ready: this is as impossible as trying to get your baby to walk or talk at the same time as other babies. Sleep is a need, not a habit. However, it is important to establish routines that are associated with sleep and bedtime, such as a warm bath, a rocking chair, dim lights, and later reading a book.

THE ADVANTAGES OF COSLEEPING

On September 30, 1999, La Leche League International, the world's foremost authority on breastfeeding, issued a statement citing studies that show that "co-sleeping with a breastfeeding infant promotes bonding, regulates the mother and baby's sleep patterns, and helps the mother become more responsive to her baby's cues."

Penelope Leach, London psychologist and author of *Your Baby and Child* wrote in an October 1, 1999, *New York Times* opinion piece, "Three studies, in the United States, New Zealand and Britain, reported no direct risks to babies from sleeping in their parents' beds." And according to James McKenna, Ph.D., director of the Mother-Baby Behavioral Sleep Laboratory at the University of Notre Dame, "Fifteen years of carefully designed and controlled research on mother-infant bedsharing, and more than 20 peer-reviewed scientific papers, confirm what in some cases amounts to 'intuitive' knowledge. Further, cosleeping parents are not lethal weapons, over which neither they nor their infants have any control; even in the deepest stages of sleep, a mother responds within seconds to an odd noise or movement of her infant."

Most of the world's cultures practice cosleeping, as did the forefathers of our country. It was not until the 1900s that babies began to sleep on their own, in their own beds. Prior to this time, a child would always sleep with a parent, sibling, grandparent, or servant. This was not because of lack of available bed space. Nor is lack of space the reason that many modern-day cultures practice cosleeping. In India,

even wealthy families with large homes will generally choose just one bedroom to be the "sleeping room." As children get older they will branch out to their own rooms, knowing they can always go back and sleep with their parents if they like.

The bottom line, as anthropologists have always observed, is that human beings like to sleep together. It enhances the bond of attachment.

Most new moms, especially if they breastfeed, learn early on that having the baby nearby means the nights are easier. You don't need to climb out of bed, walk down the hall to another room to a crying baby, and then stay awake until the baby has once again gone to sleep. Babies who sleep with their parents rarely cry to begin with. When they wake up in the night, often the mere presence of a warm body nearby is enough to comfort and lull them back to sleep.

There are a number of different ways to cosleep. One is the family bed, where everyone shares one bed together. Another popular method is the "sidecar." This is a type of crib that attaches to one side of the parents' bed and is open on that side. Another type of cosleeping is to have a crib or bassinet next to the parent's bed, within easy reach.

Whichever method you use, there are some important safety considerations to keep in mind about babies and sleeping:

- Babies should be put to sleep on their backs until they are at least six months old. Sleeping on the sides or the stomach can increase chances of blocked air passages. However, they can and should be placed on their stomachs sometimes while playing.
- Don't cosleep on a free-floating waterbed, extremely soft or pliable mattress, or couch. These soft surfaces can be a suffocation hazard.
- Partners should keep the baby between them rather than against the wall or the open side of the bed.
- Remove all extra bedding, pillows, and stuffed animals from any bed the baby is sleeping in.
- Do not use deep-pile lambskin (more than 1 1/4 inches) as a sleeping surface for baby. This

can be a suffocation hazard and also collects dust, which can affect breathing.

- Allow baby's limbs to be free. Do not swaddle her tightly in blankets while she is sleeping. Babies should not be overheated while sleeping. Do not put a hat on baby's head during indoor sleep times.
- Do not let baby sleep unsupervised in a carriage or stroller.
- Do not sleep with your baby if you have been drinking alcohol or are under the influence of any tranquilizing medications.
- Do not encourage other people, such as baby-sitters or grandparents, to sleep with a small baby. They are unlikely to have the type of awareness of the baby during the night that you have.
- Do not allow siblings to sleep with a baby younger than nine months.
- Do not allow anyone to smoke in any room where a baby sleeps.

Following these basic guidelines will ensure that you and your baby can safely share sleep together, just as millions of parents and babies do, all over the world.

Increasing both the rates of breastfeeding initiation and duration is a national health objective.

—RUTH LAWRENCE, M.D., *Breastfeeding and the Use of Human Milk*

The breastfeeding relationship is a very special one indeed. When you breastfeed, you and your baby are communicating with each other. You are giving her more than just food specially calculated for her age and constitution—you're giving her reassurance, warmth, and a clear message of love and safety. In return, your baby lets you know that she feels loved.

Chapter 9 discussed the importance of breastmilk to your baby's development, and about breastfeeding's benefits to you, as well. But because it can be tricky to get started, this chapter covers the how-tos of breastfeeding.

Getting Started

Most experts now recommend that you nurse your newborn within the first hour of birth. A newborn baby's sucking reflex will probably begin about twenty or thirty minutes after he is born. In fact, when placed on their mother's stomach, most newborns will actually maneuver their way to the breast on their own and begin to suck.

As soon as you're ready after giving birth, hold your baby close and try to get her to latch on, as described in the following sections. The most important thing to do now is to be close and get to know your baby. Don't worry if breastfeeding doesn't go

perfectly for the moment—it probably will take practice for both of you. The baby may suck for a minute and then look around. Newborns are incredibly alert during the first hour after birth.

The first liquid your baby receives is called colostrum. You may have even noticed a bit of this thick, clear liquid leaking from your breasts in the latter weeks of pregnancy. Colostrum is especially formulated for newborn babies. While all breastmilk contains antibodies that protect your baby, colostrum has particularly high concentrations of antibodies. It is easy to digest, contains high amounts of protein, and is precisely what your newborn baby needs right now.

Somewhere between two and four days after birth, your milk will start to come in, and over the next several days it will slowly replace colostrum. If you had a cesarean, your milk may take a little longer, between four and six days after the birth. You will notice this true milk right away because the liquid will suddenly appear milkier.

You may feel a change in your breasts, as well. This tingling or prickling sensation, called the "letdown reflex," can sometimes be triggered just by thinking about your baby, or by hearing him cry.

You may notice, in the early days, that breastfeeding causes uterine contractions. These can feel as strong as birth contractions, but they don't last as long, nor do they continue. Instead, they come sporadically during the first few days postpartum. The contractions occur because breastfeeding stimulates the production of oxytocin, the same hormone that caused uterine contractions during the birth. These contractions help to gradually shrink your uterus back to its prepregnancy size.

Over the first few days your baby's weight may drop a little, particularly if your milk doesn't come in right away. This is normal, but makes many new mothers quite nervous. Once your milk comes in full force, the baby will begin to gain weight more quickly. As long as you continue to breastfeed, and the baby is soaking six to eight diapers a day, weight gain should continue.

How often should my baby be fed? Most mothers worry about this, but the answer is actually quite simple: Feed the baby on demand. Let your baby breastfeed at will. The baby is the one who should decide when it is time to nurse. This is because it is the baby's sucking that produces your milk supply. The frequency and duration of your baby's sucking will be related to his nutritional needs and is designed to produce just the right amount of milk for him. In the first few days, the baby might nurse every forty-five minutes, or may wait three to four hours between feedings. There may not be a regular pattern to feedings. After the second or third day, the baby will probably become hungry more often, but the pattern will continue to vary from day to day. Babies go through growth spurts when they nurse more often, as well as "frequency days" when they nurse constantly, building up your milk supply in anticipation of a growth spurt. Babies who are allowed to determine their own feeding schedules have been shown to gain weight more quickly and to continue breastfeeding successfully for longer periods of time than those who have a schedule imposed upon them.[1]

The baby is also the best one to decide how *long* to nurse. Starting out slowly to "break in" the nipples has not been shown to reduce nipple soreness.[2] Breastfeeding doesn't work that way. Nipple soreness is not inevitable and is often related to the position of the baby. As a new mother's breasts get accustomed to breastfeeding during the first few days, any soreness diminishes.

Another reason it's important for the baby to regulate feeding is the composition of breastmilk. Breastmilk changes even during a single feeding session. The first milk to come out, the "foremilk," is different in both composition and rate of flow from the "hindmilk." The hindmilk is higher in fat content, and it is important that the baby nurse long enough to get this milk.

LATCHING ON

The baby's hold on your areola with her mouth is called "latching on." Latching on properly will ensure that the baby gets enough milk without hurting your nipples. Follow the steps below to help you and your baby latch on:

1. First, get comfortable. In the early hours after birth, this will probably mean sitting up in bed. Try sitting up straight and supporting your back with pillows, and keep more pillows nearby to support your arm, neck, or knees. Later on, you will find other spots that feel right, such as the couch or a rocking chair. Eventually, you will able to breastfeed anywhere.

2. Place the baby's head in the crook of either elbow and support her back and buttocks with your forearm and hand. The baby should be lying on her side; do not lay the baby on her back and expect her to turn her head toward you to feed, as this is not a comfortable position in which to swallow.

3. With your free hand, grasp your breast, with the thumb on top, and tickle the baby's lips or cheek with the nipple. This will cause a rooting reflex in the baby, if he is hungry, and he will try to reach for the breast with his mouth. It is important that the baby's mouth be wide open because

you want most of the areola, not just the nipple, to go in. A correct nursing position requires this because the baby's entire tongue stimulates the bottom of the areola, causing the milk ducts to express milk. If the whole areola is not inside the baby's mouth, the ducts will not receive enough stimulation to send out large amounts of milk. In addition, if the sucking pressure is not fully on the areola, your nipples will be sore.

4. When the baby's mouth is wide open, press her to you (do not lean forward to her) and make sure most of the areola is inside her mouth. If the baby is correctly positioned, you should be able to actually see her tongue sticking out a bit between your breast and her lower lip. If the baby does not achieve the correct position, use your forefinger to gently break the seal between your breast and her mouth and remove your nipple. Then try again. It may take a few tries at first.

5. Soon after the baby is sucking properly, you will feel the letdown reflex. You should then see his jaws moving up and down and a swallowing action. You should not feel pain in your nipples if the baby is positioned correctly. Nurse the baby at least ten to fifteen minutes on the first side and then change to the second side and let him nurse until he falls asleep. He will be done when the breast falls out of his mouth.

6. Burp the baby when she is done eating, or between breasts. Pick her up, rest her head against your shoulder, and gently pat her on the back. You can also try to sit her up, supporting her head, or put her on her tummy in your lap. She may spit up a bit of milk with her burp. This is normal. Most breastfed babies don't need to burp, but some do. You will soon find which category yours falls into.

BREASTFEEDING POSITIONS

At first, the position described above will probably be the most comfortable for you. If you had surgery, you may need to carefully surround yourself with supportive pillows to keep pressure off your abdomen for a few days. In more extreme cases, you might lie down, though this may make breastfeeding a bit more difficult at first.

To breastfeed while lying down, lie on either side. Lay baby on his side, facing you with his head at the level of your breast. You might need to use a pillow to raise either the baby, or your breast, to the right height. You may also need to place a pillow against his back, to keep him from rolling away from you. Put one arm, or a pillow, under your own head for support and use the other to position your breast. Some women like to place a pillow between their knees for better back support. You might need some help with this position at first from your partner, doula, or La Leche League leader.

The "football hold" is good for some babies who have trouble latching on. It is also the best way to nurse two babies at once, in the case of twins, or when tandem nursing with an older baby or toddler. The baby's body rests along your left side, lying on her back with her head resting in your left hand. You will need to use a pillow to get her up to the level of your breast. Use your other hand to position your left breast.

Getting Help with Breastfeeding

New mothers often receive advice and support from other breastfeeding mothers. The importance of mother-to-mother support was discussed in chapter 6. Being with other nursing mothers is crucial in the first few weeks and can make all the difference in the world to your comfort level and success.

You may find that you need additional information and support, either from La Leche League meetings or through a lactation consultant, a professional who is trained to help you troubleshoot nursing problems.

If you are giving birth at home or in a birth center, your midwife or doula will be able to assist you with nursing. If you are at a hospital, ask to speak to the

BODY WISE
Shoulder Releasers

Breastfeeding your baby gives you both so much, and yet it can also leave you with neck and shoulder tension. Here are two poses that help relieve upper body tension.

1. Stand erect. Reach your right arm up and over your head to cover your left ear. Pull your head gently toward your right shoulder as you keep your left shoulder even. Hold your head for a count of 10. Release and let your head float up on its own. Repeat on the left side.

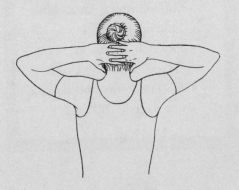

2. Clasp your hands behind the middle of the back of your head with your elbows flared. Bow your head toward your chest. Relax 30 seconds in this position. Raise your head slowly as you sit up. Take three deep breaths.

lactation consultant. You can also hire a consultant independently through a referral from your midwife, pediatrician's office, or a friend, or call La Leche League for help (see appendix 2).

A good lactation consultant will gently guide you through the steps to nursing. You should feel better after the session, not more pressured. If you don't feel comfortable with the person, do not hesitate to seek out help from someone else.

Dressing for Nursing

Consider purchasing good nursing bras before the baby is born, keeping in mind that your breasts will be larger when your milk comes in. For this reason, you need a bra with plenty of support, but one that is not too tight. Tight bras can increase your chances of breast infection, and have even been implicated in breast cancer.

The ideal nursing bra can be opened up with one hand. When you have a hungry baby, or you are out in public, putting the baby down may be difficult.

You may also want to have a supply of nursing pads on hand. Your breasts will probably leak frequently during the first few weeks. You may notice that when you feed the baby on one breast, milk leaks out of the other one at the same time. Eventually this will stop, but for now buy some pads, or make your own from cloth diapers. You can buy nursing pads that can be washed and reused, or disposable ones. Avoid any pads that are made from plastic, or have a plastic lining, as these will keep your nipples from getting the air they need.

There are many companies that make fashionable clothing for nursing moms. You can find pajamas, casual shirts, and even fancy dresses with cleverly designed openings for discreet breastfeeding. Some companies manufacture nursing outfits from organic fabrics. (See appendix 2 for some suggestions.)

Many women find that regular clothes work well and are quite discreet. A loose-fitting shirt that can be pulled up can be draped around the baby, and very little of you is actually revealed. Button-down shirts are less discreet, unless you use a blanket or shawl to cover the baby while you nurse.

Breastfeeding and Sex

Breastfeeding does change patterns of lovemaking between partners. Any woman who has just had a baby may experience a lessening of her sexual drive, perhaps for several months, because of the hormonal shift in her body. Increased levels of prolactin, the "mothering hormone," the major hormone of breast-milk synthesis and breastfeeding, and oxytocin, the "feel-good" hormone, tend to overwhelm the hormones associated with sexual desire.

During the early months of breastfeeding, it may take some effort on both your part and your husband's to shift into your new sexual patterns. Your breastfeeding relationship supplies you with a lot of physical contact and closeness. Your partner, on the other hand, is not experiencing breastfeeding in this way and, even if he or she is supportive of it, may feel a bit left out. Talk openly about what is happening, and try to find ways to stay close. Chapter 24 contains suggestions on negotiating the early weeks of new parenthood.

Breastfeeding is a natural contraceptive. If the baby is nursing exclusively both day and night, you may not get your period until six months. Some women do not get a period until one year. However, while breastfeeding does offer some contraceptive protection, it is not foolproof, and ovulation can begin before your first period. Learn more about the ovulation method of birth control during breastfeeding in the classic book *The Art of Natural Family Planning* by Sheila and John Kippley. Estrogen-based birth control pills have been shown to suppress lactation, but progestin-only mini-pills are safe.[3] You might prefer a barrier method, such as a condom, diaphragm, or cervical cap. Do not use the diaphragm or cap you used before pregnancy, however, as you may now need a larger size. Contact your health care provider for a checkup.

HIGHER GROUND
Rock-a-Bye Baby

A rocking chair is a must for a new mother. Rocking not only soothes fussy babies, it also soothes mothers. Scientific evidence now documents the benefits of rocking, which stimulates the balance mechanism in the inner ear. Rocking assists an infant's biological development and promotes her ability to be alert and attentive.

Rocking even burns a few calories, about 150 an hour. It will help you recover from childbirth more quickly. Here are some things to look for in a rocker:

- Is the seat cushioned? Is it very comfortable? Could you sit in it for hours?
- Are the arms of the rocker a comfortable place for you to rest your arms while holding the baby?
- Does it have an even, steady, comfortable rock?
- Is it attractive, and do you like its style and design?

Difficulties with Breastfeeding

Just because breastfeeding is natural does not mean it will come naturally—or that you won't have problems. With a little time and attention, you should be able to nurse successfully. Try these self-help techniques, but don't forget to enlist the support of a La Leche League leader, lactation consultant, midwife, or doctor:

- *Engorgement.* Many women experience engorgement when their milk first starts coming in. It can feel like your breasts are as hard as rocks. If you nurse your baby regularly, engorgement will decrease quickly. You might want to feed the baby at least every two hours, even if he doesn't seem hungry. Having a warm shower can alleviate the discomfort. Occasionally, a woman will become so engorged that she develops a mild fever. Both warm compresses and ice packs can offer relief. An old home remedy that seems to be quite effective is to line your bra with cabbage leaves. Remove the hard vein from the center of the leaf, and cut out a hole for your nipple. Replace the leaves every few hours. If your breasts are so engorged that the baby has trouble latching on, use a pump, or manually express a little milk, to reduce the fullness.

- *Sore nipples.* It may take a little time to get breastfeeding right, and you may have to contend with sore or, more rarely, cracked nipples. Adjust your position to make nursing more comfortable. Try the football hold described above. If the discomfort continues for more than a day or two, use a little vitamin E oil, a product made especially for sore nipples such as Lansinoh, or pure lanolin on the painful area. Although none of these products will harm your baby in small amounts, wipe any excess off prior to nursing. Avoid using antibiotic or other creams, since these may not be good for the baby. Another soothing remedy is to squeeze out a few drops of breastmilk and rub it into your nipples, as human milk has many healing properties. You may also consult a homeopath for a remedy that is formulated for your symptoms. In general, it is best to avoid using soap on the nipples when breastfeeding, as it can dry them out, but especially avoid it when they are painful.

- *Plugged ducts or breast infections.* If you find a tender spot or sore lump in your breast, you may have a plugged duct or an infection. This can be caused by a sudden change in the amount the baby is nursing, or the nursing pattern itself. Perhaps the baby slept an unusually long amount for a couple of nights. Plugged ducts can also be caused by too-tight clothing or bras, or inadequate ventilation. You may also be trying to do too much. Both problems are best treated by applying either wet or dry heat, getting plenty of rest, and continuing to nurse frequently to keep milk flowing through the breasts.[4] If possible, get into bed with the baby and stay there until you feel better. Nurse first on the affected side. Pumping a bit and massaging the affected breast can also help. Cool compresses may also feel good between heat applications. Try adding 2 drops of rose, 1 drop lavender, 1 drop clary sage, and 1 drop geranium essential oil to 2 cups of cool water. Dip a clean cloth into the water, wring, and apply to the sore area. You can also try the homeopathic remedy *Phytolacca,* which can be applied in lotion form to the breasts. If the plugged duct turns into an infection, accompanied by fever or flulike symptoms, flush your system with plenty of water and vitamin C. Drink orange juice,

NATURAL SOOTHER

Fenugreek Tea

More than thirty herbs are considered to be powerful galactagogues—agents that promote the secretion and flow of breastmilk. The best known is fenugreek. Numerous anecdotal accounts testify to the restorative powers of this herb.

To make fenugreek tea, brew 1 teaspoon of fenugreek seeds in 1 cup of water for 5 minutes. Strain and drink four or five times a day.

cranberry juice, and water with lemon. Take up to 1,000 mg of vitamin C in supplement form. Take it throughout the day, no more than 250 mg at a time, and take it after rather than before a nursing. See your midwife or doctor if your symptoms fail to improve within twenty-four hours. Although antibiotics are usually not needed, if one is prescribed, make sure it is safe for breastfeeding mothers. Do not stop nursing on the affected side. Continued rest and nursing will make your breast heal more quickly.

- *Not enough milk.* Many women think they do not have enough milk, when in reality they have more than enough. For example, if your baby seems to never want to stop nursing or seems to still be fussy after a feeding, you may think she is not getting enough to eat. In fact, that type of behavior could indicate that the baby is going through a sudden growth spurt, or simply that he wants to suck a lot or craves body contact with you. According to La Leche League,[5] you know you're providing adequate milk if, after the first week, your baby: soaks six to eight diapers a day; has two or more bowel movements a day; is gaining four to eight ounces per week; nurses frequently; is not being supplemented with formula or water; and appears healthy. Check with your health-care provider if you are concerned, but don't feel worried if your baby is meeting these guidelines. If you truly do not have enough milk, which is rare, work with a lactation specialist to determine the cause. You may be eating poorly, or not getting enough rest. Your baby may have been sidetracked with supplemental feedings or a pacifier, which is causing her to nurse poorly. One of the best old-time remedies for lack of breastmilk is to go to bed with the baby and stay there. There is probably some validity to this suggestion, as rest may help you to relax and produce more milk and will certainly promote feeding on the baby's part.

Breastfeeding, Alcohol Consumption, and Medications

As breastfeeding is on the rise, more information is becoming available about the effect of medications on newborns. Most medications—even those known to be safe—come with disclaimers about lactating women. For this reason, many physicians instruct their patients who must take medicine to pump their breasts and discard the milk. This is virtually impossible for the breastfeeding mother, as is discontinuing breastfeeding during the course of medication and continuing it again later.

Fortunately, most drugs are safe to consume while breastfeeding. A mother's body is designed to screen out many harmful chemicals through a complex system of membrane barriers within her cells. Less than 1 percent of a nursing mother's dose of medication is actually transferred to the infant, according to Thomas W. Hale, Ph.D., a professor of pediatrics at Texas Tech University School of Medicine and the leading U.S. authority in the pharmacology of lactation.

While it is good to know that there are safe medications for breastfeeding mothers, you should avoid using medication while you're nursing, if at all possible. If avoiding medications isn't possible, consult your health care provider to determine which medication would be best for you. The American Academy of Pediatrics publishes a list of drugs that are acceptable for use by nursing mothers. The trouble is, most physicians prefer to err on the side of caution and advise against using any medication while breastfeeding.

Here is Dr. Hale's brief rundown on commonly taken drugs and their safety for breastfeeding infants:

- *Painkillers:* Acetaminophen (Tylenol) and ibuprofen (Advil) are safe to use occasionally. Long-acting nonsteroidal anti-inflammatory drugs (NSAIDs) such as naproxen (Aleve) should be avoided.

- *Antihistamines:* Choose nonsedating antihistamines (such as Claritin and Zyrtec). Avoid pseudoephedrine (used in many cold remedies), because it may suppress milk production. For seasonal allergies, ask your health care provider about using a steroidal nasal spray (such as Flonase). These are not as easily absorbed into your system as other forms of steroids.

- *Antibiotics:* Almost all are safe for breastfeeding mothers to use, except for the Cipro family and sulfonamides. Very rarely, an infant might display a mild allergic reaction (in the form of a rash, diarrhea, or thrush) to penicillin or another antibiotic.

- *Antidepressants:* Zoloft is probably the best choice, if you need to take an antidepressant. So far, studies have shown no ill effects on nursing infants. Prozac is not a good choice, since colic, vomiting, poor sleep, and even coma have been associated with this drug.

- *Steroids:* Oral prednisone, used to treat inflammation, does not seem to transfer into milk and is probably safe unless the dosage level is extremely high. Check with your health care provider.

Because alcohol will not transfer to human milk in small amounts, you should limit your intake to no more than two small drinks per day. Some infants may balk at the taste of breastmilk after alcohol consumption.[6]

When Breastfeeding Is Questioned

Fortunately, as new research on the benefits of breastmilk is conducted, most health care providers now recognize that advising against breastfeeding is rarely in the best interest of the newborn. However, there are still times when health care professionals may erroneously advise against breastfeeding, or suggest that it be curtailed, when there is really no need to do this. Let's take a look at some of the situations where a woman might be advised to avoid or reduce breastfeeding.

- *Jaundice.* Newborn jaundice is very common, occurring in almost half of all babies. In healthy, full-term babies, this condition is usually identified between the second and fourth day of life. It is a yellow color of the skin, eyes, and other bodily organs that results from an increased concentration of the pigment bilirubin in the baby's body. The baby's relatively immature liver must excrete this increased concentration. In almost all cases, this condition is harmless and will resolve itself over a period of a few days, or sometimes weeks. In fact, many experts now believe that jaundice may be totally natural, and perhaps even beneficial to the newborn.[7] One reason for this perspective is that jaundice levels are higher in breastfed babies. Holding your baby in the sunlight can help reduce the bilirubin level.

  If bilirubin levels become too high, there is a rare chance that brain damage could occur, so your baby might be given phototherapy to help reduce the levels. In phototherapy, your baby is placed on a table under a set of strong lights. He will wear a special pair of eyeshields to protect his eyes from the bright lights.

  In very rare cases, a baby might be born with abnormal jaundice. This is usually the result of Rh or ABO blood incompatibilities. Other culprits can be infections or gastrointestinal obstruction. The baby will be treated with phototherapy to reduce bilirubin levels.

  At one time, jaundice that persisted for several days was referred to as "breastmilk jaundice." Women were told to stop nursing for a couple of days and to use formula in the meantime, in order to help the jaundice go away. Research now shows that this is not necessary; in fact, frequent nursing helps to shorten the duration of jaundice. Unfortunately, a few practitioners still don't know this, and might suggest stopping for a time. Stopping breastfeeding for a day or two has been shown to result in higher levels of early weaning, however, and is not recommended for jaundice.

Research also shows that supplementing a jaundiced baby with water is not necessary.[8] Supplementing with water, or anything else, has been shown to compromise the success of the breastfeeding relationship. If you are in a hospital, ask the nursing staff not to give your baby any water without your permission.

If your baby has jaundice, try to nurse often. Your baby especially needs more liquid if he is receiving phototherapy, which can dehydrate his system. Phototherapy does not need to be absolutely continuous to be effective. It is fine to either remove the baby from the lights while you nurse, or to nurse under the lights.

- *Hypoglycemia:* Some infants are born with low blood sugar levels. As with adults with this condition, the best thing to do is to consume many small meals throughout the day. Frequent breastfeeding is the solution. Keep the baby nearby at all times to make this easier. In some hospitals, glucose is given to babies with low blood sugar in an attempt to get their levels to go up. However, blood sugar levels fluctuate after consumption of glucose. Ask your practitioner to avoid glucose supplements unless it is imperative. If it does become necessary to use them, make sure you breastfeed first. Then give the glucose with a dropper or spoon, rather than with a bottle, which could create nipple confusion.

- *Metabolic problems:* Breastfeeding can usually be incorporated into the diet of babies with all kinds of metabolic diseases and disorders. Babies born with celiac disease, cystic fibrosis, and similar metabolic diseases can usually be fed solely on mother's milk. PKU, which is discussed more fully on page 178, is a metabolic

disorder in which the body is unable to metabolize phenylketonuria. Because of this, eating foods that contain phenylalanine will eventually result in abnormal brain development and could lead to retardation and other problems. Fortunately, human milk is low in phenylalanine. Infants with PKU can usually be partially breastfed. Galactosemia is a very rare metabolic disorder in which a baby is not able to metabolize lactose at all. These babies usually need to be fed a lactose-free formula, and cannot breastfeed.

Very premature infants and babies with special needs can also be breastfed. In fact, these infants need the benefits that human milk provides even more than healthy, full-term infants do. Sometimes getting started can be tricky if your baby is sick or very small. Consult chapter 28 for help with breastfeeding in these situations.

BREASTFEEDING AND HIV

The topic of HIV and breastfeeding is highly controversial. Fortunately, it is still a controversy that surrounds a relatively small population of women. In one four-year study conducted in the United States, AIDS claimed the lives of less than one-tenth of 1 percent of childbearing-aged women. Ninety-five percent of AIDS cases still occur in the original health risk groups: homosexual men, heroin addicts, and in a few cases hemophiliacs.[9]

One very important fact for women to know is that pregnancy is one of sixty-four conditions that can cause a woman to have a false-positive HIV test. As women are increasingly being tested for HIV, several thousand a year will test false positive because they are pregnant. Should you receive a positive test for HIV, it is important to request that further, more refined tests be given to verify the diagnosis.

To date, the standard prescription for a woman who tests positive is that she be treated with toxic drugs, such as AZT, during pregnancy and labor, and bottle-feed her baby after birth. La Leche League, the world's foremost authority on breastfeeding, has thus far chosen not to make any specific recommendations about HIV and breastfeeding because they feel that the research and its interpretations are inconclusive. They point out that many studies that attempt to evaluate the relationship between breastfeeding and disease transmission have failed to take all factors into account, including whether or not breastfeeding is done exclusively and how child and maternal health affects the final outcome.[10]

In one study, first published in the British medical journal the *Lancet* in 1999, mothers who exclusively breastfed their babies for at least three months had no more chance of transmitting HIV to their children than mothers who never breastfed at all. In the same study, children who received a mixed diet of formula and breastmilk had the highest HIV rates over a period of six months. When tested fifteen months later, the children showed the same results.[11]

La Leche League also points out that in some recent research, breastmilk has been shown to actually slow the progression in disease of babies who are born positive.

Currently, La Leche League urges women with AIDS to weigh out all the factors and risks, as they are known so far, on an individual basis before making a decision about whether or not to breastfeed. They urge parents and health care providers to consider the well-known benefits of breastmilk in their decision making.

The new mother has not only displaced her man for the child but displaced herself, as well.
What both partners fail to realize is that this displacement is natural, necessary, and temporary.

—WILLIAM F. VAN WERT, *Tales for Expectant Fathers*

For the first week or two after your baby is born, you and your partner will most likely be so involved with the new baby, you'll hardly exchange more than a few words—and those words will probably be about the baby. Some of what you are experiencing together will be joyful, and some of it will be very challenging. All of it will be new.

After the first few weeks, you will have time to notice what's going on between you. And that may bring up some surprises.

Becoming Parents

Your baby grew gradually in your womb—and gradually you will grow into being a mother. You may even feel as though your pregnancy is continuing, in a way, and that you and the baby are still very much a single unit. Actually having a new baby enter your home, and all that goes along with it, is not gradual, however. One day there are two of you, and the next there are three!

Much of what happens between you and your partner as a result of this new presence in your lives will depend on your relationship before the baby was born. Obviously, a strong partnership will help you through the transition into parenthood. Having a new baby may strengthen your relationship and help you to grow closer. Few relationships are perfect,

though, and for many partners, the postpartum period reveals the rough spots you were able to ignore before the baby. There is nothing like sleep loss, nervousness, and confusion to bring out the skeletons in any couple's emotional closet.

Right now, you and your partner could use extra nurturing, approval, and attention—but these needs are coming up at a time when neither has the time or energy to focus on anything but the new baby.

This is completely normal—couples who get through the postpartum period without any problems are probably not being very honest with each other. If you blow up at your partner when he orders the wrong topping for the pizza or forgets to sort the colors on laundry day, don't worry. You are not the first woman to have these feelings over matters that seem trivial.

In fact, these matters aren't trivial at all. Jay Belsky, director of the Institute for the Study of Children, documented how 250 couples handled the changes in their lives after a baby arrived. He observed that the biggest problem areas for new parents are division of labor, money, work, social life, and maintaining intimacy. These are big issues that are important to your happiness as a couple—and as a family.

Ultimately, your postpartum experiences can lay the foundation for a stronger and closer relationship. This new phase of your partnership, like every

NATURAL SOOTHER

Rekindling Romance

Now is the time to find creative ways to be together physically with your partner. Aromatherapy can offer a relaxing and sensuous atmosphere. Choose your favorite combination of lavender, rose, sandalwood, and rosemary essential oils, or use all four together. For instance, add 3 drops of lavender and rose and 2 drops of sandalwood and rosemary to 1/4 cup of olive, almond, or grapeseed oil. Adjust the amount and scent to your preference.

Find a comfortable place where you and your partner can recline for a foot massage. Spread out some towels and rub your hands together to get them warm before beginning. Mix the oil with your fingers and apply a small amount to your hands. Add more as needed. Hold your partner's foot in both hands and massage the bottom with your thumbs. Rub the top of the foot, under the toes, the ankles, the heel—and let your partner direct you to the sore spots. You can take turns or give the foot massages simultaneously.

other, will take some honest communication from both of you.

New Roles

A significant area of adjustment for women is the change in the daily fabric of life. Up until the baby's birth, you have probably lived an independent lifestyle even if you're in a committed relationship. You are used to making your own plans, going out when you feel like it, even if your partner feels like staying home that night, and tailoring your meals to your own particular likes and dislikes. Even if you and your partner spend a great deal of time together,

you probably consider your relationship to be fairly equal. You both work, and you both do your share to keep the household going.

Enter your new baby. Now everything changes. If you're like most new moms, you stay at home all day, at least for a time. Once used to talking to other adults throughout the day, you now find yourself talking only to the baby. You no longer manage your own schedule, but follow irregular and unpredictable feeding and napping habits. Since you're at home all day, you are probably doing most or all of the housework. What's worse, once competent and fairly organized, you find you've become forgetful and frazzled. You're shouldering a huge burden now, most of it alone, and you aren't even sure you're doing a very good job.

No matter how well you planned this stage of your life, it's impossible to anticipate the full impact on your relationship. There are many unconscious assumptions that couples make about money, power, and division of labor. Without intending to, you may find yourself feeling dependent and resenting it. Your partner, also without intending to, may have certain expectations about what you will do around the house while he or she is at work. When your partner decides to work late, you might now resent it, when before the baby came you may have taken it in stride.

Same-sex partners may feel the shift in role changes even more acutely. Up to this point, the two of you may have done a very good job at splitting domestic chores, social responsibilities, and earnings prior to the baby's birth—better than many traditional male/female relationships. It may not be as easy to divide chores now, especially if one of you is busy breastfeeding. In addition to reading the advice about relationships in this chapter, it may be very helpful for both of you to seek out other same-sex partners with children and talk to them about how they have coped with the shifts in their relationships. The Gay and Lesbian Parents Coalition may be helpful as well (see appendix 2).

These big changes are made more acute by concerns about money, not seeing friends, seeing more of relatives than you are used to, not having time to talk to each other, and never having any time alone with yourself.

Taking Care of Your Relationship

Nurturing a relationship during the postpartum period can be difficult. Most experts suggest that you sustain your relationship in the same way you would at any other time in your lives together as a couple.

The difference now is one of time and energy. Think small—here are some easy ways to remind your partner of how much he means to you:

- Spend a few minutes together doing something enjoyable each day. It might be as simple as watching the news every evening together or going for a twenty-minute after-dinner walk with the baby. Don't allow any outside interruptions during that time—take the phone off the hook and don't answer the doorbell. This is your time together; make it a top priority!

- Keep housekeeping goals reasonable and find ways to simplify your routine. This will allow both of you more time together to focus on other things.

- Consider a ritual or ceremony to bless your relationship or your new roles as parents. Spiritual affirmations can nourish the bond between you.

- Ask for exactly what you need from your partner—for example, "I need a hug," or "Can you give the baby her bath?" One of the biggest mistakes couples make is believing that their partner should anticipate needs without prompting.

- Once you feel comfortable leaving the baby with someone for a few hours, establish a regular weekly "date" together. You can take turns deciding what the activity will be. Surprise each other!

- As often as possible, use "I" statements instead of "you" statements when discussing problems with your partner. Instead of saying, "You forgot to put the diapers out for the service to pick

HIGHER GROUND
Forgiveness

Sometimes the best way to rekindle romance is to practice forgiveness. In the early weeks, you may feel more critical and judgmental. You will be tired and need help and not always know how to ask for it. Be willing to apologize if you have criticized or humiliated your partner. Be willing to accept his or her apology as well. Let go of bad feelings over an incident in the past. Let go of grudges that keep you agitated.

You will find that forgiveness is really a gift to yourself, as it is you who carries and are affected by the bad feelings. When you can let something go from the past, you will feel lighter as well. You will find your emotions heightened in these early weeks postpartum. Be gentle with yourself and with your partner.

up," try saying, "I feel overwhelmed by details. I need your help remembering to do this task," or even, "I feel frustrated when you don't remember to do this chore."

- In general, try to share both your positive and negative feelings regularly. We often forget to share feelings of joy and appreciation. Keep the doors of communication open so that emotions don't build up inside you.

- It's a fact of parenthood: most of your conversation will now revolve around the baby. Don't forget to talk about other things from time to time.

- Talk to other parents. Ask them how they managed the early weeks together and get some tips on how they kept their love alive. Some may have more to share than others, but talking with other people helps you to realize that your challenges are not unique.
- Don't forget to laugh together. Humor is very healing.

Reliving Your Own Childhood

According to Harville Hendrix, author of *Getting the Love You Want: A Guide for Couples,* most of couples' conflict can be traced back to unmet childhood needs. As well, couples often tend to replay aspects of their parents' marriage in their own. Having your own baby can mirror—in dozens of ways—the way that you were parented.

You may not be thrilled with this idea. Many adults want nothing more than to do things differently than their own parents did. And you can. You can use your awareness to make *conscious* choices for change and improve your partnership.

Take Care of Yourself

In order to take good care of your new baby and to sustain a loving partnership, you must first take care of yourself. While you and your partner are going through big changes, your body and emotions have gone through tremendous upheavals in the last few months, leaving you feeling fragile and vulnerable. While you may love being at home with your baby, you're likely to feel isolated from other adults.

Craving the company of another adult, and wanting someone to talk with, might make your relationship with your partner your main source of stimulation. When he comes home, you may expect conversation and nurturance, while your partner, exhausted from a long day at work, may expect to relax in front of the TV. This can put a strain on your time together.

To keep your relationship strong, it can help to

have other social outlets in place for the postpartum period. Throughout this book, you've been finding ideas to build a support system. Here are a few reminders:

- Join, or start, a mother's group. Plan to meet once a week or more at someone's house, just to

---

BODY WISE
Yoga Sit-Ups

Try this exercise after you have completely stopped bleeding.

Lie on the floor, resting your calves on a chair. Keep your feet flexed. You can either cross your forearms over your chest or behind your head for better neck support. Take a deep breath. As you exhale, contract your abdominals and lift your head and shoulders 6 to 8 inches off the ground. Repeat 3 to 5 times.

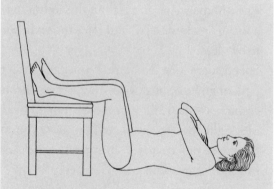

You can also do this posture to relax. Lie down with your calves resting on a chair. Place a support under your neck and head if necessary. Your arms should be at your sides, with your palms up. Allow your legs to relax and to be supported by the chair. Rest in this position, focusing on your breathing. Allow your mind to think of a pleasant memory or peaceful place you've visited. Breathe slowly as you recall how relaxed you felt.

hang out together with your babies and talk. Try to find women with infants close in age to your own. Put up signs in local stores or at your pediatrician's office. Go to La Leche League meetings. This is a great way to meet other women.

- Go to a mother/baby exercise group.
- Make a weekly date with your baby to have breakfast or lunch at a local coffee shop or diner. You will start to see the same faces and may get to know new people.
- Take your baby to the local playground. Even if she is too young for the equipment, you will meet other moms.
- Find "short and sweet" ways to reward yourself, such as brewing a cup of expensive tea, using a nicely scented shower gel, lounging in satin pajamas, reading a short, light novel you can easily pick up and put down again without losing track of the plot, taking an evening walk alone after your partner returns home, or subscribing to a fun magazine and leafing through it. Make a list of "pick-me-ups" and refer to it when you need ideas.
- Spend some time in nature, if you can. Sit in the park or go for a short walk. Take a drive through country roads. Riding in the car puts most babies right to sleep, even colicky ones. You may be able to pull over and sit or read in the car for fifteen minutes while the baby sleeps.

As you find new ways to relax and reenergize, remember Shakespeare's line, "You can't love another without loving yourself."

Sex

At your six-week checkup, your midwife or doctor will probably tell you that you can resume normal sexual relations. Many women greet this announcement with mixed feelings for a number of reasons.

For one thing, you are probably still tired. If you are breastfeeding, the changed levels of estrogen in your body make you feel quite different. Even your skin feels different, and being touched may not feel the same way it did before. Your body may still be sore, or you may have sore breasts. Your breasts might start leaking like a fountain the moment you even try to cuddle or have sex. All in all, things are not the same as they were before—your body has changed, and so have you.

Many women report that the constant physical contact they have with the baby makes them feel like they just want to be left alone the rest of the time. Some women feel as though their bodies are meant only for the baby's use in the early weeks, and are turned off at the idea of sharing it with anyone else.

Your partner, on the other hand, may have the opposite response and might be feeling left out, or even jealous of the attention the baby is getting from you.

Perhaps the best way to reinstate the physical bond with your partner in the postpartum period is to think of intimacy in terms of nurturing touch, rather than sexual activity. Until you feel ready for sex again, you might enjoy a light massage or foot rub, and your partner might enjoy sitting close together or going for a walk and holding hands. Cuddling together and taking a nap may be even better!

Once you feel ready to have intercourse, go slowly. You will probably need to spend more time on foreplay. Add candles or music, even if you never used them before. Since hormonal changes may make you feel a little dryer than usual, try a water-soluble lubricant.

Before your baby was born, you probably never had to plan sex—you could be as spontaneous as you liked. You will get some of that spontaneity back again, but for now you may have to take your chances when they come. If you plan for sex at a certain time, and the baby foils those plans by waking up and wanting to be fed, don't just abandon all chances to be close. Sit together while you nurse the baby and talk, or ask your partner for a foot rub while you take care of the baby. And find another time later. Allow this to add an element of romantic intrigue to your relationship.

It is the lack of permission to feel conflicted, inadequate, sad, angry, bored,
or irritable as well as grateful, rapturous, tingling with life, and intoxicated with love
that makes the postpartum period unnecessarily difficult and lonely.

—JENNIFER LOUDEN, *The Pregnant Woman's Comfort Book*

Practically every new mother goes through emotional turmoil in the weeks just after her baby's birth. The symptoms are classic; everyone knows about the "baby blues." You weep at the drop of a hat, can't watch the news for fear of setting off some strong emotion or another, and you alternate between intense maternal love and annoyance with your spouse over the most minor of infractions. In later months, you may laugh over some of your own behavior—it seems so crazy in retrospect.

If you have true postpartum depression (PPD), however, any description of typical baby blues will seem ridiculously trivial. Your symptoms may be so severe that you don't know how to handle them—and what's worse, very few people in your life may understand how serious it really is. Although 10 percent of women experience PPD, only a small fraction of women who have it will actually receive compassionate, effective treatment.

This chapter will examine the full range of emotional and mental changes women can go through, starting with the very common baby blues and then exploring the more serious range of postpartum depression and other postpartum mental disorders.

The Baby Blues

According to childbirth lore, the baby blues will hit you on day three. That's when the adrenaline high you've been on since the baby's birth suddenly disappears, and you are hit with short-term depression. The truth is, however, that the blues are only one part of a full spectrum of feelings that are intensified for new mothers. Somehow the early weeks of motherhood seem to give women a heightened awareness of everything, and they connect emotion-

NATURAL SOOTHER

Beat the Blues

If you're feeling depressed, take a look at your diet and make sure you're getting enough B vitamins, calcium, and magnesium. Vitamin C and zinc are also important. In addition:

- Have a cup of lemon balm tea with honey and a slice of fresh lemon in the morning upon arising.
- After you dress, put some essential oil on your hair or the collar of your shirt. Choose rose, ylang-ylang, jasmine, or neroli.
- As you prepare lunch, sip a soothing "cocktail" of Bach flower remedies. Add 2 to 4 drops each of Walnut, Willow, or Cherry Plum.

ally to all of life in ways they never did before. Many women do feel depressed, but also feel love so intense that it almost hurts, anger that seems to explode out of nothing, melancholy for lifestyles left behind, and awe for the cycles of life. We hit major emotional highs and lows on a daily, and sometimes hourly, basis.

Let's get back to the blues for a moment, though. While it's milder than postpartum depression, almost all new mothers do feel bouts of postpartum stress syndrome, or mild depression after the birth of a baby. This is normal and is not the same as postpartum depression. It can hit any time, from day one to six weeks postpartum or later. It can also happen to women who have adopted a baby.

Accepting depression is difficult for our society. Let's start by taking a look at some of the reasons new moms experience the blues:

- Everything has changed. The daily patterns of your life are totally different than they were before the baby was born. Not only do you need to get used to that, but you will, to some extent, mourn the old ways that you were accustomed to.
- Loving your new baby so intensely can leave you feeling raw and vulnerable. Fears over the baby's health and safety can seem overwhelming.
- That same love, which opens up your boundaries, can also seem like a loss of individuality at first.
- Many women report that they create awful scenarios in their heads throughout the day. As you walk down the street with your baby, you imagine bricks suddenly falling from a building and pelting the two of you. As you carry your baby up the stairs, you imagine suddenly slipping and dropping him down the entire flight. This kind of fantasizing is very common, but also very hard to live with.
- Giving birth puts you in touch with the enormity of life and all of its cycles, including death. Many mothers report a new awareness of how precious life is, and of human vulnerability.

- You simply can't accomplish in one day what you could before the baby. It's a hard truth to face, for many women.
- You are *tired,* so tired that your usual emotional defenses just aren't working right now.
- Your body has changed dramatically. You just don't feel the way you used to physically.
- Some women feel a great deal of disappointment over their birth experiences. Women who end up with C-sections or who use drugs for pain relief often feel like failures and have a lot of trouble letting go of feelings of self-hatred.

You may have your own, very specific reasons for feeling blue. The point is, depression is normal and needs to be acknowledged. Don't allow anyone, including yourself, to downplay your emotional experience.

OTHER EMOTIONS

Another aspect of depression deserves special mention, that of strong feelings of regret. Some feelings are much more difficult to accept in yourself than others. The idea you made a mistake in getting pregnant to begin with is particularly hard to feel okay about. Sometimes your new life feels so overwhelming, and the freedom of your old life so very tantalizing, that you just can't help wishing you could go back to it, even for a few moments.

Another emotion that is even more difficult to admit is anger at the baby. If your baby has been screaming for two hours straight, and nothing you do makes any difference, you may be horrified to find yourself imagining what it would be like to just walk out the door.

Don't worry—you're not a bad mother for having these seemingly negative thoughts and feelings. Most women probably have at least a glimmer of regret at some point in the early postpartum weeks, though they may not admit it, even to themselves. It's better to acknowledge these tough feelings, accept them, and carry on.

How to Deal with the Blues

Here are some ideas to help you through this time:

- Connect with others. Support groups can help you to feel more connected, but can also result in friendships that go beyond meeting times. Your life has changed, and you will need to change and expand your friendships as well.
- Be alone. Try to arrange a bit of alone time occasionally. Even a fifteen-minute break can be refreshing. Go for a short walk, take a hot bath, or go out for a cup of tea by yourself.
- Talk to a therapist. A couple of sessions might make all the difference in the world.
- Cry. Think of your tears as a soothing balm that will make you feel better.
- Call for help. Post a phone number for a good parent stress line near the telephone (see appendix 2 for contact information). If you find yourself experiencing despair or intense anger, call. The people who man these lines are familiar with what you're going through, and they can help.
- Use aromatherapy. To raise your spirits, try combinations of ylang-ylang, clary sage, geranium, and rose essential oils in an aromatherapy diffuser, or added to a hot bath.
- Try homeopathy. *Ignatia* and *Natrum muriaticum* are good for weepiness and moodiness. *Kali carbonicum* is good for irritability and fatigue.

Beyond the Blues

About 400,000 women a year have true postpartum depression (PPD). Less often, women have other postpartum mental disorders such as panic disorder or obsessive-compulsive postpartum disorder. Another two thousand have the more severe postpartum psychosis.[1]

For these women, the symptoms described in the previous section barely scratch the surface. Crying jags may not be a once-in-a-while occurrence but may happen almost continuously. Insomnia may be

BODY WISE
Get Out of the House

Life with a baby can feel overwhelming, but getting outside for a while can give you a new perspective on life. If you're not in the mood to juggle slings, carriers, and strollers, why not just take your baby outside to lie on a blanket on the porch or the grass? Sit and enjoy the fresh air.

very severe, such that they are getting only three or four hours of sleep every night. Feelings of anger toward the baby, or imaginary scenarios in which the baby is hurt or sick, may become overwhelming or obsessive. In very serious cases, women may even feel suicidal.

POSTPARTUM DEPRESSION (PPD)

The term *postpartum depression* has been used as a synonym for the baby blues or basic depression. In fact, it is a clinical condition that, unlike a mild case of the baby blues, will not resolve on its own and just go away.

Symptoms of PPD or other postpartum mental disorders may not be present until six to eight weeks after the baby's birth, making it even harder for many women and their partners to understand that there is a serious problem. They may have felt fine until six weeks postpartum, when things changed and they became severely depressed. It's easy to think it's just temporary and will go away in a day or so.

The diagnosis of PPD is difficult. Even now, with greater awareness of the potential severity of this condition, many doctors advise their patients that the depression will pass. And women with PPD are often so confused and distraught that they do not recognize the seriousness of their depression. In addition, we live in a culture that still has difficulty accepting psychiatric disorders, making it even easier to avoid dealing with PPD.

Five areas of disturbance characterize severe maternal depression. An easy way to remember them is to think of the acronym, SEE IF, as in "See if you are depressed." The symptoms of disturbance surface in one's:

- **S**leeping patterns
- **E**ating habits
- **E**nergy level
- **I**nterests and cognition, and
- **F**eelings

Here are some more specific danger signs:

- Difficulty falling asleep, staying asleep, or getting out of bed
- Frequent wakefulness due to vivid, frightening dreams
- Loss of interest in food or extreme food cravings for high-carbohydrate or high-caffeine snacks
- Unusual weight loss or gain
- Sustained interest in alcoholic beverages, sedatives, or other medication
- Feeling sluggish, slowed down, fidgety, or agitated
- Feeling exhausted and unable to complete routine tasks
- Having accidents related to fatigue or inattention
- Difficulty concentrating, remembering, organizing, or making choices
- Lack of interest in or overconcern for the baby
- Loss of interest in or difficulty planning and implementing hobbies and pastimes that you once loved
- Planning or attempting suicide or injury to oneself, the baby, or other children
- Feelings of hopelessness, anxiety, or panic
- Extreme mood swings
- Social withdrawal
- Uncontrollable crying
- Thoughts or fantasies of death or of hurting oneself or the children

While the cause of PPD has not yet been determined, suspected factors include genetic predisposition, chronic sleep deprivation and fatigue, dramatic hormonal changes, severely colicky babies, medical complications for either mother or child, previous clinical mental disorders, isolation, and lack of support.[2] There may be other factors as well, and it is likely that these factors play different roles in individual women.

LIVING WITH PPD

Perhaps the most difficult part of having PPD is living with shattered dreams. Our culture has romanticized the postpartum period so much that almost all women end up feeling cheated by the reality—that it is both wonderful and extremely challenging. Women with PPD end up feeling even more disappointed. You are likely to look upon the months following your baby's birth as "lost time."

Talk to your therapist about your losses and the unmet expectations of early motherhood and ask for help in searching for ways to move on. You may have gotten off to a rocky start, but with help, your future as a mom can be as good as anyone else's.

OTHER POSTPARTUM MENTAL DISORDERS

PPD is the most common of postpartum mental disorders. There are others, though, that do not necessarily have anything to do with depression (although depression is sometimes a problem).

- *Postpartum panic disorder.* This disabling disease was first recognized in the 1850s. It is most common among women with a preexisting history of mild anxiety disorders. Signs and symptoms include extreme anxiety, fear, tightness in the chest, and increased heart rate. Onset typically occurs two to three weeks after childbirth.[3]

- *Postpartum obsessive-compulsive disorder.* This was first documented in 1993. For years, women with this illness were misdiagnosed with postpartum depression or psychosis, and usually remained unresponsive to the treatment they received.[4] Signs and symptoms include intrusive, obsessive thoughts of harming the baby, sleep, and bizarre behavior. Onset typically occurs within the first week after childbirth. Postpartum psychosis afflicts about 2 or 3 out of every 1,000 childbearing women every year.[5]

If you are like most postpartum women, you will recognize some of these symptoms as ones you've already experienced. All new mothers will experience some confusion, inability to sleep, and overprotectiveness. The difference is in degree—for women who have these disorders, the symptoms are so severe that they are prevented from leading a normal life, and they are often a danger to themselves and their infants.

TREATING POSTPARTUM MENTAL DISORDERS

If you are concerned that you may have one of the mental disorders discussed here, *you must seek professional help as soon as possible.* Do not try to work through the problem on your own. Find someone who is experienced with treating these problems. You can call Depression After Delivery (DAD), Inc. at 800-944-4PPD if you need to talk to someone right away.

Treatment for these disorders will vary from woman to woman but may include therapy sessions, medication, and in some cases hospitalization. The road to recovery may be rocky, with days where you feel much better, and other days where you seem to backslide a bit.

> ### HIGHER GROUND
>
> What I kept saying those first months was "I just haven't got it!" My husband kept asking me what "it" was and I couldn't tell him. Then my mother decided to come for a visit. When she hugged and kissed me, I turned to my husband and said, "This is what it was! I needed some mothering myself."
>
> —EDA LeSHAN,
> *Conspiracy against Childhood*

anxiety, fear of being left alone with the baby, depression, and vigilant protectiveness of the baby. Onset typically occurs one day to six weeks after childbirth.

- *Postpartum psychosis.* This extremely frightening illness, identified in the 1850s, tends to come on suddenly, shortly after childbirth. It is associated with grave danger to mother and child, and must be treated immediately in a hospital setting. Signs and symptoms include confusion, agitation, hallucinations, delusions, inability to

Children are the most valuable natural resource.

—HERBERT HOOVER

You may have had clear plans about working after the baby was born. Most women make such plans: stay at home with the baby until she is ready for school; stay at home for three months and then return to work; stay at home for six weeks and then go back to work part-time; stay at home. Many women also have plans for child care if they return to work: full- or part-time baby-sitters; day-care facilities; a stay-at-home partner; or relatives.

Once they become mothers, however, many women find they need to reevaluate these plans. Motherhood may have dealt you a few surprises. You might not have realized, for example, how much you would want to stay with your baby. If your baby has special needs, or had to be hospitalized, you may not feel you've had enough time with him before returning to work. Perhaps you hadn't realized how financially difficult it would be to stay at home, and you need to return to work sooner than you'd hoped.

I'm Not Ready to Go Back to Work

This is a very common predicament. Many women, even the most die-hard career-driven executives, are shocked to discover that going back to work is not as easy as they thought it would be. Even when you are eight months pregnant, you cannot imagine

how you will feel about this new creature in your life. Some women simply never expect to be so in love with their babies.

For the lucky ones, the solution might be as simple as calling up the boss to say *au revoir*. Other women will struggle with conflicting feelings of love

---

NATURAL SOOTHER

Belly Warming with Moxibustion

Moxa, made with the dried leaves of the herb mugwort, is traditionally used to strengthen the mother's overall system and tonify her uterus after birth. This hot-burning herb, commonly used as an accompaniment to acupuncture, can be purchased in stick form at health food stores.

Light the moxa stick and blow on the tip until it starts to glow. Hold the moxa stick over your belly, 1 to 2 inches from your navel, and slowly move it around in a circle. With your other hand, rub your belly to disperse the heat. After 5 to 10 minutes, stop and extinguish the moxa stick by cutting off the end and allowing it to burn out. Repeat once a day for the first few days after birth.

for their child and the enjoyment of their careers. Even women who don't love their jobs may find that financial considerations are a major problem.

Some women who give up careers to stay at home will struggle with their new roles. Others relish the freedom that being at home offers. Whatever choices you make, there will be an adjustment period. In addition, while many employers have compassion for the different needs of working parents, many do not, and mothers struggle to adapt to a work environment that does not acknowledge their needs. Having to choose between the demands of your job and the needs of your children can be very stressful.

Let's take a look at some options to consider if you are weighing the advantages and disadvantages of work versus home.

CRUNCHING THE NUMBERS

If you have a choice about whether or not to return to work, add the numbers up and see if going back to work is going to be as lucrative as you thought. Some women find that when they total up the costs of everything from child care to transportation, their profit margin is actually quite low.

Take the following potential costs into account:
- *Child care:* baby-sitting or day care. Don't forget to include extra costs, such as fees for extended days at day care, overtime for sitters if you work late sometimes, or vacation and holiday days for baby-sitters, and year-end bonuses for full-time sitters or private-school teachers. If day care is your choice, check their schedules. Are there days they are closed when you will have to go to work? If so, you will need a sitter to cover you.
- Extra activities that you sign your child up for so that she and the sitter will have something to do, such as music classes or tots gymnastics. Don't include these costs if you would be doing them with your child if you were at home.
- Transportation to and from your workplace.
- The cost of business suits or uniforms. Also include dry-cleaning costs for your work clothes, if this is a factor.

- Your lunch at work, unless you bring a bag lunch.
- Any cleaning or home maintenance costs that you or your partner would do, if one of you were not working away from home.
- Extra cost of preprepared or takeout foods for dinner because you may not have the time or inclination to prepare a meal from scratch.

Doing the numbers is a good start to your decision-making process, if finances are a main consideration.

LEAVE OF ABSENCE

Even though you did not arrange to do this ahead of time, you might consider a leave of absence now. Unfortunately there is no consistent plan for new mothers in the United States to take a leave of absence from their jobs, as there is in some countries (see "Family-Friendly Policies," below), so what you can work out will depend almost entirely on the policy of your specific workplace.

The Family Medical Leave Act (FMLA) is the closest thing we have to national maternity leave in the United States. It requires that businesses of over 100 employees allow up to twelve weeks of unpaid maternity leave, with a guarantee that the employee's job (or a similar one) will be held until she returns. Many employers find ways to get around this requirement, and you and your employer may not agree on the definition of a "similar job."

Even if you are lucky enough to be employed by one of the 2 percent of companies that grant paid maternity leave to their employees, there is still no guarantee that you can have your job back if you decide to stay at home longer than agreed. You need to work this out with your boss—and try to get your agreement in writing.

You will be best off if you approach your employer with a plan, in writing, that outlines exactly what you want, when you will be back, and your expectations when you return. You may have more success with this than you might think. It costs companies money

BODY WISE
Kitchen Yoga

Your lower back may sometimes ache because of the temporary loss of muscle tone in your abdomen and the weight of carrying the baby. Don't worry; your body will get stronger. In the meantime, here is a posture that alleviates lower back pain. It is helpful to the pelvis, as it lengthens the psoas muscle, which extends from the lumbar spine to the upper thigh and commonly contracts during pregnancy.

Lie on your back with your legs straight and the soles of your feet touching a wall. Inhale and bend your right knee. Exhale and bring your knee to your chest as you hold your shin with both hands. If you're recovering from a cesarean, you may want to hold the back of your thigh instead.

Continue to press your left foot firmly against the wall. Don't tighten your abdomen. Hold for three to five deep breaths. As you exhale, release your right leg back to the wall and switch legs.

When you're finished, inhale and bend both your knees. Exhale and roll over to one side to come out of the pose.

to train new workers. If you are of value to them, they may be willing to accommodate your requests. At any rate, it doesn't hurt to try.

PART-TIME WORK

You might be able to arrange part-time work with your boss, or find a new job on a part-time basis. That might mean working two or three days a week, or it might mean working three or four hours, four or five days out of the week.

If you once worked full-time, and plan to return to the same job on a part-time basis, be aware that there might be an unspoken assumption that you will fulfill all your former duties—only in less time. It pays to spell everything out ahead of time, in great detail, so that no one is surprised.

FLEXTIME

With this option, an employee works the same amount of hours, but spreads them out differently. This might mean that a portion of the workweek is accomplished at home in the evening, after the baby has been put to bed for the night, or during naps. Or it might mean compressing the workweek by working four ten-hour days and having one extra day a week at home. It could also mean mother hours: working 8:30 to 3:00, when your children are in school, for example.

JOB SHARING

In job sharing, two or more people share the responsibilities, and the work hours, normally performed by a single person. The benefits to your family are clear. You will in effect be working part-time and will be able to spend more time with your baby. The employer benefits as well. One person is rarely equally gifted or qualified for all facets of a single job. Having more than one person doing a job means the employer can capitalize on the different strengths each one brings to the table. One of you might be better with organization, for example, while the other is better on the phone. The employer also gains a happier employee, one who does not feel so torn by time not spent with her baby. Depending on the requirements of the company, both may be eligible for benefits.

A new, untried work arrangement can be intimidating to employers, though, and convincing them to give it a try can be a challenge. As mentioned earlier, it helps if you can outline every aspect of the work and time division between you and your coworker. Who will do which tasks, who will be in on what days, and for how long? How much will each party expect to be paid, and how will the benefits be split between you? How will you and your coworker communicate with each other and your boss?

The partner you choose must be someone equally invested in making job sharing work and with whom you feel you can communicate effectively. It will be hard to make it work out if one of you is neat and the other messy, and you are sharing a single workspace. Look for compatibility.

WORK AT HOME

More and more women are working at home, at least part of the time. Modern technology has made this option a realistic possibility. Even meetings can sometimes be conducted with people who are in multiple locations. In some situations it is necessary to see coworkers face-to-face and to be in the office from time to time. Again, you need to work out the details with your employer ahead of time to avoid unmet expectations or potential conflicts.

A number of women have successfully started up their own businesses working at home. The possibilities are endless—women do everything from jewelry making to freelance writing to telemarketing from their homes.

Another at-home possibility is to do some child care with your own child in tow. This could be done either part- or full-time, in your own home, or at the other person's. It can be a great way to be with your child all day long and also make some extra money. If you've got a friend who also wants part-time child care, you might arrange a switch—taking care of each other's children along with your own on a rotating basis.

TAKE YOUR CHILD TO WORK

Once upon a time, going into the local general store and seeing the whole family behind the counter, including the youngest members, was not at all unusual. Nowadays it is not as common. The importance we place on "professional" behavior inhibits our willingness to incorporate children into the workplace. This is especially important for women, who have struggled long and hard to be considered viable professionals and who have sometimes had to hide their domestic lives in order to be taken seriously. Fortunately, this is changing, and taking children to work is becoming more common.

Of course, there are jobs where it is simply not possible to have a baby with you. If you work in a factory, in a department store, or as a surgeon or a judge, it may be impossible to have your little one with you. Even in those situations, though, some type of compromise might be possible. Perhaps there is a spare room in the building that could be used for child care. You and other employees with small children could hire someone together and share the costs. Maybe you can negotiate a different job in the same company that will allow you to have your baby nearby.

There are some unexpected benefits to having your child with you at work, aside from the obvious ones like being able to breastfeed more easily and not missing your baby's first attempts to crawl and other milestones. Some people report that having a baby around completely changes the work environment in a positive way. People are friendlier and more casual. Clients get to know the baby and look forward to visiting and seeing his progress. A company that publishes children's books allows their employees to bring their newborns to work and reports that it doesn't seem to impede their work. This company found that, in fact, employees are even more productive, perhaps because they aren't worried about their children.

There is no doubt that having a child at work means that sometimes you will get less done, and that you will have to sharpen your organizational skills and sometimes take work home. This type of arrangement will not appeal to everyone. For some parents, and their employees, however, the benefits far outweigh the disadvantages. Parents who bring a child to work will not need to take as many days off for the frequent mild illnesses children get. Many employees will prefer the inconvenience to losing the employee who has decided to stay home with her baby. Some parents offer to skip their next raise, or take a slight pay cut, to balance out their lessened productivity in exchange for the chance to have their child with them. This may be an option worth exploring.

NEW CAREERS

Babies seem to inspire changes in every part of women's lives, and work is no exception. This is the time when returning to a career you had doubts about to begin with seems all but impossible. "If I'm going to leave my child, it better be for something important," you may say.

Many women are inspired by their babies to start a new career that fits in better with their new lives as mothers. That may mean a job with more flexible or family-friendly hours. Or it may mean a career that is not so high-powered that they have to work late into the night.

Still other women find that motherhood inspires them to think up a new career that will do some good in the world. Having a child raises sensitivity to the many areas in our world where things are less than ideal. Women start not-for-profit agencies to aid other families, help assuage hunger, or improve education. Other women become inspired to become doulas, midwives, or childbirth educators, careers they knew very little about before they had children.

Family-Friendly Policies

Unfortunately, the United States lags behind more than 120 other countries when it comes to paid maternity leave and other policies that make life easier for working parents.

In Canada, women earn twenty-five weeks of paid maternity leave. Mexican women only get twelve weeks, the same as some American women, but theirs is a paid leave, unlike ours. British women get eighteen paid weeks, and Japanese women get fourteen paid weeks.

Sweden is the country most often held up as an example of family-friendly policies that work. Parents of all newborns or newly adopted children receive 450 paid days to care for that child. This can be

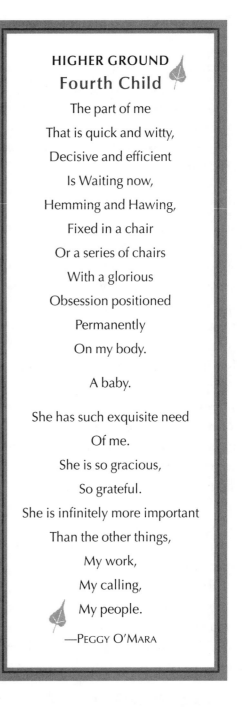

HIGHER GROUND
Fourth Child

The part of me
That is quick and witty,
Decisive and efficient
Is Waiting now,
Hemming and Hawing,
Fixed in a chair
Or a series of chairs
With a glorious
Obsession positioned
Permanently
On my body.

A baby.

She has such exquisite need
Of me.
She is so gracious,
So grateful.
She is infinitely more important
Than the other things,
My work,
My calling,
My people.

—PEGGY O'MARA

shared between the parents, or used by just one of them. In addition, a parent is entitled to work reduced hours until the child is eight years old, and has up to sixty paid days per year to take care of a sick child. Women who return to work while their babies are still nursing have protected time during the workday to breastfeed, even if their partner is at home with the baby.

And there's more. Throughout Sweden, there are hundreds of small indicators of the important place that children and families hold. Trains have play areas for kids, many institutions have small-scale toilets and sinks for toddlers, and children are welcome everywhere.

All of this is mandated by public policy. A Swedish employer is obligated to help employees gracefully combine parenthood and work.

The Swedes have discovered something that American corporations and government have yet to learn. When you support women and families, you get, in return, increased morale, loyalty, and productivity. In other words—it pays.

By contrast, the United States has few policies that protect families and offer them support. Paid maternity leave and subsidized child care are not a part of the average American parent's life, and it is the exceptional company that provides either.

Having a baby is the best way to see how clearly public policy in our country affects the family. Once you've got the little one in your arms and see how hard it is to leave her for any length of time, you know much more about the dilemma at hand. Perhaps our children's children will not have to face these difficulties if we make our voices heard now and ask for a more family-friendly world, in their names.

Work and Breastfeeding

A decision to return to work does not necessarily mean an end to breastfeeding. While there are, at present, a number of pending bills that will help ensure a woman's right to pump breastmilk at work, and some proposed tax incentives for companies that will support women to continue breastfeeding on the job, there is nothing solidly in place as of yet. The best you can hope for is to have an understanding boss who will support you in a decision to keep nursing your child.

There are some real benefits to your employer in helping you. Working women who breastfeed their babies take less time off, have higher morale, and amazingly, tend to take shorter maternity leaves, perhaps because they are less concerned about the effect of their return on the nursing relationship.

These suggestions can help you to keep nursing after you return to work:

- Find a place at your job where you can pump. If you choose the spot ahead of time and troubleshoot any potential problems with it, it will make your plan seem clearer. The bathroom should be your last choice, unless it is a particularly nice bathroom where you can lock the door and have privacy. Try to find a room with a nice atmosphere, which will make your letdown reflex happen more easily. If you use your own office, make sure the door locks and create some type of Do Not Disturb sign.

- Plan out when, during the day, you will express milk. You will probably need to do this twice, if you work a regular nine-to-five job. If you can fit it into preestablished break times, that's all the better. Otherwise, see if you can take time out of your lunch hour for pumping breaks, have it deducted from your pay, or stay a bit later to make up the time.

- Share some literature with your boss, such as *Women, Work, and Breastfeeding: Everyone Benefits!* which is published by La Leche League. You can also supply them with information about the pending legislation on pumping on the job. See appendix 2 for information on how to obtain these.

Once you have a plan in place, and have worked out some details with your employer, use these ideas to make it all go more smoothly:

- Bring a picture of the baby with you to work. Looking at a picture may make your letdown reflex happen more quickly and may help you to produce more milk.

- Do whatever you can to improve the atmosphere of the room you pump in. Perhaps a little lavender essential oil on a tissue will help you relax, or maybe some soft music will be nice. Dim the lights, if possible. On the other hand, some women don't seem to need those touches and continue to talk on the phone and read paperwork while they are pumping. Everyone is different.

- Rent, or invest in, a pump that allows you to express milk from both breasts at once. You will spend your break time more efficiently this way. There are pumps on the market in carrying cases that look like a large handbag.

- On the other hand, a few women find they are more efficient just using their hands to manually express milk. Some women do not like the sound or the feel of the machine doing the job.

- You may be able to leave the pump at work overnight and over the weekends. Get a small cooler and an icepack to transport the expressed milk home. You will also need either a cooler or a refrigerator to store the milk in during the day while you are still at work.

- Try to ease your way into your new nursing pattern. This will be easier on both you and the baby. If you have been nursing every couple of hours during the day, you may experience some engorgement and leaking until your body has adjusted to the new pattern. Amazingly, though, your body will adjust, even when you are home all day on the weekends and breastfeeding full-time.

- Practice with the pump at home before going back to work.

PART SIX

Special Circumstances

CHAPTER 27 · *When a Baby Dies: Miscarriage, Stillbirth, and Early Loss*

> Perhaps the most important way to memorialize anyone who dies is to remove the shroud of darkness that wraps all death and to bring it into the sunshine . . . especially when the death is that of a baby.
>
> —JOY JOHNSON, *Miscarriage: The Unrecognized Grief*

When a baby dies, whether the death occurs only six weeks after conception or six days after birth, a dream dies as well. Sadly, one barely has a chance to savor this dream before it disappears completely.

Women who lose a baby during pregnancy, or shortly after birth, grieve just as anyone else would after the loss of a departed loved one. That often comes as a surprise to some friends and family who may equate the smallness of the baby, and the shortness of its life, with the amount of grief the mother should experience.

The baby is already a loved one, whether she is born or is still developing. Losing a baby to miscarriage or stillbirth proves that bonding can and does happen while a baby is still in the womb. The spiritual connection between mother and baby has nothing to do with time spent together, or even with being able to see one another.

Experts of all kinds, from psychologists to midwives, agree that our society is not very good at mourning these types of losses. Devastated parents are often left to deal with their grief completely on their own. Especially when it comes to miscarriages, there are few established ceremonies or rituals that can help parents to share their loss in a public way. We'll talk more about this, and how to help yourself or a loved one through the mourning process, later in

the chapter. First, let's take a look at what causes these sad losses.

The Terminology of Loss

In obstetrical terminology there are four types of losses: miscarriage, stillbirth, intrapartum death, and neonatal death.

Miscarriage is defined as a loss that has occurred sometime before twenty weeks' gestation. Miscarriages can occur for a wide variety of reasons, but happen most often either because of a genetic problem in the baby or because of a health problem in the mother. We will talk about these reasons in more detail later on in this chapter.

Not all pregnancy losses before twenty weeks qualify as a miscarriage, however. About 4 percent of early losses are due to ectopic pregnancy, where the egg has implanted into a fallopian tube after being fertilized, rather than implanting into the uterus.[1] The rate of ectopic pregnancy is steadily rising in the United States, although no one is sure why. Another 1 percent of early losses are due to rare occurrences such as molar pregnancy, where a nonviable egg is fertilized but develops into a mass of grapelike tissue, rather than a fetus.[2]

After twenty weeks, a baby that dies in the womb, but before labor has begun, is called a *stillbirth*.

These losses can happen for many of the same reasons that miscarriages occur, though usually not because of genetic abnormalities.

Intrapartum death is the term used to describe a baby that has died during labor or delivery. *Neonatal death* is the term for a baby who dies somewhere between birth and four weeks of age.

The Prevalence of Miscarriage

Few people know how common miscarriage actually is. Statistics vary, but some experts think that well over half of all fertilized eggs are miscarried before they even implant into the mother's uterus. In fact, most of those miscarriages probably go unnoticed by the mother, who may just think she is having a slightly heavy menstrual period, if she notices anything at all. Another 31 percent are miscarried after implantation, but before pregnancy has been confirmed.[3]

Statistics also vary as to how many miscarriages occur after confirmation of pregnancy. Some say 1 in 4, while others think it is closer to 1 in 7. As we described in the previous section, about 4 percent do not actually qualify as a miscarriage (or *spontaneous abortion,* as it is called in medical terminology) because they are due to ectopic or molar pregnancies.

The remaining miscarriages can be broken up into two rough categories: *recurring miscarriages* and *chance* or *sporadic miscarriages.* About 80 percent of miscarriages are sporadic miscarriages—onetime occurrences. Most of these women will go on to have a normal full-term pregnancy when they become pregnant again. We'll talk about those later in this section.

RECURRING MISCARRIAGES

Recurring miscarriages are another story. A woman who has had three consecutive miscarriages falls into this category (some doctors now classify two consecutive miscarriages as recurrent). These women may have many miscarriages and may experience tremendous long-term grief as a result. About 1 to 2 percent of all couples will experience recurrent miscarriages.[4]

Recurring miscarriages can happen because of hormonal imbalance, immunological problems, uterine malformations, incompetent cervix, chronic infections or viruses, inherited genetic problems, or a combination of these factors, each of which is described in more detail below. Because so many factors come into play, the reason for miscarriages can be difficult to pinpoint, and many women will never have a solid explanation for their recurring miscarriages. A woman can appear to be healthy and have no particular ailments, but can still be unable to carry a baby to term. Some women will be able to correct their health problems and go on to deliver a normal, healthy baby, while others will need to come to terms with the fact that they will never be able to experience a full-term pregnancy.

Let's look at some of the reasons for recurring miscarriages:

- *Hormonal imbalance.* Some experts think that hormonal problems may account for 10 to 15 percent of all recurrent miscarriages.[5] Luteal phase defect or corpus luteum defect is a common hormonal problem that can lead to miscarriage. The luteal phase is the time between conception and the beginning of the next menstrual cycle. Progesterone levels normally rise as soon as an egg is released from an ovary. If the egg is fertilized, those levels will continue to rise in a normal pregnancy. Women with luteal phase defect experience a drop in progesterone levels even if the egg is fertilized, which causes the egg to be aborted. However, it is still not clear whether it is the low progesterone levels that caused the miscarriage, or whether the miscarriage lowered the progesterone levels.[6] More research needs to be done in this area.

  Natural progesterone is commonly given to pregnant women in the hopes that it may prevent miscarriage, but the fact is that its true effectiveness is unknown. Some studies reviewed by the Cochrane Database, which collects evidence-based information on pregnancy and childbirth from all over the world, have shown that natural progesterone is safe, while others indicate that it may cause health problems in infants.[7] Do not ever take synthetic hormones of any kind during pregnancy, as unlike the natural hormones we've described above, many problems have been definitely identified with the consumption of these.

- *Immunological problems.* This may account for about 15 percent, or more, of recurrent miscarriages. Some researchers think immunological problems may be the cause of up to one-third of all miscarriages.[8] Women who have these problems are in a particularly gut-wrenching position because their body attacks the cells of the developing fetus, which are seen as "foreign tissue." There are a number of different problems that can fall into this category.

It is thought that if you and your partner are genetically similar, and share too many of the same antigens (proteins that trigger an antibody response by the immune system), your body may not be able to block the natural impulse to reject any foreign cells, including those of your baby. One available treatment, which is still being studied, is to inject the women with some of the man's white blood cells. So far this looks promising.

Antiphospholipid syndrome (APLS) is another example of an immunological problem. APLS signals the body to produce autoantibodies against fatty substances in cells. This causes blood clots to form. If the woman becomes pregnant, those clots will form in the placenta and can literally deprive the fetus of oxygen and nutrients, causing growth retardation or miscarriage. The drug heparin, aspirin therapy, and steroid therapy are all treatments that may help some women with immune disorders who want to remain pregnant. These treatments are all still experimental, and some of them may create

further complications, such as a higher risk of preterm delivery, for example.

Interestingly, about 2 percent of women who go through normal pregnancies also have autoimmune disorders that do not seem to affect the pregnancy at all.[9]

- *Uterine malformations.* This can include a wide variety of problems and accounts for about 12 percent of recurrent miscarriages, mostly those that take place between twelve and twenty-four weeks.[10] About half of these abnormalities are a malformation known as a bicornate or septate uterus.[11] In this condition there is a band that goes through the middle of the uterus, creating, in effect, two separate cavities. In some cases, there might even be two separate cervixes. Sometimes surgery can correct these problems to improve the chances of success in future pregnancies. Asherman's syndrome is another uterine problem where scar tissue crosses the lining of the uterus, rather like a spider's web.[12] If the scarring is extensive, it can make it hard for an egg to implant, or stay implanted, in the uterus. This condition is very often the result of infection, or from having a dilation and curettage (D&C) or a late abortion.

- *Incompetent cervix.* Incompetent cervix is a rather harsh term for an involuntary condition whereby the cervix spontaneously opens up in the early weeks of pregnancy, even if the fetus inside is completely healthy. This accounts for about 1 to 2 percent of all late pregnancy losses, after the twelfth week.[13] Incompetent cervix is sometimes the result of uterine malformations (described above) or because the cervical opening has been damaged in some way.

- *Infections and viruses.* It isn't easy to pinpoint these as the cause of miscarriage, but scientists do think that infections can cause problems in early pregnancy. Some of these might be chronic and therefore responsible for recurring miscarriages. Others might be onetime infections that cause a chance miscarriage. Syphilis, malaria, toxoplasmosis, listeria, and chlamydia are all examples of infections that might cause miscarriage.[14] Viruses such as mumps and measles may also cause miscarriage, but no one knows for sure.

- *Genetic/chromosomal problems.* Repeated genetic problems that cause miscarriage after miscarriage (as opposed to chance genetic problems discussed later in this section) are quite rare, accounting for only 6 percent, or less, of all recurring miscarriages.[15] In these cases the parents have handed down a chromosomal abnormality that they are unaware of and which has not affected their health otherwise. The fetus is unable to develop properly and is miscarried.

- *Other health problems.* Certain health conditions may increase your risk for miscarriage. Untreated diabetes and thyroid problems may cause miscarriage. Congenital heart disease may deprive the fetus of enough oxygen and cause the baby to fail.

CHANCE OR SPORADIC MISCARRIAGES

While recurrent miscarriages can be devastatingly tragic, they are not as common as chance, or sporadic miscarriages, which account for about 80 percent of all miscarriages.

While older parents are statistically at higher risk for chance miscarriages, the reasons for this are not fully known. Jonathan Scher, M.D., an expert in the field of miscarriage research, suggests that as people age they develop more health problems, and some of those problems, such as uncontrolled diabetes, might affect their risk. Older parents may also have more stress in their lives, which may be a factor in both infertility and miscarriage. Scher also points out, however, that statistics showing increased miscarriages in older women may be skewed by the fact that those women are more likely to report problems, since they may be more conscientious about their health and more aware of what their bodies are doing. In addition, older women may be trying very hard to get pregnant, and may already be under medical supervision when they do miscarry, thus making it easy to include them in statistics.[16]

GENETIC PROBLEMS

Chromosomal mix-ups account for well over half of chance miscarriages. There is no known reason why chromosomal mix-ups occur. Sometimes genetic material from both parents is assembled in the wrong way, or some material is lost. Such miscarriages generally occur before twelve weeks' gestation, and often within the first four or five weeks of pregnancy. When a chromosomal mix-up happens, a fetus will survive until some point in his growth when the incorrect chromosomes prevent the next development stage from occurring. When this happens, the fetus is usually aborted.

BLIGHTED OVUM

Age may also play a role in this condition, since women over the age of thirty-five have a higher chance of experiencing it. Blighted ovum results when a fertilized, implanted egg stops growing in the early stages of cell division. The sac, however, has not yet received the message that there is no fetus and continues to develop at the normal pace for some time. These pregnancies usually spontaneously abort early on, before eight weeks. No one knows why women over thirty-five have more cases of blighted ovum, but some experts speculate that they may be caused by chromosomal mix-ups.

OTHER FACTORS

There are other reasons why a chance miscarriage can happen. A onetime infection might be the culprit (see "Infections and viruses" on page 237). It is thought that very high fevers can also cause miscarriage. Multiple pregnancies are more likely to miscarry. Sometimes, in fact, just one fetus might be miscarried, while the other one goes on to develop normally. Prenatal testing, such as amniocentesis, can also cause chance miscarriage (see chapter 5). In-vitro fertilization also comes with a higher-than-usual miscarriage rate.

As you can see, however, there is very little definitive information about why miscarriages occur. Most women who miscarry, especially ones who have a chance miscarriage, will never know for sure why it happened to them. Much more research needs to be done in this area of reproductive medicine.

Signs of a Miscarriage

Miscarriage is often detected when a woman notices that she is bleeding. She may also have some cramping, perhaps as mild as those she gets around her period. Instead of cramps she might also feel a heaviness in the pelvic region.

Neither bleeding nor minor cramping is a definite sign of miscarriage, however. About 70 percent of women bleed sometime in early pregnancy, often around the time when they would have had their regular menstrual period.[17] Your hormones are still fluctuating during this time. The implantation of the egg into the uterus can sometimes also cause a little bleeding. If the blood is a dark reddish brown, there is probably no cause for concern.

If you are bleeding, and are at the point in your pregnancy where the baby's heartbeat can be detected (after four to five weeks), the chance you will miscarry is only 10 percent.[18] If you are just spot-bleeding, your practitioner will probably suggest you take it easy and wait to see what happens. Use a pad, rather than a tampon, to contain the blood. If the bleeding continues, is of a bright red color or accompanied by heavy cramps, or if you notice that pregnancy symptoms such as nausea or tender breasts suddenly disappear, you will probably be sent to have an ultrasound exam. Your doctor will check to see if your cervix is still closed or has opened, which would also indicate the likelihood of a miscarriage.

Cramping also happens in normal pregnancy from time to time and is not necessarily a sign of impending miscarriage. It is easy to confuse uterine cramping with gastrointestinal cramping, caused by gas. Also the uterus does contract from time to time during pregnancy, though this generally happens later. These "rehearsal" contractions are called Braxton-Hicks contractions. They are only a cause for concern if you have more than four of them in one hour.

An ultrasound exam can determine whether or not the baby is still alive as early as four or five weeks, in some cases. To date, ultrasound cannot predict, with any consistency, whether or not a fetus with a normal heartbeat is *likely* to miscarry.

If you experience bleeding and cramping, you can try the homeopathic treatments *Sabina* and *Viburnum opulus* as miscarriage preventatives. *Syphilinum* and *Bacillinum* are good for preventing recurrent miscarriages. Seek the advice of a homeopathic practitioner.

Wild yam root is an herb that is also meant to help prevent miscarriage. You can make a tea out of it and drink two cups per day, or take fifteen drops of the tincture two times per day. Remember to check with your health care practitioner before using any remedies while you're pregnant.

Treatment of Miscarriage

If you have a miscarriage before week six, your body will most likely handle the miscarriage on its own with no problems. This is called a *complete abortion,* much to the dismay of some women who associate the term *abortion* with the conscious decision to end pregnancy.

Miscarriages after six weeks are more likely to be problematic due to the increased size of the placenta. The two most common problems that occur with later miscarriages are *missed abortions* and *partial abortions.* A "missed abortion" is when, unbeknownst to the mother, the fetus has died inside the womb, but has not been expelled. A "partial abortion" means that some of the tissue is effectively expelled by the body, but some remains inside. If any tissue is left inside the womb (revealed by ultrasound examinations), it can potentially result in serious infections. In some cases a partial abortion can also result in hemorrhaging.

If you have had either a missed or partial abortion and your body does not naturally expel all the tissue, you may eventually need to have a dilation and curettage (D&C) to clean out the inside of your uterus. If you are having serious bleeding (soaking more than one full-size pad in less than half an hour), the D&C might need to be performed on an emergency basis.

Don't feel pressured to have a D&C as a preventative measure. You can miscarry safely and completely at home, but be in consultation with your health care practitioner by telephone. The duration of a miscarriage is extremely variable, and can last anywhere from a few hours to a week or two, but most bleeding will subside within a few weeks. In fact, most women who miscarry before 13 weeks are likely to do just fine. Only about 20 percent will end up needing any medical help.[19] When a woman miscarries beyond thirteen weeks, it becomes increasingly more likely that a D&C will be necessary.

A D&C, like any surgical procedure, does not come risk-free. There is a chance that your uterus might be punctured during the procedure. D&Cs can sometimes create scarring that might affect your future fertility. Any surgical procedure carries anesthesia-related risks, as well.

You will need to decide for yourself how you would like to handle an incomplete or missed miscarriage (unless you are hemorrhaging, of course, in which case you must have an emergency D&C). You might prefer to let nature take charge, or you may feel that waiting is just too hard, especially if it takes more than a week or two. Many women have trouble with the knowledge that they are carrying their dead baby around inside their bodies, while others find that this last bit of closeness is comforting.

If you miscarry at home, try to save any expelled tissue that you can. It may be possible that tests can determine the cause of the miscarriage, particularly if it is genetic. Put the expelled tissue into a sterile container or wrap it in a damp cloth and ask your doctor where you should take it. You can store tissue in the refrigerator, if necessary. Do not place the tissue in any liquid or saline solution, as this may damage the cells and make it impossible to test it properly.

After the completed miscarriage, or the D&C procedure, you will continue to bleed for two or more weeks. You should use a pad, rather than a tampon. You should also avoid intercourse and tub baths until the bleeding has stopped. Report any fevers over 100 degrees Fahrenheit to your health care provider.[20]

You may be surprised at how quickly your body goes back to its regular cycle, even while you are still actively grieving. Doctors used to recommend waiting to try to get pregnant for several cycles. Many now feel it is all right to try again after just one cycle, while others suggest at least two. Check with your midwife or doctor. Most importantly, check with yourself to see if you are emotionally ready for another pregnancy.

Keep in mind that, as far as your body is concerned, you have just given birth. Your hormones will take time to return to normal levels. You may have to contend with some postpartum depression, in addition to the grief and depression you will experience due to your loss. Read "Grieving," later in this chapter.

Preventing Miscarriage

The first trimester of pregnancy, when the majority of miscarriages occur, has not been studied as extensively as pregnancy and birth. This is surprising and unfortunate, considering that by the end of the first trimester most of the fetus's major development has already taken place. Early pregnancy, however, is difficult to study. One reason for this is that traditional double-blind studies on mothers in early pregnancy may create risks for the developing baby. More needs to be learned about this early period to better understand why miscarriages happen. This way, women may be able to prevent them.

The truth is, most of the time very little can be done to prevent a miscarriage, or to pinpoint the reasons why one did occur. Only about half of women who undergo tests ever find out why they had a miscarriage. In cases where a woman has a specific medical problem and is having recurrent miscarriages as a result of that problem, preventative measures might be taken to lower the chances of future miscarriages. For example, a woman who keeps miscarrying because she has a malformed uterus might have surgery that will correct the problem.

Chance miscarriages, however, cannot be predicted and usually come with very little warning. A practitioner may suggest that a woman who is bleeding get bed rest and avoid intercourse. There is no proof that this will change the prognosis, however. The only study ever done on the effectiveness of bed rest preventing miscarriage failed to show that it had any effect.[21] Still, if resting feels good, it is probably fine to do it, at least for a few days. Prolonged bed rest can be very disruptive to a woman's life, especially if she has other children. Bed rest can also produce a great deal of anxiety, which will not help matters. Bed rest recommended in later pregnancy is another story.

Women who have experienced a miscarriage usually blame themselves. They wonder if hanging curtains or going out dancing could have been the culprit. There is no evidence that these kinds of activities can cause miscarriage, so there is no reason to feel guilty. Even women who experience serious falls or car accidents rarely miscarry, if their fetus was healthy to begin with.

There is also no evidence, as of yet, that diet causes miscarriage. Of course it makes sense to eat well, for your health and the healthy development of your baby. Bingeing on ice cream and chocolate, however, does *not* cause miscarriage.

Other lifestyle choices are more important to consider, though. Smoking can increase your chances of miscarriage by 30 to 50 percent.[22] Consuming more than 300 mg of caffeine daily (the equivalent of about two and a half cups of caffeinated coffee) increases your miscarriage risk by up to a third. That risk may be even higher in women who consume a lot of caffeine and also experience morning sickness, though the reason is unknown.

Some studies indicate that long-term exposure to chemical solvents might also be a problem. High miscarriage rates have been reported in association with disaster sites, such as the one occurring in 1984 at the Union Carbide plant at Bhopal, India.[23] Long-term exposure to computer monitors has also been blamed for miscarriages, though studies have so far failed to back that claim up. These environmental factors need to be better studied.

Since high levels of stress and grief can reduce immunological functioning, some experts think these emotional conditions may also contribute to miscarriages. Interestingly, women who have had recurrent miscarriages seem to do better in future pregnancies when good psychological support is in place, even without any type of medical intervention.[24] Managing stress will certainly improve your pregnancy, and your life. Since it is not known whether stress can really effect a miscarriage, it is probably better not to assume it caused yours or to blame yourself for not handling stress better.

Blaming yourself for a miscarriage because you

NATURAL SOOTHER

Grief Tea

While no soother is equal to the loss of a child, you must take care of yourself even in the most difficult of times. Afternoon tea is a way to do this. Borage, said to relieve sadness and grief, is an herb known in ancient times as a tonic—it calms the heart and revitalizes the exhausted system.

In the spring, you can plant some borage for your tea. Otherwise, look for dried borage at the natural food grocery store or herb shop.

Place 4 tablespoons fresh or 2 tablespoons dried borage flowers and leaves in a teapot. Cover with 1 pint of boiling water and steep for 5 to 10 minutes. Strain and sip slowly.

Drink this relaxing tea once a day.

think you were too active or too stressed is not backed up by medical evidence. The sad truth is that miscarriages are often nature's way of solving a problem: often either the fetus or the conditions in the womb were not optimal for the production of a new life. If you have had a miscarriage, focus on appropriately processing your grief. The grieving process will be discussed later in this chapter.

Stillbirth and Intrapartum Death

After a fetus reaches the age of twenty weeks, his or her death in the womb is no longer called a miscarriage, but is instead a *stillbirth*. Stillbirths account for about 45 percent of all deaths that occur between twenty weeks' gestation and four weeks of age (after live birth). An infant that dies during birth itself has died *intrapartum*. Fortunately, both stillbirths and intrapartum deaths are rare these days. Partly because of this, when they do happen, a woman tends to feel very isolated and alone.

There are a number of reasons why stillbirths and intrapartum deaths occur. Many of them are the same reasons that cause miscarriage, particularly problems like uterine malformations, incompetent cervix, and health conditions in the mother (such as untreated diabetes). Infections can still cause problems in older fetuses, but this becomes less common as the fetus ages and is better equipped to fight infections. The reasons for many stillbirths remain mysterious; about one third of stillbirths happen for unknown reasons. Let's take a look at some of the other reasons for stillbirth or intrapartum death.

- *Multiple fetuses.* Sometimes more than one fetus overextends the uterus, forcing the cervix to open too early. This usually happens after the twentieth week.
- *Placental disorders.* Placenta abruptio occurs when the placenta separates from the wall of the uterus. This tends to happen around the thirty-fifth week and is a very serious condition that can lead to the baby's death within a few hours. An emergency cesarean section is often per-

formed. An abruption may also be accompanied by pain and high blood pressure. Very late losses in pregnancy can also occur because the placenta becomes diseased or is no longer able to provide adequate nutrition to the baby. Rarely, this can be a result of postmaturity, where the baby remains in the womb for too long. In placenta previa, the placenta grows over the cervical area. This is not as immediately dangerous as abruption. The baby will also have to be delivered via C-section, but not until he is fully matured, in most cases. Both of these conditions cause bleeding. Any bleeding, especially after the twenty-eighth week, should be reported to your doctor immediately.

- *Umbilical cord accidents.* These accidents generate a lot of publicity, perhaps because they are so dramatic. In reality, they are quite rare. Occasionally, a cord can develop a kink that cuts off oxygen and blood to the baby, causing it to die. A baby with a very long cord might end up with it wrapped tightly around its neck, but even this is not always a problem. Prolapsed cord is a condition where the umbilical cord slips out of the cervix before the baby does. The pressure on the cord could potentially cut off the baby's oxygen supply.
- *Birth defects.* Some serious birth defects, such as congenital heart disease, for example, cause the baby to die even before he is born. Many of these infants would not have survived past the first few days of life if they had made it to full-term birth.
- *Rhesus incompatibility.* This rare condition occurs when the mother's blood is Rh-negative and the fetus has inherited Rh-positive blood from the father. If, during delivery, miscarriage, or an abortion, some of the fetus's blood mixes with the mother's blood, her blood may become sensitized and develop antibodies to her baby's blood. Although this rarely presents a problem during the first pregnancy, subsequent pregnancies with an Rh-positive baby could be prob-

lematic. Most women are injected with a serum that will prevent creation of antibodies against the baby after having had a first birth, or a previous miscarriage or abortion.

- *Birth accidents.* Deaths that occur during labor and birth are very rare, and are usually due to lack of oxygen. Even more rare are accidents involving damage to the baby from a forceps delivery.

SIGNS OF STILLBIRTH

Stillbirths usually start with a gush of amniotic fluid. You might not have any other warning signs at all, or you may have noticed the baby's movements slowing down or stopping altogether. As pregnancy progresses, babies do tend to move around less, due to lack of space, so less movement does not necessarily mean the baby is in danger. Another sign that stillbirth may have occurred is sudden and extreme weight loss in the mother. Keep in mind, though, that some women do lose a couple of pounds in the last weeks of pregnancy and that weight loss does not necessarily indicate trouble.

Stillbirths tend to happen much more quickly than miscarriages, which can sometimes go on for days, or even weeks. You will go into labor, or have labor induced, just as you would have with a full-term baby. Your body, not knowing the difference, will treat this as a normal birth. In later pregnancy this is often accompanied by milk production, which can be a sad reminder of the baby who is not there to drink it.

You are also subject to postpartum depression, which can make your grieving even more complex. You will need to spend time resting in bed and healing from the delivery, and you will need as much support as possible from family and friends. Don't be afraid to ask friends to help you with household chores, and to keep you company during your recovery time. Read the postpartum sections of this book for tips on healing your body after stillbirth.

Your doctor will probably suggest that the baby's body be autopsied to determine the exact cause of

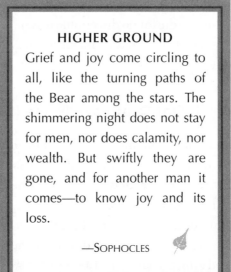

HIGHER GROUND

Grief and joy come circling to all, like the turning paths of the Bear among the stars. The shimmering night does not stay for men, nor does calamity, nor wealth. But swiftly they are gone, and for another man it comes—to know joy and its loss.

—SOPHOCLES

death. If the reasons for death were not clear, an autopsy may be helpful to you in understanding why this tragedy occurred. You may choose not to do this, however. Ask for time to think it over and discuss it with your partner.

Neonatal Deaths

A baby who dies within the first four weeks of life experiences neonatal death. Most neonatal deaths occur within the first week of life, however. The reasons for neonatal deaths are also varied, and many overlap with the reasons for miscarriage and stillbirth. Some neonatal deaths happen because a baby is born prematurely (discussed in more detail in chapter 28), or has low birth weight, and is having trouble breathing on his own.

Other neonatal deaths occur because of the opposite problem: postmaturity. These babies become deprived of nutrition during their last days in the womb because the placenta has failed to keep up with their needs, or the baby may have inhaled meconium (a dark, sticky substance that comes from the baby's intestines), which can cause pneumonia and other breathing problems.

Occasionally, neonatal death occurs because an

infant's birth defects are just too severe to support life. Still others die for no discernible reason, and this is usually classified as sudden infant death syndrome (SIDS).

Sudden Infant Death Syndrome (SIDS)

While more is now known about SIDS, it remains a largely mysterious condition. SIDS cases tend to occur between the ages of two weeks and one year, although the large majority of SIDS cases happen before six months. After the age of four weeks, SIDS is the major cause of all infant deaths in the United States and afflicts about 1 in 1,000 infants.[25] Generally speaking, an infant will have been put down for a nap, or for the night, and appears to have died during sleep, with no apparent signs of struggle. If an investigation and autopsy reveal no sign of illness or accident, then SIDS is the usual diagnosis.

There are a large number of theories as to what causes SIDS. Some think it may be because of a subtle brain abnormality. Others say it might be a type of sleep apnea, a condition causing breathing to stop during sleep, or gastroesophageal reflux (GER), where food backs up the esophagus and causes choking.

While no one knows for sure what causes SIDS, you can take the following steps to reduce the risks:

- Get adequate prenatal care. Take good care of yourself and avoid taking unnecessary drugs during pregnancy, labor, and delivery.

- Do not smoke near your baby. Smoking during or after birth can double the risk of SIDS.[26]

- Breastfeed your baby. Studies in the United States and New Zealand have shown that bottle-fed babies have been shown to be at greater risk for SIDS.

- Put your baby to sleep only on her back, not her stomach or her side. Do put her on her tummy for playtime, however.

- Remove any loose bedding from where the baby sleeps. Do not use a pillow or a thick comforter. Do not allow the baby to become overheated.

- Use nontoxic mattresses and bedding for the baby (see chapter 12 and appendix 2 for more information).

- Sleep with your baby. According to sleep expert Dr. James McKenna, infants who sleep with their parents may be at lower risk for SIDS.

Grieving

In Japan, special temples are created specifically to honor babies who have died, even ones who died in utero. Parents can place a statue in the temple in honor of the lost baby. Many women dress the statues with baby hats or bibs. In some West African cultures, there are specific grief ceremonies for women who have suffered a miscarriage. Although the Japanese and the West Africans handle miscarriage differently, they have some important things in common. Both countries publicly acknowledge the reality and the depth of the grief that women experience when they lose a baby. This grief is acknowledged by special ceremonies, rituals, and public memorials.

In the United States there are very few such rituals. A baby who is born alive and then dies in the early weeks will probably have a funeral. There is likely to be a bit more compassion and understanding for parents who lose a full-term baby. An early stillborn baby, or one who is miscarried, is not customarily given a funeral or any type of ceremony. One exception to this is in some Orthodox Jewish sects, where a new ceremony for grieving miscarriage has recently been initiated. In general, though, our culture's general affluence and good health has really distanced us from death. We just don't know how to grieve very well.

Until a loss like this has happened to you, or someone very close to you, you may not understand the depth of grieving that parents go through. In some cases there is even misunderstanding between partners about how much grief is appropriate. When a woman becomes pregnant, major hormonal changes occur immediately. Even before she looks pregnant, she is pregnant—with a capital P. Mothers usually feel a bond with their babies sooner than fathers, who may not feel such a bond until the pregnancy becomes more obvious.

You are likely to feel as though friends and family just don't understand. People will say things that don't make sense to you, such as "It was probably for the best." While that may ultimately be true, it certainly doesn't feel "best" to you and doesn't demonstrate respect for your feelings of loss. You may receive some thoughtful treatment at first, but as the months go by, you may be saddened to find that some people don't understand why you are *still* grieving. "Isn't it time to move on?" they may ask. It is unlikely that they would expect this of you if you had lost a spouse or a parent.

Hospitals and medical personnel are even less likely to treat devastated parents with gentle compassion. "This happens all the time," you might be told. While it is true that miscarriage is common, it certainly doesn't feel "usual" to the parents. This is a unique and personal loss of the baby they'd hoped to soon hold in their arms. Many women are kept waiting for hours between treatments, spoken to in a curt manner, and then sent home with no suggestions on how to handle their grief.

Most experts recommend that you actually see your baby, whether you've had a miscarriage or a stillbirth. "All those feelings about having a real baby are completely confirmed when a mother sees her baby," says Perry-Lynn Moffitt, a pregnancy loss counselor and coauthor of *A Silent Sorrow.* This is important even if all there is to look at is tissue. A miscarried or stillborn fetus usually looks peaceful. Even the appearance of a malformed fetus is rarely as bad as a woman's imagination might lead her to believe. If you possibly can, try to hold your baby for a time.

It is also helpful to visit your newborn baby in the intensive care unit even if death is imminent. Some women worry that seeing the baby too much will make the eventual loss more painful. Evidence shows that mothering your baby actually helps to ease the pain of loss.

In addition, it can help to name your baby. Use the name you'd planned, rather than saving it for a future child. This also helps to confirm the importance this baby had in your life, and can help to make the loss seem more real.

If you have older children, you will probably need to give them some explanation for what has happened. This is true even if you had not yet told your child about the pregnancy. Children can always sense when their parents are sad or disturbed about something. Children have a tendency to make things up if they are not given accurate information. Often they blame themselves when Mommy seems sad.

Find an age-appropriate way to tell your children what's going on. You might tell a two-year-old simply "Mommy feels very sad, but it is not your fault." A three- or four-year-old might need more information, "Mommy had a baby in her tummy, but the baby was sick and could not grow, so it died. Now Mommy feels very sad." Never tell a child that death is like going to sleep. This could cause your child to become fearful of sleep in general. Your child may ask you many questions over the weeks to come. Don't force a conversation, but try to answer all questions simply and clearly.

RITUALS AND CEREMONIES

While our culture does not have many established rituals to acknowledge the loss you've experienced, you can find solace, as well as acknowledge your grief to a larger community, if you wish, by creating rituals of your own. Here are some suggestions to help you through the grieving process:

- Take photographs. Most hospitals routinely photograph infants who die, including stillbirths. They keep the photos for several months, even if parents say they don't want them. Hospitals report that, in almost all cases, the photographs are eventually claimed. If you can, take your own photos of the baby as well. Although it may be too painful to look at them now, they may be very meaningful to you in future months and years.

- Claim as many mementos as you can. Some hospitals prepare a package for parents with photos, certificates, or other items having to do with the baby. They are less likely to do something like this for miscarriages, so you might need to ask for specific things. Some other items to save could include your positive pregnancy test, names of people who cared for you or the baby in the hospital, a blanket or clothing that the baby was wrapped in, a lock of hair, and foot or hand prints, which are possible for even the smallest of babies. When you are ready, you might put these items into a beautiful box or scrapbook.
- Hold a funeral or memorial service. Most funeral homes will work with parents who have stillbirths. If you decide to use a coffin or a cremation urn, you might want to place a small toy, or other meaningful memento, inside with the baby. You can also hold your own memorial ceremony in a park, or by the water, or wherever else feels special to you. The organization SHARE Pregnancy and Infant Loss Support, provides small coffins for parents who have had a miscarriage (see appendix 2). Some states are now making it mandatory for hospitals and doctors to ask the parents of miscarried babies what they would like to do with the remains. In other states, you will have to inquire what is being done with the remains, and hope for cooperation if you have something specific you would like to do.
- Plant a tree or a small garden in honor of the baby. Create a special area outdoors, using plants, rocks, candles, or a small statue.
- Make an annual contribution to a charity on the anniversary of your baby's death. You could contribute to an organization having to do with

BODY WISE
Quick Relaxers

Your grief and sadness may make it hard to relax. Here are a couple of quick exercises you can do anywhere, anytime you feel nervous or tense.

Just Breathe
- Stand up straight.
- Place one hand on your abdomen.
- Breathe in deeply and slowly as you expand your stomach muscles.
- Drop your shoulders.
- Repeat 5 times.

Hang Loose
- Place your feet shoulder width apart and slightly turned in.
- Exhale as you lower your head to your knees.
- Let your arms dangle.
- If your hands touch the floor, you can bend your arms and hold your elbows with your hands.
- Just dangle. Don't stretch; just hang loose.
- Hold for 30 seconds, and breathe deeply from your abdomen.

the baby's specific cause of death, or any other that you feel strongly about.
- Have your baby's birthstone set in a ring or necklace that you can wear. You can use either the month your baby died, or the month of his projected birth date. This will serve as a tangible reminder of the baby you still love.
- Create art in the baby's memory, whether it's a drawing, a watercolor, a framed poem that is meaningful to you, or a dried bouquet of flowers that you press. Frame the artwork and hang it in a special place in your home.

- Many groups like SHARE offer participation in memorial walls for parents or newsletter memorial statements. See appendix 2 for the names of support groups. An Internet search will reveal dozens of similar Internet memorial walls.

SUPPORT GROUPS

One of the best things you and your partner can do to help yourself work through grief, anger, and fear is to join one of the many support groups that are just for parents who, like you, have lost a child. Most of them open their arms to parents who have had any type of loss: miscarriage, stillbirth, and early infant loss. You can attend a support meeting and meet others who have gone through just what you have had to face. As well, these groups can help you to find a grief therapist, provide you with helpful information and the names of useful books, and tell you about places where you can memorialize your lost baby.

You may find, after some time, that you can offer support to parents who have lost a baby as well. Helping them through their grief can help you with yours.

There is no easy way to get through the loss of a child. You have to move through the pain, one step at a time—at your own pace. You may feel better for a time, then find yourself slipping back into sadness again. You may find the yearly anniversary of the baby's loss or due date to be difficult. In two years, you may find yourself wondering what the baby would have looked like, and how many words she would be using by now.

You know now, if you did not know before, how strong the love is between a mother and a baby, even an unborn one. Soon you'll find a way to put that love to a good purpose—whether that means trying to find a way to ease the pain of others, supporting research to help prevent early loss, or finding strength to carry on with your own life.

CHAPTER 28 *Prematurity and Multiple Births*

Nature, time, and patience are the three great physicians.

—GREEK PROVERB

When a baby arrives into the world long before he or she is due, our best-laid plans are obliterated. Parents of premature infants go through enormous emotional turmoil just at the time they were planning to settle down for the last few weeks of pregnancy. While other parents are having childbirth education classes, parents of "preemies" are dealing with matters of survival and learning medical lingo they never thought they'd need to know.

What about the premature infant himself? So much focus is put on the medical needs of these tiny babies that most people never consider their emotional needs. Their very beginnings are clouded with the struggle of trying to breathe and the pain of being constantly poked and prodded. Many are placed in incubators immediately and are too small and too fragile to be held at first.

Not so long ago, the chances of a premature infant living for more than a few hours or days were very slim. There were no special treatments for premature infants. Medical breakthroughs have changed all of that. Treatment is now available that can help most early babies go on to live full and normal lives. Now more than 90 percent of premature babies who weigh 800 grams or more (which is a bit less than 2 pounds) will survive, and those who weigh more than 500 grams (a little more than 1 pound) have a

40 to 50 percent chance of survival (with greater chances of complications, however). As younger and younger infants are kept alive, though, questions of ethics are being raised. How hard should doctors fight to save a child who will be left with severe disabilities? Parents are usually the ones left to make these heartbreaking decisions.

Parents of twins, or other multiple births, are often the parents of premature infants as well. The day they are finally able to take home their babies is at once joyful and intimidating. Taking care of more than one infant is a challenge that requires good planning and plenty of support. We'll talk more about multiples later in this chapter.

Causes of Prematurity

The internationally agreed definition of a premature infant is one who is born prior to thirty-seven weeks' gestation. Most premature babies are born between thirty-two and thirty-seven weeks—only one-quarter of all premature babies are born before thirty-two weeks.[1] The label of prematurity has less to do with birth weight than it does with how well the baby's vital organs have developed, particularly the lungs.

Infants are born prematurely either because of spontaneous labor, or because of early elective delivery, when it seems that continued pregnancy might place the baby at risk.

Spontaneous labor can occur because of a variety of health problems in the mother, including:

- Preeclampsia or high blood pressure
- Severe infection, such as pneumonia or a urinary tract infection
- High levels of stress in the mother

Certain women go into early labor in all their pregnancies. Some researchers think these women may suffer from some type of subtle, underlying uterine infection that existed before they even became pregnant.

The reasons for early labor can also stem from the baby. Some reasons include:

- Intrauterine growth restriction (IUGR). IUGR means that the baby is not growing properly in the womb.
- Multiple fetuses. In fact, about half of all twins, and other multiples, are born prematurely.[2]
- Problems with the placenta or insufficient nutrition.

The fact is, though, that very little is known about the causes of prematurity. Many infants are born prematurely for no discernible reason.

Early elective delivery might be necessary if either the baby's or the mother's health would be severely compromised by continuing the pregnancy. Problems with the placenta, such as placenta abruptio (where the nutrient-providing placenta detaches from the uterine wall), might indicate the need for early elective delivery. Preeclampsia is another condition that can affect the placenta's ability to adequately nourish a fetus, and could necessitate an early delivery. Monoamniotic twins, where identical twins share one amniotic sac rather than each having their own, are often delivered early to avoid the danger of getting tied up in each other's umbilical cords. In some cases, early elective delivery is controversial. For example, many women with diabetes (both gestational and true, or mellitus, diabetes) are given early C-sections to avoid larger-than-average baby size. Research does not show this to be necessary.[3]

Low-birth-weight babies (also called small-for-date babies) are born at their projected due dates, but are much smaller than they should be. They can have many of the same health problems as premature babies, such as difficulties with breathing and maintaining normal body temperatures. Many are also seriously undernourished.

In most cases, the reasons for a low-birth-weight baby are simply not known. In some cases the reasons can be attributed to maternal smoking or poor prenatal care. Preeclampsia or high blood pressure in the mother may also be factors. Many twins are small-for-date, even if they do manage to go full-term and the mother has taken good care of herself.

Premature Birth

If you go into labor early, you may be given medication, either in the form of pills or IV, in a hospital. These drugs are designed to inhibit the hormones that cause labor, buying a little more time for the baby's development in the womb. You may be put on bed rest for the rest of your pregnancy to prolong pregnancy as long as possible. Sometimes the treatment is effective, but in other cases it simply does not work, and the baby's birth becomes imminent.

CORTICOSTEROID INJECTIONS

Your practitioner will probably suggest an injection of corticosteroids if you begin labor prior to thirty-four weeks (although some might even do this up until thirty-seven weeks). A single injection of steroids has been shown to help speed up the maturation process in babies' lungs and circulatory systems. The more mature these systems are, the less likely that the baby will have respiratory distress problems and other difficulties, such as brain hemorrhage.

Steroid injections are most effective for about a week after they are administered, after which they do not continue to produce the same results. Because of this, doctors often repeat the procedure, giving women weekly injections until the baby is born or is no longer deemed premature.

This practice has now become quite common, even though preliminary research on the safety of this practice has caused a great deal of concern. Repeated injections may be associated with lower birth weight, growth retardation, neurological deficits, and infections (in both mother and child).[4] In addition, higher rates of death were reported in babies whose mothers received multiple injections.

Experts from thirteen different major medical centers, as well as AGOG are now recommending against the routine use of weekly treatments. Further studies need to be completed on this issue.

HOSPITAL BIRTH

If it looks like your baby is going to be born prematurely despite efforts to delay the birth, you must give birth in a hospital that is equipped to deal with the needs of a premature baby of the specific age of yours. A baby born at thirty-six weeks may not need significantly different care than one born full-term, for example. Babies born before thirty-two weeks, on the other hand, are prone to an array of complications that some hospitals cannot manage.

Giving birth in a hospital may be a letdown if you'd dreamed of a home birth, or had picked out the birth center that seemed just right for you. You will need to acknowledge this disappointment, but you do not necessarily need to give up on all your plans. It is possible that your midwife, or your birthing doula, can still be a part of your delivery experience. In fact, a doula will be especially appreciated in a high-tension situation such as the birth of a premature baby. If you have had time to prepare items, such as your favorite music or aromatherapy scents, that you wanted to use during labor, by all means bring them along.

VAGINAL BIRTH VERSUS CESAREAN

If an early delivery is imminent, you and your doctor will need to decide whether this is going to hap-

pen vaginally or via cesarean section. There is a certain amount of controversy surrounding this decision. Some doctors and medical facilities feel that cesarean section is safer for all preterm infants. According to the Cochrane Database, a clearinghouse of international obstetrical research, there is no medical evidence to support the belief that cesarean sections are safer for preterm infants than vaginal birth. Proper controlled trials need to be done to compare the outcomes. In the meantime, most hospitals are likely to encourage cesarean sections when there is time to do so—sometimes spontaneous preterm labor happens too quickly for cesarean sections to be done.

Preterm babies are more likely to be in a breech presentation (where the infant comes out feet- or buttocks-first, rather than headfirst), because they have not had time to turn around. Many doctors are unfamiliar with vaginal breech birth to begin with, and even more unlikely to try it for one that is preterm.

In many vaginal deliveries at hospitals, episiotomies and forceps are routinely used for premature infants. Many doctors believe that this will reduce trauma to the infant's skull. The Cochrane Database reports there is no evidence to support this practice.[5]

UMBILICAL CORD CLAMPING

The controversy between early and late umbilical cord clamping is even bigger when it comes to premature babies. Some doctors believe that clamping the cord right away will prevent swelling and reduce the chance of hemorrhage. Some studies indicate that later clamping may decrease the amount of time an infant needs supplemental oxygen. Advocates of the latter suggest that the large infusion of blood from the cord to the baby may help prevent respiratory problems and provide nutrition.[6] Discuss this with your physician, if you have the time to do so before the birth occurs.

BONDING WITH YOUR PREEMIE

Unfortunately, in many hospitals, preterm infants are even more likely than full-term babies to be whisked away from their mothers right after delivery. There is sometimes good reason for this, particularly if your baby is born in a state of extreme distress and needs urgent attention. Otherwise, it is important that you be able to see and touch your baby as soon as he is born. This is essential for promoting bonding between you and your baby and will also help to reassure you. Your partner or other advocate should insist on this if you aren't able. Talk to each other about this ahead of time, if possible, and to the staff of the hospital.

Your baby's length of stay in the hospital's neonatal intensive care unit (NICU) will be determined by many factors. Weight and size are not necessarily the main determinants. Doctors will be more concerned with your baby's age and the development of her vital organs, particularly the lungs, as well as any congenital deformities or other health problems. Hospital stays can range anywhere between one or two extra days to several months.

Mothering Your Premature Baby

If you're fortunate, giving birth prematurely will not be very different than having a normal full-term birth. Your baby may be monitored for an extra day or so and then sent home as any newborn baby would. In other cases, though, you might have to deal with recovering under very trying circumstances. The birth itself may have been unexpected and frightening. The chances of your baby's survival may be uncertain for some time. It is likely that you will be leaving the hospital many days, or weeks, before your baby can join you.

Quite often, the parents of a newborn premature infant feel helpless and unnecessary. Your first view of your tiny, fragile baby in the intensive care unit, hooked up to wires and machines, may be overwhelming. The baby may not even look quite real to you. Many parents have to continuously fight off the feeling that their baby belongs to the hospital, rather than to them. Research has shown, however, that the parents' role is vital to the baby's health and survival.

NATURAL SOOTHER

Sleepy Tea

With twins or a premature baby, sleep will become precious. This tea will help you to relax and get a good night's sleep. It is a tonic as well as a relaxant. In a ceramic or glass teapot, put:

> 1 tablespoon dried chamomile
>
> 1 tablespoon dried hops
>
> 1 tablespoon dried lemon balm
>
> Add 1 pint boiling water.
>
> Steep for no more than 10 minutes; sip in the evenings before bed.

TOUCH

Without a doubt, touch is the most important thing you can do for your premature baby. All newborns thrive on close bodily contact and warmth, but preemies in particular need this. In fact, it is every bit as important as the medical care your child receives from the hospital. As more and more doctors begin to learn about this, hospitals are beginning to encourage touch as a tool for healing.

The treatment known as "Kangaroo Care" has received a great deal of publicity in the past few years. Kangaroo Care is the practice of holding your premature baby skin-to-skin for several hours every day. This technique was first developed in Columbia in the early 1980s in a maternity hospital that serviced a population of poor mothers with high rates of premature birth and high rates of loss. The hospital, unable to provide enough incubators, began to experiment with skin-to-skin contact out of desperation. The results were dramatic. More infants began to survive the first few days of life and had fewer complications. Furthermore, the mothers took better care of their infants once they were discharged.

A study in Spain showed that infants receiving Kangaroo Care were more likely to learn to spontaneously breastfeed.[7] Many other studies show positive effects, including hospital stays that are 50 percent shorter.[8] In addition, most parents report the emotional benefits to them are very large.

To practice Kangaroo Care, the baby is placed in an upright position against the mother or father's bare chest, and then both of them are covered with a blanket or shirt. This not only provides reassuring skin-to-skin contact but also allows the baby to hear your voice and heartbeat, familiar sounds that probably also contribute to a feeling of safety.

Doing Kangaroo Care while in a rocking chair may increase the soothing benefits for both of you. Rocking has the effect of organizing small babies' nervous systems and helping them to feel calmer and safer. You can also offer a fingertip for the baby to suck on, or direct the baby's finger into his mouth, for added comfort.

Other kinds of touch are important for your baby, as well. A parent's reassuring hand can actually reduce a baby's heart rate if he is stressed during medical procedures.

MASSAGE

Massage is another form of touch that can help your baby to thrive. It is hard, at first, to believe that you can actually massage a tiny premature infant. You need to start out slowly, both for the baby's sake and for yours. Your confidence that you can hold your baby without hurting her will increase each time you do it.

Start by simply cupping the baby in your hands. Focus on your own breathing—watch your breaths go in and out. This will help you to focus calmly on the baby. Then simply hold each part of the baby's body one at a time. Place a hand around a foot and feel the warmth exchange between you. Then hold the baby's calf and move on. You might like to rub a small amount of almond oil on your hands first.

Some preemies have a condition called hyperflexia, which means that their bodies are tightly contracted. If your baby's arms are clutched to his chest,

for example, do not try to pry them away. Respect his need to protect himself and stroke his arms without pulling them away from his body. Watch your baby carefully for subtle signs of pulling away that may indicate an area is sensitive to touch. If you see signs of relaxation, on the other hand, take note of what you have done so that you can repeat it.

After some time, you will be able to proceed to real infant massage (see page 201). Use miniature versions of each step at first. Use two fingers to rub her back, for example, rather than your whole hand, as you would for a larger baby. Be gentle, but make sure your touch is also firm, or it will not be effective.

SOUND

Your soothing voice can make all the difference in the world to your baby. Talk to her often, using the low, soothing voice that will probably come naturally to you anyway. NICUs contain many loud, harsh sounds. Your voice will help to counteract the beeps of machinery, ringing telephones, and loud voices. You can also play some relaxing music, such as lullabies. Make a tape of your voice to leave in the NICU when you can't be there and ask one of the nurses to play it for your baby as often as she can. If your baby's incubator is in a high-traffic or noisy area, ask that he be moved to another part of the room. Suggest, also, that the door to the incubator be closed gently and not slammed shut.

LIGHT

Just as you appreciate soft lighting when you are sick or tired, your premature baby needs to be protected from harsh lighting. When you are in the NICU, you can place a folded towel on top of the incubator over the area of the baby's head, to shade his eyes. When he is placed on a warming table under bright lamps, find a creative way to shield his eyes. One idea is to cut the sides off an empty box, such as the type sterile gloves come in, and create a shade. If you feel your baby's incubator is in a particularly bright spot, ask if it can be moved to a darker spot.

EYE CONTACT

Preemies may need some help establishing eye contact at first. Lower the lights, if you can, and position yourself so that you are in her line of vision. If the baby's eye contact becomes "locked," and she appears to be stressed by the inability to refocus, gently unlock the baby's gaze by passing a hand in front of her face or shifting her position.

OTHER HELPFUL TOOLS

As you interact with your baby, be on the lookout for signs that she is becoming overstimulated. This happens rather easily to preemies. If you are holding your baby, maintaining eye contact, and singing to her all at once, that may be too much stimulation at one time. If she begins to cry or squirm, these may be cues for you to remove one or more of these stimulants until she is calm once again.

You may feel as though your baby is not aware of your presence at first. It may seem as though nothing you do has any effect. Unresponsiveness is very common in preemies. You must persevere, though. In time, you will begin to see signs that your baby

knows who you are. Some parents report seeing their baby's oxygen levels rise while they are speaking to her, showing them that the baby recognizes them and benefits from their presence. Others soon begin to notice that their voices and their touch can calm a distressed preemie when the nurse cannot.

A very important part of mothering your premature baby in the hospital is becoming as comfortable as you can with the NICU and the staff. Ask to help perform baby-care tasks. You may be able to take the baby's temperature, change his diaper, or give him a sponge bath. Get as involved as you can. Ask a lot of questions. Get enough information to feel comfortable about every aspect of the baby's care, as well as the instruments and medications used to treat him. If you begin to feel overwhelmed by information, take a break until later.

FEEDING YOUR PREMATURE BABY

Without a doubt, breastmilk is the best food for your premature baby. A number of well-conducted studies have shown that breastmilk offers premature infants significant health benefits, even when parent-child closeness is not present. A study done in New Zealand also showed that the more breastmilk a very low birthweight (VLBW) infant receives, the better his cognitive development is. The babies who were breastfed for eight months or longer had scores of up to 10 points higher on IQ tests than those who were not.[9]

Other studies show that breastmilk decreases the tendency toward distractibility and hyperactivity displayed by many children who were born prematurely. The last weeks of pregnancy are the time when a great deal of growth occurs in the brain. Premature babies, who are born without this extra developmental time, receive significant benefits from breastmilk in preventing nutritionally based brain deficits.

The milk of a woman who has delivered a premature baby is composed differently than that of a woman who has carried to term. Not only does it contain higher concentrations of nutrients, such as protein, that a preemie needs, it also contains higher levels of antibodies to help protect the fragile new baby. Human milk is also much more easily digested than formula, which is especially important for preemies, who often have immature digestive systems.

Feeding a preemie can sometimes present a challenge. Very premature babies are sometimes unable to suck. In this case, they are often fed by a tube, which is inserted into the stomach through either the nose or mouth. Until your baby can nurse from your breast, your best course of action is to pump your milk and store it for tube feeding. You can refrigerate the milk for five to eight days, or freeze it for up to thirty days. Your doctor may also recommend supplementing with vitamins or other nutrients, depending on your baby's particular needs.

Pumping can be a challenge if you have not yet had the experience of putting a baby to your breast, and felt the letdown reflex. It is possible, however. You will need to pump your breasts approximately every three to four hours, for about twenty minutes per session. Be sure to wash your hands thoroughly before beginning, and always store the expressed milk in a sterile container. At first you may not need to pump during the night. Once the baby is able to breastfeed during hospital visits, you will need to replicate her feeding pattern as much as possible, pumping throughout the day and night in order to keep up your milk supply to provide her with milk when you are not there.

Practicing Kangaroo Care while pumping has been shown to be very helpful for mothers of preemies. The close contact with your baby will make it easier for your milk to come down. It will also help your baby to nurse spontaneously when she is ready. The letdown reflex can also be encouraged by pumping in the hospital with the baby in view, or with a photo of the baby nearby, or while holding a blanket or shirt with the baby's scent on it.

Many women report that their milk supply seems to decrease after two or three weeks of continuous pumping. Don't despair if this happens to you. Your milk will not "dry up." Try increasing your pumping schedule or experiment with other types of pumps. A hospital-style pump that does both breasts at a time may be your best bet. Electric pumps, in general, tend to be more efficient for frequent pumping. A few women prefer to hand-pump, using their own hand to extract the milk, rather than a machine.

When it is time to put the baby to your breast, keep your expectations small, just at first. Focus on closeness and cuddling the first couple of times. Your baby may not do more than lick your nipple or hold it in his mouth for a few seconds. That's okay. You need to be patient and plan on going slowly. Premature infants sometimes have a very hard time staying awake while breastfeeding and will need gentle coaxing to keep nursing. Some also tend to have a strong gag response. Experiment with different positions and use pillows to support yourself. You may need to have one hand free to hold the breast in place for the baby at first.

Don't forget to seek breastfeeding help from the hospital's lactation consultant, as well as La Leche League, your best resource for getting help with breastfeeding a premature baby.

Some hospital employees still believe that premature babies need to "learn" to suck using a special preemie nipple and bottle before they can manage breastfeeding. There is no evidence that this is true, and there is a danger that adding one more element to the experience may confuse the baby. Make sure the NICU staff understand from the start that you are determined to breastfeed your baby.

COMPLICATIONS

The smaller and younger a baby is at birth, the more likely he is to experience one of many medical complications, including:

- *Anemia.* Very small infants may require blood transfusions to replenish their red blood cell supply.
- *Apnea.* This is when a baby suddenly stops breathing. All newborns are prone to apnea, and some experts believe it is the cause of sudden infant death syndrome (SIDS). Premature babies experience apnea with much greater fre-

quency. For this reason, they are hooked up to a monitoring system that alerts nurses to an episode. Although the alarms—often false—can be terrifying to parents, it is usually quite easy to revive the baby. Often nothing more than a gentle touch is needed.

- *Bradycardia.* Bradycardia refers to a sudden decrease of the baby's heart rate. This might occur after an episode of apnea, or it could be a reflex response to interventions, such as the insertion of a feeding tube.

- *Jaundice.* A yellowing of the skin caused by an excess of a component in the blood called bilirubin. Jaundice is quite common, affecting almost 50 percent of all newborns. It usually resolves itself, although very high levels can potentially cause brain damage.

- *Infections.* Premature infants are prone to infection because they don't have the defenses they need to fight them off effectively. As well, they spend the first few weeks of their lives in hospitals, where the chances of getting infections are higher.

- *Necrotizing enterocolitis (NEC).* Premature infants have fragile intestines and are more prone to intestinal infection or inflammation that can injure or destroy parts of the bowel. Surgery is sometimes required. Preemies are often fed very slowly at first to help prevent NEC.

- *Respiratory distress syndrome (RDS).* This is the most common form of breathing difficulty in premature infants. Their immature lungs do not produce enough of a substance called surfactant, which allows the inner surface of the lungs to expand properly when the infant leaves the womb. This condition responds well to treatment. You may be given an injection of corticosteroids while you are in labor that can help prevent this condition. Your baby will probably be given oxygen to help with breathing and may also receive artificial surfactant via a breathing tube that has been inserted into the baby's windpipe, several times after birth.

- *Retinopathy of prematurity (ROP).* For unknown reasons, about 7 percent of smaller premature infants have abnormal growth of the blood vessels in their eyes. The result can be damage to the eyes that might be mild, requiring glasses, or severe, resulting in blindness.

Dealing with Your Own Emotions

Women experience a huge range of emotions when a premature baby comes into their lives. The first emotion most women feel is guilt. You may wonder if it was your fault that the baby was born so soon, if you did or ate something that harmed the baby in your womb. Some women are afraid to look at their baby at first, and others are frightened or appalled at the way the baby looks. This can compound your feelings of guilt—after all, a mother is supposed to adore her new baby.

You may also feel a sense of loss from an experience that was far from the image of the perfect birth of a "normal" baby. Instead of sitting in a rocker at home with your baby in your arms, surrounded by admiring relatives, you are parked in a neonatal intensive care unit. You may be dealing with matters of life and death on a daily basis—but even if you aren't, you are surrounded by machines and dependent on people you hardly know.

The truth is that you will probably go through a grieving process, even if your baby survives and goes home with you in a few short weeks. You may feel you were cheated out of those last few precious weeks of pregnancy, which were vital to your sense of readiness. You may not have had time to prepare your home for a baby, to finish your childbirth education classes, or even to have your baby shower.

You and your partner need to get these feelings out into the open in order to comfort one another as you navigate the next few crucial weeks. Talk to each other; talk to friends and relatives. There are many good support groups available for the parents of premature babies. See appendix 2 for ideas, or ask for contact information at your hospital. There are many on-line support groups and message boards available as well.

At Last! Bringing Your Premature Baby Home

When the much-anticipated day to take your baby home arrives, you may feel equal parts of joy and trepidation. This is the day you've been wanting for so long, but now you may wonder if you can handle it on your own.

Of course you can, but like any new parent, you need a good support system. Look through part 5 of this book for suggestions on easing the transition to life with your new baby. For example, having a post-partum doula come by for a few days can boost your confidence level, and playgroups or mothers' groups in your area can help you to stay connected with other adults. In addition, do what you can to simplify your life before bringing your baby home. Keep your expectations small when it comes to housekeeping and other chores or social obligations, and make some time for yourself.

If your baby has special needs, you may be taking home equipment or medications. Learn how to use these before your baby leaves the hospital. Ask whether a visiting nurse is appropriate to your situation.

Twins and Other Multiple Births

Many women suspect they are carrying twins even before a doctor tells them so. Dreaming that you are having twins is common. You may also notice that you are gaining weight very rapidly, even though you are not overeating. You might also feel movements quite early in the second trimester. You might even be able to discern separate fetal movements later on in your pregnancy. Women who are carrying twins tend to have more dramatic early pregnancy symptoms such as morning sickness, nausea, and tender breasts.

An experienced midwife or doctor can usually confirm the presence of twins by feeling the mother's abdomen, or by listening carefully with a stethoscope for more than one heartbeat. The more multiples there are, the greater the difficulty in pinpointing the exact number. Twins are usually confirmed with the use of ultrasound. Even ultrasound is not infallible, and occasional misdiagnosis of twins does occur.

How Multiples Happen

There are two types of twins: fraternal and identical. Fraternal or dizygotic (two-egg) twins happen when two eggs are fertilized by two separate sperm during one cycle. This accounts for about 7 out of 10 cases of twins. The fertilized eggs implant into the uterus separately, and each has its own sac and placenta, although occasionally the eggs may implant so closely together that the two placentas seem to fuse into one. Fraternal twins may be of the same sex, or one male and one female. They will not look any more alike than any other brothers and sisters do.

You have a greater chance of having fraternal twins if there is a history of twins in your family. You are also more likely to have fraternal twins if you are between the ages of thirty-five and forty and if you have already had at least one child. Taking fertility drugs, such as Clomid, can increase your chances of having multiple births by up to 20 percent, depending on the particular drug you are taking. Fertility drugs often cause the ovum to release several eggs in a cycle. It is possible to end up with two, three, or even more fertilized eggs at once!

Identical or monozygotic (one-egg) twins are less common than fraternal twins, occurring in about 4 out of every 1,000 births. In this case, a single egg is fertilized by a single sperm. The egg implants and cell division begins, just as it would for any fetus. For unknown reasons, though, during the first stages of cell division, the egg separates into two completely different units (or even more rarely, three), which develop into two separate babies. These babies are always of the same sex, and will look identical when they are born.

There is no inherited tendency to have identical twins, or any other predisposing factors that scientists are aware of. This phenomenon seems to be a fluke of nature.

In most cases, identical twins will have their own sac, although they almost always share a placenta. In very rare cases, identical twins will also share an amniotic sac and are known as monoamniotic twins. This is potentially problematic because the two babies are at risk for getting tangled up in each other's umbilical cords or for having cord compression (which could deprive one baby of oxygen and nutrients).

Delivering More than One Baby

No one knows for sure why twins tend to be born earlier, because no one knows for sure what triggers labor to begin with. Perhaps the increasing size of twins "tricks" the mother's body into thinking that it is time for them to be born. If, as some experts theorize, it is actually chemicals in the baby's brain that start labor, then perhaps the double amounts of those chemicals in twins' brains causes labor to begin early. In any case, about half of all twins don't make it full-term and are born prematurely. The average single baby is born weighing seven pounds, seven ounces. The average twin weighs only five pounds, five ounces.

Some experts think that good prenatal care plays an important role in how long twins will stay in the womb. Perhaps inadequate nutrition signals the body that the babies need to come out early. A woman who is carrying twins needs to be extremely vigilant about taking good care of herself during pregnancy, getting adequate prenatal care, and, most importantly, eating well. The more fetuses there are in your womb, the more high-quality calories you need to consume.

The fact is, though, that it is possible to carry twins to full term, or close, and deliver them naturally. The choice of a practitioner is critical, since delivering twins is becoming something of a lost art.

Many doctors prefer to deliver all twins by cesarean section, even when the mother is healthy, strong, and complication-free.

However, many women have even given birth to their twins at home and in birth centers. You must seek out a midwife or doctor with a good track record of success in vaginal deliveries of twins, and with experience delivering breech babies, since one twin is often in the breech position. In this case, the heads-down baby will usually be born first, opening up the birth canal to ease the birth of the breech sibling, usually within an hour. Twins are also frequently both in a heads-down position. If both twins are breech, vaginal birth is more challenging, but not necessarily impossible. If one twin is in a transverse (sideways) position, cesarean is usually performed, unless the baby can be successfully turned around.

In any event, your midwife or doctor should have experience with these situations. Make sure the practitioner understands your goals clearly and will work with you to meet them.

Prepare Ahead of Time for Your Babies

It's hard to imagine what life will be like with one new baby in the house, never mind two! If you know you are carrying twins, you'll need to be even more prepared, perhaps even sooner, since twins are often born early. In addition to the ideas you'll find in chapter 12, look through part 5 of this book for some ideas on what to expect. Here are some tips from mothers of twins for the early weeks at home with your babies.

- Decide ahead of time what your priorities are. You are going to have to let some things go—the question is, what? What is it that makes you feel good: Having home-cooked meals instead of takeout? Making the bed every morning? Keeping in touch with friends? Choose the things that matter most to you.

- All new mothers need help. It can be hard to ask for it. If you are having twins, you *must* get over that! When friends and family offer to help, be ready with an idea of what would be really useful. Perhaps the gift you would like most for your shower is someone to come in and clean your house or do your laundry for you. Ask a good friend to coordinate a rotating circle of friends to make dinner and help you as needed in the first few weeks.

- A postpartum doula might make all the difference in the world on your postpartum stress levels. Read "Postpartum Doulas" on page 189 for more details on how this can help you.

- Seek out other mothers of twins both before and after you give birth. You can get valuable tips ahead of time from them. After all, they are the only ones who will truly understand what your life will be like. There are also many support groups, play groups, and clubs just for the parents of multiples.

- You will need two of some things, such as slings or other baby carriers, and car seats. You don't need twice the amount of clothing, however. One and a half the amount of clothes you need for a single baby will do, at least in the early months. If cost is a factor, remember that most people usually buy much more than they need for even one baby. Check with friends for baby items they no longer need. Check out thrift stores and garage sales for gently used things.

- Stock up on dry goods and paper supplies. Keep a month's supply of these things in storage, if you can, and buy your perishables just once a week.

Breastfeeding Multiples

The breasts are indeed miraculous. Your body can produce the right amount of milk to feed one, two, or more babies. If you have decided that you want to

---

BODY WISE
Side Twist

This is a simple yoga posture that you can even do on the floor of a hospital room. It strengthens the buttocks, which relieves lower-back tension and also stretches the front of the thighs.

Lie on the floor with your knees bent and your feet flat on the floor. Place your arms out to your sides with your palms up.

Keeping your feet planted, lift your hips off the floor. Stretch them to the left a few inches, then put them back down.

Inhale, take your feet off the floor and draw your knees to your chest.

As you exhale, rotate your knees to your right side and then gently let them down to the floor.

Turn your head to look at your left hand and put your right hand on your right knee.

Relax and breathe for 10 to 30 seconds.

When ready, let gravity pull the top leg up, and the bottom leg will follow.

Repeat on your left side.

---

nurse your babies, there is every reason to believe that you will be able to do so. La Leche League meetings and consultations with a lactation consultant can help you to make this happen smoothly.

Most mothers of twins report that, although nursing one infant at a time is more satisfying, nursing both babies at once (tandem nursing) works best, especially in the early weeks when babies need to be fed often. In the beginning you may need some help with this, especially if this is your first experience with motherhood. While many partners tend to feel left out of the breastfeeding experience, partners of twins almost never do! Their extra hands are needed to coordinate a good breastfeeding posi-

Breastfeeding Twins

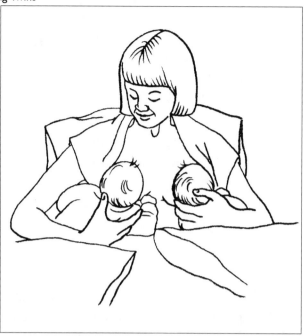

tion, or to hold one infant while the other one is being fed.

There are a couple of different tandem nursing positions you can try (see above). Some women hold one baby in the classic nursing position, with the baby held in front of her body with one arm, while the other baby is in a football hold to one side. You can also hold both babies in the football-hold position. When they are small, you may even be able to hold both in front of you, with one tucked close to your body and the other splayed slightly out.

If one infant latches on more quickly than his sibling, start him nursing first. This will cause your let-down reflex to occur, making it easier for the second baby to feed. Try to have the babies take turns on each breast. If one infant consumes more milk than the other, and you don't switch them, you could end up with a much greater milk supply on one side than on the other.

Sleeping with the babies in your bed, or at least in your room, will make nighttime nursing easier. Turning from one side to the other is much easier

than getting up and out of bed every time you need to feed one of them.

If you are nursing twins, you will need extra nourishment. You will probably need around 3,000 calories a day of quality food. It's a good idea to keep a high-protein snack, such as nuts, near your bed. You may find yourself hungry in the middle of the night after a couple of nursing sessions. Also keep a glass of water nearby at night and while you are nursing during the day. Your need for fluids will be noticeably higher than usual.

You may want to keep a nursing log during the early weeks. It's hard to remember which infant you fed last, and which breast he or she fed on! Some women also use a system of colored diaper pins to remember which side each baby nursed on last. Tack the pink pin onto diaper or shirt of the baby who last nursed on the right breast, for example.

While having twins may be challenging at times, you will adjust before you know it. Your children will be blessed with lifelong companionship, and soon you won't be able to imagine life without them.

CHAPTER 29

Birth Defects and Hospitalization

Ask many of us who are disabled what we would like in life and you would be surprised
how few would say, "Not to be disabled." We accept our limitations.

—ITZHAK PERLMAN

When parents are first told that their child has a defect, they experience a death—that of their dream of the "perfect child," who will never be. The grieving process may be short or long, and the disability may be minor and correctable, or lifelong. No matter what your situation, being told that there is something wrong with your baby may be the hardest thing you will ever have to hear. What was supposed to be one of the happiest days of your life suddenly becomes one of the saddest and most frightening.

It may seem, at first, as though you can't go on. You may want to blame someone. You are being led down a path you never expected to travel, and navigating it may seem impossible. You will find your way, though, and the dark days will not last forever.

Defects and Disabilities

About 120,000 infants are born each year with birth defects, according to the Centers for Disease Control (CDC). About 8,000 of these children will not live past the first year of their lives. In fact, birth defects account for 20 percent of all infant deaths.

Genetics and environment both play a role in the causes of birth defects. Birth defects that happen for genetic reasons can be the result of one or both parents passing on a disease-causing gene, such the gene causing cystic fibrosis or Tay-Sachs disease. Some-

times genetic errors occur after conception, while the baby is developing, as in the case of Down syndrome. Environmental factors can include exposure to an infectious disease or a dangerous drug, herbicide, or environmental toxin. Poor nutrition, such as a deficit of folic acid, can cause neural tube defects.

Sometimes both genetics and environmental factors can play a part in a defect. It is thought that cleft lip and palate, for example, may be caused by both a genetic predisposition and pregnancy disturbance such as a flu or fever in the early weeks. Amazingly, even though 1 out of every 28 couples will have to hear that there is some kind of a problem, large or small, with their child, up to 70 percent of those problems happen for unknown reasons.[1]

The range of potential disabilities and problems is so large that it seems incredible that they should all be encompassed into the one term *birth defects*. Birth defects are generally divided into three different categories:

- *Structural/metabolic abnormalities.* One example of this type is heart problems, which are the most common of the structural defects. Others include neural tube defects, absence of kidneys, and metabolic disorders, such as PKU. There are many more.

- *Congenital infections.* Rubella (or German measles) is probably the best known of these. Exposure to rubella in the first trimester of pregnancy can cause deafness, blindness, and mental retardation. Untreated syphilis also falls into this category.

- *Other causes.* Fetal alcohol syndrome is caused by alcohol abuse during pregnancy. Exposure to certain drugs, such as Accutane (which is used to treat acne), during pregnancy can also cause birth defects. Smoking and excessive caffeine consumption are implicated in cleft lip and palate.

Here is a look at just a few of the more common birth defects:

- *Heart defects.* One out of every 125 to 150 babies has some type of heart defect.[2] Some defects are so minor that they do not become apparent for years. Others require urgent surgical intervention. Advances in surgery have improved the outlook for babies born with this problem. The cause of heart defects is still unknown, although researchers believe that both genetic and environmental causes are factors. Defects usually occur in the first few weeks after conception, when the heart is first developing.

- *Down syndrome.* Babies with Down syndrome have an extra chromosome (number 21) in each of their cells. This error, which affects approximately 1 in 800 to one in 1,000 babies, causes the fetus to develop differently. As a result, children with Down syndrome have a characteristic look: almond-shaped eyes, small ears, a flattened nasal bridge, or puffiness in the face and neck. As well, the error in chromosome information can cause children with Down syndrome to have congenital defects, such as congenital heart disease or visual impairments, although not all will have problems. Children with Down syndrome can have a wide range of intelligence that has nothing to do with her

appearance. In less than 10 percent of cases, children may be severely retarded, while others will have only minor IQ problems. Many Down syndrome children do very well, and are able to go to regular schools and live semi-independently as adults. As of yet, no one knows the reason for the genetic accident that results in Down syndrome. Some recent research suggests that mothers of Down syndrome babies may have problems metabolizing B vitamins. It could be that folic acid supplements may help prevent the occurrence of Down syndrome, although no one knows for sure.

- *Spina bifida.* Spina bifida is the most common of the birth defects known as neural tube defects. It affects about 1 in every 2,000 births. Between the seventeenth and thirtieth day after conception the neural tube forms, and then closes, in most fetuses. The neural tube later develops into the spinal cord, brain, and skull. If it fails to close properly, the brain and/or spine are left exposed to the amniotic fluid, leaving the baby prone to infection. Some forms of spina bifida are mild and may require minor or no surgery. The child will develop normally. In more severe forms some degree of leg paralysis and bladder or bowel control problems may occur. There has been recent experimental surgery on babies with severe spina bifida while they are still in the womb. So far the results are promising. Taking folic acid in the first weeks of pregnancy lowers the risk of spina bifida and other neural tube defects significantly.

- *Cerebral palsy.* A child with cerebral palsy has sustained damage to one or more parts of her brain, affecting muscle movement. This condition may be quite mild, or severe. Some children with cerebral palsy also suffer from mental retardation, learning disabilities, and speech problems. In about 70 percent of cases, the brain damage that causes cerebral palsy occurs in the womb during development. This might be because of an infection in the mother, such as rubella or toxoplasmosis, or because insufficient oxygen has reached the baby while in the womb; in a very few cases it can occur during the birth itself. It can also occur during the early months after birth. In many cases, the cause is unknown.[3] Cerebral palsy patients respond well to therapy, depending on the level of severity.

- *Clefts.* The lip and palate normally close by the end of the first trimester. In a few cases this fails to occur, leaving the baby with a visible split in her lip or palate. Cleft lip/palate affect approximately 1 out of every 1,000 white babies born in the United States.[4] For unknown reasons, African Americans are much less likely to be afflicted with this defect, while certain groups of American Indians are more likely to be. Males are more commonly affected than are females. Cleft palate alone (without cleft lip) occurs less often. Researchers think genetics are partially responsible, and environmental causes (such as infections, alcohol use, or vitamin B deficiency) also play a role except in cases of isolated cleft palate, which appears to be solely genetic. Up to 13 percent of babies with both cleft lip and palate, and up to half of babies with only cleft palate, have other birth defects as well. Therefore, if your baby has a cleft, it's a good idea to insist on a very thorough evaluation to rule out other troubles. Cleft disorders can vary in severity. Most will require surgery, usually within the first year of life. Future surgeries may also be necessary. See the section on breastfeeding below for tips on nursing a baby with a cleft defect.

- *Genital/urinary tract disorders.* These affect 1 out of every 135 babies. Sometimes the disorder is minor, as in urinary tract blockages or hypospadias, where the urinary opening in male babies is placed abnormally. This is easily corrected with surgery. In more severe disorders a baby might be born with one or both kidneys missing. Babies born with both kidneys missing

are unable to live longer than a few hours after birth.

There are many other types of birth defects; for more information on a condition not listed here, see appendix 2 at the end of this book.

Nursing a Child with a Disability

Since breastmilk has been shown to provide tailor-made nutrition for all babies, it stands to reason that a baby with special needs will benefit even more. Mothers benefit, too. The stress of learning that you have had a baby with a birth defect can seriously affect the bonding process with your baby. Nursing can ease the stress and help you to realize that you have a real effect on your child.

You can breastfeed a baby with almost any type of birth defect. It was once thought that children with PKU, a metabolic disorder, could not breastfeed. More recent research has shown that breastmilk is naturally low in phenylalanine, the amino acid that PKU sufferers cannot metabolize; it is possible to partially breastfeed these babies along with supplements of a special formula. PKU children who breastfed as babies show higher IQ scores in school than those who were only formula-fed.[5]

Galactosemia is the only metabolic disorder that calls for avoidance of breastmilk. These babies cannot tolerate any lactose. Fortunately, this is quite rare. Babies with other metabolic disorders, such as cystic fibrosis, need mother's milk.

Babies with Down syndrome especially need to breastfeed. They are much more prone to infections than other children. This will continue to be true for most of their lives. The added immunity boost that breastmilk provides is a big plus for them. In addition, babies with Down syndrome respond well to closeness and affection, and generally give affection back generously.

Babies with Down syndrome may take longer to learn to latch on. You will need to be patient and persistent. They may fall asleep more easily than other

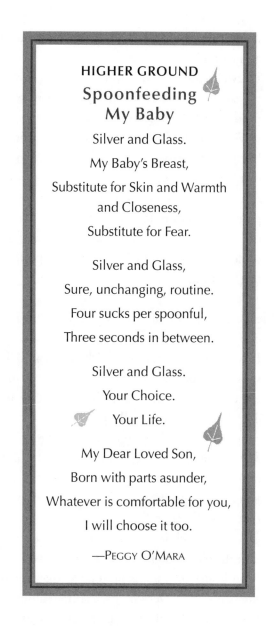

Spoonfeeding My Baby

Silver and Glass.

My Baby's Breast,

Substitute for Skin and Warmth
and Closeness,

Substitute for Fear.

Silver and Glass,

Sure, unchanging, routine.

Four sucks per spoonful,

Three seconds in between.

Silver and Glass.

Your Choice.

Your Life.

My Dear Loved Son,

Born with parts asunder,

Whatever is comfortable for you,

I will choose it too.

—PEGGY O'MARA

Cleft lip usually presents less of a problem than cleft palate. By adjusting your position, or holding your breast tissue in a way that fills the gap created by the cleft, your baby should be able to get enough suction to feed effectively. Cleft palate can be more challenging because the gap in the roof of the mouth can more seriously interfere with the suction needed to pull milk out of the breast.

Try to start with a full breast, which will make it easier for the baby to get the milk. Hold your baby in a semi-upright position, with the baby's body tilted slightly backward. Try sitting on the floor against a couch, with your knees bent and the baby straddling your legs. You can also nurse in a reclining position, as long as the baby's body and head are upright. Hold your baby very close to your breast. Place your index finger on the top of the areola and your middle finger on the bottom of it, and press your nipple out between these fingers. Try to close up the cleft with your breast in this way and create suction. Direct the flow of milk toward the inside of the baby's cheek, not the back of the throat. Give yourself plenty of time to do this, and be patient. Your baby may nurse quite slowly, especially at first.

You will know your baby is receiving enough milk if he soaks six to eight diapers per day, and has frequent bowel movements. Weigh your baby regularly, and keep an eye on his skin tone and general state of alertness.

Hospitalization and Surgery

Unfortunately, babies with defects often need surgery, tests, and hospitalization in the early weeks and months of their lives. Your baby may be kept in the hospital for some time after birth. You may be discharged well before your baby is. This is extraordinarily painful for most parents, who had hoped to proudly bear their new infant home soon after birth.

If your baby needs to spend time in the neonatal intensive care unit (NICU) after birth, see chapter 28 for tips on caring for her there.

If you have taken your baby home and then need

babies while feeding. If they are unable to consume enough milk via breastfeeding in the very beginning, you can help them by pumping. This will increase your supply, making it easier for them to feed. You can also give them some of the pumped milk with a dropper or a cup, if they are having trouble sucking.

Cleft lip and palate might present some special challenges to breastfeeding, depending on the severity of the cleft. For some babies, only minor adjustments will be necessary. For others, it may be necessary to supplement, or substitute, nursing at the breast by spoon- or cup-feeding pumped breastmilk, or using a feeding tube device.

to return to the hospital to have tests or surgery performed, it can be especially difficult. If an emergency comes up, such as a sudden infection, you may have to be prepared to spend several days in a hospital with your young baby.

The idea that you would willingly subject your child to pain or discomfort is foreign to the very concept of mothering. Every bone in your body wants to protect him and keep him from potential pain. This holds true even when you know that a procedure is in your child's best interest.

PREPARING FOR HOSPITALIZATION AND SURGERY

To begin with, you must take care of yourself, so that you can take good care of your child. Here are some ideas to explore:

- Take it moment by moment. You've heard the expression, "Take it one day at a time." When it comes to caring for a sick baby, even one day seems like an eternity of worry. As Shakespeare said, "In a minute there are many days." Just try to go through each minute as it comes along, only thinking ahead as much as you need to prepare.
- Prepare to experience a wide range of emotions. You may be surprised at what comes up. Anger and fear are to be expected. Some parents feel guilty when they find themselves giggling together in the waiting room. But laughing in situations of high stress is normal and a necessary relief.
- Prepare for uncertainty. This can be the most difficult aspect of dealing with medical treatments and children with defects. It isn't always possible to predict the outcome of any certain procedure. Every child responds differently to treatments.
- You will not always be able to stand between your child and pain, as much as you would like to.
- Avoid exhaustion. You will not help matters by staying up all night. This kind of vigilance won't

help your child, and will leave you exhausted and irritable.

- Eat well. You may not feel like eating much at all, so make sure that what does go into your mouth provides maximum nutrition. It isn't always easy to find healthy snacks in a hospital, so bring along easy-to-eat nutritious snacks and drinks like bottled water, nuts, and fruits.
- Ask your friends and family to help. If you can, prepare a list of tasks ahead of time. When they offer to help, you'll know just what to ask them to do. This will help you, and also help them to feel involved.

Here are ways you can help your child while in the hospital:

- If at all possible, room in with your child. This should not be a problem in most pediatric units, even if he is staying in an intensive care unit. The hospital can usually put you in a nearby room. If needed, be assertive in your request. A few hospitals have accommodations for entire families who have traveled from out of town. If you are in a position to choose, pick a hospital that is family-friendly.
- Once your child is more than a couple of months old, it makes sense to bring something from home that she is familiar with: a blanket she sleeps with every night, a stuffed animal, or a brightly colored toy. These things will smell and look familiar to your baby and may offer a bit of reassurance.
- Bring along music, such as lullabies, to play at the hospital. If you've been playing music at home, this will be especially helpful.
- It can be easy to feel unnecessary in the hospital environment, or to feel as if the baby belongs to the hospital. Remember that your baby's main comfort from pain and stress is *you*.
- Ask if you can go into the operating room with your child and stay until after anesthesia is administered. Most anesthesiologists will cooperate with this, though some may not feel it is

NATURAL SOOTHER

Rest Your Eyes

Having a baby with a birth defect may send you into a whirlwind of new emotions and unfamiliar procedures. It may be hard to find time to take care of yourself, but here's a simple treatment for your tired eyes.

Steep one chamomile tea bag in 1 cup boiling water in a large mug for 5 minutes. Remove the tea bag and allow the tea to cool. Add 1 cup rosewater to tea. Chill in refrigerator. Soak two cotton pads in the mixture. Place them on your eyelids and leave on for 5 minutes.

Try this any time of the day you get a few minutes or at bedtime. You can purchase rosewater in any grocery store.

necessary for a very small baby. Be politely persistent.

- By the same token, try to be there as your child is waking up from surgery so that yours is the first face she sees. Be prepared for the fact that most children are very disoriented upon waking up from anesthesia.
- Ask if you can hold your child, or stand close by, while even simple procedures, such as taking blood or reading blood pressure, are performed.
- Take notes whenever someone talks to you about your child's condition. If needed, ask how things are spelled. Keep a record of all the procedures and medications your child receives. Ask lots of questions: "Why do you want this blood test, doctor?" "What sorts of results are you hoping to find?" "How often will this medication be given to my baby?"
- Ask how machines work and what they do. Keep a close watch on tubes or IVs hooked up to your child. You will probably notice some-

thing awry, such as a line that has worked loose, before a nurse does.

COMING HOME AFTER SURGERY

There is a lot you can do to help the healing process along when you return home from the hospital. Your baby will need to heal on both a physical and an emotional level, and there is no doubt that they supplement each other. Helping your little one feel safe and nurtured will increase her ability to heal physically. As well, you need to heal and recover from a process that has most likely been draining.

- *Rest and touch.* The first few days at home need to be gentle and slow. Turn the pace of your life down to a fraction of what it normally is. Hold your baby as much as you can. Take lots of naps together.
- *Talk to your baby about what happened.* A baby who is a few months old will understand some of what you have to say about what happened in the hospital. Even those who are way too young to comprehend, though, will benefit from the soothing and matter-of-fact way your voice sounds. It will help you, too, to go over what happened in simple language.
- *Expect crying.* Crying is the only way your baby has to express the fear and frustration he may feel at having been poked and prodded while in the hospital. If you can, try to welcome this form of expression and respond to it as lovingly as you can. Think of it as talk.
- *Learn to do baby massage.* Page 201 teaches you how to do infant massage. You will need to take your baby's physical state into account, of course. Consult with the baby's doctor to make sure you understand where to avoid placing pressure.
- *Use aromatherapy.* Put lavender or chamomile essential oils into a diffuser for a soothing atmosphere at home.
- *Consult with a homeopath.* A homeopathic doctor may be able to help with the healing process.

Find one who has had plenty of experience caring for small children.

Older Siblings

It isn't easy to be the sibling of a baby with a disability. Even if your baby's troubles are managed quickly, the short-term intensive concern over her health may have long-term repercussions for your older child.

Older children can experience jealousy over the attention the new baby is getting, but they can also have a range of other complicated emotions. Like you, they may feel fear and anger over what has happened to the baby. They may worry that their jealousy or ambivalence about becoming a sibling has actually caused the baby to become sick or disabled. They need to be able to discuss their feelings, and they need to be reassured that what has happened is not their fault.

Try to involve your older sibling in the baby's care as much as possible. If your child is allowed in the hospital, bring him often. As we discussed in chapter 8, children's fantasies are often much more terrible than the truth. Don't try to shield your older child from what is going on. He can handle it, as long as he has your support. Once the baby is home, your child will be able to do much more to help by fetching things the baby needs, drawing baths, and keeping the baby company.

It's hard to find balance as a parent when you have a sick baby in the hospital and a well one at home. You may need to take turns spending special time with your older child and being with the baby.

Exploring Painful Emotions

You may come to feel that your child is perfect, just the way he or she is. Before you can get to that point, though, you'll need to allow yourself to explore all your feelings. Sadness is to be expected. You may need to deal with feelings of guilt. Some mothers wonder endlessly if they could have done some-

---

BODY WISE
Baby and You

Here are two exercises that you and baby will both enjoy. They strengthen the arms and work the abdominal muscles.

Baby Bench Presses
- Lie on your back with your baby on your stomach.
- Hold the baby under and around the waist and lift her up until your arms are fully extended.
- Bring baby slowly back down, and greet her with a kiss.
- Repeat.

Baby Push-Ups
- Lay the baby down on his back on a blanket.
- Do modified push-ups, placing your palms shoulder width apart on the floor on either side of your baby's head, and resting your knees together. Kiss him each time you bend your arms.

---

thing during pregnancy that caused their child's disability. You may find yourself feeling moments of regret that you ever got pregnant to begin with, and that can bring on more guilty feelings. Anger may also play a part in your feelings. Where can you direct your anger? Who or what is responsible for what happened to your child?

It isn't only parents of children with severe birth defects who have to contend with these difficult emotions. Your child may have a very treatable problem, such as cleft palate. You may know that your child is going to be okay and will have a normal childhood. Yet your images of a healthy, perfect child have been shattered, and it is normal to grieve for hat. Your emotions may be difficult to understand at first. The bottom line is that you must give yourself permission to have all your feelings. Recognize that what you feel is normal, under the circumstances.

Give yourself the gift of support. Almost every birth defect has a support group tailored just for the needs of families who are dealing with it. See appendix 2 for contact information for several of these groups. If you don't find the one you are looking for, ask your hospital's social worker or staff psychologist for help, or do a search on the Internet. You may want to see a therapist for help as well. If you don't have a good lead on a therapist, ask for a reference from your hospital.

Be mindful of the stress that difficult situations can cause between partners. People often handle difficult emotions in different ways. One of you may be calmer than the other. One of you may have greater fear of hospitals than the other. It can be all too easy to assume that your partner does not care as much about the baby because he or she is having trouble being present, physically or emotionally. Talk openly to each other about the pain you're experiencing, and consider attending support groups or seeing a therapist together.

Feelings of anger lead many parents of children with birth defects to become activists. Parents have been responsible for most of the funding and advocacy for disabled children that have occurred in recent years. This can be a good outlet for difficult emotions. If you allow yourself time to process these painful emotions, you will soon discover that your child's unique personality, and your budding relationship with him, will overshadow everything else. Parents of children with disabilities report that bonding makes it possible for them to put themselves in their child's shoes. Doing this can help you to better understand how the world works for your child, and therefore how you can best help him.

PART SEVEN

Especially for Fathers

Having a child, I discovered, makes you dream again and,
at the same time, makes the dreams utterly real.

—CHARLES KRAUTHAMMER, *Washington Post*

Now that you are about to have a child, you will be asking yourself what it means to be a father. While your definition of fatherhood will be unique, and is likely based on your childhood and your experiences with your own father, much of what you think about fatherhood has been influenced by society.

Our changing world has had a profound impact on fatherhood in ways both subtle and obvious. The shifting roles of women have given men new opportunities to bond with and nurture their children. The age of information has made it easier for men to work at home and see more of their families. It has also resulted in friction in the workplace, as more and more men seek careers that offer them flexibility to care for their families.

A Historical View of Fatherhood

Only thirty or forty years ago, a man wouldn't dream of witnessing his child's birth. Now most men wouldn't dream of missing it.

Before the Industrial Revolution, personal involvement with their children was a part of most men's lives. Most men worked on home farms or ran their own small businesses, with their children working or playing nearby. Children understood the de-

tails of their fathers' lives and were most likely involved with the family business. Men were also more involved with their wives' pregnancies.

Once fathers left their farms and stores for factories and offices, however, mothers became more exclusively central to children's lives. It was mothers who attended to almost all of the child's needs and who taught children much of what they knew about life, values, and love.

Soon it was assumed that only women were able to supply this day-to-day nurturing. Men were expected to express their love for their children by bringing home a paycheck and providing their children with food, clothing, and shelter.

During World War II, the division of labor changed as many women took jobs outside the home, in factories and stores, filling in for the thousands of men who were fighting overseas. After the war was over, however, men reclaimed their places in the workforce, and women returned to their roles as homemakers and primary nurturers of children.

At the same time, pregnancy began to be seen as a medical event. Babies were no longer born at home. Women went to the hospital to give birth, and only doctors and nurses were allowed to be present. In fact, the mother herself was barely present, since she was often anesthetized once labor began. The father remained in a waiting room, pacing for hours and waiting for word of the birth from the doctor. His first experience of his child took place through the nursery window.

This began to change in the 1970s, when the concept of the father as a labor coach began to catch on. Dads began to attend births and even cut the umbilical cord. While fathers initially had to fight for the right to attend the birth, today it's assumed that they will be there. When men began to attend the births of their children, they also became much more comfortable handling and caring for them. A new interest and preoccupation with their infants turned men into active fathers.

Today, nurturing by fathers is considered not only normal, but essential. The type of special nurturing a man has to offer is seen as an integral part of child rearing. Studies have shown how important a father's involvement is. Children from "father-deprived" families have greater difficulty developing self-esteem, adjusting socially and sexually, and coping with frustration.

Stereotypes

Examining stereotypes about dads can help you to see how societal definitions of fatherhood have affected your own perceptions.

Television in the 1940s and '50s gave us some powerful father icons that are still with us today. Jim Anderson, played by Robert Young in the classic *Father Knows Best,* stands out in particular. He was the absolute Head of the House, albeit a kindly one. Once he got home from his office, his word was final. He was strong, steadfast, and always right.

Today's media often portrays fathers as bumbling, fumbling guys trying desperately to be dads, but ineptly blowing it every time. These images usually appear in comedies like *Mrs. Doubtfire,* where Robin Williams portrays a desperate, divorced dad trying to spend more time with his kids by impersonating a nanny, or *Three Men and a Baby,* where three single men are clueless when it comes to caring for an infant. Sadly, these stereotypes reveal our mixed feel-

HIGHER GROUND
Common Concerns

As your child's birth approaches, you may find yourself overwhelmed by a stream of worries. You're not alone: a survey of several hundred fathers at the University of California at Davis revealed concerns that are common to new dads.

The early months of pregnancy bring ambivalence, with fathers bouncing between pride, joy, and an overwhelming sense of impending responsibility.

Later, most men experience a fervent desire for father-child intimacy and a nagging anxiety that they won't measure up to their own expectations, as well as fears about their finances, their relationships, and the health and safety of their partners and babies.

The majority of men interviewed were "very anxious" about being the primary support person during labor and birth. They felt burdened by the enormous responsibility of providing support, while having no support of their own.

The survey points to the need for new fathers to have the support of other fathers, just as mothers receive support during pregnancy. It also suggests that the willingness to express emotions and good communication with your partner help to relieve uncertainty.

ings about men's inability to care for children, which we still view as "women's work."

Another, less amusing stereotype is the deadbeat dad, an image fueled by statistics about the number of single African-American mothers. This image conveys that abandonment and neglect are foregone conclusions—and fails to take into account that the majority of black fathers are actively involved in the lives of their children.

Take some time to remember the stereotypes of fathers you've encountered throughout your life in television, movies, and books. Which aspects of these icons do you want to emphasize or avoid in your own fatherhood?

Rediscovering Your Own Father

The journey to new fatherhood invariably includes some side trips to the past. You can't examine your upcoming role as a dad without thinking about your relationship with your own father. That may bring up memories both positive and powerful—and painful.

Your father may have been a parent at a time when fathers were "invisible." Did your father work long hours or spend more time on social activities than your mother did? Until recently, it was the norm for men to work so hard that they weren't around for some of the milestones that mattered, like birthday parties and ball games.

Many wonderful, positive memories may be conjured up when you think of your childhood and your father. It is important to pay special attention to these memories. They will offer you a powerful key to embarking on your own journey. Try to remember what felt best about that camping trip you took together. Perhaps it was the one-on-one time together, without the pressure of routine daily life and schedules. Perhaps you felt really understood by your father.

Traditionally, fathers and sons have had difficulty exploring their emotions, making many men feel that their dads were not available emotionally, even if

---

BODY WISE
Upper Body Stretches

Carrying the baby is exercise in itself! Even if you're already in great shape, you might find that your arms and back ache from their new workouts. These exercises will help stretch your back and arms in preparation for fatherhood, as well as easing the aches and helping you to relax.

Stand with your feet shoulder width apart. Clasp your hands behind you at buttocks level as you bend slightly forward from the waist. Keep your hands clasped and arms straight as you slowly lift your arms upward. Feel your chest expand.

Raise your left arm overhead and bend your elbow, letting your hand fall behind your left shoulder. Place your right palm against your elbow and press straight back. Repeat with your right arm.

---

they were around physically. It may have been possible to talk about what happened during a baseball game, but not how you felt about school. You may have been punished for bad behavior without being asked to explain your side of the story.

The importance of allowing children to express their emotions was not fully realized, even a generation ago. Many men begin to address emotions with their fathers after they become adults. Your own impending fatherhood can provide a tremendous catalyst for improving your relationship with your father. You may simply wish to know your father better, or there may be significant problems in the relationship that you need to work out.

IMPROVING YOUR RELATIONSHIP

Before addressing your concerns directly, put yourself in your father's shoes for a time. Review what you know about his life, his work, and his friendships. What was the daily fabric of his life like? Imagine his morning routine, for example, or a typical workday. Picture how he spent his lunch hour. What did he do to relax? This might not be easy if you have a stormy relationship with your father. If you need some emotional distance, imagine your father as a character in a film instead of someone you know. Above all, be mindful that your father is probably dealing with his own difficult feelings. Perhaps he resents the role of provider that he was forced to play for so long. Perhaps he regrets not having had more time to spend with his children.

Once you're ready, spend some relaxed time with your father. Take it slow and savor your time together doing something you both enjoy. Once you feel the time is right, tell your dad you want to talk about childhood memories, both happy and difficult ones. While you might worry that he will not be interested in a tense discussion, most fathers do wish to improve their relationships with their children as they age.

As you prepare for your new role as a dad, try to learn as much as you can about your father: what he liked about his work, who he admires, and how his value system works. You might even try to learn about his relationship with his own father. It can be interesting to see what he has passed on to you from the previous generation.

If your relationship with your father was particularly difficult, you may need to approach him more slowly. Don't expect dramatic changes in your relationship right away. If either of you is holding on to painful experiences from the past, you may be afraid to deal with powerful, pent-up emotions. It never helps to ignore difficult emotions, however. They will ultimately stand in your way, so go slowly. Getting to know one another slowly over time will accomplish far more than a single, huge confrontation.

IF YOUR FATHER HAS DIED

Your relationship with your dad is never really over. If your father is no longer alive, you won't be able to have a face-to-face conversation with him but you may be able to learn more about him. Look through any personal papers and belongings he left behind. While reading a diary or journal would be ideal, even invoices can reveal interesting information about him.

Speak to your mother, to other relatives, and to your father's friends or business associates. You may find out details you never knew. For example, find out who his favorite authors were so that you can read them for yourself and try to identify what he liked about them.

If your relationship with your father was rough before he died, you may be able to work through some of your emotions by writing him a letter. It will help you to crystallize your issues and express your emotions. If you'd like, imagine or write a response from your father. Try to find common ground and mutual forgiveness for mistakes that you both may have made. This can tell you more about who you are, which will build a stronger foundation for your own fatherhood.

NATURAL SOOTHER

New Father Tonic

Here's a blender pick-me-up for the early weeks of new fatherhood. It's high in vitamin C, vitamin B, potassium, magnesium, and selenium, which make it a great brain booster, as well as a source of extra energy for the man everyone's depending on.

    1 cup crushed fresh pineapple

    1 stalk of celery

    1/3 cucumber, peeled

    1 apple

Mix ingredients together in a blender or juicer. Add a dash of Tabasco, if desired.

What Kind of Father Will You Be?

Your goals as a father will be unique. Start off by formulating general objectives, such as "I would like to spend more time with my child than my father did with me," "I want my child to know he is important to me," or "I want my child to know what my work is like." Then hone them down to concrete goals, such as "I want to be there when my son takes his first steps," or "I plan to teach my children the love of the outdoors by taking them camping and hiking often." Write your goals down or share them with someone you trust.

Entering fatherhood with vague objectives may set you up for constant worry that you aren't doing enough. This is a good opportunity to talk with your partner and plan your future parenting styles together.

Looking Ahead

In the next two chapters we will talk about the journey from pregnancy to child care from the father's point of view. The focus of the coming months will be on your partner, then your new baby. With some preparation, you can avoid feeling left out of things as you recognize your vital role in your growing family.

The magic intensity that is part of this meeting is more than most men could ever imagine before they experience it. After months of watching the woman he loves experience pregnancy, and a labor during which many of us feel frustratingly helpless, the sudden separate reality of the child is overwhelming.

—KEN DRUCK, *Secrets Men Keep*

It may sound funny to talk about the "pregnant father," when after all, it is the woman who is pregnant. Perhaps we need a new word that describes a man's experience while waiting for his baby to be born. Few men are ever asked, "How are you feeling?" or "Are you nervous?" There are few rituals designed to guide fathers through this rite of passage, perhaps the most significant one of his entire life. Fathers don't usually participate in baby showers, for example.

Once the baby is born, all attention is centered on every move this new creature makes. A great deal of attention is also focused on the mother, since she needs time to heal from the experience of birth. It is a time of joy and wonder, exhaustion and stress—and change. Fathers are likely to ignore their own feelings and needs during this time. It just seems like everyone else comes first.

But to remain strong and supportive for your family, you need to take care of yourself. A part of this self-care involves acknowledging the big changes you are going through.

Pregnancy

Everyone has heard of "sympathy pains," where a man experiences psychosomatic symptoms similar to those of his partner. Weight gain, nausea, loss of ap-

petite, and moodiness are often experienced by men during the nine months of pregnancy. It can seem humorous, but in reality it is an expression of a sympathetic desire to share the pregnancy.

For fathers-to-be, it's not easy to be on the outside looking in. Your partner will go through tremendous physical changes as the baby grows inside her. At first, you'll only hear about those changes secondhand. Seeing the woman you love alternate between rapture, emotional outbursts, and nausea can make your own needs feel insignificant.

YOUR CONCERNS DURING PREGNANCY

Let's take a look at the very real emotional challenges you will face during pregnancy. Over the next nine months, you may be asking yourself these questions:

- "Can I provide for a family?" This is one of the biggest worries for a man as he contemplates fatherhood, perhaps because our society still strongly associates dads with the role of the Great Provider. This feeling is often unrealistic; even men who earn a solid and generous living feel the burden of responsibility in ways they did not before. After all, if something had happened to you before you had a child, your partner would probably have been able to provide for herself. But this new creature will be completely dependent on the two of you for everything.

- "Will I have to give up my favorite activities?" Men wonder and worry about what life will be like as a parent. You may be aware that you will have to make some sacrifices, but have no idea how much the daily fabric of life will change.

- "What do I really have to offer a child?" It's normal to wonder whether or not you will be up to the task of being a good father to a child. Most men are particularly nervous about being able to care properly for a new baby, especially if they haven't had much contact with small children.

- "Will my partner be okay?" As you watch your partner's body change, concerns for her health and safety are bound to come up. Is childbirth really safe, men wonder? What if there is an emergency?

- "What will happen to our partnership?" You may worry that becoming parents will change your relationship so drastically that you will be unhappy with each other. You may be unsure that you are really ready to give up that one-on-one quality your relationship has now. Will you ever be able to be alone together again?

- "How do I fit into the pregnancy? What is my role?" Many men watch their partners go through pregnancy and feel as if they are just going along for the ride. You might worry that you have nothing to contribute.

- "Will the baby be normal?" You may wonder what will happen if something is wrong with the baby, and if you'll be able to handle caring for a child with a disability.

You may experience one or two of these concerns, or all of them—maybe even a few more! You aren't the first man to have these feelings, and you aren't being unusually negative. It is normal to worry and fantasize when you are about to face major life changes. It is your mind's way of coping, of sorting it all out.

What can be potentially problematic is not facing up to your fears. Many men discover that simply acknowledging these seemingly irrational thoughts makes them feel better right away. Read on to learn about ways to deal with these very normal concerns.

TAKING CARE OF YOURSELF

To care for yourself emotionally during the period of pregnancy, start off by making sure you are taking care of your body. Eat a healthy diet and get plenty of exercise. During times of stress, we need extra nutrition. What's more, exercise actually reduces stress, and it is a good way of dispelling nervous energy. Consider yoga, which will help you keep fit and alert while soothing you during this often-nervous time.

To keep yourself emotionally fit and to prepare for the new life that is about to become a part of yours, try these suggestions:

- Begin to establish a relationship with the baby while he is still in the womb. At first this may feel odd to you, or maybe even a bit silly. Remember, though, that the fetus can hear quite well by the fifth month. Some studies suggest that newborn babies can recognize the sound of their father's voices. Talking to the baby will make her seem real to you, and will help you dispel your feelings of being left out. After the twentieth week or so, you may be able to feel fetal kicks. The best time to catch these movements is right after you and your partner have settled into bed for the night, a period of high activity for babies in the womb.

- Read about pregnancy and childbirth. Lennart Nilsson's *A Child Is Born* contains famous photographs of the baby developing in the womb. You can also read the earlier chapters of this book, especially the "What's Happening in My Body?" and "What's Happening with My Baby?" sections that appear at the beginning of parts 1 through 3. If you enjoy surfing the Web, it contains a wealth of information about your developing baby. You may even learn some things your partner doesn't know!

- Although it makes good sense to examine the future from a financial point of view, don't allow concern about money to take over your life. If you find yourself spending more than a couple of minutes comparing the price of one brand of toilet paper to another (or counting sheets to see which roll is bigger), you may be using this to cover up stress about other areas of parenting or pregnancy. Release yourself from your fears about money, at least long enough to get to the bottom of your emotions. Some men find affirmations helpful. Try this one: "I trust that we will be provided for."

- Dads feel the nesting instinct, too. In fact, you may be more impatient than your partner to get things ready. Some fathers like to make something special for the baby during pregnancy, such as a cradle or a toy chest. Visit the library and look for how-to books, or design your own, if you're handy. You may be the best candidate for repainting or floor refinishing, as well. Your partner needs to avoid breathing in paint and chemical fumes while she is pregnant.

- Gather information about home birth, if that is what you and your partner have chosen. Research birth centers or hospitals. Find out what sorts of childbirth education courses are available in your area.

- Ask for personal attention from your partner. Don't assume she knows what you need, or that she "should" know without being told. Make your needs known, whether you want to spend time talking, go to the movies, or make love.

- Find other dads to talk to. If you've got friends who are already fathers, spend a little extra time with them. You will do this with new eyes. Watch their interactions with their children. Observe how they schedule their time. Ask questions. If you feel close to one of them, he may be the right person to share your concerns with. He will undoubtedly recognize your fears, having gone through this already. If you are closer to your own father, uncle, or grandfather,

> ### HIGHER GROUND
> We live in an age in which many men sense that fatherhood may be the most mysterious and fulfilling journey a man can make.
>
> —RICHARD LOUV, *FatherLove*

talk to him as well about his experience with fatherhood. You can also volunteer to do a bit of baby-sitting, if you like. This can be a real confidence booster.

- Meditate, or find other ways to be quietly with yourself for a few minutes each day. Going for a walk or run outdoors can be very meditative. As you walk, try to keep your focus on your feet one step at a time. When your mind wanders, guide it gently back to paying attention to each step. Breathe deeply and slowly as you walk.

- Plan for the future with your partner. Explore the options for the first few months of your baby's life. This doesn't mean you have to figure it all out. Your plans will change and grow over time, but talking about these things now can help ease your mind about how things will be. It is good for your relationship, as well, to keep talking and trying to understand each other's concerns about what life will be like with a new baby.

Sex during Pregnancy

It is difficult to predict how your sex life might change during pregnancy. Some couples find there is no difference at all. Some pregnant women feel a heightened sense of sexuality during pregnancy, while others find they are less interested than usual. Morning sickness, changing hormones, fatigue, and other pregnancy symptoms may also be factors in our partner's level of sexual desire, especially in the first trimester.

Some men worry about the safety of sex during pregnancy. They wonder if sexual intercourse can harm the baby. There is no reason to be concerned about this. Sex is perfectly safe during pregnancy, unless your partner's health care provider has specifically suggested that you refrain, which only happens rarely. As pregnancy progresses, certain positions may become uncomfortable for your partner. For example, you will need to avoid placing the full weight of your body on your partner's abdomen.

If sex seems to be on the wane during pregnancy, try not to take it personally. Make an extra effort to stay close in other ways. Cuddling, kissing, and even holding hands during a romantic movie can provide both of you with the physical intimacy you need. Make sure you are talking to each other about what is happening to avoid misunderstanding and built-up resentments.

Labor and Birth

The prospect of labor and birth might be especially frightening to you, and you may be wondering how you can best help your partner through the experience. A childbirth education course can teach you a great deal about the stages of labor, breathing exercises, and home birth, birth center, or hospital routines.

The bottom line, however, is that you are indeed walking into a new situation. It helps to accept this fact right from the start. By nature, birth is unpredictable, and planning can be difficult. Your best bet may be to stay open to the moment. Even if you knew everything that would happen during your baby's birth, your unique responses to this experience are almost impossible to predict.

LABOR COACHING

These days, most fathers attend the births of their children. This is a far cry from the isolation men experienced prior to the 1960s during labor and birth.

Now men can feel a part of the birthing experience. They can witness the first moments of their child's life, images they will retain forever. A father's loving presence is especially reassuring to birthing mothers, who have had to go through this process with relative strangers in days gone by.

Accepting men into the birthing room has had its difficulties. The emphasis on the husband as the primary coach has put a great deal of pressure on men to fit into a role that may not be perfect for them—or worse, a role that may keep them from managing their own transitions into fatherhood.

When a man chooses to perform the duties of a labor coach at the birth of his child, he is often expected to bury his own needs and feelings completely, attending solely to the needs of his wife. This expectation sets many couples up for trouble. Men sometimes end up feeling inadequate, and women feel let down. Many men find they haven't had the right kind of training to make the birth experience satisfying for them. Socialized to handle difficult situations by fixing them and getting results, many men are overwhelmed by a situation that requires patience rather than action. The very term *coach* can be a bit misleading. Coaching someone is often associated, in the sports world, with winning, achievement, and success. Coaching is action-oriented. Often, during labor, the last thing a woman needs is to be coached. There may be times when your partner will simply need the comfort of your presence, without any pressure to try harder, be stronger, or rush things along.

Of course, many men handle the role of coach superbly and feel satisfied with their roles. Like anything else in life, different people thrive in different situations. If the birth will take place at home, with a midwife you feel comfortable with, you will likely experience less pressure to be the "perfect" coach than you will in a hospital, where you may be the only constant presence during your partner's labor.

FATHERHOOD IN OTHER CULTURES

If your own father paced the floor as he waited for your birth in a hospital waiting room, you unfortunately cannot rely on previous generations to help you through this situation. It can help, however, to talk with other fathers and to examine cultures where men take a far more active role in the birthing process. In many indigenous cultures, men experience birth through a practice called couvade. In couvade, men actually act out the labor. They lay on the ground and pant and moan. In some South American groups, men cut themselves with animal teeth to feel the pain, paint their joints and the soles of their feet with red dye to mimic blood, and take to their hammocks for three days to recover from ritual birth.

In eastern Paraguay, fathers-to-be stop eating certain foods, such as armadillo, thought to cause breech birth; they refrain from tying knots, believed to cause knotting of the umbilical cord; and they avoid touching sharp objects such as machetes, believed to cause bleeding, in late pregnancy. At the same time, the pregnant woman is following rituals of her own. In the Guarani culture in South America, both parents spend the final days of pregnancy resting in their hammocks and quietly socializing with family and friends. The birth is usually attended by women, but the man cuts the umbilical cord with a bamboo knife. Fathers are then expected to rest and stay near the child. Until the child's umbilical cord falls off, the father has a special connection with the baby's soul, which is believed to enter the world slowly; as it does, fathers are responsible for assuring it's safe transition. Even after the cord drops off and men return to normal life, the child's spirit remains with the father. When he goes into the forest to hunt, a father is expected to carry the spirit of his new child in a sling over his left shoulder. In the case of a son, fathers make and carry a miniature set of bow and arrows that allow the child's spirit to hunt.

Although you may want to avoid armadillo meat, you probably don't want to pattern your child's birth experience after the Guarani. Like most men today, you won't want to miss seeing your baby's birth, and our culture doesn't encourage rituals like acting out the labor and delivery. However, many cultures view as normal a man's feelings concerning the birth of his child. These cultures acknowledge that the birth affects him, too.

YOUR ROLE IN THE BIRTH

To determine how you can best contribute, consider where your strengths lie. What does your partner think she will need from you during labor? What things does she think you can best provide? Do you think you can give the specific kind of support she wants?

No matter where you decide to give birth or how you choose to participate, it can be very helpful to hire a doula for labor support. The word *doula* is derived from ancient Greek, and means "woman caregiver of another woman." In today's world, a doula is a woman, hired by the expectant mother and her partner, to "mother the mother." Countless studies have shown the benefit of the one-on-one, woman-to-woman support provided by doulas. (For more details about doulas, read chapter 7.)

Hiring a doula means that you will not be the one and only support person for your partner. You can do as much, or as little, as you are able to, or you and your partner agree upon. If you become overwhelmed or very emotional at any point, you can step back for a moment and take care of yourself, or just experience what's going on.

Some men also find it helps to have someone special who is there just for them. You and your partner may not want your best friend to be right in the labor and delivery room with you, but your relative or close friend could wait nearby, or could come to see you right after birth occurs. It can be great to share this experience with and show off your minutes-old baby to someone who knows you well and cares about you.

HOW YOU CAN HELP DURING LABOR

Throughout the years, men have provided tremendous reassurance and support during labor and delivery. Here are some ways that you may wish to help your partner.

- Give massages to your partner. This can be particularly helpful if she is experiencing "back labor," where the baby's body is facing away from the spine, instead of toward it, which is more common. (See chapter 13 for more ideas on natural pain relief during labor.)

- Handle paperwork or other routine matters if you are in a hospital.
- Keep too many people from coming into the room and disturbing your peace and privacy.
- Carry out plans the two of you had decided upon ahead of time, such as playing specific music or having aromatherapy scents in the room.
- Help your partner to focus when she seems to be getting overwhelmed by the labor.
- Help your partner to stick to decisions she made ahead of time about the use of painkillers or labor augmentation (where chemicals are used to speed labor up).
- Support your partner in a variety of positions, especially the squat position. Upright positions have been shown to speed up labor. (See "a Potpourri of Birth Positions" in chapter 17 for more on this subject.)

While these ideas may not work for all couples, discuss them with your partner ahead of time. There is plenty you can do that really makes a difference.

After Your Baby Is Born

Be prepared for some intense feelings once the baby is actually born. Many men report that no matter how involved they were with their partner's pregnancy and labor, the reality of the baby didn't truly hit until the moment of birth. You may experience stronger feelings of love than you can imagine when you hold your baby for the first time. Some men feel torn between wanting to cry and wanting to "keep it together" in order to fulfill the role of the strong supporter. It's important to let yourself experience all of your feelings.

The first place a baby needs to go directly after

NATURAL SOOTHER

Sunday Morning Coffee Cake

For the next few weeks, you'll probably be doing a lot of cooking. Here's an easy breakfast dish; you can add fruit, juice and hot tea for a light meal or a frittata for a more hearty meal.

Mix together 2 cups of any kind of flour, 2 teaspoons double-acting baking powder, and 1 tsp. salt.

Cut in 1 cup butter with a pastry cutter.

Drop 1 egg into a glass measuring cup, and add enough cow, rice, or soy milk to raise the level to 1 cup. Add 1 teaspoon vanilla to the liquid. Mix well.

Add the milk mixture to the dry ingredients. Add 1 cup of honey to the mixture. Mix well. The mixture will be thick.

Pour into a buttered pie pan or small, square cake or loaf pan. Spread the batter evenly in the pan.

In a small pan on the stove, melt equal parts honey and butter (between 1/8 cup and 1 cup each, depending on your preference). Sprinkle in 1 teaspoon cinnamon and 1 teaspoon cardamom. Pour this mixture over the top of the coffee cake. Create a swirl pattern with a spoon or spatula.

Bake at 350 degrees for 25 to 30 minutes.

---

birth is into the mother's arms. Fathers need their time with the new baby, too. Try to make sure you have a chance to hold the baby, feel her warmth, and look into her eyes for at least a few minutes soon after delivery. If, however, your partner has a cesarean section, you are the best person to hold the baby first.

THE FIRST FEW WEEKS

No matter how well prepared you are, those first few weeks at home with a new baby will be unexplored terrain. This exciting adventure is like no other you will experience. The world looks different when you are a dad.

Some men struggle with feelings of uselessness. It may seem like all the baby does is sleep and nurse. In reality, though, there is nothing that can replace the contribution of a loving father. You can make all the difference in creating an environment at home that will nurture the new baby, your partner, and yourself.

In the postpartum period, your partner needs to heal from pregnancy and delivery. She will be experiencing large hormonal adjustments, and also mastering the fine art of breastfeeding (one of the most natural things in the world, but not always easy to learn). Here are some ways you can help to provide the peaceful environment that is so critical during this time:

- Take as much paternity leave from your job as you can. Try to organize your home ahead of time so that your partner can rest and relax. Either take over housekeeping duties, enlist help from friends, or hire someone. Start each day by walking through the house and taking an inventory of what needs to be done.

- Splurge where possible on items such as takeout meals, or having a laundry service wash and fold your clothes by the pound. Hire a diaper service to pick up and clean soiled cloth diapers.

- Whenever possible, run interference between your partner and well-meaning friends and relatives who want to visit. Take the phone off the hook when mother and baby are sleeping.

- On the other hand, if people ask whether they can help, take them up on it! Ask friends and relatives to prepare a meal that can be reheated for dinner, run errands, take older children to school, or do a little housekeeping for you.

- Don't forget to compliment your partner on how well she's doing as a new mom.

As you take on these new responsibilities, bear in mind that women often have a very difficult time asking for—and accepting—help. Your partner may fear she will not seem competent in her new role as mother if she needs help. Reassure her that she can rely on you and still be a wonderful new mom.

How to Hold Your Baby

Men who are not used to holding small babies worry about doing this properly. In short order, you will feel so comfortable that you will wonder what the fuss was about. The traditional cradle hold doesn't always work well for men, since babies tend to associate this position with nursing. Here are some others to try:

- Hold the baby high on your shoulder, with her front facing yours. Her head can nestle into your neck area; later, she can look over your shoulder. If your baby is fussy or colicky, place her body higher up, so that her belly is against your shoulder and her upper body drapes over the top. The pressure on the baby's abdomen is often quite soothing.

- With the baby tucked into a sling or front carrier, you can run errands or do chores around the house. Very small babies benefit from constant closeness. The rocking motion they feel when they are in a carrier is believed to "organize" their nervous systems.

- Lean back, or lie down, with the baby stomach-down against your chest or stomach, with his head placed either over your heart or nestled under your chin. Straddle the baby's arms and legs on either side of your chest and stomach. Aside from the closeness and warmth this position brings, it also provides the baby with the soothing sound of your heartbeat, a sound she may associate with her time in the womb. You can also sing or hum while holding her, or just talk. Your baby will be soothed by the familiar sound of your voice.

> ## BODY WISE
> ### Flying Babies
>
> Here's a fun exercise you can do with baby while building strength in your arms, back and chest. At six weeks, do it with the baby facing toward you. At twelve weeks, let the baby face outward.
>
> - Stand with your feet hip width apart.
> - Hold your baby against your chest. If he's facing toward you, place one hand under his buttocks and one hand across his back; if he's facing outward, place one hand under his buttocks and one hand across his chest.
> - Inhale, exhale, and slowly and gently lift your baby up and to the right as you shift your weight to the right side and bend your knees.
> - Inhale, exhale, and straighten your legs as you bring your baby back to your chest.
> - Repeat on the left side.

The "Nursing Father"

The health benefits of breastfeeding are overwhelming, both in terms of the baby's health and the parents' convenience. It may be that neither you nor your wife were breastfed, so you may not have had much exposure to nursing. Many new parents, both male and female, are surprised to discover that breastfeeding is a learned technique for both mother and child. While it is a natural process, it takes practice.

While it's common for men to feel "out of the loop" when it comes to breastfeeding, new fathers can contribute a great deal to this experience.

- Learn more about breastfeeding. Chapters 9 and 23 of this book are good places to start. Become a "breastfeeding cheerleader." The first

few days can make or break the breastfeeding relationship. Perseverance is the key, and your encouragement can make all the difference in the world. A few patient and kind words from you might include, "I know you can do this, honey. It's going to get easier."

- Help your partner to find a comfortable position. Most women use pillows to support themselves and the baby. You can help your partner to get settled, and hand the baby to her once she is in position.

- Make sure your wife has plenty of water nearby. Lactating women need extra liquids to encourage milk production.

- Don't press your partner to nurse in situations where she isn't comfortable. Even some women who are committed to breastfeeding may feel uncomfortable about doing so in public. While she will most likely overcome this shyness quickly, help her to find private places to nurse the baby during the first few weeks. Perhaps you can help by strategically holding a baby blanket in the right place.

Crying

It can sometimes be hard to remember that, for babies, crying is a form of communication, a language they use to tell us what they need. Crying often does have a particular message. It might mean your baby is hungry. It could mean she is having stomach pains, or is too warm. A detailed description of the different types of cries, and how to interpret them, is found in chapter 22, on page 200.

But crying is sometimes just a form of release, similar to the release you get from venting to a coworker or your wife after a frustrating day at work. This type of crying requires sympathy and support. It can help to try to understand what crying means to you. When we were small, many of us were taught that crying was "bad" and that emotions should be concealed. It can be hard to ignore those cultural messages when you hear your own baby crying.

At first, you may find it challenging to soothe your new baby. She may prefer Mom, and most often will be soothed by nursing. However, there are plenty of things you can do to help your crying baby. Physical contact is the most important. Hold your baby securely. Walk around with her. Sing to her. Pat her on the back. Rock with her in a porch swing or rocking chair. In time, the calmness of your touch and the rhythm of your movement will calm her crying.

CHAPTER 32 *Balancing Work and Family*

The best time of my life has been the three instances where I have been there
for the birth of my children. That is, nothing [else] has ever come close.

—STEVEN SPIELBERG

Men in today's world are trying to figure out a new way of fitting work into their lives, one that allows them to spend more time with their families. More and more fathers are unwilling to settle for leaving work early just once in a blue moon to catch a school play or see an after-school soccer game. They want more. They want jobs that allow them to routinely be a part of their children's daily lives—jobs that won't keep them tied to their desks until 8:00 P.M., and all day Saturday. They want to prepare meals, go to the playground, and put their children to bed.

Even though many men feel this way, those who choose to do something about it face an often unsympathetic culture. We live in a culture that glorifies career, long workdays, and multitasking. Working parents are fighting against the tide when they ask for different kinds of work arrangements. Men who insist on leaving the office by 5:00 or request limited travel schedules may worry that they aren't being "team players" or pulling their own weight.

Dads who choose to stay at home or work limited hours are certainly better accepted now than they were fifteen or twenty years ago, but there is still a stigma attached to the man who stays home with the kids while his wife brings home the paycheck.

Balancing Fatherhood and a Career

There's an old saying: Nobody's deathbed wish has ever been, "I wish I'd spent more time at the office." Your children will grow up in a flash, and you'll never get another chance to see your little one take his first step or say his first word.

On the other side of the scale is the very real need to earn money. And even if you don't want work to take over your life, it does bring unique satisfactions that family life doesn't offer. Many men find deep gratification in meeting deadlines and working with colleagues.

Now that you're a father, your time will be at a premium. It's the perfect time to reexamine your priorities so that your time can be spent doing what you feel is really important. If you find that your career simply isn't as important as it once was, consider ways that you can change your current situation. Here are some creative options many men are using to balance work and home life.

- *Sharing child care.* Some couples are able to manipulate their work schedules so that one parent is always at home with the baby. There are many different ways to do this: you can each have a part-time job, working different days of the week; you can work different shifts on the same days; or you can each bring work home on certain days of the week.

- *Working at home.* Many men are able to work at home, at least part of the time. This allows them to spend more time with their children. Some men even change careers to make this possible. Employee studies show that work at home can be more productive for the company.

- *Working part-time or flextime.* If you can afford a pay cut, part-time work may satisfy your current needs. With flextime, you can find a mutually agreeable schedule, for example, compressing your workweek into four days or leaving early two days a week. Flextime often proves to be a satisfying situation for both employee and employer. Men who are able to manipulate their work hours in ways that positively benefit their family lives are usually better, more satisfied workers.

- *Job sharing.* In this arrangement, two people work the equivalent of a full-time job. This won't work for all jobs, of course. You'll need to get permission from your supervisor and find a work partner with whom you're compatible and can communicate effectively. An advantage to the employer in this arrangement is that she gains the expertise of two different people and can take advantage of each person's unique strengths.

- *Freelancing.* Some men are able to leave permanent jobs and become freelancers or outside consultants. This may mean that you can work full-time for a few weeks, and then take time off for a week or two before taking on another assignment. While this won't allow you to be at home full-time, it will allow you to see more of your children.

- *Staying at home.* This might work if your partner has a full-time job she wishes to keep. This arrangement will be discussed later in this chapter.

NATURAL SOOTHER

A Trio of Allies

Try these natural soothers during the first few months of new fatherhood:

1. *Saint-John's-wort tincture.* This herb gives a gentle lift to the spirits. Add one dropper to your morning glass of water or juice.

2. *Elm and Oak Bach flower remedies.* Elm is used when you feel overwhelmed; Oak is recommended when you feel despondent but struggle on. Place 2 to 3 drops of each into a small glass of water, and sip with your lunch.

3. *Chamomile and passionflower tea.* Both of these herbs help you to sleep. Place one chamomile and one passionflower tea bag into a large mug; add boiling water and steep for 3 to 5 minutes. Sip at bedtime.

KEEPING WORK IN ITS PLACE

No matter what your job situation—full-time, part-time, or flextime—there will be times when one will infringe upon the other, creating stress for you and your family. This potpourri of suggestions can help you to keep everything running smoothly:

- *Leave work on time.* Though it may not always be easy, this single act can make an enormous difference in the amount of time you spend with your family. While some coworkers may initially resent your new limits, time will prove that you are just as productive as you were when you stayed until the wee hours. Bring work home with you only if absolutely necessary.

- *Schedule "family time" in advance.* Plan ahead for special circumstances such as trips to the pediatrician or visits with family. Some employers allow you to use sick time for doctor's visits; others allow you to split sick and vacation days in half.

- *Telecommuting.* Even if working at home is not possible on a regular basis, there may be times when a specific project can be done from home. Your employer may allow this on a regular basis if you are able to demonstrate its effectiveness. If you are able to work at home, you'll need to balance your career and family responsibilities carefully: Can you work and also care for your baby? Can you work during naps or in the evening after the kids' bedtime? Do you need a sitter who will either bring your children into your workspace or leave you alone, as needed?

- *Schedule a "transition time."* Going from one demanding set of stimuli into another can be difficult. If possible, give yourself a few minutes to breathe between your job and your home life. Sit in the car for a few minutes and listen to the radio before going inside, or head straight for the bedroom and change into comfortable clothes. Leave home a few minutes early in the morning and read the newspaper at your desk before starting work.

- *Give the kids attention first.* It often works best to play with your children as soon as you get home from work. Play with them for fifteen minutes before opening the mail, chatting with your partner, or doing anything else. This will make it easier to break away and attend to other matters.

- *Minimize business travel.* Explore alternatives to business trips. Can the goals of the trip be accomplished by other means, such as video or teleconferencing? Can another associate travel to gather data or deliver information? There may be times when diplomacy requires your personal attendance, but there may also be

---

HIGHER GROUND

The New Dad

According to a *Redbook* poll, 70 percent of fathers would like the opportunity to stay home and care for their children full-time. In fact, over 2 million fathers nationwide are staying home with their young children. Men are forming play groups, starting home businesses, and redefining their identities.

Gone are the days of the aloof patriarch, the stern disciplinarian, and the ominous "Wait until your father comes home." Fatherhood is being reinvented by dads who—in the words of one observer—are "determined above all that their sons and daughters will feel their living presence and their love."

Ninety percent of dads are present at the birth of their baby; 96 percent of fathers change their baby's diapers; 86 percent take their child to the doctor; 75 percent leave work to take care of their children.

The paternal shift from breadwinner to coparent is spawning a number of societal shifts—from generous leave policies at Fortune 500 companies to changing tables in airport men's rooms. And although a Boy Scout cannot yet earn a merit badge for child care, attitudes about masculine attentiveness have moved well beyond what James Levine of the Fatherhood Project at New York City's Families and Work Institute, calls the "deficit model": "What we are witnessing is a new stage of awareness about fathers as critical forces and contributors to family life."

times when your supervisor has not considered less time-intensive choices.

- *Synchronize your calendars.* While this notion may conjure a corporate image, it refers to spending time each week talking with your partner. Spend a few minutes on a "business meeting," reviewing the week's goals and agendas as well as financial matters. Schedule time when you can give one another your full attention, perhaps in the evening after the baby is asleep. If your spouse wants to get to the gym twice next week, and you need to work late on Friday, you can figure out how to accomplish both of your goals.

The Stay-at-Home Dad

Doing something different can be a challenge. This year, about 2 million dads did something different by staying at home with their children, while their spouses earned the bulk of the family income. While our culture is becoming more open-minded about these arrangements, there are still many preconceived notions about men who stay at home with the children.

STAYING CONNECTED

Stay-at-home dads face a number of obstacles. Most men have been trained to identify strongly with their work and derive much of their self-esteem from their careers. What they do is who they are. Men can therefore be especially sensitive to criticisms such as remarks that they are allowing their partners to support them, or that they are too lazy to go out and get real jobs.

Isolation is experienced by both men and women who stay at home with their children. Women have more opportunities to meet with others, however. Mothers' groups and exercise classes are normally geared toward women. Men who take their children to infant groups or toddler classes may find themselves the only man in the group. In larger cities, there is a better chance of finding other stay-at-home fathers to bond with, but in a smaller town, it can be difficult to feel connected. You will most likely meet other dads at places where your children play together or through friends.

JOB SATISFACTION

It can also be difficult for stay-at-home dads to find the recognition and rewards that a typical job offers. Taught for most of their lives that jobs yield tangible results, new dads may find that parenting's rewards are largely intangible. Bonuses and plaques are a thing of the past. After all, your baby is not likely to say, "I like the way you handled that messy diaper, Dad. Keep up the good work."

Satisfaction has to come from within. When your child is a bit older, praise will be plentiful. You will delight in the beaming smile from your six-week-old son or in seeing your three-year-old girl run to you for comfort when she suffers a scraped knee. But in the early weeks, keep in mind that your child will retain the benefits and memories of your fathering skills for the rest of her life.

Choosing to stay home with the kids can cause unexpected difficulties in your relationship as well. It isn't only men who have to adjust to a new role, and all the stereotypes associated with it. Women often find they have a great deal of difficulty letting go of their expected role of homemaker. This might result in her expecting you to do things just as she would have done them. She may also have to deal with criticism from family and friends because she is not home nurturing the baby. Communication between the two of you is even more critical now, as each of you needs encouragement and support, along with reminders that you have made the right decision for your family.

The Politics of Housework

Conflicts over housework—who should do it, when it should be done, and how much should even be done—are an age-old cliché of the "war" between the genders. This issue seems to bring out impas-

...oned opinions on both sides, which isn't surprising ...ecause the bottom line is this: nobody wants to do ...e dirty work.

Men are doing more domestic tasks than ever, but ...tudies show that women still do the lion's share of ...vork around the house, whether or not they have ...obs outside the home. A study at Cornell University ...evealed that men in the United States do only 27 ...ercent of the housework. Even in homes where ...ousework is supposedly split down the middle, ...some men are reluctant to do the advance planning; ...or example, they will cook dinner, but they won't ...shop for ingredients. Women, on the other hand, ...will often automatically abdicate responsibility to ...men in areas of household repair and maintenance. Each sex tends to overlook the unseen things the other does around the house.

Just why is this ever-present thorn in the side of family life still around? One obvious answer has to do with how you were raised. If you grew up in a home where women did the housework and men simply helped when they were asked—or not at all—these images may be a part of your belief system, as well as your sense of self. If your partner confronts you about housework without compassion, you are likely to respond with some hostility.

Society is also responsible for our attitudes about work around the home. Our government's lack of support for family-friendly programs, such as paid maternity leave, give the message that domestic work is not worth very much, and is not even "real work" at all. Despite the fact that doing laundry and cleaning the house are paid work for some people, when parents do it, it isn't even included in the Gross National Product. Stringent work schedules do little to help. In France there is a nationwide thirty-six-hour workweek. Here in the United States, fifty-hour workweeks are not unusual, leaving many parents without the energy to go home and do more work.

Some men are reluctant to do housework because they fear they will be unable to live up to their partner's standards. There may be good reason for this concern. The "Supermom" phenomenon has

---

BODY WISE
Give Yourself a Hand

Doing extra housework can leave your hands aching. Here's a quick, simple hand massage that you can do anywhere:

Starting at the tips, squeeze each finger of your right hand for two to three seconds as if it's a nearly empty tube of toothpaste.

Massage your right palm with the knuckle of your left index finger with small, slow, circular motions. Concentrate on loosening the meaty area below your thumb and the web between your thumb and index finger. Repeat with the other hand.

To stimulate circulation and revitalize the backs of your hands, rake your left fingers along the knuckles of your right hand, beginning at your fingertips and continuing to just below your wrist.

---

many women running like mad to have the perfect home, the perfectly behaved child, and the perfect job. This can inadvertently give their partners a mixed message: "You don't do enough, and even the bit you do accomplish is not good enough."

The key to success in negotiating these difficult issues is awareness and sensitivity. Tackle one issue at a time. Sit down together and talk about housework—not when either of you is angry, but when you're both calm and open to discussion. Who did the chores in your families of origin? Discuss what each of you believes it means to be a man or a woman, and how these beliefs shape your ideas about housework.

Next, discuss how you'd each like to handle things in your home now that you have children. Try to come to an agreement about what is necessary and what isn't. Discuss your expectations about cleanliness and order. Once you agree, make a list of the necessary chores and divide them fairly based on your personal preferences. One of you may hate to cook, but enjoy doing the laundry.

Keep an open mind throughout this process. It will be necessary for each of you to make concessions: unless you're fortunate enough to be able to hire a cleaning staff, you won't have a perfect home without negotiation and work. This process of negotiation will leave you both feeling satisfied and can strengthen your relationship considerably.

Finding Time for Sex

During the postpartum period, which usually lasts about six weeks, women need to refrain from having intercourse while they heal from childbirth. That sounds like a long time, but most couples barely miss it in the flurry of activity that surrounds the care of a newborn. Truth be told, most parents are too excited, wound up, and just plain tired to think about sex during this time.

However, many men find that once they are interested in sex again, it's the last thing on their partner's mind. This can be emotionally painful for both parties, with men feeling unloved and women feeling pressured. It can help both of you to temporarily redefine "sex" to include all expressions of intimacy. Consider these possibilities:

- Rediscover romance. Spend time holding hands, cuddling, or kissing. Create a romantic atmosphere with food, candles, scents, or music. Most important, make time to talk: compliment one another, reminisce about your first date, or talk about sex, if you like.

- Try massage. You don't have to be a pro. A simple hand or foot massage works wonders. The beauty of massage is that giving one can be

as pleasurable as receiving one. Make it a rul[e] that the more exhausted parent gets the firs[t] massage.

- Take a nap together somewhere new, just fo[r] fun. Pile blankets and pillows on the livin[g] room floor and cuddle up together.

Sex starts out in the mind. If you concentrate o[n] enjoying intimacy, with or without the act of sex, you will maintain the strong foundation you have as a couple. Then, when sex comes back into your lives, it will be an even more powerful expression of your love.

When you are ready for sex again, prepare to be a bit more spontaneous and flexible than you were before the baby was born. You may need to "steal the moment" and grab opportunities for sexual intimacy when you can. Waiting for just the right moment may not be possible. Many new parents report that their babies seem to wake up at the most inopportune times, so be prepared for a few interruptions as well!

Beyond the Family

Many fathers find that becoming a parent opens their eyes to their world in a new way. To begin with, the type of love they feel for their newborn child is an altogether new one. This love is wrapped up with a protectiveness that may be far more intense than even romantic love. There is a selflessness that develops when a man falls in love with his own child. You may now understand why parents would sacrifice anything for their children.

Appendix 1:
Birth Report Card

This report card can help you to evaluate your choices for place of birth and birth attendant. Make copies for each practitioner and birth location you are considering. Part A reviews the birth interventions that should be avoided, if possible; part B discusses standards of care that are encouraged.

PART A

When you visit birth locations or interview birth attendants, ask them about their rates of the interventions listed below, noting the answers in column 3. Then compare their rates to the rates in columns 1 and 2.

Column 1 shows the rates recommended by the World Health Organization (WHO); these recommendations are based on a multidisciplinary consensus review of the international scientific literature.

Column 2 shows the rates recommended by the Coalition to Improve Maternity Services (CIMS), a U.S.-based consensus group made up of the Association of Women's Health, Obstetric and Neonatal Nurses (AWHON), the American College of Nurse-Midwives (ACNM), the Midwives Alliance of North America (MANA), and over 100 other health care organizations.

Interventions	Column 1	Column 2	Column 3
Early rupture of the amniotic sac	0%	0%	_____
Induction of labor	<10%	<10%	_____
Augmentation of labor	<10%	<10%	_____
Epidural anesthesia	0%	0%	_____
Narcotic anesthesia	0%	0%	_____
Electronic fetal monitoring	0%	0%	_____
Episiotomy	0%	<5%	_____
Cesarean (community hospitals)	<10%	<10%	_____
Cesarean (large hospitals)	<15%	<15%	_____

Early rupture of the amniotic sac is the intentional breaking of the "bag of waters" that encases the baby prior to the onset of labor.

Induction of labor occurs when drugs or procedures are introduced to end pregnancy and stimulate labor to begin.

Augmentation of labor is the use of drugs during labor to increase the strength or effectiveness of labor contractions.

Epidural anesthesia is the administration of regional anesthesia to block pain and sensation only in the pelvic area.

Narcotic anesthesia is systemic pain management through the use of intravenous narcotic drugs including morphine, Demerol, Stadol, codeine, Nubain, Talwin, and Sublimaze.

Electronic fetal monitoring is the use of belt, telemetry unit, catheter, or electrode to monitor contractions and fetal heartbeat.

Episiotomy is the surgical cutting of the perineal tissues during delivery.

Cesarean is surgical birth in which the baby is taken from the mother's womb through an incision in her abdomen.

PART B

Use this section to review the standards of care you want implemented at your place of birth and by your birth attendant. According to the Coalition to Improve Maternity Services (CIMS), hospitals, birth centers, and home-birth practices utilizing these standards are considered "mother-friendly." Check off each of the standards that are available at the places of birth you are considering.

_____ Will I be offered access to the birth companions of my choice?

_____ Will professional midwifery care be available to me?

_____ Will accurate, descriptive, and statistical information be provided to me about birth-care practices and procedures?

_____ Will the care I receive be culturally sensitive?

_____ Will I be able to move around during labor?

_____ Will I be encouraged to birth in an upright position?

_____ Does this place of birth have clearly defined policies supporting continuity of care, follow-up, well-baby care, and breastfeeding support?

_____ Does this place of birth routinely employ practices and procedures supported by scientific evidence?

_____ Will my attendants be educated in nondrug pain relief, and will I be discouraged from using analgesic or anesthetic drugs?

_____ Will I be encouraged to touch, hold, and breastfeed my baby?

_____ Will medical circumcision be discouraged?

_____ Will the standards of the Baby-Friendly Hospital Initiative (page 87) be upheld?

Appendix 2:
Resources

Mothering magazine maintains a list of helpful publications, organizations, and Web sites. Since finding a midwife will probably be your first priority, this list begins with tips to guide you through that process, followed by resources on each stage of pregnancy, labor and delivery, and caring for your new baby.

HOW TO FIND A MIDWIFE

Books

Armstrong, Penny, and Feldman, S. *Wise Birth.* New York: William Morrow and Company, 1990.

Davis, Elizabeth. *Heart and Hands: A Midwife's Guide to Pregnancy and Birth.* Berkeley, CA: Celestial Arts, 1987.

Ehrenreich, Barbara. *Witches, Midwives and Nurses: A History of Women Healers.* Old Westbury, NY: Feminist Press, 1973.

Frye, Anne. *A Comprehensive Textbook for Midwives in Homebirth Practice.* Portland, OR: Labrys Press, 1995.

Gaskin, Ina May. *Spiritual Midwifery.* 3d ed. Summertown, TN: Book Publishing Company, 1990.

Katz-Rothman, Barbara. *In Labor: Women and Power in the Birthplace.* New York: W. W. Norton, 1982.

Kitzinger, Sheila. *The Midwife Challenge.* London: Pandora Press, 1988.

Lang, Raven. *The Birth Book.* Palo Alto, CA: Genesis Press, 1972. Look for this classic at libraries or used-book stores.

Rooks, Judith Pence. *Midwifery and Childbirth in America.* Philadelphia, PA: Temple University Press, 1997.

Varney, Helen. *Nurse-Midwifery.* Boston, MA: Blackwell, 1987.

Publications

Midwifery Today, Inc.
P.O. Box 2672-350
Eugene, OR 97402
800-743-0974
www.midwiferytoday.com
Search under "Finding a Midwife Today" and "Finding a Doula Today."

Organizations

American College of Nurse-Midwives
818 Connecticut Avenue, Suite 900
Washington, DC 20006
202-728-9860
E-mail: info@acnm.org
www.acnm.org
"Find a Midwife" at the bottom of the home page will help you search for a certified nurse-midwife in your area.

Citizens for Midwifery (CFM)
P.O. Box 82227
Athens, GA 30608-2227
888-CFM-4880
E-mail: shodesmwy@peachnet.campus.mci.net
www.cfmidwifery.org
Go to "About Midwifery" on the home page, and select "Finding a Midwife." Also includes
great information on midwives and midwifery care.

The Farm
42 The Farm
Summertown, TN 38483
931-964-2293
The Farm is an international community founded in the 1970s. The Farm's midwives,
including Ina May Gaskin, are world renowned for their excellent birth statistics.

Midwives Alliance of North America
P.O. Box 175
Newton, Kansas 67114
888-923-6262
www.mana.org
"Find a Midwife" under "Resources" will help you search for a certified professional midwife
in your area.

National Association of Childbearing Centers (NACC)
3123 Gottschall Road
Perkiomenville, PA 18074
215-234-8068
E-mail: reachnacc@birthcenters.org
www.birthcenters.org
This Web site can help you find a freestanding birth center in your area.

Web Sites

www.birthpartners.com
> Comprehensive search for midwives, doulas, childbirth educators, breastfeeding
> support, birth photographers, massage therapists, and homeopathic physicians.

www.midwifeinfo.com
> This site is full of information on midwifery and has a Midwifery Directory on the
> home page.

www.mfom.org
> This site of the Massachusetts Friends of Midwives offers a search function for New
> England midwives, doulas, and childbirth educators, as well as *The Directory of
> Birthing Resources,* a print version of New England resources.

THE FIRST TRIMESTER

Books

Arms, Suzanne. *Immaculate Deception II: A Fresh Look at Childbirth.* Berkeley, CA: Celestial Arts, 1994.

Baker, Jeannine Parvati, Frederick Baker, and Tamara Slayton. *Conscious Conception: Elemental Journey through the Labyrinth of Sexuality.* Monroe, UT: Freestone, 1986.

Balaskas, Janet. *New Natural Pregnancy: Practical Wellbeing from Conception to Birth.* Brooklyn, NY: Interlink, 1999.

———. *Preparing for Birth with Yoga.* Boston, MA: Element, 1994.

Balaskas, Janet and Gayle Peterson. *Natural Pregnancy: A Practical Holistic Guide to Wellbeing from Conception to Birth.* Brooklyn, NY: Interlink, 1991.

Baldwin, Rahima. *Special Delivery.* Berkeley, CA: Celestial Arts, 1995.

Chamberlain, David B. *Babies Remember Birth.* Los Angeles: Jeremy P. Tarcher, 1988.

Cheatham, King. *Childbirth Education for Women with Disabilities and Their Partners.* Minneapolis: International Childbirth Education Association, 1994.

Cohen, Nancy Wainer, and Lois J. Estner. *Silent Knife.* South Hadley, MA: Bergin & Garvey, 1983.

Cohen, Nancy Wainer. *Open Season: A Survival Guide for Natural Childbirth and VBAC in the '90s.* Westport, CT: Bergin & Garvey, 1991.

Crawford, Karis, Charles S. Mahan, and Johanne Walters. *Natural Childbirth after Cesarean.* Malden, MA: Blackwell, 1996.

Dick-Read, Grantly. *Childbirth without Fear.* New York: Harper & Row, 1984.

Freedom, Lois Haizel. *Birth as a Healing Experience: The Emotional Journey of Pregnancy through Postpartum.* Binghamtom, NY: Harrington Park Press, 1999.

Feingold, D. S., and Deborah Gordon. *Getting Pregnant the Natural Way.* Berkeley, CA: Healing Arts Press, 1999.

Haire, Doris. *Cultural Warping of Childbirth.* Minneapolis, MN: International Childbirth Education Association, 1972. Available from ICEA at *www.icea.org* or 800-624-4934.

Klassen, Pamela E. *Blessed Events: Religion and Home Birth in America.* Princeton, NJ: Princeton University Press, 2001.

Louden, Jennifer. *The Pregnant Woman's Comfort Book.* San Francisco: Harpers, 1995.

Kitzinger, Sheila. *The Complete Book of Pregnancy and Childbirth.* New York: Alfred A. Knopf, 1996.

———. *Your Baby Your Way: Making Pregnancy Decisions and Birth Plans.* New York: Pantheon, 1987.

Korte, Diana. *The VBAC Companion: The Expectant Mother's Guide to Vaginal Birth after Cesarean.* Boston: Harvard Common Press, 1997.

Korte, Diana, and Roberta Scaer. *A Good Birth, a Safe Birth.* 3d ed. Boston: Harvard Common Press, 1992.

Marti, James, with Heather Burton. *Holistic Pregnancy and Childbirth: A Month-by-Month Guide.* New York: John Wiley & Sons, 1999.

Montagu, Ashley. *Life before Birth.* New York: New American Library, 1964. (Out of print.)

Nilsson, Lennart. *A Child Is Born.* New York: Delacorte Press, 1990.

Noble, Elizabeth. *Essential Exercises for the Childbearing Year.* 4th ed. Harwich, MA: New Life Images, 1995.

Olkin, Sylvia Klein. *Positive Pregnancy Fitness: A Guide to a More Comfortable Pregnancy and Easier Childbirth through Exercise and Relaxation.* Garden City, NY: Avery, 1987.

Paris, Raina M. *The Mother-to-Be's Dream Book: Understanding the Dreams of Pregnancy.* New York: Warner Books, 2000.

Raphael, Dana. *The Tender Gift.* New York: Schocken Books, 1974.

Sears, William, and Martha Sears. *The Pregnancy Book: A Month-by-Month Guide.* Boston: Little, Brown, 1997.

Schwartz, Leni. *Bonding before Birth: A Guide to Becoming a Family.* Boston: Sigo Press, 1991.

Stern, Sue Ellen. *I'm Having a Baby: Meditations for Expectant Mothers.* New York: Dell, 1993.

Verny, Thomas R. *Nurturing the Unborn Child: A Nine-Month Program for Soothing, Stimulating and Communicating with Your Baby.* Milford, CT: Olmstead Press, 2000.

———. *Tomorrow's Baby: The Art and Science of Parenting from Conception through Infancy.* New York: Simon and Schuster, 2002.

Verny, Thomas R., with John Kelly. *The Secret Life of the Unborn Child.* New York: Dell, 1986.

Wesson, Nicky. *Enhancing Fertility Naturally: Holistic Therapies for a Successful Pregnancy.* Rochester, VT: Healing Arts Press, 1999.

Winsor, Mari, with Mark Laska. *The Pilates Pregnancy: Maintaining Strength, Flexibility, and Your Figure.* New York: Perseus, 2001.

Organizations

Association of Prenatal and Perinatal Psychology and Health (APPPAH)
P.O. Box 1398
Forestville, CA 95436
Phone/Fax: 707-887-2838
E-mail: apppah@aol.com
www.birthpsychology.com

American College of Obstetricians and Gynecologists (ACOG)
409 12th Street SW, P.O. Box 96920
Washington, DC 20090-6920
202-638-5577
www.acog.org

Association of Women's Health, Obstetric and Neonatal Nurses (AWHON)
2000 L Street, NW, Suite 740
Washington, DC 20036
800-673-8499 (US)
800-245-0231 (Canada)
Fax: 202-728-0575
www.awhonn.org

Coalition to Improve Maternity Services (CIMS)
P.O. Box 2346
Ponte Vedra Beach, FL 32004
904-285-1613
Fax: 904-285-2120
www.motherfriendly.org

Informed Homebirth and Informed Parenting
P.O. Box 1733
Fair Oaks, CA 95628
916-961-6923

Web Sites

www.birthpsychology.com
> This unique site explores mental and emotional dimensions of pregnancy.

www.light-hearts.com
> Information on prebirth communication, prenatal bonding, and soul contact before conception and during pregnancy.

www.mindfulnesstapes.com
> Jon Kabat-Zinn's meditation tapes.

www.pregnancy.about.com
> Large site with pregnancy calendar and other features.

www.pregnancy.com
> This Web site has a lunar month pregnancy calculator.

THE SECOND TRIMESTER

Books

Bing, Elisabeth, and Libby Colman. *Making Love during Pregnancy.* New York: Bantam, 1989.

Baldwin, Rahima, and Tierra Palmarini Richardson. *Pregnant Feelings: Developing Trust in Birth.* Berkeley, CA: Celestial Arts, 1995.

Brackbill, Yvonne. *The Birth Trap.* New York: C. V. Mosby, 1984.

Dahl, Gail. *Pregnancy and Childbirth Tips.* Boston: Innovative Publishing, 1998.

Edwards, Margot, and Mary Waldorf. *Reclaiming Birth.* Santa Cruz, CA: Crossing Press, 1984.

England, Pam, and Rob Horowitz. *Birthing from Within: An Extra-ordinary Guide to Childbirth Preparation.* Albuquerque, NM: Partera Press, 1998.

Enkin, Murray, et al. *A Guide to Effective Care in Pregnancy and Childbirth.* New York: Oxford University Press, 2000.

Erickson, Jim. *Mother.* Petaluma, CA: Dillon Beach Press, 2001.

Harper-Roth, Jaqulene. *The Pregnancy Herbal: Holistic Remedies, Nutritional Therapies, and Soothing Treatments from Nature's Pharmacy for the Mother-to-Be.* New York: Three Rivers Press, 2001.

Kitzinger, Sheila. *Sex during Pregnancy.* Minneapolis, MN: International Childbirth Education Association, 1979. Available from ICEA at *ww.icea.org* or 800-624-4934.

Leboyer, Frederick. *Birth without Violence: The Book That Revolutionized the Way We Bring Our Children into the World.* Rochester, VT: Inner Traditions, 1995.

Machover, Ivana, Angels Drake, and Jonathan Drake. *The Alexander Technique Birth Book: A Guide to Better Pregnancy, Natural Birth and Parenthood.* New York: Sterling, 1993.

McCutcheon, Susan, and Peter Rosegg. *Natural Childbirth the Bradley Way.* New York: Penguin Putnam, 1999.

Odent, Michel. *Birth Reborn.* New York: Birth Works, 1994.

———. *The Scientification of Love.* New York: Free Association Books, 1999.

O'Mara, Peggy. *Natural Family Living: The Mothering Magazine Guide to Parenting.* New York: Pocket Books, 2000.

Peterson, Gayle. *Birthing Normally: A Personal Growth Approach to Childbirth.* 2d. ed. Berkeley, CA: Shadow & Light, 1991.

———. *An Easier Childbirth: A Mother's Workbook for Health and Emotional Well-Being during Pregnancy and Delivery.* Los Angeles: Jeremy P. Tarcher, 1991.

Romalis, Shelly. *Childbirth: Alternatives to Medical Control.* Austin: University of Texas Press, 1981.

Rothman, Barbara Katz. *The Tentative Pregnancy.* New York: W. W. Norton, 1993.

Sears, William, and Martha Sears. *The Birth Book: Everything You Need to Know to Have a Safe and Satisfying Birth.* Boston: Little, Brown, 1994.

Steingraber, Sandra. *Having Faith: An Ecologist's Journey to Motherhood.* Cambridge, MA: Perseus, 2001.

Weed, Susun S. *Wise Woman Herbal for the Childbearing Years.* Woodstock, NY: Ash Tree, 1986.

Organizations

Association of Labor Assistants and Childbirth Educators (ALACE)
P.O. Box 390436
Cambridge, MA 02139
617-441-2500
888-22-ALACE
E-mail: alacehq@aol.com
www.alace.org

The Bradley Method
American Academy of Husband-Coached Childbirth
P.O. Box 5224
Sherman Oaks, CA 91413-5224
Phone: 800-4-A-BIRTH or 800-423-2397
818-788-6662
www.bradleybirth.com

Birthing From Within
Pam England, CNM
P.O. Box 4528
Albuquerque, NM 87196
505-254-4884
www.birthingfromwithin.com

BirthWorks
P.O. Box 2045
Medford, NJ 08055
888-862-4784
www.birthworks.org

Doulas of North America (DONA)
P.O. Box 626
Jasper, IN 47547
888-788-3662
E-mail: Doula@DONA.org
www.DONA.com

International Childbirth Education Association (ICEA)
P.O. Box 20048
Minneapolis, MN 55420
952-854-8660, 800-624-4934
Fax: 612-854-8772
www.icea.org

Lamaze International
2025 M Street NW, Suite 800
Washington, DC 20036
Phone: 800-368-4404 or 202-857-1128
www.lamaze.org

Web Sites

www.childbirth.org
   Searchable site with many links on numerous aspects of pregnancy and birth, including a labor and delivery guide.
www.sheilakitzinger.com
   The Web site of author and birth expert Sheila Kitzinger.
www.thelaboroflove.com/index.shtml
   Comprehensive site that offers a pregnancy and parenting search engine covering many Web sites.

THE THIRD TRIMESTER

Books

Gardner, Joy. *Healing Yourself during Pregnancy.* Freedom, CA: Crossing Press, 1987.

Haire, Doris, and members of ICEA. *The Pregnant Patient's Bill of Rights/The Pregnant Patient's Responsibilities.* Minneapolis: International Childbirth Education Association, 1975. Available from ICEA at *www.icea.org* or 800-624-4934.

Balaskas, Janet. *Active Birth.* Rev. ed. Boston: Harvard Common Press, 1992.

Castro, Miranda. *Homeopathy for Pregnancy, Birth, and Your Baby's First Year.* New York: St. Martin's Press, 1993.

Davis-Floyd, Robbie. *Birth as an American Rite of Passage.* Berkeley: University of California Press, 1992.

Elkins, Valmai Howe. *The Rights of the Pregnant Patient.* New York: Schocken Press, 1980.

Flamm, Bruce. *Birth after Cesarean: The Medical Facts.* New York: Fireside, 1990. (Out of print.)

Goer, Henci. *Obstetric Myths versus Research Realities: A Guide to the Medical Literature.* Westport, CT: Bergin & Garvey, 1995.

Jordon, Brigitte. *Birth in Four Cultures: A Cross Cultural Investigation of Childbirth in Yucatan, Holland, Sweden, and the United States.* 4th ed. Prospect Heights, IL: Waveland Press, 1993.

Kitzinger, Sheila. *The Experience of Childbirth.* London: Penguin, 1987.

Peterson, Gayle. *An Easier Childbirth: A Mother's Guide for Birthing Normally.* 2d ed. Berkeley, CA: Shadow & Light, 1993.

Rothman, Barbara Katz. *The Encyclopedia of Childbearing.* New York: Henry Holt, 1994.

Scarry, Elaine. *The Body in Pain: The Making and Unmaking of the World.* Oxford, England: Oxford University Press, 1985.

Simkin, Penny. *Turning a Breech Baby to Vertex.* Minneapolis: International Childbirth Education Association, 1983.

Simkin, Penny, Janet Whalley, and Ann Keppler. *Pregnancy, Childbirth, and the NewBorn: The Complete Guide.* New York: Meadowbrook Press, 1991.

Small, Meredith F. *Our Babies, Ourselves.* New York: Anchor Books, 1998.

Tew, Marjorie. *Safer Childbirth? A Critical History of Maternity Care.* New York: Chapman and Hall, 1990.

Wagner, Marsden. *Pursuing the Birth Machine: The Search for Appropriate Technology.* Campertown, Australia: ACE Graphics, 1994.

Werz, Richard W., and Dorothy C. Werz. *Lying In: A History of Childbirth in America.* New Haven, CT: Free Press, 1977.

Young, Diony, and Charles Mahan. *Unnecessary Cesareans: Ways to Avoid Them.* 2d ed. Minneapolis: International Childbirth Education Association, 1989.

Organizations

Cesareans/Support, Education and Concern, Inc. (CSEC)
22 Forest Road
Framingham, MA 01701
508 877-8266
Include SASE if contacting by mail.

Children's Environmental Health Network
1604 Solano Avenue
Berkeley, CA 94707
510-526-0081
Fax: 510-526-3672
www.cehn.org

Environmental Building News
122 Bierge Street, Suite 30
Brattleboro, VT 05301
802-257-7300
Publishes a newsletter and pamphlets such as *Carpeting, Indoor Air Quality and the Environment.*

International Cesarean Awareness Network (ICAN)
1304 Kingsdale Avenue
Redondo Beach, CA 90278
800-686-ICAN
Fax: 310-542-5368
www.ican-online.org

National Lead Information Center and Clearinghouse
800-LEAD-FYI
Provides information and referrals about lead and lead removal.

Organic Trade Association
P.O. Box 1078
Greenfield, MA 01301
413-774-7511

U.S. Consumer Product Safety Commission (CPSC)
Washington, DC 20207-0001
800-638-2772
E-mail: info@cpsc.gov
www.cpsc.gov
Publishes a free "Baby Safety Checklist."

LABOR AND DELIVERY

Books

Baldwin, Rahima. *Special Delivery.* Berkeley, CA: Celestial Arts, 1995.
Gillmor, Mickey. *Squatting for Labor and Birth.* Minneapolis: International Childbirth Education Association, 1989.
Jones, Carl, and Jan Jones. *The Birth Partner's Handbook.* New York: Meadowbrook Press, 1989.
Jones, Carl, Henci Goer, and Penny Simkin. *The Labor Support Guide: For Fathers,*

Family and Friends. Minneapolis: International Childbirth Education Association, 1984.

Kitzinger, Sheila. *Being Born.* Rutherford, NJ: Berkeley, 1992.

———. *A Celebration of Birth.* Minneapolis: International Childbirth Education Association, 1986.

———. *Giving Birth: How It Really Feels.* New York: Farrar, Straus, and Giroux, 1989.

Kitzinger, Sheila, and Penny Simkin. *Episiotomy and the Second Stage of Labor.* Minneapolis: International Childbirth Education Association, 1986.

Maguer, Benig. *Spirituality of Birth: Healing for Mothers and Babies.* Rochester, VT: Healing Arts Press 2000.

Moskowitz, Richard. *Homeopathic Medicines for Pregnancy and Childbirth.* Berkeley, CA: North Atlantic Books, 1992.

Simkin, Penny. *The Birth Partner: Everything You Need to Know to Help a Woman through Childbirth.* Boston: Harvard Common Press, 1989.

Organizations

Lotus Birth
Jeannine Parvati Baker
Freestone
40 North State Street
Joseph, UT 84739
435-527-3738
www.freestone.org
Info packet: $15

Publications

BIRTH, published quarterly
Blackwell Science, Inc.
Commerce Place
350 Main Street
Malden, MA 02148
617-388-8250 or 888-661-5800
Fax: 617-388-8255
www.blacksci.co.uk/usa

Web Sites

Mango Mama's Natural Parenting Website
    www.geocities.com/Heartland/Woods/2924/lotus.html
    Eclectic natural parenting site with information on Lotus Birth.

POSTPARTUM

Books

Bing, Elizabeth, and Libby Colman. *Laughter and Tears: A Complete Guide to the Emotional Life of New Mothers.* New York: Henry Holt, 1997.

Belsky, Jay, and John Kelly. *The Transition to Parenthood.* New York: Delacorte, 1994.

Bossi, Lisa Burnett. *Mother's Nature: Calm and Confidence for the Motherhood Journey.* San Rafael, CA: Cedco, 2001.

Boyer, Ernest L. *A Way in the World: Family Life as Spiritual Discipline.* New York: Harper & Row, 1985.

Campbell, Leslie Kirk. *Journey into Motherhood.* New York: Riverhead, 1996.

Canadian Society for the Prevention of Cruelty to Children. *A Certificate for Parenting.* CD-ROM, 2001. Also available in text form at *www.empathicparenting.org.*

Choquette, Sonia. *The Wise Child: A Spiritual Guide to Nurturing Your Child's Intuition.* New York: Three Rivers Press, 1999.

Crittenden, Ann. *The Price of Motherhood: Why the Most Important Job in the World Is Still the Least Valued.* New York: Metropolitan Books, 2001.

Erlich, Louise. *The Bluejay's Dance: A Birth Year.* New York: HarperCollins, 1995.

Frymer-Kensky, Tiva. *Motherprayer.* New York: Riverhead, 1995.

Fuchs-Kreimer, Rabbi Nancy. *Parenting as a Spiritual Journey: Deepening Ordinary and Extraordinary Events into Sacred Occasions.* Woodstock, VT: Jewish Lights, 1996.

Gosline, Andrea Alban. *Welcoming Ways: Creating Your Baby's Welcome Ceremony with the Wisdom of the World's Traditions.* San Rafael, CA: Cedco, 2000.

Greenspan, Stanley I. *The Four-Thirds Solution: Solving the Child-Care Crisis in America Today.* New York: Perseus, 2001.

Kabat-Zinn, Myla, and Jon Kabat-Zinn. *Everyday Blessings: The Inner Work of Mindful Parenting.* New York: Hyperion, 1997.

Kitzinger, Sheila. *The Year after Childbirth.* New York: Fireside Books, 1994.

Kleiman, Karen R., and Valerie D. Raskin. *This Isn't What I Expected.* New York: Bantam Books, 1994.

Lamott, Anne. *Operating Instructions: A Journal of My Son's First Year.* New York: Fawcett Books, 1994.

Lewis, Cynthia Copeland. *Mother's First Year: How to Cope with the Exhausting, Exasperating, Exhilarating Experience Called Motherhood.* New York: Berkeley, 1992.

Lim, Robin. *After the Baby's Birth, a Woman's Way to Wellness: A Complete Guide for Postpartum Women.* Rev. ed. Berkeley, CA: Celestial Arts, 2001.

Martin, April. *Lesbian and Gay Parenting Handbook.* New York: HarperCollins, 1993.

Martin, William. *The Parent's Tao Te Ching: Ancient Advice for Modern Parents.* New York: Marlowe & Co., 1999.

McClure, Vimala. *Infant Massage: A Handbook for Loving Parents.* New York: Bantam Books, 2000.

———. *The Tao of Mothering.* Novato, CA: New World Library, 1997.

McGinnus, Kathleen, and James McGinnus. *Parenting for Peace and Justice.* Maryknoll, NY: Orbis, 1981.

Palmer, Linda Folden. *Baby Matters: What Your Doctor May Not Tell You about Caring for Your Baby.* Lancaster, OH: Lucky Press, 2001.

Parlapiano, Ellen H., and Patricia Cobe. *Mompreneurs.* New York: Berkeley, 1996.

Placksin, Sally. *Mothering the New Mother: Women's Feelings and Needs after Childbirth.* New York: Newmarket Press, 2000.

Resnick, Susan Kushner. *Sleepless Days: One Woman's Journey through Postpartum Depression.* New York: St. Martin's Press, 2000.

Riddell, Chris. *Tao of Babies.* Berkeley, CA: Ulysses Press, 2001.

Robinson, Janice. *Pride and Joy: African-American Baby Celebrations.* New York: Pocket Books, 2001.

Saavedra, Beth Wilson. *Restoring Balance to a Mother's Busy Life.* Chicago: Contemporary Books, 1996.

West, Cornel, and Sylvia Ann Hewlitt. *The War against Parents.* New York: Houghton Mifflin, 1998.

Wolf, Naomi. *Misconceptions: Truth, Lies and the Unexpected Journey to Motherhood.* New York: Doubleday, 2001.

Wolfson, Paula Ethel, and Lloyd Wolfson. *Jewish Mothers: Strength, Wisdom, Compassion.* San Francisco: Chronicle Books, 2000.

Organizations

Attachment Parenting International
2906 Berry Hill Drive
Nashville, TN 37204
615-298-4334
www.attachmentparenting.org

Child Friendly Initiative
322 Cortland Avenue
PMP #200
San Francisco, CA 94110
800-500-5234
www.childfriendly.org

Depression After Delivery, Inc. (DAD)
P.O. Box 1282
Morrisville, PA 19067
800-944-4773
215-295-3994
www.depressionafterdelivery.com

Parents, Families and Friends of Lesbians and Gays (PFLAG)
1726 M Street NW
Suite 400
Washington, DC 20036
202-467-8180
Fax: 202-467-8194
www.pflag.org

Postpartum Support International (PSI)
927 North Kellog Avenue
Santa Barbara, CA 93111
805-967-7636
www.postpartum.net

Web Sites

www.amagicalchild.com
> A return to simple play and preserving childhood.

www.iamyourchild.org
> Key issues, research findings and parenting advice for early childhood.

www.bygpub.com/natural
> "The Natural Family Site."

www.gentleparenting.com
> Site for stay-at-home moms.

www.humaneparenting.com
> A pediatrician mom offers information and advice.

www.instituteforplay.com
> The benefits of play for adults and children.

www.life.ca
> Natural Life Online offers an extensive collection of articles and detailed information on many aspects of natural living.

www.naturalchild.com
> Dedicated to parenting and education that respects children.

www.nd.edu/~alfac/mckenna
> Site of the Mother and Baby Behavioral Sleep Lab of Notre Dame, the lab of Dr. James McKenna, world-renowned cosleeping researcher.

www.pages.ivillage.com/gentlegoodnight
> The Gentle to Sleep Resource Page. Bedtime help that is not coercive.

www.parentsplace.com
> Large site that covers everything from pregnancy to household management.

www.promom.org
> ProMom site offers parenting advice and support.

www.rebozoway.com
> Advantages of wearing the baby in a traditional cloth wrap carrier.

www.seldomfar.com/nurturing
> Information on "The Nature of Nurturing."

www.salonmagazine.com/mwt
> Salon site department that considers "how motherhood reshapes our lives as women."

www.wearsthebaby.com
> Site that encourages baby wearing and attachment parenting.

www.workoptions.com
> Helps women to make a plan to negotiate flexible work arrangements.

BREASTFEEDING

Books

Adamson, Eve, and Mauren Kays. *Breastfeeding: a Holistic Handbook.* New York: Berkeley, 1999.

Auerbach, Kathleen G., and Jan Riordan. *Study Guide for Breastfeeding and Human Lactation.* 2d ed., Boston: Jones & Bartlett, 1999.

Baumgarner, Norma Jane. *Mothering Your Nursing Toddler.* Rev. ed. Schaumburg, IL: La Leche League, 1999.

Bengson, Diane. *How Weaning Happens.* Schaumburg, IL: La Leche League, 1999.

Franz, Kittie. *Breastfeeding Product Guide Supplement.* Los Angeles: Geddes, 1994.

Hale, Thomas. *Medications and Mothers' Milk: 1998–1999.* Amarillo, TX: Pharmasoft Medical Publishing, 1998.

Herzog-Isler, Christa, and Klaus Honigmann. *Give Us a Little Time: How Babies with a Cleft Lip or Cleft Palate Can Be Breastfed.* Baar, Switzerland: Medela AG, 1996.

Huggins, Kathleen. *The Nursing Mother's Companion.* 3d ed. Boston: Harvard Common Press, 1995.

Huggins, Kathleen, and Linda Ziedrich. *The Nursing Mother's Guide to Weaning.* Boston: Harvard Common Press, 1994.

Kippley, Sheila. *Breastfeeding and Natural Child Spacing.* Cincinnati: Couple to Couple League International, 1989.

Kitzinger, Sheila. *Breastfeeding Your Baby.* Rev. ed. New York: Knopf, 1998.

La Leche League International. *The Womanly Art of Breastfeeding.* New York: Plume, New American Library, 1997.

Lawrence, Ruth A. *A Review of the Medical Benefits and Contraindications to Breastfeeding in the United States.* Arlington, VA: National Center for Education in Maternal and Child Health, 1997.

Lee, Nikki, and Margot Edwards. *An Employed Mother Can Breastfeed When.* Minneapolis: International Childbirth Education Association, 1991.

Mohrbacher, Nancy, and Julie Stock. *The Breastfeeding Answer Book.* Rev. ed. Franklin Park, IL: La Leche League International, 1997.

Moran, Elaine. *Bon Appetit, Baby! The Breastfeeding Kit.* Freedom, CA: Treasured Child, 2000.

Newman, Jack, and Teresa Pitman. *Dr. Jack Newman's Guide to Breastfeeding.* New York: HarperCollins, 2000.

Odent, Michel. *The Nature of Birth and Breastfeeding.* Westport, CT: Bergin & Garvey, 1992.

Pryor, Karen and Gale. *Nursing Your Baby.* New York: Pocket Books, 1991.

Sears, Martha, and William Sears. *The Breastfeeding Book: Everything You Need to Know about Nursing Your Child from Birth through Weaning.* New York: Little, Brown, 2000.

Organizations

International Lactation Consultants Association (ILCA)
4101 Lake Boone Trail, Suite 201
Raleigh, NC 27607
919-787-5181
Fax: 919-787-4916
E-mail: ilca@erols.com
www.ilca.org

La Leche League International
1400 N. Meacham Road
Schaumburg, IL 60173-4048
847-519-7730
Breastfeeding Helpline: 800-525-3243
Taped Message: 900-448-7475, ext. 26
Fax: 847-519-0035
www.lalecheleague.org

The Parent Center for Breastfeeding and Parenting Services
6145 N. Beulah
Ferndale, WA 98248
360-384-1755
Fax: 360-384-2694
E-mail: kga@telcomplus.net

Web Sites

www.breastfeeding.asn.au
> Site of the Breastfeeding Mothers of Australia.

www.breastfeeding.com
> Comprehensive breastfeeding site.

www.prairienet.org/laleche/dettwyler.html
> Site of Katherine Dettwyler, professor of anthropology and expert on cross-cultural breastfeeding practices.

www.lactivist.com
> The Lactivist is a warehouse of breastfeeding information.

www.members.tripod.com/~breastfeedingtwins/
> Breastfeeding and attachment parenting of twins.

www.motherwear.com
> Fashions for the mother-to-be.

www.waba.org.br/
> World Alliance for Breastfeeding Action is a site devoted to international breastfeeding advocacy.

CIRCUMCISION

Books

Bigelow, Jim. *The Joy of Uncircumcising! Exploring Circumcision: History, Myths, Psychology, Restoration, Sexual Pleasure and Human Rights.* 2d ed. Aptos, CA: Hourglass, 1995.

Goldman, Ronald. *Circumcision, The Hidden Trauma: How an American Cultural Practice Affects Infants and Ultimately Us All.* Boston: Vanguard, 1997.

———. *Questioning Circumcision: A Jewish Perspective.* 2d ed. Boston: Vanguard, 1997.

O'Mara, Peggy, ed. *Circumcision: The Rest of the Story—A Selection of Articles, Letters, and Resources, 1979–1993.* Santa Fe, NM: Mothering, 1993.

Ritter, Thomas J. *Doctors Re-examine Circumcision.* Hurricane, WV: Third Millennium, 2002.

Ritter, Thomas J., and George C. Denniston. *Say No to Circumcision! 40 Compelling Reasons Why You Should Respect His Birthright and Keep Your Son Whole.* 2d ed. Aptos, CA: Hourglass, 1996.

Wallerstein, Edward. *The Circumcision Decision.* Minneapolis: International Childbirth Education Association, 1990.

Publications

Whose Body, Whose Rights? Examining the Ethics and the Human Rights Issue of Infant Male Circumcision. 56 min. VHS. Request personal-use videotapes of this award-winning documentary through VideoFinders, 1-800-343-4727.

Organizations

Doctors Opposing Circumcision (DOC)
2442 NW Market Street, Suite 42
Seattle, WA 98107
206-368-8358
www.u.washington.edu/~gcd/DOC

National Organization of Circumcision Information Resource Center (NOCIRC)
P.O. Box 2512
San Anselmo, CA 94979-2512
415-488-9883
E-mail: nocirc@concentric.net
www.nocirc.org

National Organization to Halt the Abuse and Routine Mutilation of Males (NOHARMM)
P.O. Box 460795
San Francisco, CA 94146-0795
415-826-9351
Fax: 415-642-3700
www.noharmm.org

Nurses for the Rights of the Child
369 Montezuma, Suite 354
Santa Fe, NM 87501
505-989-7377
www.cirp.org/nrc

VACCINATIONS

Books

Cave, Stephanie. *What Your Doctor May Not Tell You about Children's Vaccinations: Hidden Dangers, Pros and Cons, and Safety Measures That Can Protect Your Child.* New York: Warner Books, 2001.

Coulter, Harris L., and Barbara Loe Fisher. *DPT, A Shot in the Dark: Why the P in the DPT Vaccination May Be Hazardous to Your Child's Health.* Garden City Park, NY: Avery, 1991.

James, Walene. *Immunization: The Reality Behind the Myth.* 2d ed. Westport, CT: Bergin & Garvey, 1995.

Lange, Robert W. *The Doctor's Guide to Protecting Your Health Before, During, and After International Travel.* Greenport, NY: Pilot Books, 1997.

Neustaedter, Randall. *The Vaccine Guide: Making an Informed Choice.* Berkeley, CA: North Atlantic Books, 1996.

O'Mara, Peggy, ed. *Vaccination: The Issue of Our Times.* Santa Fe: *Mothering* magazine, 1997.

Offit, Paul A., and Louis M. Bell. *What Every Parent Should Know about Vaccines.* New York: Macmillan, 1998.

Plotkin, Stanley A., and Edward A. Mortimer. Jr. *Vaccines.* 2d ed. Philadelphia: W. B. Saunders, 1994.

Rozario, Diane. *The Immunization Resource Guide.* 3d ed. Burlington, IA: Patter Publications, 1998.

Romm, Aviva Jill. *Vaccinations: A Thoughtful Parent's Guide—How To Make Safe, Sensible Decisions about the Risks, Benefits and Alternatives.* Rochester, VT: Healing Arts Press, 2001.

Stratton, Kathleen, Cynthia Howe, and Richard Johnston. Jr., eds. *Adverse Events Associated with Childhood Vaccines: Evidence Bearing on Causality.* Washington, DC: National Academy Press, 1994.

Publications

The Case against Immunizations
Reprints of the vaccination lectures of Richard Moskowitz, M.D.
173 Mt. Auburn Street
Watertown, MA 02172
Dr. Moskowitz is a national expert on the biochemistry of vaccines. His lectures can be ordered by sending $3.00 to the address above.

Organizations

Autism Research Institute
4182 Adams Avenue
San Diego, CA 92116
619-281-7165
Fax: 619-563-6840

The Bell of Atri, Inc.
J. Anthony Morris
23-E Ridge Road
Greenbelt, MD 20770
301-474-5031

Determined Parents to Stop Hurting Our Tots (DPTSHOT)
Marge Grant
915 S. University Avenue
Beaverdam, WI 53916
920-887-1133
dptshot@powerweb.net

Steiner Medical Associates
Gilpin Street Holistic Center
Philip Incao, Anthroposophic and Homeopathic Medicine
1624 Gilpin Street
Denver, CO 80218
303-321-2100
Fax: 303-321-3737

Michigan Opposing Mandatory Vaccines
P.O. Box 1121
Troy, MI 48099-1121
586-447-2418

Missouri Citizens' Coalition for Freedom in Health Care
P.O. Box 190318
St. Louis, MO 63119-0318
314-353-8012

National Vaccine Information Center (NVIC)
421 E. Church Street
Vienna, VA 22180
800-909-SHOT or 703-938-0342
Fax: 703-938-5768
www.909shot.com
NVIC publishes *The Consumer's Guide to Childhood Vaccines,* available
for $9.00 plus $2.00 shipping.

National Vaccine Injury Compensation Program (NVICP)
U.S. Department of Health and Human Services
Health Resources and Services Administration
Parklawn Building, Room 8A-35
5600 Fishers Lane
Rockville, MD 20857
800-338-2382
www.hrsa.dhhs.gov/bhpr/vicp

Naturopathic Healthcare
Amy Rothenberg, N.D.
Paul Herscu, N.D.
115 Elm Street, Suite 210
Enfield, CT 06082
860-763-1225

Vaccine Policy Institute
Kristine Severyn, R.Ph., Ph.D.
251 W. Ridgeway Drive
Dayton, OH 45459
937-435-4750

Optimal Wellness Center
Dr. Joseph Mercola
1443 W. Schaumburg Road
Schaumburg, IL 60194
(847) 985-1777
www.mercola.com

Vaccine Adverse Events Reporting System (VAERS)
Department of Health and Human Services
P.O. Box 1100
Rockville, MD 20849-1100
800-882-7267
www.fda.gov/cber/vaers.htm

Vaccine Information and Awareness (VIA)
Karin Schumacher
12799 La Tortola
San Diego, CA 92129
858-484-3197
E-mail: via@access1.net
www.access1.net/via

Web Sites

www.altcorp.com
    Web site of Boyd Haley, Ph.D., head of the chemistry department of the University of
    Kentucky. Includes research on mercury toxicity.
www.autismfraud.com
    This is the site of the law firm Walters and Kraus, which is involved in lawsuits in ten
    states regarding mercury toxicity and autism.
www.autism-mercury.com
    The site of Lynn Redwood, one of the founders and current president of
    SAFEMINDS.
www.cdc.gov
    Site of the Centers for Disease Control and Prevention. Look under National Vaccine
    Policy (NIP) and Advisory Committee on Immunization Policy (ACIP).
www.iom.edu
    Site of the Institutes of Medicine, part of the National Academy of Sciences.
    Site includes IOM forums on vaccine related issues.
www.safeminds.org
    Site of SAFEMINDS, an organization founded by parents whose children have
    mercury-induced neurological disorders.

SPECIAL CIRCUMSTANCES—
PREMATURE BABIES AND CHILDREN WITH DISABILITIES

Books

Campion, M. J. *The Baby Challenge: A Handbook on Pregnancy for Women with a Physical Disability.* New York: Routledge, 1990.

Cowen-Fletcher, J. *Mama Zooms.* New York: Scholastic, 1993.

Doron, Mia Wechsler, et al. *Preemies: The Essential Guide for Parents of Premature Babies.* New York: Pocket Books, 2000.

Klein, Stan, and Kim Schive. *You Will Dream New Dreams.* New York: Kensington Books, 2001.

Madden, Susan. *The Preemie Parents' Companion: The Essential Guide to Caring for Your Premature Baby in the Hospital, at Home, and through the First Years.* Boston: Harvard Common Press, 2000.

Preston, P. *Mother Father Deaf: Living between Sound and Silence.* Cambridge, MA: Harvard University Press, 1994.

Rogers, J., and M. Matsumara. *Mother to Be: A Guide to Pregnancy and Birth for Women with Disabilities.* New York: Demos, 1991.

Segal, Marilyn, et al. *In Time and with Love: Caring for Infants and Toddlers with Special Needs.* New York: Newmarket Press, 2001.

Publications

It's Okay! Adults Write about Living and Loving with a Disability
Phoenix Counsel
1 Springbank Drive
St. Catharines
Ontario, Canada L2S 2K1
905-685-0486

Parenting with a Disability Newsletter
Through the Looking Glass
2198 6th Street, Suite 100
Berkeley, CA 94710-2204
510-848-1112
800-644-2666 (voice and TDD)
www.lookingglass.org

Organizations

March of Dimes
1275 Mamaroneck Avenue
White Plains, NY 10605
914-997-4629
www.modimes.org

Mothers from Hell
P.O. Box 19
German Valley, IL 61039
818-362-5303
Fax: 303-374-3151
www.mothersfromhell2.org

Project STAR
Parenting with Disabilities Project
Children's Institute
6301 Northumberland Street
Pittsburgh, PA 15217
412-244-3081
www.trfn.clpgh.org/star/

Through the Looking Glass
Research and Training Center for Families with Adults with Disabilities
2198 6th Street, Suite 100
Berkeley, CA 94707
800-644-2666 (voice and TDD)
E-mail: TLG@lookingglass.org
www.lookingglass.org

Web Sites

www.geocities.com/roopage
   A site on the benefits of Kangaroo Care, and skin-to-skin contact, for premature babies.
www.ourworld.compuserve.com/homepages/Trish-and-John/disabilitycool
   A one-stop resource for parents with disabilities.

SPECIAL CIRCUMSTANCES—
MISCARRIAGE, STILLBIRTH, AND EARLY INFANT DEATH

Books

Allen, Marie, and Shelly Marks. *Miscarriage: Women Sharing from the Heart.* New York: John
   Wiley and Sons, 1993.
Davis, Deborah L. *Empty Cradle, Broken Heart: Surviving the Death of Your Baby.* Golden,
   CO: Fulcrum, 1996.
Doka, Kenneth, ed. *Children Mourning, Mourning Children.* Washington, DC: Hospice
   Foundation of America, 1995.
Fitzgerald, Helen. *The Grieving Child: A Parent's Guide.* New York: Simon & Schuster, 1992.
Fumia, Molly. *A Piece of My Heart: Living through the Grief of Miscarriage, Stillbirth, or Infant
   Death.* Emeryville, CA: Conari Press, 2000.
Huntley, Theresa. *Helping Children Grieve: When Someone They Love Dies.* Minneapolis:
   Augsburg, 1991.
Ilse, Sherokee. *Empty Arms: Coping after Miscarriage, Stillbirth, and Infant Death.* Rev. ed.
   Maple Plain, MN: Wintergreen Press, 1990.
Jarratt, Claudia Jewett. *Helping Children Cope with Separation and Loss.* Boston: Harvard
   Common Press, 1994.

Johnson, Joy, and Marvin Johnson. *Grief: What It Is and What You Can Do.* Omaha: Centering Corporation, 1995.

——. *Tell Me, Papa: A Funeral Book for Children.* Rev. ed. Omaha: Centering Corporation, 1996.

Krementz, Jill. *How It Feels When a Parent Dies.* New York: Alfred Knopf, 1999.

Kubler-Ross, Elisabeth. *Questions and Answers on Death and Dying.* New York: Macmillan, 1974.

Kohn, Ingrid, and Perry-Lynn Moffit. *A Silent Sorrow.* New York: Routledge, 2000.

McCue, Kathleen. *How to Help Children through a Parent's Serious Illness.* New York: St. Martin's Press, 1996.

Mellonie, Bryan, and Robert Ingpen. *Lifetimes: The Beautiful Way to Explain Death to Children.* New York: Bantam Books, 1983.

Moulder, Christine. *Miscarriage: Women's Experiences and Needs.* New York: Routledge, 2001.

Roberts, Janice, and Joy Johnson. *Thank You for Coming to Say Goodbye: A Funeral Home Orientation for Children.* Omaha: Centering Corporation, 1994.

Schaefer, Dan, and Christine Lyons. *How Do We Tell the Children? A Step-by-Step Guide for Helping Children Two to Teen Cope When Someone Dies.* New York: Newmarket Press, 1993.

Scher, Jonathan, and Carol Dix. *Preventing Miscarriage: The Good News.* New York: Harper Perennial, 1991.

Sha, Janet L. *Mothers of Thyme: Customs and Rituals of Infertility and Miscarriage.* Ann Arbor, MI: Lida Rose Press, 1990.

Traisman, Enid. *Fire in My Heart, Ice in My Veins: A Journal for Teens Experiencing a Loss.* Omaha: Centering Corporation, 1992.

Wheeler, Sara Rich, and Margaret M. Pike. *Goodbye My Child: A Gentle Guide for Parents Whose Child Has Died.* Omaha: Centering Corporation, 1992.

Woods, James R., and Jennifer L. Esposito. *Loss during Pregnancy or in the Newborn Period.* Pittman, NJ: Jennetti, 1997.

Organizations

Centering Corporation
P.O. Box 4600
Omaha, NE 68104
402-553-1200
A nonprofit organization that supports and provides resources for bereaved children and their families.

Children's Hospice International
901 North Pitt Street, Suite 220
Alexandria, VA 22314
Toll-free: 800-24-CHILD (242-4453)
Fax: 703-684-0226
E-mail: info@chionline.org
www.chionline.org
Information on children's hospice care for the general public, referrals to local hospice programs or health professionals, and printed materials.

The Compassionate Friends
P.O. Box 3696
Oak Brook, IL 60522-3696
630-990-0010
Fax: 630-990-0246
E-mail: nationaloffice@compassionatefriends.org
A national self-help organization for families who have lost a child.

Hospice Education Institute
3 Unity Square
Machiasport, ME 04655-0090
"Hospice Link" toll-free hotline: 800-331-1620
Fax: 207-255-8008
E-mail: hospiceall@aol.com
www.hospiceworld.org
Referrals to a regularly updated directory of hospice and palliative care
programs nationwide, plus general information on hospice care and
bereavement services.

National Council of Jewish Women Pregnancy Support Program
820 Second Avenue
New York NY 10017
212-687-5030

National Hospice and Palliative Care Organization
1700 Diagonal Road, Suite 625
Alexandria, VA 22314
703-837-1500
For referrals to hospices in your area, call 800-658-8898
www.nho.org

National SHARE Pregnancy & Infant Loss Support Inc.
Joseph Health Center
300 First Capitol Drive
St. Charles, MO 63301-2893
800-821-6819
www.nationalshareoffice.com
This organization sells memory books and remembrance boxes, along with other items
helpful in creating rituals appropriate for miscarriage loss.

Web Sites

www.fertilityplus.org/faq/miscarriage/resources.html
> Huge clearinghouse for information on support groups, chat groups, medical information, and on-line memorials. Offers many books about miscarriage.

JUST FOR FATHERS

Books

Churchwell, Gordon. *Pregnant Man: How Nature Makes Fathers Out of Men.* New York: Quill, 2001.

Cosby, Bill. *Fatherhood.* New York: Simon & Schuster, 1986.

Ehrensaft, Diane. *Parenting Together: Men and Women Sharing the Care of Their Children.* Champaign: University of Illinois Press, 1990.

Franklin, John B., and Cher Martin. *Fatherbirth: A Close Encounter of the Fourth Kind.* Eagle, PA: FatherBirth, 2001.

Glennon, Will. *Fathering: Strengthening Connection with Your Children No Matter Where You Are.* Emeryville, CA: Conari Press, 1995.

Greenberg, Martin. *The Birth of a Father.* New York: Continuum, 1985.

Hall, Nor, and William R. Dawson. *Broodmales.* Dallas: Spring, 1989.

Heinowitz, Jack. *Fathering Right from the Start: Straight Talk about Pregnancy, Birth and Beyond.* Novato, CA: New World Library, 2001.

Levine, James A. *Who Will Raise the Children? New Options for Fathers (and Mothers).* Philadelphia: Lippincott, 1976. (Out of print.)

Louv, Richard. *FatherLove: What We Need, What We Seek, What We Must Create.* New York: Simon & Schuster, 1993.

Osherson, Samuel. *Finding Our Fathers.* New York: Ballantine/Fawcett, 1987.

Pittman, Frank. *Man Enough: Fathers, Sons and the Search for Masculinity.* New York: G. P. Putnam, 1993.

Pruett, Kyle. *The Nurturing Father: Journey toward the Complete Man.* New York: Warner, 1987.

Spacek, Tim. *Fathers: There at the Birth.* Chicago: Chicago Review Press, 1985.

Thevenin, Tine. *Mothering and Fathering: The Gender Differences in Parenting.* Garden City Park, NY: Avery, 1993.

Thorndike, John. *Another Way Home: A Single Father's Story.* New York: Crown, 1996.

Vanwert, William F. *Tales for Expectant Fathers.* New York: Dial, 1982.

Web Sites

www.fathersjournal.com
> Reflective writings on fatherhood.

www.fathermag.com
> Online magazine for fathers.

NATURAL FOOD FOR PREGNANCY AND BREASTFEEDING

Books

Colbin, Annemarie. *Balanced Eating.* New York: Ballantine, 1991.

————. *The Book of Whole Meals: A Seasonal Guide to Assembling Balanced Vegetarian Breakfasts, Lunches and Dinners.* New York: Ballantine, 1985.

Johnson, Roberta, ed. *Whole Foods for the Whole Family.* 2d ed. Schaumburg, IL: La Leche League International, 1993.

Katzen, Mollie. *Enchanted Broccoli Forest.* Rev. ed. Berkeley, CA: Ten Speed Press, 1995.

————. *The Moosewood Cookbook.* Rev. ed. Berkeley, CA: Ten Speed Press, 1992.

————. *Still Life with Menu Cookbook.* Rev. ed. Berkeley, CA: Ten Speed Press, 1994.

Katzen, Mollie, and Ann Henderson. *Pretend Soup and Other Real Recipes: A Cookbook for Preschoolers and Up.* Berkeley, CA: Tricycle Press, 1994.

Lappe, Frances M. *Diet for a Small Planet.* 20th ed. New York: Ballantine, 1991.

Madison, Deborah, and Edward Espe Brown. *The Greens Cookbook: Extraordinary Vegetarian Cuisine from the Celebrated Restaurant.* 5th ed. New York: Bantam, 1988.

Robertson, Laurel, Carol Flinders, and Brian Ruppenthal. *The New Laurel's Kitchen.* Berkeley, CA: Ten Speed Press, 1986.

Weil, Andrew. *Eating Well for Optimum Health.* New York: Quill, 2000.

Yntema, Sharon. *Vegetarian Pregnancy: The Definitive Nutritional Guide to Having a Healthy Baby.* Ithaca, NY: McBooks Press, 1994.

Web Sites

www.crha-health.ab.ca/hlthconn/items/preg1

A public service site on nutrition during pregnancy sponsored by Calgary Educational Services.

www.vrg.org/nutrition/veganpregnancy

Good article entitled "The Vegan Diet during Pregnancy and Lactation."

www.vegfamily.com

Comprehensive site on vegan pregnancy, birth and parenting.

www.greenguideonline.com

The Green Guide offers environmental updates on food, clothing, and health issues relevant to children and families.

www.epa.gov/oas/mercury.html

The Environmental Protection Agency's site on mercury levels in fish.

COMPLEMENTARY AND ALTERNATIVE MEDICINE

These resources offer more information on the alternative and complementary practices we suggest in this book; many of the organizations listed can refer you to a local practitioner.

Books

American Pharmaceutical Association. *American Pharmaceutical Association Practical Guide to Natural Medicines.* New York: William Morrow, 1999.

Annas, George. *The Rights of Patients: The Basic ACLU Guide to Patient Rights.* (An American Civil Liberties Union Handbook.) Totowa, NJ: Humana Press, 1992.

Bach, Edward, and F. J. Wheeler. *The Bach Flower Remedies.* New Canaan, CT: Keats, 1979.

Castro, Miranda. *The Complete Homeopathy Handbook.* New York: St. Martin's, 1990.

Gladstar, Rosemary. *Family Herbal: A Guide to Living Life with Energy, Health and Vitality.* North Adams, MA: Storey Books, 2001.

Grist, Liz. *A Woman's Guide to Alternative Medicine.* Chicago: Contemporary Books, 1988.

Keville, K., and M. Green. *Aromatherapy: A Complete Guide to the Healing Art.* Freedom, CA: Crossing Press, 1995.

Korte, Diana. *Every Woman's Body: Everything You Need to Know to Make Informed Choices about Your Health.* New York: Ballantine, 1994.

Lad, Vasant. *Ayurveda: The Science of Self-Healing.* Santa Fe, NM: Lotus, 1984.

Morton, Mary, and Michael Morton. *Five Steps to Selecting the Best Alternative Medicine: A Guide to Complementary and Integrative Health Care.* Novato, CA: New World Library, 1996.

Murray, Michael. *Natural Alternatives to Over-the-Counter and Prescription Drugs.* New York: Quill, 1999.

Norman, L. *Feet First: A Guide to Foot Reflexology.* New York: Simon & Schuster, 1988.

Merck Research Laboratories. *The Merck Manual of Medical Information: Home Edition.* Whitehouse Station, NJ: Merck Research Laboratories, 1997. (Text available online at *www.MerckHomeEdition.com*.)

Oster, Nancy, Lucy Thomas, and Darol Josef. *Making Informed Medical Decisions: Where to Look and How to Use What You Find.* New York: O'Reilly & Associates, 2000.

Panos, Maesimund B., and Jane Heimlich. *Homeopathic Medicine at Home.* New York: Jeremy P. Tarcher, 1980.

Schmidt, Michael A., Lendon H. Smith, and Keith W. Sehnert. *Beyond Antibiotics: 50 (or so) Ways to Boost Immunity and Avoid Antibiotics.* Berkeley, CA: North Atlantic Books, 1994.

Trivieri, Larry Jr. *The American Holistic Medical Association Guide to Holistic Health: Healing Therapies for Optimal Wellness.* New York: John Wiley & Sons, 2001.

Organizations

American Association of Naturopathic Physicians
3201 New Mexico Avenue NW
Suite 350
Washington, DC 20016
866-538-2267
www.naturopathic.org

American Chiropractic Association
1701 Clarendon Boulevard
Arlington, VA 22209
703-276-8800
Fax: 703-243-2593
E-mail: memberinfo@amerchiro.org

American Holistic Health Association
P.O. Box 17400
Anaheim, CA 92817-7400
714-779-6152
E-mail: mail@ahha.org
www.ahha.org

American Holistic Medical Association
12101 Menaul Blvd., NE
Suite C
Albuquerque, NM 87112
505-292-7780
www.holisticmedicine.org

Associated Bodywork and Massage Professionals
1271 Sugarbush Drive
Evergreen, CO 80439-7347
800-458-2267
Fax: 303-674-0859
www.abmp.com

National Acupuncture and Oriental Medicine Alliance
6405 43rd Avenue NE
Suite B
Gig Harbour, WA 98335
253-851-6896

National Certification Commission for Acupuncture and
    Oriental Medicine
11 Canal Center Plaza, Suite 300
Alexandria, VA 22314
703-548-9004
Fax: 703-548-9079

The National Institute of Ayurvedic Medicine
584 Milltown Road
Brewster, NY 10509
Voice/Fax: 914-278-8700
888-246-NIAM
www.niam.com

North American Society of Homeopaths (NASH)
1122 East Pike Street, Suite 1122
Seattle, WA 98122
206-720-7000
www.homeopathy.org

The Office of Alternative Medicine (OAM)
National Institutes of Health
9000 Rockville Pike
Building 31, Rooms 5B-38
Bethesda, MD 20892
888-644-6226
Fax: 301-402-4741
altmed.od.nih.gov

Physician's Association for Anthroposophical Medicine
1923 Geddes Avenue
Ann Arbor, MI 48104-1797
734-930-9462
Fax: 734-662-1727
www.paam.net

The Reflexology Association of America
4012 S. Rainbow Boulevard
Box K585
Las Vegas, NV 89103-2059
508-364-4234

CHILDREN'S BOOKS ABOUT BIRTH AND BREASTFEEDING

These books will help your older children to learn more about their new baby brother or sister; appropriate ages for each book are included.

Ahlberg, Janet, and Allan Ahlberg. *The Baby's Catalogue.* Boston: Little, Brown, 1982. (Ages 1–10.)

Anderson, Sandra VanDam, and Georgeanne DelGiudice. *Siblings, Birth, and the Newborn.* Seattle: Pennypress, 1983. (Ages 3 and up.)

Arnott, Joanne. *Ma MacDonald.* Mildord, CT: Women's Press, 1993. (Ages 2–6.)

Cole, Joanna. *How You Were Born.* New York: Morrow Junior Books, 1993. (Ages 3–11.)

Corey, Dorothy. *Will There Be a Lap for Me?* Morton Grove, IL: Albert Whitman, 1992. (Ages 3–8.)

Cushman, Karen. *The Midwife's Apprentice.* New York: Clarion Books, 1995. (Ages 5 and up.)

Dragonwagon, Crescent. *Wind Rose.* New York: Harper and Row, 1976. (Ages 5 and up.)

Falwell, Cathryn. *We Have a Baby.* New York: Clarion Books, 1993. (Ages 1–3.)

Fagerstrom, Grethe, and Gunilla Hansson. *Our New Baby.* Hauppauge, NY: Barron's Educational Series, 1982. (Ages 6 and up.)

Gewing, Lisa. *Mama, Daddy, Baby and Me.* Santa Cruz, CA: Spirit Press, 1989. (Ages 2–4.)

Harris, Robie H. *Happy Birth Day!* Cambridge, MA: Candlewick Press, 1996. (Ages 3–10.)

Isadora, Rachel. *Over the Green Hills.* New York: Greenwillow, 1992. (Ages 4–8.)

Kitzinger, Sheila. *Being Born.* New York: Putnam, 1986. (Ages 6 and up.)

MacLachlan, Patricia. *All the Places to Love.* New York: Harper Collins Juvenile Books, 1994. (Ages 4–8.)

Malecki, Maryann. *Mom and Dad and I Are Having a Baby.* Seattle: Pennypress, 1979. (All ages. Also available in Spanish.)

———. *Our Brand New Baby.* Seattle: Pennypress, 1980. (All ages.)

Manning, Mick, and Brita Granstorm. *The World Is Full of Babies.* New York: Doubleday, 1996. (Ages 2–6.)

Martin, Chia. *We Like to Nurse.* Prescott, AZ: Hohm Press, 1995. (Ages 1–3.)

Mennen, Ingrid. *One Round Moon and a Star for Me.* New York: Orchard Books, 1994. (Ages 3–8.)

Nilsson, Lennart, and Lena Katarina Swanberg. *How Was I Born?* New York: Delacorte Press, 1994. (Ages 3–8.)

Overend, Jenni. *Welcome with Love.* Brooklyn, NY: Kane/Miller, 2000. (Ages 2–6.)

Pearse, Patricia. *See How You Grow: A Lift-the-Flap Body Book.* Hauppauge, NY: Barron's Educational Series, 1988. (Ages 3–8.)

Sears, William, Martha Sears, and Christie Watts Kelly. *Baby on the Way.* New York: Little, Brown, 2001.

Sheffield, Margaret. *Before You Were Born.* New York: Knopf, 1984. (Ages 5–8.)

Stein, Sara Bonnett. *That New Baby.* New York: Walker & Co., 1974. (Ages 3–8.)

Walter, Mildred Pitts. *My Mama Needs Me.* New York: Lothrop, Lee & Shepard Books, 1983. (Ages 3–6.)

Wolff, Ashley. *Only the Cat Saw.* New York: Walker & Co, 1996. (Ages 3–8.)

Appendix 3:
Range of Costs for Various Birth Settings

	Home Birth	Birth Center	Hospital	Cesarean
Fees for professional services of midwife or physician for prenatal care, delivery, and postpartum care	$2,300–5,000	$2,300–5,500	$1,800–6,000	$1,800–6,000
Facility fee		$1,200–2,800	$2,500–10,000	$2,500–10,000
Surgeons, anesthesiologist, and additional hospital time				$5,000–6,000
Total approximate costs	**$2,300–5,000**	**$3,500–8,300**	**$4,300–16,000**	**$9,300–26,000**

These ranges of costs have mostly to do with location. The high for a hospital birth, for example, was reported from the San Francisco Bay Area in California. The high for both professional fees and birth centers is in New York City, and the low for a birth center is in south Texas. The facility fee is related to how long you stay at the facility. The most recent figures released by the National Association of Childbearing Centers (NACC) indicate that the average birth-center birth costs $3,641—$2,105 for professional fees and $1,536 for facility fees. Midwife-attended home births average under $3,000, with the high of $5,000 coming from a physician home birth service in Chicago. There will be additional charges wherever the birth occurs. Professional fees, for example, do not include lab work, diagnostic tests (ultrasounds, for example, cost about $250 each), and medications. Childbirth classes may also require an additional fee.

A 1998 study at the San Diego Birth Center showed that midwife/birth center collaborative care saved parents 21 percent as compared with hospital birth. A study published in 1999 in the *Journal of Nurse-Midwifery* on the cost-effectiveness of home birth revealed that the average uncomplicated vaginal birth costs 68 percent less in a home than in a hospital.

NACC reports that most major health insurers contract with birth centers for reimbursement. Insurers are required by law to cover the services of certified nurse-midwives, and most cover direct-entry midwives as well. In addition, midwifery practices and birth centers often offer sliding scales for those who are uninsured or not covered by Medicaid.

Adapted from D. Jackson, W. Swartz, J. Lang, et al., Outcomes from the San Diego Birth Center; *presented at the Association for Health Services Research 15th Annual Meeting, Washington, D.C., June 22, 1998; and R. E. Anderson and D. A. Anderson, "The Cost-Effectiveness of Home Birth,"* Journal of Nurse-Midwifery, *44 (Jan.–Feb. 1999): 30–35.*

References

PART ONE: THE FIRST TRIMESTER

Chapter 1: How You Feel

1. Sheila Kitzinger, *The Complete Book of Pregnancy and Childbirth* (New York: Knopf, 1996), 20.
2. *www.nv.essortment.com.*
3. *www.sids-networks.org.*
4. *www.ospinet.org; www.holymtn.com.*
5. Kitzinger, *Complete Book of Pregnancy,* 103.
6. Statistics are from the Alberta Tobacco Reduction Alliance: *www.atra.ab.ca.*
7. American Society of Plastic Surgeons: *www.medem.com.*
8. Ibid.
9. Ibid.
10. Information from Maureen Hatch, Ph.D., director of the Division of Epidemiology at the Mt. Sinai School of Medicine.
11. American College of Obstetricians and Gynecologists: *www.acog.com.*
12. Murray Enkin et al., *A Guide to Effective Care in Pregnancy and Childbirth* (New York: Oxford University Press, 2000), 96.
13. Ibid., 97.
14. Kitzinger, *The Complete Book of Pregnancy,* 136.
15. Ibid., 134.
16. Ibid., 136.
17. *www.medem.com.*
18. F. Lorscheider, M. J. Vimy, and A. O. Summers, "Mercury Exposure from 'Silver' Tooth Fillings: Emerging Evidence Questions a Traditional Dental Paradigm," *FASEB Journal* 9 (1995): 504–8; *www.home.online.no/~reiersol/friberg.htm.*
19. Kitzinger, *Complete Book of Pregnancy,* 108.
20. *www.medem.com.*
21. Enkin et al., *A Guide to Effective Care,* 100.
22. Kitzinger, *Complete Book of Pregnancy,* 108.
23. *www.herpes.com.*
24. Ibid.
25. Enkin et al., *A Guide to Effective Care,* 63.

Chapter 2: What You're Eating

1. Murray Enkin et al., *A Guide to Effective Care in Pregnancy and Childbirth* (New York: Oxford University Press, 2000), 44.
2. Karin B. Michels and Kristine Napier, *The Gift of Health* (New York: Pocket Books, 2002), 19–20.
3. Ibid., 32.
4. Andrew Weil, *Eating Well for Optimum Health* (New York: Quill, 2000), 46.
5. Andrew Weil, "Omega-3s: What You Need to Know," *Self Healing,* December 2001.
6. Michels and Napier, *Gift of Health,* 107.
7. Enkin et al., *A Guide to Effective Care,* 43.
8. National Institutes of Health, *www.cc.nih.gov.*
9. Weil, *Eating Well,* 132.
10. Michels and Napier, *Gift of Health,* 94.
11. Mothers & Others; *www.mothers.org.*
12. *www.cyberdiet.com.*

13. Michael Gallo et al., "Pregnancy Outcome Following Gestational Exposure to Echinacea," *Archives of Internal Medicine* (November 13, 2000).

14. Kitzinger, *Complete Book of Pregnancy,* 39.

Chapter 3: Making Birth Choices— Choosing Your Place of Birth and Your Birth Attendant

1. Peter F. Schlenzka, *Safety of Alternative Approaches to Childbirth* (Palo Alto, Calif.: Stanford University Press, 1999).

2. National Association of Childbearing Centers; *www.birthcenters.org.*

3. Mark Durand, "The Safety of Homebirth: The Farm Study," *American Journal of Public Health* 82 (1992): 450–52.

4. National Association of Childbearing Centers.

5. American College of Nurse-Midwives: *www.midwife.org.*

6. Lloyd K. Mitler, John A. Rizzo, and Sarah M. Horwitz, "Physician Gender and Cesarean Sections," *Journal of Clinical Epidemiology,* vol. 53, no. 10, pp. 1030–1035, September 2000.

PART TWO: THE SECOND TRIMESTER

Chapter 4. Self-Awareness and Self-Appreciation

1. Jennifer Louden, *The Pregnant Women's Comfort Book* (San Francisco: Harper, 1995), 70.

2. Ibid., 26.

3. Sheila Kitzinger, *The Complete Book of Pregnancy and Childbirth* (New York: Knopf, 1996), 133.

4. Murray Enkin et al., *A Guide to Effective Care in Pregnancy and Childbirth* (New York: Oxford University Press, 2000), 160.

5. Kitzinger, *Complete Book of Pregnancy,* 134.

6. Enkin et al., *A Guide to Effective Care,* 101.

7. Ibid., 102.

8. Enkin et al., *A Guide to Effective Care,* 98.

Chapter 5: Prenatal Testing

1. B. G. Ewigman et al., "Effect of Prenatal Ultrasound Screening on Perinatal Outcome," *New England Journal of Medicine* 329, no. 12 (1993): 821–27.

2. *ACOG Technical Bulletin,* no. 87 (December 1993).

3. O. R. Brand et al., "Specificity of Antenatal Ultrasound in the Yorkshire Region: A Prospective Study of 2261 Ultrasound Detected Anomalies," *British Journal of Obstetrics and Gynaecology* 101, no. 5 (1994): 392–97.

4. J. Cnattingius, "Screening for Intrauterine Growth Retardation" (Ph.D. diss., Uppsala University, Sweden, 1984).

5. F. Y. Chan, "Limitations of Ultrasound" (paper presented at Perinatal Society of Australia and New Zealand 1st Annual Congress, Freemantle, 1997).

6. *ACOG Technical Bulletin,* no. 187 (December 1993).

7. *"Diagnostic Ultrasound Imaging in Pregnancy,"* Consensus Development Conference Statement 5, no. 1 (Washington, D.C.) NIH 1984.

8. World Health Organization, "Diagnostic Ultrasound in Pregnancy, WHO view on routine screening," *Lancet* 2 (1984): 361.

9. Murray Enkin et al., *A Guide to Effective Care in Pregnancy and Childbirth* (New York: Oxford University Press, 2000), 58.

10. Patrick Brennan et al., "Shadow of a Doubt," *New Scientist,* vol 12, no. 1476 (June 10, 1999), p. 23.

11. Helle Kieler et al., "Sinistrality a Side Effect of Prenatal Sonography: A Comparative Study of Young Men," *Epidemiology* 12 (2001): 610–23.

12. ACOG: *www.medem.com.*

13. Sheila Kitzinger, *The Complete Book of Pregnancy and Childbirth* (New York: Knopf, 1996), 220–21.

14. ACOG: *www.medem.com.*

. Enkin et al., *A Guide to Effective Care,* 6.

. Ibid., p. 64.

Chapter 7: Doulas for Labor Support

1. *www.birthworks.org.*

2. Murray Enkin et al., *A Guide to Effective Care in Pregnancy and Childbirth* (New York: Oxford University Press, 2000), 253.

3. Mayri Sagady, *Professional Labor Support: Your Newest Option in Childbirth; www.server4.hypermart.net/alacehg/article.htm.*

Chapter 9: Preparing for Breastfeeding

1. Naomi Baumslag and Dia L. Michels, *Milk, Money, and Madness: The Culture and Politics of Breastfeeding* (Westport, Conn.: Bergin and Garvey, 1995).

2. Meredith F. Small, *Our Babies, Ourselves* (New York: Anchor Books, 1998), 193.

3. Baumslag and Michels, *Milk, Money, and Madness,* 25.

4. "American Academy of Pediatrics Policy Statement," *Pediatrics* 100, no. 6 (December 1997)

5. Ibid.

6. Baumslag and Michels, *Milk, Money, and Madness.*

7. Ibid.

8. "American Academy of Pediatrics Policy Statement."

9. T. Greiner, "Breastfeeding and LAM (Lactation Amenorrhea Method of Contraception): Beyond Conventional Approaches" (World Alliance for Breastfeeding Action (WABA) research paper no. 95, presented to Georgetown University Institute for Reproductive Health, Washington, D.C., May 1997), 69.

10. "American Academy of Pediatrics Policy Statement."

11. Ibid.

12. Ibid.

13. Baumslag and Michels, *Milk, Money, and Madness,* 140.

14. *www.lalecheleague.org.*

15. Murray Enkin et al., *A Guide to Effective Care in Pregnancy and Childbirth* (New York: Oxford University Press, 2000), 441.

16. La Leche League International, *Nursing with Breast Implants,* publication no. 24 (Schaumburg, IL: La Leche League International, 1992).

PART THREE: THE THIRD TRIMESTER

Chapter 10: Revisit Your Fears

1. Excerpt from Claudia Panuthos, "Transformation through Birth," *Mothering* 36 (1985), 64–65.

2. Barry J. Jacobson and Jodi A. Mindell, "Sleep Disturbance During Pregnancy," *Journal of Obstetric Gynecologic, and Neonatal Nursing,* 2000 29, pp. 590–597.

3. Murray Enkin et al., *A Guide to Effective Care in Pregnancy and Childbirth* (New York: Oxford University Press, 2000), 104.

4. Ibid.

5. Ibid.

6. Ibid.

7. Ibid., 77.

8. William Sears and Martha Sears, *The Birth Book* (New York: Little, Brown and Company, 1994), 97.

9. Sheila Kitzinger, *The Complete Book of Pregnancy and Childbirth* (New York: Knopf, 1996), 139.

10. Enkin et al., *A Guide to Effective Care,* 123–24.

11. Ibid., 122–23.

Chapter 12: Getting Ready for Baby

1. Meredith F. Small, *Our Babies, Ourselves* (New York: Anchor Books, 1998), 112–13.
2. Ibid., 130.
3. Ibid., 132.
4. J. J. McKenna, "The Potential Benefits of Infant-Parent Co-Sleeping in Relation to SIDS Prevention: Overview and Critiqu of Epidemiological Bed Sharing Studies," in *Sudden Infant Death Syndrome: New Trends in the Nineties,* ed. T. O. Rognu (Oslo: Scandinavian University Press, 1995): 256–65.
5. Rosalind Anderson and Julius Anderson, "Acute Respiratory Effects of Diaper Emissions," *Archives of Environmental Healt* 54 (October 1999).
6. C. J. Partxch, M. Aukamp, and W. G. Sippell, "Scrotal Temperature Is Increased in Disposable Plastic Lined Nappies, *Archives of Disease in Childhood* 83 (October 2000): 364–68.
7. Nan Scott, "Diapering: A Biased Mother's View," *Mothering* magazine, no. 43, pp. 33–36.

Chapter 13: Pain in Labor

1. *Obstetrics and Gynecology,* April 1988.
2. William Sears and Martha Sears, *The Birth Book* (New York: Little, Brown and Company, 1994), 168.
3. Murray Enkin et al., *A Guide to Effective Care in Pregnancy and Childbirth* (New York: Oxford University Press, 2000), 325.
4. B. Jacobson et al., "Opiate Addiction in Adult Offspring through Possible Imprinting after Obstetric Treatment," *British Medical Journal* 301 (1990): 1067–70.
5. Sheila Kitzinger, *The Complete Book of Pregnancy and Childbirth* (New York: Knopf, 1996), 323.
6. 1993 study by Kennell, Klaus, and Kennell, as reported by *www.birthworks.org.*
7. Adrienne Lieberman, *Easing Labor Pain* (New York: Doubleday & Company, 1987), 3.
8. *International Journal of Childbirth Education* 3, no. 4 (November 1988): 43–44.
9. Kitzinger, *Complete Book of Pregnancy,* 302.
10. *Obstetrics and Gynecology* 160, no. 3 (1989): 707–12.
11. Kitzinger, *Complete Book of Pregnancy,* 301.
12. Enkin et al., *A Guide to Effective Care,* 322.
13. Ibid., p. 328.

Chapter 14: Avoiding the Cascade of Medical Interventions

1. *Assessment of the Postterm Pregnancy,* American Academy of Family Physicians, 1996.
2. Murray Enkin et al., *A Guide to Effective Care in Pregnancy and Childbirth* (New York: Oxford University Press, 2000), 90.
3. William Sears and Martha Sears, *The Birth Book* (New York: Little, Brown and Company, 1994), 98.
4. Ibid.
5. Enkin et al., *A Guide to Effective Care,* 88.
6. Ibid.
7. Ibid.
8. Ibid., 85–86.
9. Ibid., 87.
10. Michael J. McMahon, Jeffrey A. Kuller, and Jerome Yankowitz, "Assessment of the Postterm Pregnancy," *American Family Physicians,* vol. 54, 2, August 1996, p. 63.
11. Zhang J. Rayburn, "Rising Rates of Labor Induction: Present Concerns and Future Strategies," *Journal of Obstetrics and Gynecology,* vol. 100(1), July 2002, pp. 164–167.
12. W. J. Huston et al., "Practice Variations Between Family Physicians and Obstetricians in the Management of Low-Risk Pregnancies," *Journal of Family Practice,* vol. 40 (no. 4), April 1995, pp. 345–351.
13. Henci Goer, *Obstetrical Myths v. Research Realities* (Westport, Conn.: Bergin and Garvey, 1995).

. "Care in Normal Birth: Report of a Technical Working Group," The World Health Organization, and "Life in a Parallel World: A Bold New Approach to the Mystery of Autism," *Newsweek,* May 13, 1996.

. "Induction of Labor," *American College of Obstetricians and Gynecologists Technical Bulletin,* no. 217 (December 1995). *Bulletin who/frh/msm/96.24, order no. 1930104.*

. Ibid.

. B. Chayen, N. Tejani, and U. Verma, "Induction of Labor with an Electric Breast Pump," *Journal of Reproductive Medicine* 31 (1986):116–18.

. M. Castro, *Homeopathy for Pregnancy, Birth and Your Baby's First Year* (New York: St. Martin's Press, 1994).

. Lisa Summers, "Methods of Cervical Ripening and Labor Induction," *Journal of Nurse-Midwifery* 42, no. 2 (March/April 1997): 77.

0. Sheila Kitzinger, *The Complete Book of Pregnancy and Childbirth* (New York: Knopf, 1996), 334.

1. Ibid., 333.

2. Enkin et al., *A Guide to Effective Care,* 271.

3. Kitzinger, *Complete Book of Pregnancy,* 339.

4. Enkin et al., *A Guide to Effective Care,* 186.

5. American College of Nurse-Midwives; *www.midwife.org.*

6. Francisco A. R. Garcia, Helen Bowman Miller, George R. Huggins, and Toby A. Gordon, "Effect of Academic Affiliation and Obstetric Volume on Clinical Outcome and Cost of Childbirth," *Obstetrics and Gynecology* 97, no. 4 (April 2001): 567–76.

27. J. B. Gould et al., "Socioeconomic Differences in Rates of Cesarean Section," *New England Journal of Medicine* 321 (1989): 233–39; S. Rock, "Malpractice Premiums and Primary Cesarean Section Rates in New York and Illinois," *Public Health Reports* 103 (1989): 459–63; K. Kizer and A. Ellis, "C-Section Rate Related to Payment Source," *American Journal of Public Health,* 78, no. 1 (1988): 96–97.

28. *Obstetrics and Gynecology,* May 1990, 821–25.

29. Enkin et al., *A Guide to Effective Care,* 188.

30. Kitzinger, *Complete Book of Pregnancy,* 338.

31. Ibid., 346.

32. Sears and Sears, *The Birth Book,* 117.

33. E. Hemminki and J. Merilainen, "Long-term Effects of Cesarean Sections: Ectopic Pregnancies and Placental Problems," *American Journal of Obstetrics and Gynecology* 174 (May 1996): 1569–74.

34. E. L. Ryding, "Experiences of Emergency Cesarean Section; A Phenomenal Study of 53 Women," *Birth* 25 (December 1998): 246–51.

35. M. Gabay and S. M. Wolfe, "Encouraging the Use of Nurse-Midwives: A Report for Policymakers," *Public Citizen Health Research Group Booklet,* Washington D.C., *Delivering a Better Childbirth Experience: A Consumer's Guide to Nurse Midwifery,* November 1995, 13–29.

36. Sears and Sears, *The Birth Book.*

PART FOUR: LABOR AND DELIVERY

Chapter 16: Early Labor

1. Sheila Kitzinger, *The Complete Book of Pregnancy and Childbirth* (New York: Knopf, 1996), 243.

Chapter 17: The First Stage of Labor

1. M. Mead and N. Newton, "Cultural Patterning," in *Childbearing: Its Social and Psychological Aspects,* eds. Stephen A. Richardson and Alan F. Guttmacher (Baltimore: Williams and Wilkins, 1967).

2. Murray Enkin et al., *A Guide to Effective Care in Pregnancy and Childbirth* (New York: Oxford University Press, 2000), 263.

3. Roberto Caldeyo-Barcia, "The Influence of Maternal Positioning during the Second Stage of Labor," M. D. Mauk et al., "Tonic Immobility Produces Hyperalgesia and Antagonizes Morphine Analgesia," *Science* 213 (1981): 353.

4. Doris Haire, *The Cultural Warping of Childbirth* (Minneapolis, MN: International Childbirth Education Association, 197 and A. Blankfield, "The Optimum Position for Childbirth," *The Medical Journal of Australia,* 1965, pp. 666–668.

5. Enkin, *Guide to Effective Care,* 264.

6. Ibid., 263.

7. Ibid.

8. Sheila Kitzinger, *The Complete Book of Pregnancy and Childbirth* (New York: Knopf, 1996), 262.

9. Ibid., 266.

Chapter 18: The Second Stage of Labor

1. Sheila Kitzinger, *The Complete Book of Pregnancy and Childbirth* (New York: Knopf, 1996), 251.

2. Murray Enkin et al., *A Guide to Effective Care in Pregnancy and Childbirth* (New York: Oxford University Press, 2000 290–91.

3. Ibid., 290.

4. Enkin, *Guide to Effective Care,* 291.

5. Erica Eason and Perle Feldman, "Much Ado about a Little Cut: Is Episiotomy Worthwhile?" *Obstetrics and Gynecology* 95, no 4 (April 2000): 616–18.

6. Watson Bowes, "Should Routine Episiotomy be Performed Routinely in Primiparous Women?" *Ob/Gyn Forum* 5, no. 4 (1991): 1–4.

7. Enkin et al., *Guide to Effective Care,* 295.

8. Marsden Wagner, *Pursuing the Birth Machine: The Search for Appropriate Birth Technology* (Camperdown, New South Wales, Australia: ACE Graphics, 1994), 165–74.

9. Kitzinger, *Complete Book of Pregnancy,* 322.

Chapter 19: The Third Stage of Labor

1. Murray Enkin et al., *A Guide to Effective Care in Pregnancy and Childbirth* (New York: Oxford University Press, 2000), 304.

2. Sheila Kitzinger, *The Complete Book of Pregnancy and Childbirth* (New York: Knopf, 1996), 324.

Chapter 20: Newborn Decisions

1. Murray Enkin et al., *A Guide to Effective Care in Pregnancy and Childbirth* (New York: Oxford University Press, 2000), 420.

2. "Forced Medication of Healthy Newborns with Vitamin K in New York State"; *www.home.att.net/~waterbird/.*

3. Enkin et al., *Guide to Effective Care,* 421.

4. B. A. Larsson, G. Tannfeldt, H. Lagercrantz, and G. L. Olsson, "Venipuncture Is More Effective and Less Painful than Heel Lancing for Blood Tests in Neonates," *Pediatrics* 101 (May 1998): 882–86.

5. National Center for Health Statistics (NCHS); *www.cirp.org/library/statistics/bollinger3/.*

6. See photographic series, J. A. Erickson, "Three Zones of Penile Skin," in M. M. Lander, "The Human Prepuce," in G. C. Denniston and M. F. Milos, eds., *Sexual Mutilations: A Human Tragedy* (New York: Plenum Press, 1997), 70–81.

7. From the *Lancet,* March 1, 1997; as reported by the New York State Society of Anesthesiologists.

8. R. E. Marshall et al., "Circumcision: II. Effects upon Mother-Infant Interaction," *Early Human Development* 7 (1982): 367–74.

9. W. F. Gee and J. S. Ansell, "Neonatal Circumcision, a Ten-Year Overview: With Comparison of the Gomco Clamp and the Plastibell Device," *Pediatrics* 58 (1976): 824–27.

10. National Center for Health Statistics (NCHS).

11. Lisa Reagan, "Show Us the Science: Report on the Second International Public Conference of the National Vaccine Information Center," *Mothering,* March/April 2001, 28.

12. Anderson & Krieger, APLC; *www.vaccineinfo.net/autismHg.htm.*

PART FIVE: POSTPARTUM

Chapter 22: Getting to Know Your Baby

1. Meredith F. Small, *Our Babies, Ourselves* (New York: Anchor Books, 1998), 6.
2. Ibid., p. 81.
3. M. Shostak, *Nisa: The Life and Words of a !Kung Woman* (New York: Vintage Books, 1981), 45.
4. Steven Bell and M. Ainsworth, "Infant Crying and Maternal Responsiveness," *Child Development* 43 (1972): 1171–1190.
5. Richard Restak, *The Brain* (New York: Doubleday, 1979), 122.
6. Steven Bell, "Long-Term Effects of Responsive Parenting" (Ph.D. diss., Berry College, Berry, Ga., (1972).
7. Belinda J. Pinyerd, "Strategies for Consoling the Infant with Colic: Fact or Fiction?" *Journal of Pediatric Nursing* 7, no. 7 (1992): 403.
8. David Chapman-Smith, "Infantile Colic: A New Study from Denmark," *Chiropractic Report* 4, no. 1 (November 1989): 1–4.
9. Murray Enkin et al., *A Guide to Effective Care in Pregnancy and Childbirth* (New York: Oxford University Press, 2000), 445.

Chapter 23: The How-Tos of Breastfeeding

1. Murray Enkin et al., *A Guide to Effective Care in Pregnancy and Childbirth* (New York: Oxford University Press, 2000), 446.
2. Thomas W. Hale, "But Is It Safe for My Baby? Medications and Breastfeeding," *Mothering* magazine, March/April 2002, 63–69.
3. La Leche League International, *The Womanly Art of Breastfeeding* (New York: Penguin, 1997), 130–34.
4. Ibid., pp. 138–40.
5. Hale, op. cit.
6. Enkin et al., *Guide to Effective Care,* 447.
7. Ibid., p. 447.
8. Peter H. Duesberg, *Inventing the AIDS Virus* (Washington, D.C.: Regnery 1996).
9. Breastfeeding and HIV Media Release, July 4, 2001; *www.lalecheleague.org/Release/HIV.html.*
10. Anna Coutsoudis et al., "Method of Feeding and Transmission of HIV-1 from Mothers to Children by 15 Months of Age: Prospective Cohort Study from Durban, South Africa." *AIDS* 15 (2001): 379–87.
11. Ibid., pp. 379–87.

Chapter 25: The Blues and Beyond

1. Karen R. Kleiman and Valerie D. Raskin, *This Isn't What I Expected* (New York: Bantam Books, 1994), 2.
2. Ibid., 7.
3. Telephone interview with Dr. Deborah A. Sichel, conducted by Sara Kirschenbaum (June 1994), *Mothering* magazine.
4. Deborah A. Sichel et al., "Postpartum Obsessive Compulsive Disorder: A Case Series," *Journal of Clinical Psychiatry,* vol. 54 (April 1993): 156–59.
5. Kleiman and Raskin, *This Isn't What I Expected,* 2.

PART SIX: SPECIAL CIRCUMSTANCES

Chapter 27: When a Baby Dies: Miscarriage, Stillbirth, and Early Loss

1. Ingrid Kohn, Perry-Lynn Moffitt, and Isabelle A. Wilkins, *A Silent Sorrow* (New York: Routledge, 2000).
2. Ibid.
3. Jonathan Scher, *Preventing Miscarriage* (New York: Harper Perennial, 1991), 8.
4. Murray Enkin et al., *A Guide to Effective Care in Pregnancy and Childbirth* (New York: Oxford University Press, 2000), 109.
5. Scher, *Preventing Miscarriage,* 68.
6. Enkin et al., *Guide to Effective Care,* 112.

7. Ibid.

8. Scher, *Preventing Miscarriage,* 127.

9. Enkin et al., *Guide to Effective Care,* 113.

10. Scher, *Preventing Miscarriage,* 107.

11. Ibid., 102.

12. Ibid., 106.

13. Ibid., 112.

14. Ibid., 151–54.

15. Kohn, Moffitt, and Wilkins, *A Silent Sorrow.*

16. Scher, *Preventing Miscarriage,* 163.

17. Ibid., 25.

18. Sheila Kitzinger, *The Complete Book of Pregnancy and Childbirth* (New York: Knopf, 1996), 373.

19. Enkin et al., *Guide to Effective Care,* 115.

20. Scher, *Preventing Miscarriage,* 50.

21. Enkin et al., *Guide to Effective Care,* 110.

22. Claire Infante-Rivard, et al. "Fetal Loss Associated with Caffeine Intake before and during Pregnancy," *Journal of the American Medical Association,* vol. 270(24), (December 22, 1993), pp. 2940–2943.

23. Scher, *Preventing Miscarriage,* 182.

24. Enkin et al., *Guide to Effective Care,* 109.

25. *www.askdrsears.com.*

26. Ibid.

Chapter 28: Prematurity and Multiple Births

1. Murray Enkin et al., *A Guide to Effective Care in Pregnancy and Childbirth* (New York: Oxford University Press, 2000), 347.

2. Ibid., 350.

3. Ibid., 175.

4. Ibid., 227; Jane E. Brody, "New Doubts about Treatment for Premature Babies," *New York Times,* December 2001.

5. Enkin et al., *Guide to Effective Care,* 355.

6. Ibid.

7. Papi A. Gomez, *Anales Españoles de Pediatría* 48, no. 6 (June 1998): 631–33.

8. N. Charpak et al., *Pediatrics* 100, no. 4 (October 1997): 682–89.

9. Brian Darlow, John Horwood, and Nina Mogridge, "Receipt of Breast Milk and Subsequent Cognitive Ability at 7–8 Years amongst a National Cohort of VLBW Infants," *Pediatric Research* 43 (1998): 211A, abstract 1233.

Chapter 29: Birth Defects and Hospitalization

1. Centers for Disease Control; *www.cdc.gov/nchs/fastats/bdefects.htm.*

2. March of Dimes; *www.modimes.org.*

3. Ibid.

4. Ibid.

5. La Leche League International, *The Womanly Art of Breastfeeding* (New York: Penguin, 1997), 296.

Index